POPE PIUS IX
THE MAN AND THE MYTH

POPE PIUS IX
THE MAN AND THE MYTH

YVES CHIRON

Translated by Graham Harrison

ANGELUS PRESS
2915 FOREST AVENUE,
KANSAS CITY, MISSOURI 64109

Originally published in French as *Pie IX, pape moderne,* by Publications du Courrier de Rome, ©1999. Yves Chiron, born in 1960, is Professor of History and a member of the Society of the Ecclesiastical History of France. He has published numerous works on religious history, including *Padre Pio the Stigmatist* (1999, 2nd ed.), *Paul VI* (1993), *Inquiry on the Apparitions of the Virgin* (1995); *Pius IX: Modern Pope* (1995); and *Inquiry on Canonizations* (1998).

The drawing of Blessed Pope Pius IX on the cover was drawn by Christoph Häfliger of Design Atelier Häfliger, Opfikon, Switzerland.

Library of Congress Cataloging-in-Publication Data
Chiron, Yves, 1960-
  [Pie IX, pape moderne. English]
  Pope Pius IX : the man and the myth / Yves Chiron ; translated by Graham Harrison.
     p. cm.
  Includes bibliographical references and index.
  ISBN 1-892331-31-4 (alk. paper)
  1. Pius IX, Pope, 1792-1878. I. Title.

  BX1373.C4513 2005
  282'.092--dc22

                                                              2005008420

ANGELUS PRESS
2915 Forest Avenue
Kansas City, Missouri 64109
Phone (816) 753-3150
Fax (816) 753-3557
Order Line 1-800-966-7337
www.angeluspress.org

ISBN 1-892331-31-4
First Printing–July 2005

Printed in the United States of America

CONTENTS

INTRODUCTION

Of all the popes of modern times, Pius IX is the most controversial pope—a position he shares, no doubt, with Paul VI, for different and even opposite reasons. Perhaps we should have said "was the most controversial pope," for today his pontificate seems to be largely forgotten. Nonetheless this pontificate (1846-78), the longest in the Church's history, dominated the second half of the nineteenth century.

A brief tour of his achievement reveals that many things he did are still regarded as milestones in the history of the Church:

- He was the first pope to condemn Communism (1846).
- After several centuries in which the Church's hierarchy was eclipsed in certain Protestant countries, he re-established it in England (1850), Holland (1853), and Scotland (1878).
- He defined the dogma of the Immaculate Conception (1854).
- In a full and practically exhaustive way, he issued a renewed condemnation of modern errors in philosophy and theology through his Encyclical *Quanta Cura* and the Syllabus (1864).
- He laid the foundation for Catholic Action by approving its first core section, the "Society of Italian Catholic Youth" (1868) and then the "*Opera dei Congressi*" (1874).
- He summoned the Vatican Council (1869-1870), the first in modern times since the Council of Trent, in which, notably, the dogma of Papal Infallibility would be defined.

All this was achieved in one of the most troubled historical contexts, namely that of post-Revolution and post-Napoleonic Europe, which was characterized at the same time by revolutions, changes of regime, the development of industrialization and secularization, as well as the obliteration of the Papal States—a political fact which dominated Pius IX's pontificate.

Even during his lifetime, as G. Mollat observed, "he was equally hated and loved."[1] He had as many detractors as he had admirers. Some of his adversaries were outside the Church, notably the partisans of Italian unity, to which the popes' temporal sovereignty constituted an obstacle. Some were his own flock, notably the liberal Catholics of various countries who reproached the pope with failing to come to terms with the values of the modern world. There can be no doubt, however, that during his lifetime the vast majority of the faithful, the clergy and the episcopate, were in harmony with his teaching and his government of the Church.

---

[1]   G. Mollat, "Pie IX" in *Dictionnaire de Théologie Catholique*, 1935, XII, col.1686.

OPE PIUS IX

Catholics in Rome and in the entire world took the opportunity of
solemn ceremonies such as the eighteenth centenary of the martyrdom of
Saints Peter and Paul in 1867, Pius IX's priestly jubilee in 1869, and the
fiftieth anniversary of his episcopal consecration in 1877, to demonstrate
their enthusiasm and loyalty.

Nowadays most of the Catholic Church's faithful know nothing, or
almost nothing, of Pius IX. While in Italy, particularly thanks to the efforts of the Postulator of the cause of beatification of Pope Mastai, there
has been no lack of historiographical studies of more or less high quality,
the last biography of Pius IX to appear in France was published thirty
years ago.[2] While it was a disorderly work of compilation, abounding in
errors as to dates and names, it did have the merit of being the first book
in French to be based on the "informative process" of the cause of beatification and on the Secret Vatican Archives, which were closed at that time
except to a few rare researchers.

This is the place to mention a pioneering work that dates from the
same time, namely, *Le Pontificat de Pie IX*, by Roger Aubert. This book was
concerned only with the pontificate and did not discuss the earlier years,
which are so important for an understanding of Pius IX's governance of
the Church; even today, however, it remains a work of reference, albeit
many of its interpretations can be disputed. What Roger Aubert said at
the time is still true in France today: "There is as yet no critical biography
of Pius IX. Most of the biographies which were published during his lifetime or shortly after his death...are hardly more than panegyrics."[3]

What we are presenting to the reader today is, therefore, a critical
biography. This book will not be a complete history of the Church under
the pontificate of Pius IX. It does not give a detailed presentation of the
religious history of the different Catholic countries in the nineteenth century. Its purpose, more modestly, is to give a portrait of Pius IX that is not
restricted to the years of his pontificate but also considers the childhood,
youth, and ecclesiastical career of the man who was to become pope in
1846. In our view, great importance attaches to the young man's formation, and notably his spiritual formation, to the relationships which were
cemented in Rome in the early years of his priesthood, to his mission to
Chile, and to the episcopal charges he exercised in Spoleto and then in
Imola. All this is important if we are to understand the actions of the
pontificate that followed.

Although we are not writing a history of the Church under Pius IX,
but rather setting forth a biography that will be as complete and precise
as possible, we shall use the pontifical acts to throw light on the religious

---

[2] Pierre Fernessole, *Pie IX*, 2 vols. (Lethielleux, 1960-63).
[3] Roger Aubert, *Le Pontificat de Pius IX*, 2nd ed. (Bloud & Gay, 1963), p.6.

situation of different countries at one time or another. Our intention, in writing this biography of Pius IX, is to contribute to a better perspective on the development of the Church in the nineteenth century, without Manichaeism or anachronism.

There are many diverse sources, both printed and handwritten, for such a task. First and foremost there is the abundant Italian historical writing of recent decades. After the first biographies which appeared even during the pope's lifetime or in the years following his death, an initial synthesis was published at the beginning of the twentieth century.[4] This enterprise was premature, however, for it could not take account of most of the Roman and foreign archives, which remained untapped, nor could it have recourse to the many particular testimonies which were assembled during the Informative Process of the Cause. Later, Alberto Serafini started writing an enormous biography which he was unable to complete.[5] Roger Aubert judged it somewhat severely, including it, together with that of Fernessole, among those works which "belong to an obsolete hagiographical genre lacking all historical perspective."[6] All the same it must be said that Fernessole's 1,760 pages do contain many very interesting letters and documents.

From the 1970's, with the nomination of a new Postulator of the cause of beatification and canonization, Pius IX studies experienced a new impetus in Italy. A trimestrial review was initiated, dedicated to Pius IX's life and the history of his pontificate, a collection of *"Studi Piani"* was started at the Libreria Editrice Vaticana, and various colloquia have been organized.

In recent decades, independently of the above initiatives, Fr. Giacomo Martina, S.J., published an enormous study in three volumes, dedicated (like that of Roger Aubert) entirely to the pontificate.[7] It contains an exceptional wealth of documentary evidence, particularly from the Secret Vatican Archives, and will long remain a standard reference work for the political and diplomatic aspects of the pontificate. Certain major religious questions are also presented in detail. However, a number of the judg-

---

[4] Giuseppe Sebastiano Pelczar, *Pio IX e il suo pontificato*, 3 vols. (Turin: G. B. Berruti, 1909-11).

[5] *Pio Nono* (Tipografia Poliglotta Vaticana, 1958). Only the first volume was published, dealing with the years prior to the pontificate.

[6] Aubert, *Le Pontificat de Pie IX*, p.6.

[7] *Pio IX, 1846-1850* (Rome: Editrice Università Gregoriana, 1974); *Pio IX, 1851-1866* (Editrice Pontificia Università Gregoriana, 1986); *Pio IX, 1867-1878* (Editrice Pontificia Università Gregoriana, 1990).

ments and evaluations found in Fr. Martina's three weighty volumes are debatable.[8]

The 1980's also saw the publication of a *Life of Pius IX* by the archpriest of the cathedral of Senigallia, Pius IX's native town.[9] While this book does not always observe the rules of critical historical scholarship and restricts itself essentially to Italian sources, it does present a picture that is entirely favorable to Pius IX's beatification.

A further source which the historian cannot neglect is the evidence gathered for the process of beatification and canonization of Pius IX, insofar as he can gain access to it. In our final chapter we shall list the various stages of this process, which [at the time of writing was] still ongoing. The procedure was started at the beginning of the twentieth century with a detailed interrogation of 243 witnesses, lay and clerical, who knew Pius IX well. These depositions were collected into twelve large volumes and are at present in the possession of the Congregation for the Cause of Saints. These volumes are not available for consultation. On the other hand, thanks to the kindness of the current Postulator of the Cause, we were able to use the voluminous *Summarium* drawn up in 1954 by the Sacred Congregation of Rites. The *Summarium's* 1,159 pages is a distillation of the most important depositions. They contain many facts shedding interesting light on the different aspects of the life of the one who was proclaimed "Venerable" by John Paul II in 1985.

A third documentary source is composed of the various testimonies of Roman, Italian, and foreign contemporaries, and the numerous historical studies of this or that aspect of the pontificate. Many are the varied and important elements to be taken into account here, bearing in mind G. Mollat's strict requirement "to pass the works of Pius IX's apologists and his detractors through the sieve of a severe criticism."[10]

Finally, it proved valuable to look at certain archives again. The Secret Vatican Archives had been widely used by Giacomo Martina and Alberto Polverari. Since the works of these two authors appeared, a certain number of documents—particularly correspondence—from other archive collections (diocesan archives, State Archives of Spoleto, Macerata, Gaeta, Naples, *etc.*) have been published in several volumes, in a very limited number of copies, by Msgr. Cittadini. Not all these documents are free from the editor's hand; it is a pity that the correspondence has not been published as a critical edition, but interesting items can be found there.

---

[8]   Fr. Martina, who in 1987 was a member of the commission of seven experts charged with examining whether the beatification of Pius IX was "opportune," was the only one to regard it as inopportune. We shall return to this question at the conclusion of the present study.

[9]   Msgr. Alberto Polverari, *Vita di Pio IX,* 3 vols. (Editrice la Postulazione della causa di Pio IX, Libreria Editrice Vaticana, 1986-1988).

[10] Mollat, "Pie IX," col.1686.

It also proved fruitful to take a second look at the French archives, *i.e.*, the diplomatic dispatches preserved in the Archives of the Ministry of Foreign Affairs, letters and other writings held in the Archives of Saint-Sulpice, and various letters found in the Department of Manuscripts in the Bibliothèque Nationale. Some of these had been consulted in part by various historians, some of them were completely unedited; they furnish a number of valuable facts and analyses relating to different aspects of the pontificate.

Generally speaking, the Italian works on Pius IX are strongly marked by the problems surrounding Italian Unification and sometimes, consequently, tend to neglect the other issues, particularly religious issues; they also do not take foreign archival material into account.

The present book was written in two places: in Senigallia (where the residence where Pius IX was born houses a study center and an interesting museum) and in Rome where, for nearly ten years, Msgr. Piolanti, the Postulator of the cause, has honored me with his kind attention.

ACKNOWLEDGMENTS OF THE AUTHOR

My thanks go first to Msgr. Antonio Piolanti, Postulator of the cause of beatification of Pius IX. For almost a decade, in Rome, he encouraged me in various ways to pursue my work. Most importantly, he provided me with the *Summarium,* which is often cited in this book, an exceptional documentary source which is usually available only to members of the Congregation for the Cause of Saints.

Msgr. Angelo Mencucci, Director of the Pius IX Study Center and Museum at Senigallia, received me warmly and permitted me to work at my leisure in the rich library he superintends.

My thanks also to Fr. Irénée Noye, P.S.S., who generously admitted me to the Archives of the Seminary of Saint-Sulpice.

Many people allowed me to consult documentation that proved very useful to me, and I thank them here: Msgr. Pietro Biggio, Apostolic Nuncio to Santiago de Chile, Fr. Jésus Leceo of the General Curia of the Piarist Fathers (Scolopes), Fr. Luis Enrique Bernal, Archivist of the Congregation of Passionists, and the Archivist of the Institute of Masonic Studies and Research of the Grand Orient of France.

Finally, I record my gratitude to René Rancoeur and Grégoire Celier, who generously allowed me to consult their extensive libraries.

ABBREVIATIONS OF
FREQUENTLY CITED SOURCES

A.M.A.E., C.P. Rome: Archives of the Ministry of Foreign Affairs, Paris, Political Correspondence, Rome.

Annales I: *Annales ecclésiastiques de 1846 à 1866,* ed. Joseph Chantrel (Gaume & Co., 1887).

Annales II: *Annales ecclésiastiques de 1867 à 1868*, ed. Joseph Chantrel (Gaume & Co., 1896).

Annales III: *Annales ecclésiastiques de 1869 à 1873*, ed. Rev. François Chamard (Gaume & Co., 1893).

Annales IV: Joseph Chantrel, *Annales ecclésiastiques de 1873 à 1879* (Gaume & Co., 1896).

Aubert: Roger Aubert, *Le Pontificat de Pie IX*, 2nd ed. (Bloud & Gay, 1963).

Encyclicals I or II: *Encycliques et documents en français et en latin*, ed. Rev. Raulx, 2 volumes (L. Guerin, 1865).

Fernessole I or II: Pierre Fernessole, *Pie IX*, 2 volumes (Lethielleux, 1960, 1963).

Martina I, II, or III: Giacomo Martina, *Pio IX,* 3 volumes (Pontifical Gregorian University Press, 1974-1990).

Polverari I, II, or III: Msgr. Alberto Polverari, *Vita di Pio IX*, 3 volumes (La Postulazione della causa di Pio IX/Vatican Library Press, 1986-1988).

Serafini: Alberto Serafini, *Pio Nono* (Tipografia Poliglotta Vaticana, 1958).

Summarium: Sacred Congregation of Rites, *Positio super Introductione Causae*, Volume I: *Tabella testium et Summarium*, 1954.

CHAPTER 1

THE FIRST YEARS

Pius IX came from a noble family, the Mastai, who had lived in Senigallia for several generations. Nowadays Senigallia, which used to be spelled "Sinigaglia," is a seaside resort of 40,000 inhabitants, situated on the Adriatic coast between Ancona and Rimini.[1] The town's name comes from the Latin, Sena Gallica or Seno Gallia, witnessing to the fact that in the third century B.C. it was inhabited by a colony of Gauls from Sens.[2]

When the future Pius IX was born, Senigallia was part of the Papal States, which at that time included the Marches, Umbria, and Romagna, as well as Rome and Latium. The town had not yet become the sizeable resort it now is: it was a city of 8,000 inhabitants, with a prestigious past, but which had lost some of its former glory. Until the Middle Ages it had been a port city of some commercial importance; its markets enjoyed repute in the entire peninsula. At the beginning of the fourteenth century, however, the port of Trieste, on the opposite coast of the Adriatic, was liberated from the tutelage of Venice and began to develop vigorously; it became a formidable rival to the port of Senigallia, which began to slow down as a commercial center.

Apart from fishing, the annual fair was the town's only notable activity. The latter, which lasted for more than a month during the summer, was the most important fair in the Papal States. In its best years it attracted 300 to 400 ships with cargoes of all kinds from France, Greece, Dalmatia, Turkey, *etc*. Merchants used to come from all parts of the Italian peninsula. During the month of the fair the town teemed with people, and the population tripled or quadrupled. For the local inhabitants it was both a time of distractions and a source of profit. For the rest of the year the town's economy was generally dependent on its hinterland, and drew significant revenue from farming.

Pius IX belonged to one of the important Senigallia families, the Mastai. The family came from Crema in Lombardy.[3] In documents concern-

---

[1] Throughout this work, apart from exceptions, we shall observe the Italian orthography of proper names. Thus we shall speak of "St. Peter's," but of "Giovanni Maria Mastai."

[2] Luigi Salvatorelli, *Histoire de l'Italie* (Saint-Étienne: Editions Horvath, 1973), p.19.

[3] Msgr. Angelo Mencucci, *La genealogia della famiglia Mastai-Ferretti dal Mille ad oggi* (Senigallia: Rotary Club, 1992).

ing the town of Cremona from the eleventh to the end of the thirteenth century we find surnames close to that of the Mastai: De Mastaleis, De Mastaliis, Mastallia, Mastagius, Mastallius, Mastaius. However, it is in the nearby city of Crema that we find, in all certainty, the origins of this family.

One Francesco Mastai was born in Crema in 1520 and settled in Venice in 1540. His two sons, Pompeo and Giovanni Maria, moved to Senigallia between 1570 and 1580. They became town notables. Although he had only recently come to the town, Giovanni Maria was appointed first *regolatore* and then *gonfaloniere,* which, in modern terms, means that he became something like the town clerk and, subsequently, supreme magistrate. He was also regarded as a *nobile, i.e.,* indisputably noble. In 1653 the marriage of another Giovanni Maria Mastai to Margherita Ferretti, the daughter of a noble family of Ancona, resulted in the addition of a second surname. The coat of arms of the Mastai-Ferretti family expanded: the golden lion, crowned, on an azure ground (the Mastai arms) was quartered with red bars on a white ground (the Ferretti arms). A century later, in 1750, a third Giovanni Maria would receive the title of Count from the Duke of Parma.

This Mastai family (later Mastai-Ferretti) played an eminent role in Senigallia at the beginning of the seventeenth century. Having supplied the *regolatore* or *gonfaloniere* in that first generation, it did so several times subsequently. But members of the family also served as members of the city council or as *caporione*–which may be translated as commandant of the militia.

One also finds many ecclesiastics in the Mastai-Ferretti family: male and female religious, canons, beneficiary or conventual clergy, two consultors of the Holy Office, and a vicar-general. Three of the future Pius IX's four uncles were ecclesiastics. One, Andrea, having been canon of Senigallia cathedral, would become Bishop of Pesaro; the second, Gabriele, who was also a canon in Senigallia, was already dead when the future pope was born; the third, Paolino, had an ecclesiastical career in Rome, where he was secretary to the Rota and canon of the Basilica of Santa Maria Maggiore.

It was into this family of the minor nobility, devoted to the Church and the city, that Giovanni Maria Mastai-Ferretti, the future pope, was born. His father, Count Girolamo Mastai-Ferretti, had been born in 1750. The Pius IX Museum (the former Mastai residence) preserves a little print which portrays Count Girolamo in wig and jabot, showing the same smile which Giovanni Maria was to inherit. In 1780 Girolamo Mastai-Ferretti had married Caterina Solazzi di Faro, who was also a native of Senigallia. Count Girolamo was an important person in the town. Numerous authors indicate that he was several times elected *gonfaloniere* of Senigallia. We must be careful, however, not to lend too much importance to this office. Carlo Falconi, at the conclusion of a detailed study of the running of the municipality at this period, mentions that between 1782 and 1807 Girolamo Mastai was designated *gonfaloniere* eighteen times.[4] The office was temporary, however, and only lasted for twenty days; it was exercised by one of the twenty-six members of the council of nobles who administered the town. So, while the Count was indeed chosen eighteen times, which shows that he enjoyed his peers' esteem and confidence, he only administered the town for short and discontinuous periods. In any case, the *gonfaloniere* was not the town's chief administrator. He had to render account to a governor and to the local representative of the papal legate of Pesaro-Urbino.

Count Mastai had inherited certain property from his family which made him a comfortably well-off noble, but he had no dazzling fortune. At that time the Mastai palace was a large, square, brick-faced, three-story building. (Today it is only two-storied, since the upper story was destroyed as a result of an earthquake.) The only really noteworthy exterior ornaments are two doors with colonnades, surmounted by the arms of the family. As regards the first floor interior, mention should be made of a large reception-room decorated with seventeenth-century paintings, and a little private chapel including stations of the cross.

At Roncitelli, in the country, four miles from the town, the Mastai possessed another *palazzo* next to the little town's castle. This *palazzo*, of which practically nothing remains today, was in fact a modest house of several floors where the family regularly came on holiday. From there Count Girolamo could visit the farms which belonged to him. There is still a lively tradition which says that the future Pius IX was born at Roncitelli, where his mother was resting, and not in Senigallia;[5] but in fact there can be no doubt that the future Pius IX was born in the Mastai palace in Senigallia.

He was the last child of a family of four boys and five girls. First came three boys: Gabriele in 1781, Giuseppe in 1782, and Gaetano in 1783. The family's fourth child was a girl, Maria Virginia, born in 1784, but she died the following year. Four other girls followed: Maria Teresa in 1786, Maria Isabella in 1787, Maria Tecla in 1788, and Maria Virginia in 1790. Then, two years later, came Giovanni Maria, born May 13, 1792. He was baptized that very day in the Cathedral of St. Peter by his uncle Andrea.

4   Carlo Falconi, *Il giovane Mastai* (Milan: Rusconi, 1981), p.636.
5   Cf. Renato Lucchetti, "Pio IX e il Castello di Roncitelli," *Atti del II. Convegno di ricerca storica sulla figura e sull'opera di papa Pio IX, October 9, 10, 11, 1977* (Senigallia: Centro Studi Pio IX), pp.435-446; hereafter, *Atti del II. Convegno.*

His Christian names were: Giovanni Maria, Giovanni Battista, Pietro, Pellegrino, Isidoro; he was usually called by the first two.

We also know that, on the very day of his birth, he was consecrated to the Virgin Mary by his mother; in this she was following a pious custom that was widespread at the time. One of the first acts of Giovanni Maria, once he had become Pope, was to renew this consecration. Thus he showed that he desired to place the second part of his life under the special protection of the Virgin Mary, just as the first had been.

Family Piety

We know relatively little about the early childhood of Pius IX apart from what he himself or members of his family reported later.

As was usual at the time in noble and middle-class families, Giovanni Maria was given to a wet-nurse shortly after birth. The Mastai family possessed several farms in and around Senigallia, and they entrusted the new-born infant to their Roncitelli farming folk. The farmer's wife, Marianna Chiarini, had a child of the same age as Giovanni Maria, called Domenico. So the two boys were nourished by the same milk and brought up in the same farming milieu: there was a one-story farmhouse with extensive yards, near to the village. The farm no longer exists.

Marianna Chiarini used to call the Mastai child "Giovaninno" (or, more usually, "Giuanin" in the local dialect). This nickname stuck with him even after he had returned to Senigallia.

Giovaninno received his first Christian education from his mother. Recently some writers, in order to counteract the "hagiographical" portrayals of his early childhood, have insisted on the importance of the personality of Caterina Mastai, describing her as a thrifty housewife "lacking any aura of aristocratic refinement, a real woman of the people–even if she was not actually that."[6] Such descriptions, based solely on a portrait kept in the Resorgimento Museum in Milan, are given the lie by certain facts. The Pius IX Museum contains a number of pious artifacts which belonged to Caterina Mastai, showing that she had a solid piety. This she knew how to transmit to her children.

Later, Pius IX was happy to speak of several features of this religious education.[7] It was his mother who taught him to pray every morning and evening. It was she who taught him the habit of renouncing the first of every fruit which, according to the season, appeared on the table, and offering this little sacrifice to the Blessed Virgin. As Pius IX one day said to some women religious: "I learned this practice at my mother's knee, and I

---

[6] Falconi, *Il giovane Mastai*, p.35.
[7] All these features are given in the *Summarium*.
[8] *Summarium* §355. The 1,159 pages of the *Summarium* are divided into 3,603 numbered paragraphs. The references here are to the paragraphs, not the pages.

have always maintained it. Now that I am Pope, I still do it."[8] His mother also went to the early Mass every day, celebrated at the church of San Martino, which was under the care of the Servite Fathers. In the church there is a tableau representing Our Lady of the Seven Dolors, traditionally shown as a Virgin whose heart is pierced by seven knives. Caterina Mastai had great devotion to her. As soon as Giovanni Maria had reached the age of reason he used to accompany his mother to this daily morning Mass.

Did his brothers and sisters do the same? Probably not; but whether it was his mother who encouraged the child to accompany her every morning, or Giovanni Maria himself who asked to be allowed to go with her, there can be no doubt that Caterina Mastai had a notable religious influence on her son. We see this same influence some decades later in the case of the mother of St. John Bosco or the mother of St. Pius X. In all these instances the influence of the mother, even if it did not determine the child's vocation, was of great and lasting importance.

Another devotion to which Pius IX remained very attached, and with which he was acquainted from his earliest years, was the devotion to Our Lady of Loreto.

Loreto is only about thirty miles from Senigallia. On many occasions the Mastai family went on pilgrimage to the Holy House, the house of the Virgin Mary which, according to tradition, had been miraculously brought there from Nazareth. Every year, on December 10, like many families of the region, the Mastai family would spend part of the night in prayer, celebrating the Translation of the Holy House. At different moments of his life–as a priest, a bishop, and a pope–Pius IX would go back on pilgrimage to Our Lady of Loreto.[9]

His early childhood was not taken up solely with acts of piety, however. It is reported that he was "a naturally lively child who loved conversation,"[10] that he willingly took part in the games appropriate at his age. As an old man, Pius IX recalled that he had played "with the son of a Jacobin" who eventually became a revolutionary.[11] Later on, he loved playing ball, hunting, and swimming in the canal which flows into the sea.

Little Giovanni Maria's childhood was marked by an accident. One day in 1797, while playing in the Roncitelli farmyard, he fell into a large well and was almost drowned. The farmer himself jumped into the well and saved him.[12] This incident is more than anecdotal, for some of his contemporaries expressed the view that the attacks of epilepsy, from which

[9] Aldo Alberoni, "Caratteristiche della spiritualità di Pio IX," *Atti del II. Convegno*, p.399.
[10] *Summarium* §2815.
[11] Audience of December 29, 1872; in *Actes et paroles de Pie IX captif au Vatican* (Paris: Victor Palmé, 1974), p.312; hereafter, *Actes et paroles*.
[12] *Summarium* §356 and §692; but the testimonies differ regarding the place: a stream, a fishpond, *etc.*

the Mastai youth suffered as he emerged from adolescence, originated in this terrifying childhood experience.

Another fact that made a deep impression on the childhood of the future pope was the French invasion of the Papal States. At that time Italy was divided into a number of sovereign states. The most important, in the northwest, was the Kingdom of Sardinia (or Piedmont-Sardinia); in the north-east Austria controlled Lombardy, with Milan and Venetia.

The Directoire decided to send the young general Napoleon Bonaparte to northern Italy with the mission of separating the Piedmontese from the Austrians, both of whom were at war with France, and re-floating the state coffers.

It is well known that this first Italian campaign, begun in April 1796, was a dazzling success for Bonaparte. He forced the Piedmontese to ask for a separate peace, and obliged Austria to sign an armistice in 1797. Then he turned his attention to the Papal States. The orders given by one head of the Directoire, La Revellière-Lepeaux, give a clear idea of the hatred of the Church which inspired this invasion: he wrote that "Rome's Pius the Last must be overthrown; the hydra of priestly fanaticism must be crushed in its lair." Of course, the young General Bonaparte was not motivated by this kind of hatred, but all the same he obeyed the orders he was given and allowed his troops to ill-treat the clergy and pillage the churches. In Tolentino Pius VI was forced to sign a peace treaty in which he ceded a part of his territory, namely the Legations of Bologna and Ferrara. During these operations Napoleon Bonaparte stopped at Senigallia on two occasions.

Napoleon had already returned to France when, at the beginning of 1798, on the pretext of incidents which had taken place in Rome, the Directoire ordered General Berthier to invade what remained of the Papal States. Senigallia was occupied by troops who, as everywhere else in Italy, behaved brutally and were not slow to lay hands on church treasures.

Rome too was occupied, the Roman Republic was proclaimed, and Pius VI, in spite of his great age and failing health, was taken prisoner.[13] He was transferred to Siena, where he remained for three months, and then to the Florence Charterhouse. There was question of him being deported to Sardinia. In the end he was taken to Parma, where he stayed for some days; then his forced exile continued via Turin, the Col du Montgenèvre, Gap, Grenoble, Romans, and finally Valence, where he died of exhaustion in August 1799. The Conclave could not meet until the fol-

---

[13] A detailed account of his tribulations is given in *Histoire civile, politique et religieuse de Pie VI*, "compiled from authentic memoranda by a French Roman Catholic" (Avignon, n.d. [1802?]), pp.347-390.

[14] Elected March 14, 1800, Pius VII entered Rome the following July. Coming from Venice, he spent the night of June 21 at Senigallia. So it was that the young Mastai saw for the first time the pope who would play an important role in his path to the priesthood.

lowing December, in Venice. Cardinal Chiaramonti was elected Pope and took the name of Pius VII.[14]

The French occupation, the disorders it brought about, and the violence offered to the Pope aroused much emotion in the Mastai family. Caterina taught her son, at this time, to "pray for the Church's enemies"[15] and to add to his evening prayers one *Pater* and one *Ave* for the intentions of the Pope, now a prisoner, and for the conversion of his persecutors.

It was in this context of upheaval that Giovanni Maria received the sacrament of Confirmation on June 6, 1799. At this period it was customary to admit children to the sacrament of Confirmation at the age of seven, whereas they were not admitted to First Communion until around the age of eleven. His private teacher, Don Francesco Teloni, prepared the young Mastai boy for Confirmation. The ceremony took place in the chapel of the episcopal palace, and the sacrament was conferred by Cardinal Honorati, Bishop of Senigallia.

Giovanni Maria was a devout and charitable child. As a witness reported at the canonization process, "from childhood he showed himself aloof from all deliberate sin."[16] He was "very kind and friendly, generous to the poor, and he was always happy to be able to give alms, never hesitating to deprive himself."[17] Nor is this portrayal overdone: at Senigallia he was commonly called *Giovaninno il Buono* ("good little Giovanni"). In the beatification process it was also reported that, even as a child, he loved to play the part of the street-preacher, holding up a cross and addressing an improvised sermon to his comrades as he urged them to follow him to the church.[18]

He made his First Communion on the Feast of the Purification, February 2, 1803, in the cathedral of Senigallia. It was also the Feast of the *Madonna della Speranza* (Our Lady of Hope), honored in a chapel in the cathedral. As a memento of this twofold event, Giovanni's mother gave him a picture of the *Madonna della Speranza*. He kept it always, for it reminded him of the first great religious emotion he had felt. He made his Communion fervently. In all probability his desire to become a priest dates from this day.[19]

It is worth noting that he was not yet eleven when he made his First Communion, whereas the other communicants were twelve or thirteen. No doubt he was thought sufficiently prepared to make his Communion earlier than the prescribed age at that time. Once he was Pope he began, by various acts, to work against this custom of administering First Com-

---

[15] *Summarium* §54.
[16] *Summarium* §57.
[17] *Summarium* §51.
[18] This cross can be seen today in the Pius IX Museum.
[19] *Summarium* §2855.

munion relatively late; it remained for a later pontificate–that of Saint Pius X–to see the age of First Communion officially lowered to seven years.

At the College of St. Michael

Having completed his initial schooling at home under the direction of his teacher, Don Teloni, Giovanni Maria was sent to a college of the Piarist Fathers ("Scolopes") at Volterra.[20]

This religious order was founded in the seventeenth century, devoted especially to Christian education. In Italy and elsewhere it had about ten colleges of high reputation. One of Giovanni Maria's uncles on his father's side, Canon Andrea Mastai, had completed his studies at the Roman college of the order, and was acquainted with some of the teachers at the Volterra college. It was he who persuaded Count Mastai to send his youngest son to this distant college.

Volterra is situated some 185 miles from Senigallia, to the west of Siena. As is attested by important remains, it had a prominent Etruscan, and subsequently Roman past. At the beginning of the nineteenth century it was a little city of 2,500 inhabitants belonging to the Grand Duchy of Tuscany. For those times, therefore, the journey the Mastai boy had to undertake, outside the Papal States, was a long one. His uncle the canon accompanied him.

The college, founded in 1710, was dedicated to St. Michael and accommodated sixty boys from noble or well-to-do families. Most of them were boarders. Giovanni Maria arrived there on October 20, 1803. He was eleven, and he stayed there until 1809.[21]

The education given at the College of St. Michael was solid; it was organized over seven years, with three cycles: *scuola di grammatica, scuola d'umanità, scuola di rettorica* (schools of "grammar, humanities, and rhetoric"). The first cycle, which lasted for two years, was basically concerned with the teaching of Italian and "general principles of geography and history." Arithmetic and penmanship were also taught. Young Mastai only spent one year in this cycle because he had already learned the rudiments of these various subjects from his own teacher. The *scuola d'umanità* lasted for three years, and consisted of Italian, Latin, Greek, history, geography, and mythology. Finally, the last two years (*scuola di rettorica*) were

---

[20] The Scolopes Fathers—the word is a corruption of the Italian "Scuole Pie," "religious schools"—are also called "Piarists" from the name of their religious order: the *Ordo Clericorum Regularium Pauperum Matris Dei Scholarum Piarum.* They should not be confused, as various authors have done, with the Christian Brothers. In France they are also called *"Calasantins"* after their founder, Giuseppe Calasanz.

[21] Certain authors say that he arrived on August 20, 1803, or 1802. The wealth of archive documents reproduced by Giovanni Ausenda and Claudio Vilà Palà, in *Pio IX y las escuelas pias* (Rome: Editiones Calasanctianae, 1979), provide us with exact knowledge of these college years.

particularly devoted to mathematics, physics, and philosophy. Literature, however, was not ignored, and there was also some teaching of "civil institutions" and of mineralogy.

All these subjects were taught by the Piarist Fathers. One of them, Fr. Giovanni Inghirami, became an astronomer and cartographer of repute. When Giovanni Maria arrived at the college, Fr. Inghirami was teaching philosophy, physics, mathematics, and Greek. He was the young Mastai's teacher of Greek from 1803 to 1805, before leaving the college for other duties in his order.

The boys were also able to attend optional courses in other subjects: French, music, singing, drawing, decorative arts, painting, civil or military architecture, and dancing. These courses were given by external teachers.

Giovanni Maria must also have attended courses in French, because later he was able to make himself understood in that language. In addition, as we know, he learned to play the flute and the cello; in later life he remained fond of these instruments. Drama, poetry, dancing, and music were regularly given a prominent place at the college: there were public performances of plays, religious or profane, and of ballets, and there were recitals of music.

Naturally, religious instruction and practice occupied an important place in the boys' daily life. Each one had a book of prayers and hymns so that he could take part in the day's various religious devotions. They were taught to begin the day with private prayer. Then the *Miserere* was recited in common. All the pupils assembled in the chapel for daily Mass. The midday meal was preceded by the recitation of the *Angelus* and a private examination of conscience. The day ended with the recitation of the Rosary and the Litany of the Saints. On Sunday, before Mass, the boys listened to a spiritual talk followed by an explanation of the Gospel of the day. Confession and Holy Communion were obligatory once a month.

Discipline was severe. The intention was to give the boys a solid education. The head of the college was the Father Rector, and the Father Minister was in charge of discipline. The latter was assisted in this task by "prefects" (*camerata* in Italian) who were chosen from among the most serious boys. Giovanni Maria was a prefect for several years. Discipline did not consist only in the observance of a detailed rule, but also in the acquisition of a style of behavior that was imbued with dignity and poise. Thus the rule stipulated that "The young gentlemen of the college should treat each other with the greatest civility. Among themselves, accordingly, they must not use nicknames or other improper terms...nor show too much familiarity."[22]

---

[22] Cited by Ausenda and Vilà Palà, *op. cit.*, p.51.

Every evening they were allowed to go out into the countryside beyond the town gates, but it was forbidden to go into Volterra itself, except
in order to take a meal with some family in the town, with the permission
of the Father Rector or Father Minister. It was forbidden to take meals
outside on religious feast days or during the Carnival. There was a further
exception: from June 1 to September 1 the boys could go and play ball
or football in an enclosed field in the town, taking it in turns by dormi-
tory. The only games allowed within the college itself were draughts and
chess.

The pupils saw their families only once a year, for forty days in the autumn, unless the family came to visit Volterra or the surrounding region.
The Mastai family used to stay in Santa Margherita or Pignano—which
were near the college—from May to October. It seems that young Mastai
did not see Senigallia again until 1809.

So, from the age of eleven to seventeen, the Mastai boy received a very
varied education, sustained by a discipline which, while strict, was not
harsh. Pius IX recalled one of the Father Ministers he had known during
his last two years as a boarder, Fr. Ceccherini: he was "severe and inflexible
in keeping discipline, but extremely kind at the same time."

Zeal and discipline, just as much as the study of school subjects, were
stimulated by an "Academy." This Academy consisted of three sections
(Literature, Philosophy, and Arts), and its membership was made up of
the teachers and the best pupils. It was not sufficient, to gain admission
to this Academy, to shine in this or that subject; prospective members also
had to have obtained the "good conduct medal" and to present a certifi-
cate from the Father Minister. The Academy organized "tournaments" in
which teams of pupils competed. A topic was announced, and they would
have to produce a literary composition; the festivities would also include a
ballet, a fencing match, a concert of music, or some other entertainment.
The Academy had a hierarchical structure, with the best pupils gradually
ascending the various rungs of the ladder.

Giovanni Maria was a candidate for the Arts Section of the Academy,
most probably in 1806, but he was not a member at that time. We do
not know whether his candidature was rejected, or if he failed to attain a
satisfactory level in one of the three obligatory subjects for this section,
namely, mathematics, penmanship, and French. Eventually he was admitted to the Literature Section in August 1807. The following December
18 he was elected as "censor." On March 30, 1809, he was elected to the
Philosophy Section. Finally, in July 1809 he was elected "consul."

The "consulate" was the highest degree of the Academy. According to
the Academy's regulations, the consul "should set an example to the others by his zeal in studies and his application." Giovanni Maria, no doubt,

had merited this honor in virtue of his undeniable intellectual and moral qualities. His conduct and piety made him a model pupil. At the beatification process Fr. Raphael Cianfrocca, the assistant general of the Piarist Fathers, recorded the impression the Mastai youth made on the fathers of the College: "Throughout the six years he spent at our College, he showed himself to be a model of piety and assiduous study."[23]

Another important feature should be mentioned in connection with these years at Volterra, namely, the great Marian devotion, and particularly the devotion to the Immaculate Conception, which the Piarist Fathers promoted in their colleges. Giovanni Maria, who was already, under his mother's influence, devoted to the *Addolorata* ("Our Lady of Sorrows") and Our Lady of Loreto, found in Volterra an atmosphere conducive to the development of his Marian devotion.

According to their statutes, the Piarist Fathers are "clerks regular of the Mother of God." Their founder, St. Joseph Calasanz (1558-1648), had invented the devotion of the "Crown of Twelve Stars"–a daily invocation of the twelve privileges of the Virgin Mary. The Virgin's fourth privilege, according to Calasanz's devotion, is her having been preserved from original sin: "Praised be God the Father who preserved the Virgin Mary unspotted when she was conceived." This belief in the Virgin's Immaculate Conception was not a dogma of faith at the time; everyone knows that it was Pius IX who defined it in 1854.

Certain authors have suggested that this devotion of the Twelve Privileges was promoted at the College of St. Michael and that the Immaculate Conception was celebrated there in grand style. They think that, once he had become a priest, Giovanni Maria Mastai remained attached to the devotion. In this view, the College's pious practice of the "Crown of Twelve Stars" was one of the factors influencing him to promulgate the dogma of the Immaculate Conception. They see the proof of this in the fact that, three months after the dogma was proclaimed, Pius IX enriched the "Crown of Twelve Stars" with spiritual favors.

However attractive it may be, this reconstruction is not based on any conclusive fact. In the (very detailed) regulations of the College of St. Michael, enumerating the prayers and pious practices to be made every day or at different moments in the liturgical year, there is no mention whatsoever of the "Crown of Twelve Stars."

At Volterra there is no picture or statue from this period which can be linked to this devotion. Nor is it mentioned in the prayer-books used at the College as far as we know. It seems legitimate to conclude, therefore, that this "Crown of Twelve Stars" was not current at Volterra when young

---

[23] *Summarium* §2016.

Mastai was a pupil there. He only became acquainted with it later, in Rome, or more likely when he became Bishop of Spoleto.

Nonetheless, devotion to the Immaculate was certainly present in Volterra in other forms. The "Academy" was explicitly placed under her patronage, and every year a triduum of prayers in honor of the "Conception of the Virgin Mary" was celebrated. In other words, Pius IX had been familiar with devotion to the Immaculate Virgin from his youth, even if there is no direct link with later practices.

The Great Trial

Between 1807 and 1809, while he was at the College of St. Michael, Giovanni Maria had the first of his epileptic attacks which made life difficult for him and obstructed his vocation for several years.

Writers differ as to the precise date, but a statement of Pius IX himself allows us to be certain of the location where it took place. Returning to Volterra in 1857, having conducted an important pastoral journey to his estates, he expressed the desire to see his old College. On entering the little ante-room next door to the Father Minister's room, he turned to the Grand Duke of Tuscany who was accompanying him and said: "That's where I had my first epileptic attack; that seemed to be the end of everything as far as I was concerned, but Providence...."[24] But the Pope did not go into the details of this dramatic event. At the beatification process one witness stated that the attack came after a violent quarrel with another pupil.[25] Today it is still difficult to ascertain the exact nature of the illness from which the Mastai youth suffered. In the absence of authoritative medical archives it is impossible to say whether it was a generalized or partial epilepsy. All the same, witnesses agree that the attacks were violent and followed by a loss of consciousness. Can a link be established between the boys' quarrel and the child's fear of drowning? Would these incidents be enough to provoke epileptic attacks? Psychologists are still debating the issue.[26]

In the years to come Giovanni Maria would experience many other epileptic attacks, but they were intermittent. He was able to complete his school studies at St. Michael's College in the normal way. On September 7, 1809, in the presence of the Bishop of Volterra, the Sub-Prefect, and the Mayor of the town, he successfully passed an examination in physics and mathematics concerning "optical machines" and was awarded the

---

[24] Cited by Ausenda and Vilà Palà, *Pio IX y las escuelas pias*, p.95.

[25] *Summarium* §2412.

[26] In the nineteenth century, most of the biographers-hagiographers of Pius IX did not dare to mention epilepsy but spoke of a "sickness thought to be fatal," miraculously cured. Cf. Alex de Saint-Albin, *Histoire de Pie IX et de son pontificat* (Paris: Victor Palmé; Brussels: Joseph Albanel, 1878), I, 9.

prize of a mathematics book. Two days later, as Academy "consul," he opened a session devoted to "Greek historical records" with a dithyrambic ode entitled "The Genius of Homer."

Thus brilliantly he concluded his school days, which had given him a considerable humanistic and scientific training. His subsequent theological formation may have been somewhat desultory, but at Volterra he had received a solid basis in profane scholarship.

Finally, on October 7, he received the clerical tonsure at the hands of Msgr. Incontri, Bishop of Volterra, after having obtained letters dimissory from Cardinal Gabriella, Bishop of Senigallia.[27] Certain writers have chosen to see this as the sign not of a definite vocation, but of opportunism, i.e., of the desire to follow an ecclesiastical career.[28] They surmise that his family's financial difficulties in the wake of the French occupation prompted him to ask for the tonsure in order to obtain ecclesiastical benefices, such as a prelature, without having to embrace the priesthood.

At the very outset, however, this explanation is involved in contradiction. Why would the young Mastai have wanted to receive the tonsure at Volterra if his aim was only to seek a profitable ecclesiastical career in Senigallia? He would only have had to wait a few days, and he would have been at home again. This strongly suggests that receiving the tonsure at Volterra was evidence of perfect sincerity on his part.

We can imagine that, by taking this first step towards the priesthood in the college he was about to leave, Giovanni Maria wanted to show the great spiritual debt he owed to his "Scolopes" (Piarist) teachers. This tonsure, and the adoption of the soutane which accompanies it, is also the first commitment of a soul that has long been impregnated with a profound faith. We have already mentioned the young boy's desire, at the time of his First Communion, to become a priest. There was also the example of his two canon uncles, and in general the regular life of piety which was lived at the college.

This, surely, allows us to regard the first clerical step of October 1809 as being utterly sincere. In a letter to Msgr. Incontri, Mastai himself, when he had just received the cardinal's hat, recalled this ceremony at St. Michael's College as "the first stone" of an edifice willed by God.[29]

---

[27] Many works repeat the error of the college chronicler and situate this first step towards the priesthood on September 26. However, the Volterra episcopal registers give us the exact date.

[28] Falconi, *Il giovane Mastai*, pp.98-99.

[29] Cited by Vilà Palà. *Pio IX y las escuelas pias*, p.77.

CHAPTER 2

A DIFFICULT PATH TO THE PRIESTHOOD

Having stayed for a while in Senigallia, Giovanni Maria left for Rome in December 1809.[1] In recent times an author has constructed a kind of popular novel about the youth of the future Pius IX–with all the appearance of a serious and erudite work–in which he portrayed the young Mastai's first visit to Rome as "a few weeks' tourism."[2] All the evidence is contrary to this interpretation.

Giovanni Maria went to Rome to pursue his studies for the priesthood. He lived with one of his uncles on his father's side, Canon Paolino Mastai, who worked at the Curia as an under-secretary at the Memorials. His functions allowed the canon to reside in the Apostolic Palace of the Quirinal, where, at that time, Pius VII himself lived.

Later, with his own hand, Pius IX would himself correct the account of a Jesuit historian, Fr. Ballerini, who had undertaken to write his biography. Ballerini had written that the Mastai youth had gone to Rome "for his apprenticeship in theology." Pius IX corrected the manuscript, pointing out that he had come "to attend courses in philosophy, physics, and mathematics…at the Roman College under the direction of Professor Fr. Conti."[3] Was it his intention to go on to some seminary or other? Doubtless, yes. At that time the young man was dressed as a cleric and there is no indication that he had abandoned the idea of the priesthood.[4]

However, this stay in Rome was short. Historical events obliged the young Mastai to return to Senigallia. Some months before, in June 1809, following the annexation of the Papal States by Napoleon I, Pius VII had issued a bull of excommunication against the "usurpers, instigators, advisors, and executors" of the temporal violation of the Holy See. In response, on the night of July 5-6, Napoleon had the pope arrested and imprisoned in Savona.

Rome and Latium were divided into two departments, Tiber and Trasimeno, and completely integrated into the French Empire. Institutions were re-fashioned after the French model.[5] So the city the young Mastai

---

[1] Fernessole says that he arrived in Rome "at the start of 1809" (I, 2). This dating contradicts all the archives making reference to the last months of his stay in Volterra.
[2] Falconi, *Il giovane Mastai*, p.114.
[3] Cited by Polverari, I, 33.
[4] *Summarium* §362 and §2415.

found in December 1809 was in upheaval. Eventually the Curia was entirely dispersed, Canon Paolino Mastai had to leave, and Giovanni Maria abandoned the clerical habit and returned to Senigallia, probably before the end of the university year, 1810.[6]

Years of Trial

It was due to the edicts of the new French administration that he abandoned clerical attire and left Rome. Giovanni Maria was not able to resume his studies until 1814. The years 1810-1814 have been the subject of the most colorful hypotheses, during the pope's own lifetime and right up to the present day.

In 1854, in a biography of the pope then reigning, a well-intentioned author wrote:

> The decree of 1811, by which Napoleon established the Guards of Honor, found Mastai in one of those hours of indecision when he was not sure where to apply his activities. At the age of nineteen, not yet having heard the irresistible call of God, the young count joined the 1st Squadron of the 1st Regiment....Then he set out and served for two years in these elite regiments. When Napoleon fell and the Empire was dismembered, Mastai entered an Austrian regiment, but did not stay there: there was too little in common, in terms of character and ideas, between the other officers and himself. Once he was free again, he requested and—with great difficulty—obtained admittance to the Noble Guard which had been reconstituted by Pope Pius VII.[7]

Later, two months after the death of Pius IX, a Masonic magazine, amplifying some rumors which had already been published in former years, published what was claimed to be the testimony of a former comrade-in-arms of the young Mastai. Not only did the witness quoted say that he had acted as sponsor at the future pope's initiation into Freemasonry, he even went on in these terms:

> At the time I was sub-lieutenant and he was in the same squadron. He was a very lively character. Like all the rest of us, he had some amorous escapades at Thionville....After the fall of Napoleon, Mastai, like all the other Italian nobles, was eager to leave France. Mastai was of a military turn of mind and entered Pius VII's dragoons, where he reached the rank of captain. He was to be married. When his fiancée was burned to death at a ball, his grief drove him to a monastery, where he received orders and became pope.[8]

---

[5]   Jean-Marcel Champion, "Pie VII," and Jacques Godechot, "Rome," *Dictionnaire Napoléon*, ed. Jean Tulard (Paris: Fayard 1987).
[6]   During this period his Uncle Andrea, who had become Bishop of Pesaro in 1806, was arrested, ejected from this diocese, and exiled to northern Italy.
[7]   E. de Saint-Hermel, *Pie IX* (Paris: Lib. Hachette & Cie, 1854), pp.25-26.

More recently, not without a certain finesse, Carlo Falconi revived these suppositions. He presents the young Mastai at this time as a "daring young dandy" and tries to reconstruct the story of his "forbidden romance."[9]

None of these more or less crude reconstructions can stand up to the facts. Certain documents of indisputable authenticity provide us with indications shedding light, to some extent, on these hidden years. There can be no question of establishing a year-by-year account of his life at that time, and sometimes we have to be content with hypotheses. All the same, these documents are quite adequate to dispatch rumors and guesswork.

Something the young Mastai wrote dated April 10, 1810, reveals to us his state of mind at the moment he was leaving Rome. This is found in the notes he took during a course of the Spiritual Exercises.[10] This text is interesting for three reasons: it is the earliest manuscript of the future Pius IX that we possess; it shows us that, at this time, he was accustomed to make the Spiritual Exercises; and finally, by putting the words "in the lay state" after the date, he shows indisputably that the fact of having abandoned clerical dress was not unimportant in the eyes of the young Mastai. Above all, it shows that this young man, who was nearly nineteen, had already achieved a great spiritual maturity, and that there was nothing superficial about his religious life:

> In the name of the Most Holy Trinity, the Most Blessed Virgin, Saints Joseph, John the Baptist, John the Evangelist, Louis Gonzaga, Philip Neri, Joseph Calasanz, Francis of Assisi, and my Guardian Angel.
>
> My soul, reform your conduct; repent of so many sins committed and keep your faults ever before your eyes. Give thanks to God who has been waiting for you until this very day, and resolve to live always, and as much as possible, in his grace.
>
> Flee the occasions of sin. It is much better for you to keep away from company which has nothing holy about it and which you never leave without having committed at least some venial sin. Let there be no more of these speculative and earth-bound ideas that attach you to gold or to vanity; never take thought for tomorrow's needs; submit yourself to the will of God in all things. Remember that voluntary venial sins incline those who commit them to be scornful of the divine Majesty; furthermore, it seems to me that, up to now, you avoid mortal sins for fear of hell rather than for the love which you owe to God.

---

[8] "Pie IX fut-il reçu franc-maçon avant d'être pape?" *La Chaîne d'Union*, April 1878, pp.138-39.

[9] Falconi, *Il giovane Mastai*, pp.127ff.

[10] Fernessole publishes the photograph of the manuscript and offers a translation (pp. 21-23). We have completed and corrected his translation by using the version given by Polverari I, 35. The date is erroneously given as March 10 in Serafini, p.29, and Luigi Bogliolo, *Pio IX: Profilo spirituale* (Vatican City: Editrice la Postulazione della causa di Pio IX/Libreria Editrice Vaticana, 1989).

Humble yourself often, and hate pride with all your strength; check these motions of anger; answer everyone with a good grace. Always try to walk with eyes cast down; control all human respect. To avoid irreligious, impure, and other thoughts, frequently raise your mind to God; make ejaculatory prayers very frequently, but make them from the bottom of your heart. Out of charity, flee venial sins, which are the escorts of mortal sins: if you feel drawn to taste, experience, or be curious about anything, lower your eyes.

Remember that, if God gives you ability and health, you must study in order to learn and in order to be instructed in the path of grace, not out of the ambition to know things. Every time you sit down at your desk, lift your soul to God with this in mind.

Do not be weak; show courage in resisting those who would try to inveigle you into dangerous pursuits.

Remember, finally, that life is short and that we have nothing to bring before God, at his terrible Judgment, except what we have done in life. Be at peace, therefore, and carry out the divine design which has been set before you.

There follow extracts in Latin from the Bible and various spiritual authors, and then personal reflections in the form of maxims. *E.g.*, "The pillars of the heavens have fallen: who shall guarantee that I shall stand upright?"; "Woe to those who, living in the world, delay penitence until the point of death. Woe also to the religious who slumber until death overtakes them."

Such determination, on the threshold of difficult years, shows that the young Mastai was possessed of a great clarity of vision. He knew his weaknesses and was striving to combat them. Furthermore, he had resolved to remain faithful to God's design for him (the text says *sistema divina*). Yet this was also the start of a period characterized by much uncertainty for him. Was his serious illness curable? Would his state of health and the French occupation allow him to find his way to the path of studies and the priesthood?

Different documents attest the seriousness of his illness. No medical report has come down to us, but we know that various medical examinations were made, no doubt in the wake of the first crises at Volterra. These crises were to recur after he had left the College.

Once Giovanni Maria was back in Senigallia after his brief stay in Rome, the doctors advised him to avoid prolonged periods of study. This gave rise to the practice of various distractions during these years: ball games, horse-riding, music, long walks, and holidays on the Roncitelli estate or with his parents, not far from Senigallia, at Iesi, Ostra Vetere, Ancona, and Treia.

This also explains why he was looking for some employment. One of his childhood friends, Giovanni Marchetti, had become the secretary of

Antonio Aldini, Napoleon's confidential advisor in the Kingdom of Italy. When Aldini was called to France, his secretary followed him. At that time young Mastai wrote to his friend Marchetti asking him to get him "a post in the French Imperial administration or in the Kingdom of Italy."[11] Does this mean that, at that time, the future pope had given up the idea of becoming an ecclesiastic? We cannot say for certain. It may be that he was just biding his time, and that he was seeking a paid position only in order to provide some distraction and a certain amount of income (since the family's financial situation was always precarious).

However, the epileptic attacks (and again we have no way of assessing their severity) continued to affect him. In February 1812, according to a statement made four months later by two *industrianti* of Senigallia, the young Mastai was found in a state of collapse, foaming at the mouth, at the entrance of the family's mansion-house. It was this epilepsy that excused him from military service.

Some months after this event, in his twentieth year, like all the young men of his age, he was included in the list of conscripts, drawn up by the Senigallia magistrate, who were to form part of the Guard of Honor of the Kingdom of Italy. (Napoleon had proclaimed himself King of Italy in 1805.) Conscription began on November 4. Mastai presented himself, but the same day he wrote to a friend: "I am tormented by horrible cramps; perhaps they will exempt me"[12]–which is what happened. On several occasions the French Vice-Prefect in Senigallia had been present at the Mastai palace when the family's youngest son had had an epileptic attack. He decided to exempt him from military service. However, his superior, the Prefect of Ancona, in a letter dated November 12, demanded that the Mastai boy pay an exemption tax of 1,151 écus before December 5.[13] Giovanni Maria asked to be dispensed from this tax, but his request was refused in a letter of January 27, 1813.

Certain authors, including even the first Postulator of the cause of beatification, have suggested that the young Mastai "immediately went to Saint-Cloud to implore the intervention of Napoleon I. Fortunately the latter gave him a rescript exempting him."[14] In fact, if he was indeed given an exemption, it was after measures taken at Bologna. One of his childhood friends, Giacinta Marchetti, had married a colonel of the Guards of Honor of the Kingdom of Italy, Count Francesco Milzetti. Count Milzetti, as commanding officer of the 4th Company of the Romagna, was also responsible for conscription in the Marches. He was therefore the man

---

[11] Letter of April 12, 1812.
[12] Letter cited by Polverari, I, 36-37.
[13] Msgr. Cani, *Procès romain pour la cause de beatification et de canonisation du Serviteur de Dieu le pape Pie IX* (Paris: Bayard, 1910), p.8; hereafter *Procès romain*.
[14] *Ibid.*, p.8.

of the moment. Giovanni Maria decided to go and plead his cause with
this influential man. It was upon this visit to Bologna that Carlo Falconi
undertook to construct a romantic story on the "forbidden grand passion,"[15] imagining the young Mastai setting out for Bologna "inflamed"
by the idea of seeing his childhood sweetheart again. On the basis of later
letters he concludes that in Bologna the future pope experienced a "torrid
affair."

In many ways this reconstruction is erected on completely unfounded
hypotheses. We do not know exactly how long he spent in Bologna. Carlo
Falconi suggests that he may have spent eighteen months there up to the
end of January 1814, because the first extant letter to Giacinta Milzetti is
dated the 16th of the following month. But there is nothing to say that
there were not earlier letters, now lost. Nor is there any evidence that the
young Mastai wrote to his friends in Bologna immediately after his return
to Senigallia.

These letters from Giovanni Maria to Giacinta had not been unknown
prior to Falconi's interpretation of them. There are nine of them, from
March 1814 to April 1816, and they are kept in the Vatican Archives.
They were published, along with much other correspondence, in the third
volume of the *Positio* of the cause of beatification.[16] Falconi admits that
they can be read as nothing more than a young man's warm affection for
a childhood friend, but he thinks that a careful reading can discover "expressions that are ambivalent but adequately suggestive."

We shall not follow the author in this hypothesis. Even if, in these
years 1813-1814, young Mastai could have lost sight of his priestly vocation or thought that circumstances made its fulfillment uncertain, nothing can justify the idea that he had a passionate affair with a woman seven
years married, the mother of a two year-old daughter. In these letters written by Giovanni Maria (for we know nothing of any replies that may have
been written by Giacinta) there is nothing beyond the limits of propriety.
It is true that the young Mastai, unsure about his destiny and having
abandoned clerical garb several years ago, behaved more like a young man
of the world than like a future priest. At Senigallia and Bologna he frequented the salons, the theater, and balls. But did he feel amorous passion,
did he think of marrying? We have no evidence to affirm this. The only
written evidence we have from him on this subject in fact says the opposite. In March 1814 he wrote to Giacinta:

> Since my return from charming Bologna, I have never left my own
> country; but I have had to defend myself, to this very day, against a moth-
> er who wanted to make me marry her daughter....

---

[15] Falconi, *Il giovane Mastai*, p.164.
[16] *Appendix ad Elenchorum Scriptorum* (Rome: Typis polyglottis Vaticanis, 1995).

The truth is that I had never allowed a promise of marriage to cross my lips, nor had I ever entered her house. All the same it may have been imprudent of me to regard her with a certain interest in recent months, and to pay her my compliments at the theater in the presence of her mother.

Enough of that! Here I am, rescued from the storm, and I vow that henceforth I will look at the young girls with the eyes of a holy hermit. I will do the same as regards the married women too, so long as there is one such in the whole world who makes me indifferent to all the others....[17]

Back to Rome

Once again it was the upheavals of Napoleon's Europe which changed the course of young Mastai's life. The defeats which signaled the end of the Empire and Wellington's invasion of the south of France obliged Napoleon to set Pius VII free. (He had been kept at Fontainebleau ever since 1812.) On January 21, 1814, the order was given to bring Pius VII to Savona and then, in March, the Pope was allowed to enter Rome.[18] This was a long and triumphal return journey.

In May it became known that Pius VII would break his journey in Senigallia for one night. Preparations were immediately made. The civil authorities installed by Napoleon had fled. On the Cathedral Square a bonfire was made of all the paraphernalia of the French occupation: the judges' robes and caps, portraits of Napoleon and the viceroy. The town was decorated to give fitting honor to the Pope. He arrived on the evening of May 12 and resided at the bishop's palace. We also know that he was received at the Mastai palace, among other places, and that the young Giovanni Maria was presented to him. Of course it was an entirely formal reception, but would not the young Mastai, who was celebrating his twenty-second birthday that very day, have interpreted this as a providential sign?

Whatever may have been the exact nature of his feelings and hopes on this May 13, it is a fact that he immediately decided to set out for Rome with a number of friends in order to be present at the Pope's solemn entry, which was to take place some ten days later. His uncle, Canon Paolino, was also returning to Rome, and one can imagine that the family were happy to let Giovanni Maria go, knowing that he would be in good hands. He lodged in the residence of the canons of the splendid Church of St. Mary Magdalen, thanks to his uncle, who was also staying there. On May 24, on the Piazza del Popolo, he witnessed the Pope's triumphal entry into his city after an absence of five years. Three sovereigns who had

[17] Letter of March 28, 1814, in Fernessole, I, 24.
[18] Champion, "Pie VII," *Dictionnaire Napoléon*, p.1331.

been expelled by Napoleon were also present: the King of Spain, the King of Piedmont-Sardinia, and the Grand Duke of Tuscany.

What were his intentions at the time? It is very hard to say. He himself did not know what path to take. On September 7, he wrote to his friend Marchetti, saying that he did not know how long he would be in Rome, adding, "The best course would be to adopt the soutane (*prendere il collare*), but unfortunately I do not have the vocation."[19]

This statement is unambiguous. Nonetheless, it does not permit us to say, as Falconi does, that the young Mastai had decided to undertake "a whole program of *la dolce vita*."[20] Once again, nothing we know of this period of his life would justify such a theory. What we do know of his activities suggests that he was a young man with time on his hands, but not someone who was plunging into a torrent of unbridled pleasure.

We know that he re-established contact with the Piarist Fathers and took part in the "grand academic literary congress" which was held at the end of the year in their Roman college, the *Collegio Nazareno*. We also know that he became a member of the Archconfraternity of the Holy House of Loreto, to which many clerics and laymen from the Marches belonged. Naturally, it was a pleasure to establish connections with his compatriots in joining this archconfraternity, but the latter's aim was primarily religious: divine office and Mass in the Church of Our Lady of Loreto (particularly on the Feast of the Translation, December 10), and charitable activities. While he was uncertain about his vocation, Giovanni Maria remained a pious young man. In all the writings and testimonies from this period there is no trace of any crisis that would have turned him away from the practice of religion.

His uncle Paolino was also keeping an eye on him. In November 1814 he was appointed to the Apostolic Chamber and left the house of the canons of St. Mary Magdalen for a sumptuous residence in the Piazza Montecitorio, in the magnificent Palace of the Tribunals, now the seat of the Italian parliament. There was no question of his nephew following him to this new residence. Some months later, however, he succeeded in having him admitted as a guest in the very austere house of the Fathers of the Mission (Vincentians) which was situated on the same piazza. Canon Mastai also introduced his nephew to some great Roman families: the Orsini, Colonnas, Dorias, and Piancinis. This was not a case of merely casual relationships: young Mastai was getting to know families that played an important role in all the different areas of public life.

The Doria family, for instance, was the only family in a position to give a mortgage guarantee on a loan which the Pope had to make, after the

---

[19]   Letter of September 7, 1814, cited by Polverari, I, 39. In Italian, *collare* means "collar," but the expression *prendere il collare* also means taking the soutane.

[20]   Falconi, *Il giovane Mastai*, p.164.

Treaty of Tolentino, in order to pay the one million écus demanded by the French Directoire. At the time young Mastai got to know the family, two of its members were cardinals of the Sacred College. Almost sixty years later, at an audience given to representatives of the Roman nobility, Pius IX recalled a conversation he had had with a Roman prince:

> I remember, when I was a young man, speaking with a Roman prince, very advanced in age, and who has since departed from us to enter eternity; this prince, a man of sense and of truly Catholic principles, told me that thrones had a twofold support: the clergy and the aristocracy; these are the two powers which alone can uphold monarchies.[21]

Young Mastai was particularly acquainted with two Doria princesses, both of whom were very devoted to religious and charitable works: Teresa Doria Orsini and Chiara Doria Colonna. The former was a great benefactress of the hospitals of St.James and the Holy Savior, but she was also the foundress of the religious order of the Hospitallers of the Holy Savior and of a refuge for abandoned and delinquent young people.[22] Giovanni Maria took part in these works of charity, but it is difficult to say in what capacity. It is not superfluous to mention this, because it shows the kind of apostolate which was to remain uppermost in his life, right up to his first episcopal charge.

We must also note his links—no doubt since the end of 1814—with two outstanding priests to whom he had been introduced by his uncle or some Roman prince: Pietro Caprano and Msgr. Odescalchi. The former, a professor at the Roman College, was also private chamberlain to Pius VII, consultor of the Holy Roman Inquisition and of several Roman Congregations. He followed a brilliant ecclesiastical career which led to the cardinalate. When did he get to know the young Mastai? It is hard to be precise. What we do know is that he registered his young protégé as a member of the Marian congregation of the Roman College. This took place in the spring of 1815, as we shall see. He it was, no doubt, who encouraged young Mastai to follow various courses as a guest student at the same College. Giovanni Maria would always be grateful to Caprano (who was nominated archbishop the following year) for the advice he gave him at this time, and it was his wish that the minor and major orders would be conferred on him by Caprano.

As for Msgr. Odescalchi, he belonged to one of the most illustrious families of the Roman nobility which had already given the Church a great pope of the 17th century, Innocent XII. Despite his youth (he was twenty-nine) Msgr. Odescalchi already had a brilliant career behind him in the Roman Curia, and had been promoted by Pius VII to the rank of

---

21 Allocution of December 29, 1872, in *Actes et paroles*, p.309.
22 Falconi, *Il giovane Mastai*, p.168.

"domestic prelate." This was no routine promotion. From this time on
he devoted himself to popular missions, which would remain the great
apostolate of his entire life. He had been appointed head of the "Poor
Depot," an organization which ran the pontifical services catering for two
thousand of the Eternal City's poor.[23]

He also exercised a parish ministry in the Church of Santa Maria in
Via Lata, on the Corso, and was particularly dedicated to two Roman
charitable establishments: the *Pia Casa de Ponterotto* and the *Ospizio di
Santa Galla*.[24] Finally, together with another priest who today is canonized, Gaspare del Bufalo, he had restored the ancient Pious Union of the
Priests of Santa Galla, particularly dedicated to popular preaching. This,
then, was the Roman environment in which young Mastai lived in 1814-
1815; it was anything but frivolous. The first priests with whom he became acquainted—and here we should add the name of Msgr. Vincenzo
Strambi, Passionist and Bishop of Macerata, who has also been canonized—belonged to that category of the many "holy priests" to be found in
Rome at the beginning of the nineteenth century, who, by their deep piety
and pastoral zeal, sharply contrasted with the court clergy, more numerous but less fervent.

It may have been on Msgr. Strambi's advice that Mastai made a retreat
from February 26 to March 12, 1815, in the Passionist house of St. John
and St. Paul.[25] Usually the retreats given in this house lasted for five days,
but Giovanni Maria stayed there for a fortnight. This shows the seriousness with which he took the retreat. We can be sure that the preacher
of this retreat was Fr. Paoluigi di Maria Vergine; the Passionist archives
contain a retreat plan which dates from 1815 and is entitled "Reforms to
be carried out by secular retreatants in their private exercises." The most
immediate fruit of this retreat was the young Mastai's decision, some days
later on March 25, to register with the *Prima Primaria* of the Roman
College, *i.e.*, the oldest Marian congregation created by the Jesuits. Does
this mean that this retreat with the Passionists was "connected with a resolution fully to resume the path to the priesthood"?[26] Probably not. The
months which followed this retreat show that Mastai was still experiencing a certain hesitation.

On leaving the house of the Passionists he learned that during his
retreat Napoleon had escaped from the Isle of Elba and retaken power in

---

[23] *Ibid.*, pp.171-72.
[24] The term *ospizio* in Italian does not have the restricted sense it has in French ("a
house for old men"). Rather, it means a "refuge" in a general sense, *i.e.*, a charitable
establishment for diverse categories of people.
[25] Fr. Federico Menegazzo dell'Addolorata, "Fama di santità del Servo di Dio Pio IX
nelle tradizione passionista secondo un documento inedito," *Pio IX*, September-
December 1977, pp.470-74.
[26] Bogliolo, *Pio IX: Profilo spirituale*, p.38.

France. At that time Murat, whom the allies had left at the head of the Kingdom of Naples, wanted to support the ex-Emperor, who would have to face the coalition of armies. He sent his troops to invade the Papal States, which caused Pius VII's hasty departure for Genoa.

At this point we encounter two more fabricated episodes in the life of the future Pius IX, *i.e.*, his "engagement" and his time spent in the papal army. The first allegation is well known to those who have studied the documents relating to the process of beatification. Fr. Clementi, who assisted the first Postulator of the cause at the beginning of the century, quotes two manuscript sources from the end of the nineteenth century which report the rumor. During this time, not dated with any precision, the young Mastai is supposed to have met a certain Teodora Valle Tota (or Antonia Tota) and have become engaged to her.[27] Fr. Clementi, who had access to these sources, thought that such a person indeed existed and that she had been in love with Mastai, but that there had been definitely no engagement. Carlo Falconi, in a work of considerable erudition but built on shaky foundations, without adducing any new evidence, constructed a new episode of the most romantic kind. According to him, young Mastai was indeed in love and engaged, and once Pius VII had entered Rome on June 7, 1815, he asked to be admitted to the Papal Noble Guard because he intended to "marry Tota."[28] This reconstruction—which occupies no more than half a page in Falconi's book—has no credibility and mixes up the true and the imaginary. A certain Tota may well have existed and may well have been in love with Mastai—why not? But, having just emerged from a serious retreat, surrounded by solid priests, how could he have yielded to a passion of this kind? Was it some impulsive act or a tempestuous emotion? If this had been the case, there would have been some sign of it here or there in his correspondence and life. But of this there is not a trace.

On the other hand, his request to enter the Papal Noble Guard was quite real. Almost a year earlier Giovanni Maria had observed happily that his epileptic attacks had become very much rarer.[29] The improvement in his health meant that he could envisage, not a military career, but some honorific charge in the papal service and an employment which, above all, would bring him some substantial remuneration. In his letters to friends he insists on this financial aspect and on the "diversion" it would afford him. There is no need, therefore, to invent a whole scenario of the penniless husband-to-be frantically trying to find a livelihood. Rather we should think of the frustration of a young man of twenty-three who has

---

[27] *Summarium* §§2423-24.

[28] Falconi, *Il giovane Mastai*, p.185.

[29] Letter of July 13, 1814, to Giacinta: "The time of my terrible epilepsy has greatly receded," cited by Serafini, p.19.

been staying in Rome for a year without having attained clarity about a purpose to which he might dedicate his life.

The Papal Noble Guard would not officially be reconstituted until the following October, and the slow pace of Vatican bureaucracy meant that by the time the young Mastai's request came to be examined, he had already directed his life along another path, even if he had some regrets in abandoning the idea of becoming a Noble Guard.

Priest

His acquaintance with Caprano and Odescalchi, no doubt at the end of 1814, and the long retreat with the Passionists in February-March 1815—these were important stages towards the path the young Mastai decided to take: to become a priest and be faithful to the aspirations of his childhood and adolescence.

A third stage came when, in August 1815, he took lodging in the house of the Fathers of the Mission and made the acquaintance of Chiarissimo Falconieri. We have already mentioned that it was his Uncle Paolino who succeeded, not without some difficulty, in having Giovanni Maria admitted to the residence. Rare and privileged were the guests accommodated there, particularly priests or bishops undergoing retreats.

Silence was *de rigueur* everywhere, including the refectory. It was there, some time after he arrived, that young Mastai became acquainted with a young cleric, Chiarissimo Falconieri. In this initial period he would become both a model and a friend. Through his various stages, as priest, bishop and pope, Mastai kept up friendly contact with Falconieri, who died a cardinal in 1859.[30]

The two young men had much in common: they were the same age (Falconieri was born in 1794), they had both been educated by the Scolopes Fathers (Falconieri had studied at their college in Siena), and most of all they had both aspired to enter the Papal Noble Guard. Under the advice of his spiritual director, Fr. Guidi, Falconieri had given up this idea and had come to the Vincentian house to make a retreat prior to taking up the priesthood once and for all. To young Mastai all these coincidences must have presented themselves as a new sign from Providence.

Falconieri introduced Mastai to his spiritual director, Fr. Guidi. Together with Don Cesare Storace, the latter was in charge of the *Ospizio dell'Assunta*, popularly called the *Ospizio Tata Giovanni*. This hospice was in fact one of Rome's principal charitable establishments. Its nickname came from its first founder in the eighteenth century. A stonemason,

---

[30] The vast correspondence between Mastai and Falconieri between 1826 and 1846 has been edited and presented, together with many other documents, by Msgr. Giovanni Cittadini, under the title *Giovanni Mastai-Ferretti (Pio IX) Lettere IV* (Acquasanta-Frascati, 1994); hereafter, *Lettere IV*.

Giovanni Borgi, had gathered together a number of young boys who had been sleeping on the steps of the Pantheon; what had originally been a little family had grown due to the priests who supported this modest lay-man.

When Mastai made the acquaintance of Fr. Guidi and his work, the hospice was still located in the House of the Catechumens. In 1816 the *Ospizio Tata Giovanni* would be moved to the buildings of an old convent annexed to the church of Sant'Anna dei Falegnami. It was more than a simple refuge: it had become a place of instruction and vocational educa-tion for abandoned children. Young Mastai went there frequently and the process of beatification reports that in the evenings he used to come and teach the young orphans to read and write, and on feast days he would take them for a walk on the Aventine or on Mount Testaccio. His fre-quent visits to the *Ospizio Tata Giovanni*, and also, perhaps, Falconieri's example, led him to choose Fr. Guidi as his spiritual director. The latter no doubt encouraged him to pursue his vocation seriously: should he be a Papal Noble Guard or a priest? The decision was not a sudden one.

Reading certain letters, one senses that he has become less enthusias-tic about the military path. On November 6, a few months after meeting Fr. Guidi, Mastai wrote to Giacinta:

> The Noble Guard has not yet been organized and, since everything takes place as slowly as possible, I do not know when it will start. I have certain regrets about having desired a post of this kind; I am not sure that I could bend to real discipline and be a proper military person. Perhaps it will all turn out well?[31]

A few days later something happened to put a decisive end to this military prospect. In the beatification process, according to sources worthy of belief, Fr. Clementi (whom we have already cited) made the following very important deposition:

> One Thursday evening in November the Barnabite Cardinal Gregorio Fontana was returning to his residence on the via dei Chiavari when his carriage had to stop suddenly in front of a body lying on the ground. It was the Servant of God. He had had an attack of epilepsy on his way to the school of Tata Giovanni, which at that time had its entrance on the other side. Canon Storace and others ran up to help him, and as a result of this public scene the Servant of God could no longer hide his malady. As a result there was no longer any question of his entering the Noble Guard. Nonetheless, he presented himself to the Holy Father, who confirmed his fears, but told him, "The Lord desires something else for you" and advised him to ask light from the Lord.
>
> In the papal antechamber was the Venerable Vincent Pallotti, who was very well disposed towards the young Count Giovanni Mastai; seeing him

---

[31] Letter of November 6, 1815, cited in Cani, *Procès romain*, p.10.

coming out from the papal audience sad and discouraged, his eyes full of tears, he asked him what had so upset him. Mastai replied that all hope of his being admitted to the Pope's Noble Guard had vanished. Pallotti consoled him and said the following words to him: "Instead of guarding others, you yourself will be guarded."[32]

This deposition is confirmed by some ten other depositions collected in the *Summarium*. All the accounts report the facts in a similar manner, even if some of them give greater elaboration to the remarks of Pius VII or Vincent Pallotti (now canonized).[33] We also know that it was Concionofro Concioni, the medical officer of the Papal Noble Guard, who eliminated the young Mastai from the list of candidates as a result of his November attack. Giovanni Maria tried one further time with Pius VII—which resulted in the audience to which we have just referred.

We can be sure, therefore, that in November-December 1815 the future Pope had not finally set his life on a course for the priesthood, and that it was with regret that he gave up the idea of a military career. Spiritually, however, he was mature enough to take another path. He returned to his family in Senigallia and made a pilgrimage to the sanctuary of Our Lady of Loreto. Some authors say that he was completely cured of his epilepsy on the occasion of this pilgrimage. This is going too far. Later, as we shall see, Mastai would say that it was not until 1819 that he was finally cured of his epilepsy. In the beatification process, depending on the depositions, his cure is attributed either to the Madonna del Mare (venerated in a Capuchin monastery in Fabriano, near Ancona), to a blessing which Pius VII imparted to him at the audience mentioned above, or to the intercession of St. Louis Gonzaga or of Venerable Elisabetta Canori.[34]

We should imagine, therefore, that this cure was not a sudden one; no doubt it was fervently prayed for, in various places, by the young count himself and his mother; but it was nonetheless real and permitted him to be ordained priest in 1819.

In February 1816 Mastai returned to Rome. This was the month during which he decided irrevocably to become a priest. On one occasion he was in the church of Santa Maria dell'Orazione (also called Santa Maria della Morte) on the Via Giulia, where he had served Mass, and "while praying there he made the firm resolve to put on the clerical habit and aspire once again to the priesthood if he succeeded in overcoming the obstacle of epilepsy."[35]

---

[32] *Summarium* §§2426-2427.
[33] Falconi thinks (without adducing any argument) that the meeting with St. Vincent Pallotti in the papal antechamber is "a well-constructed legend" (p. 248); in fact it is attested by sources other than the beatification process of Pius IX.
[34] *Summarium* §§854, 996, 1046, 1719.

Leaving the church after Mass, he went to find his friend Falconieri; during their conversation he told him of his decision. In March he resumed the soutane and on the 30th he wrote to Giacinta:

> Now I will tell you some news which may come as a shock, and of which you will probaby not approve. I have completely changed my way of life. I have adopted clerical dress and hope to follow an ecclesiastical career. I took serious thought before deciding on this step, and, following the advice of wise persons, I have decided once and for all.[36]

A little while later he would explain in another letter that he was not intending to pursue an ecclesiastical career towards the prelature (*giro prelatizio*)—which could see him rise to the cardinalate without being a priest—but that he wanted to pursue the path of holiness in the ecclesiastical state: "The condition of my health has made me see clearly that happiness is not in this world, and that therefore this world is the place where man must make preparation for happiness."[37]

So Mastai the cleric began to devote himself with all seriousness to theological studies in the Roman College and the Ecclesiastical Academy, and to canon law at the Roman University. His professor of theology was Canon Giuseppe Maria Graziosi, a convinced Thomist.[38] He also continued to visit the *Ospizio Tata Giovanni* and devote himself to the work of Fr. Guidi and Canon Storace. At the end of the year he attended a retreat in order to practice the Spiritual Exercises once again. This was from December 20-30, in the Passionist house where he had made his preceding retreat.[39]

At the end of this retreat he drew up a rule of life.[40]

He had decided upon the priesthood but had not entered a seminary. He was still living in the house of the Fathers of the Mission. He also adhered to a very precise rule of life which specified the time to be spent in prayer, daily Mass, and various activities.

Certain authors, including the Postulator of the cause himself, give January 5, 1817, as the date when the young cleric received the four minor orders.[41] In fact, as Alberto Polverari has shown, this ceremony must have taken place a year later.[42] It was preceded by another retreat, again conducted by the Passionists, on December 23-25, 1817.[43] We learn of

---

[35] *Summarium* §2430.
[36] Letter cited by Serafini, p.172.
[37] Letter of April 20, 1816, cited by Fernessole, I, 27.
[38] Antonio Piolanti, *Pio IX e la rinascità del tomismo* (Vatican City: Libreria Editrice Vaticana, 1974), pp.10-15.
[39] Menegazzo dell'Addolorata, "Fama de santità," p.471.
[40] The text of this "rule of life" is in Fernessole, I, 28-29.
[41] Cani, *Procès romain*, p.11.
[42] Polverari, I, 66.

the resolutions he made at the close of this retreat from a little memorandum drawn up in all simplicity and humility by the young cleric:

1. I have made a pact with my eyes, which I have not been guarding sufficiently.
2. I must avoid entering into conversations (let alone initiating them) that are derogatory to third parties.
3. I must be extremely watchful for the first signs of anger, and if any wrong is done to me I must endure it with a good grace.
4. I must submit fully to the judgments of God.
5. I must never stop begging Him to make me worthy to be admitted among His ministers.
6. I need great humility, and must practice this virtue whenever I think myself ignored or despised.[44]

On January 5, 1818, in accordance with the letters dimissory from the Bishop of Senigallia, Giovanni Maria Mastai received the four minor orders from the hands of one of his first mentors, Msgr. Caprano. Henceforth his life was entirely oriented towards prayer, the apostolate, and studies. The following April 1 he became a member of the Pious Union of the priests of Santa Galla, which was under the direction of Msgr. Odescalchi. There he renewed his acquaintance with Canon Storace, Msgr. Caprano, and Don Vincent Pallotti, and later he would get to know Msgr. Polidori, a man whom, in the future, he would esteem and trust. No doubt it was in the context of this confraternity that he was asked to teach the catechism in the parish of the Holy Savior.

It should also be noted that he took part in a popular mission given in Senigallia the following September by Msgr. Odescalchi, Msgr. Strambi, and two other clerics. Mastai, as a young cleric, may have given some sermons on this occasion. Some weeks later the bishop of the town, Cardinal Testaferrata, praised him in these terms: "He performed his duties with great presence of mind before a considerable crowd of the population. He is such a good man...."[45]

At this mission, together with Msgr. Odescalchi, he became a member of the Confraternity of the Holy Sacrament and of the Cross of Senigallia. This implied, of course, the commitment regularly to perform certain particular devotions.

We also know that he considered entering the Jesuits, and also the Passionists, but he dropped these ideas after consulting with members of these orders and on the advice of his spiritual director.[46]

---

[43] Menegazzo dell'Addolorata, "Fama de santità," p.471.
[44] Texts in Fernessole, I, 29.
[45] Letter of November 4, 1818, to Msgr. Cristaldi, cited in Polverari, I, 67.
[46] *Summarium* §2112.

Even prior to his priestly ordination, the cleric Mastai's essential apostolate was dedicated to the *Ospizio Tata Giovanni*. Fr. Guidi had died in the autumn of 1817. Then Mastai and Falconieri had chosen Canon Storace as their spiritual director. Mastai's assiduous devotion to the abandoned youngsters prompted Canon Storace to link him more closely with the work. From February 1, 1818, Mastai moved to *Tata Giovanni* and stayed there until July 2, 1823, the date of his departure for Chile.

Epilepsy is an impediment to the priesthood. For several months now Mastai had had no attacks, and he asked for this impediment to be lifted. The Bishop of Senigallia was required to produce a report on this subject, and on other aspects of the character of this candidate for the priesthood. The bishop replied on November 4: "To my knowledge he no longer suffers from the epileptic attacks to which he was subject in his more tender years. I am sure that it is many months since he has had a single attack of this malady."[47] Pius VII agreed, on condition that in future, as a priest, Mastai would only celebrate Mass with the assistance of a deacon or another priest.[48]

Having undergone a retreat prior to each ceremony, Mastai was able to receive the subdiaconate on December 19, 1818, the diaconate on March 7, and finally the priesthood on the following April 10. As in the case of the minor orders, it was Msgr. Caprano who conferred the major orders upon him. The ceremonies took place in the chapel of the Doria Palace. Thus the clerics and princes who had helped him along on the first stage of his Roman sojourn could now witness the term of a path which had sometimes seemed a tortuous one.

On April 11, Easter Sunday, the new priest celebrated his first Mass in the church of Sant'Anna dei Falegnami, annexed to the *Ospizio Tata Giovanni*. He was surrounded at the altar by his friend Falconieri, who had become a priest a few months before, his Uncle Paolino, and Canon Storace. He was nearly twenty-seven and the ecclesiastical career which was opening up before him would be very different from what he expected at that time.

---

[47] Cited by Fernessole, I, 30.
[48] Cani, *Procès romain*, p.13, and Falconi, *Il giovane Mastai*, p.106. On April 3, 1819, a few days before his ordination, Mastai succeeded in being dispensed from this obligation for a probationary period of three months. On July 4 following a new dispensation, of six months this time, was granted. Other dispensations, of longer duration, were granted in January and November 1820 and in August 1821. Then, when there was definitive confirmation of the cure, Don Mastai had no need to ask for further dispensations.

CHAPTER 3

FROM TATA GIOVANNI TO CHILE

His apostolate at the *Ospizio Tata Giovanni* still took up a good deal of his time. Even after his ordination, however, he continued to attend courses in theology and he studied certain questions on his own initiative. In his preparation for the priesthood he had not received the systematic doctrinal formation provided by a seminary, nor had he followed the different stages of a university course. For many years, also after his return from Chile, he would continue his personal study of different areas of theology.

In 1821 he made a request to be permitted to read a number of "proscribed books" (*i.e.*, books listed on the Index) which were necessary for his studies.[1] He was given the required authorization. From his personal papers from this period it appears that from 1819 to 1823 Don Mastai studied and took copious notes on various theological and moral subjects such as "the form and matter of the sacrament of confirmation" or "the just and unjust war." We also find many notes relating to his reading of Holy Scripture and the Church Fathers. Of course, Don Mastai cannot be considered to have been a theologian. Despite his close links with the Thomist Graziosi, it cannot be said that he received a real "Thomist formation."[2] Conversely, it cannot be said, as some authors do, that his theological knowledge was superficial.

This is borne out by the texts of many sermons of this period that have come down to us. These are either short homilies delivered to the children of the *Ospizio Tata Giovanni* or more elaborate sermons given in different churches in Rome.

To the children he urged the necessity of being informed about the mysteries of the faith: "Ignorance in religious matters leads to unbelief." He also preached on the Last Things. "The thought of death is salutary, for it invites us to penitence." He thought very highly of a book by Blessed Claude de la Colombière entitled *La Pensée de la mort: Règle de vie* and subsequently made much use of it in other sermons on this topic—which was dear to his heart. He presented his young protégés with a model in St. Aloysius Gonzaga; he himself had a great devotion to the saint.

---

[1] Text of the request in Serafini, p.223.
[2] Piolanti, *Pio IX e la rinascita del tomismo*, p.10.

His external sermons were even more numerous. The secret Vatican Archives for 1819-23 contain the texts of some 260 sermons, panegyrics, or spiritual homilies.[3] They were addressed to very diverse audiences: religious, students of the Roman College, or parish faithful, and they were given in the various churches of Rome or in convents.

All witnesses agree that he was a good speaker. Reading the texts that have come down to us, we can also see that they were doctrinally solid and supported by frequent scriptural and patristic quotations. Here we find explanations of the Gospel; sermons on the sacraments, on the Passion of Christ, on the gifts of the Holy Spirit, on prayer as the unique way of obtaining the divine mercy; panegyrics of St. Aloysius Gonzaga and St. Augustine; and a series of eight discourses on the souls in purgatory. There is also a discourse on the Assumption of the Blessed Virgin Mary.

No doubt this taste for preaching was grounded in a deep personal piety.

On July 11, 1819, Don Mastai, who was already a member of several pious associations, became a member of the Archconfraternity of the Sacred Heart of Jesus of the church of San Theodoro. He had two reasons for doing this. First, of course, was his devotion to the Sacred Heart, of which we have documentary evidence dating from these years; his spiritual director, Canon Storace, was also attached to this devotion. Once he had become pope, he would make his own contribution to the development of this devotion, culminating in the consecration of the world to the Sacred Heart on June 16, 1875.[4] The other reason was that the Archconfraternity was also a confraternity of penitents who were particularly dedicated to prayer for the dead, and we know that concern for a good death and concern for the destiny of the dead were important spiritual obligations for Don Mastai.[5]

In 1821 Don Mastai also became a member of the Franciscan Third Order at a ceremony which took place at the convent of St. Bonaventure on the Mount Palatine, where he had occasionally attended short retreats. This same year, 1821, he made several retreats. The first took place in February, perhaps in connection with his entry into the Franciscan Third Order. There he conducted an unsparing examination of conscience, at the end of which he noted down the faults which he would have to correct in himself:

1. Tendency to judge others too harshly.
2. Tendency to become irritated at the least affront.

---

[3] Many extracts in Fernessole, I, 36ff.

[4] Arnaldo Pedrini, "Pio IX e la devozione al Sacro Cuore di Gesù," *Pio IX,* January-August 1986, pp.82-107.

[5] The members of this Archconfraternity were also called *Sacconi,* from the name of the robes of coarse cloth they wore when performing their offices.

3. Tendency to become morose if I am not given due attention.

4. Too little attention to the Office, especially on days when it is not choral.

5. Too concerned about my own person, especially at certain times, from the spirit of pride.

6. I am downcast when I cannot find the right procedure in dealing with some abuse: this is an effect of my own spirit of pride.

7. My natural tendency (or rather, the temptation) to take pleasure in things that may prove dangerous, or other things of the same kind.

8. Being anxious.[6]

He attended the Spiritual Exercises in June and then again in November. Both times he made a strict examination of conscience and made resolutions. In June he drew up a detailed list of the various points on which he must examine himself:

- Regard for my neighbor.
- Tranquillity versus anxiety.
- Kindness and humility.
- Chastity and purity.
- The Office outside choir to be said with more attention.
- The grace to recognize temptations sooner.
- A right intention.
- Some clarity of ideas.
- The desire to do what pleases God.
- A true contempt for myself, enabling me to thank God when my neighbor is scornful of me, and when I am humiliated.
- I must not act as the lawgiver when I am only a beginner.
- Greater charity towards my neighbor.
- The grace to conquer the temptation of false scorn of myself, *etc.*, which comes from a lack of zeal for the glory of God, so that I may diligently seek it.[7]

This taste for retreats and pious confraternities clearly shows Don Mastai's desire to perfect and sanctify himself. We have no evidence of any steps he took to solicit or obtain any important post or any stepping-stone to the higher ranks of the ecclesiastical hierarchy. When he left for Chile in 1823, it was not to follow some career far away from Rome, but in order to follow a missionary ideal, completely free of self-interest.

In Chile

In 1818, at the conclusion of a two-year-long uprising against the Spanish Empire, Bernardo O'Higgins had proclaimed Chile's independence. On October 6, 1821, O'Higgins, styled "Supreme Director" of the new state, wrote a letter to Pius VII expressing his desire for the reorganization of the Catholic Church in Chile. He sent to Rome a plenipoten-

---

6 Text cited by Fernessole, I, 33.

7 Serafini, p.185.

tiary minister, Don José Ignacio de Cienfuegos, a former vicar-general of the Diocese of Santiago.[8] Canon Cienfuegos did not arrive in Italy until July 1822.

As soon as Spain learned that Chile had sent a representative to the Holy See, it expressed to the pope's Secretary of State its total hostility to the diplomatic recognition of "these rebellious provinces." Cienfuegos was received first by Cardinal Consalvi on August 3, and then, finally, some days later, by the pope himself. No doubt Pius VII had been favorably impressed by the positive attitude which the new Chilean authorities were showing: the letter indicated that "the fundamental Constitution of Chile has decreed that the Catholic, Apostolic, and Roman religion is the only one which may be professed."

Nonetheless, lest Spanish susceptibilities should be ruffled, Cienfuegos was not received as a diplomatic representative—which would have constituted an official recognition of the new state—but as a "private individual who had come to the Holy See to explain the condition of religion in Chile." Pius VII, without promising anything, had the question studied by the Secretariat of State. Cienfuegos drew up four memoranda illustrating the political and religious situation in Chile and setting forth the requirements made by the new authorities.

In the end the Pope decided to send a pontifical mission to the new state. It would be charged with the task of studying the Church's situation on the spot and the relations between the local religious authorities and the new state. This mission would be directed by a prelate with the title of Vicar Apostolic. Initially Pietro Ostini was designated for this mission. Pietro Ostini was professor of church history at the Academy of Noble Ecclesiastics, which was under the aegis of the Secretariat of State. He was also one of those many ecclesiastics who came to exercise some apostolate at the *Ospizio Tata Giovanni* from time to time. Don Mastai, therefore, was acquainted with him.

When, at the beginning of 1823, Don Mastai learned of the mission that was to be entrusted to Pietro Ostini, he was "immediately electrified," as he wrote.[9] He so wanted to go with him. He mentioned this desire to his spiritual director. Canon Storace put no obstacle in his way, even if he

---

8   The texts of this letter and of all the official documents relating to the Mission to be sent by the Holy See have been edited by Fernando Retamal Fuentes, *Escritos menores de la Mision Muzi* (Santiago: Pontificia Universidad Catolica de Chile, 1987). This collection enables us definitively to correct the errors and approximations of many authors on the subject.

9   *"Questa notizia…mi elettrizzo subito"*—the expression is found in the "relation" or "journal" which Mastai kept during his voyage and his stay in Chile. This *"Relazione"* was published in full for the first time by Alberto Serafini in 1958. We refer to the new, annotated edition, in Spanish, which has been provided by Lillian Calm, *El Chile de Pio IX: 1824* (Santiago: Editorial Andres Bello, 1987). The work also reproduces many other documents.

was hardly delighted at the prospect of his precious assistant at the *Ospizio Tata Giovanni* going away. He was already acquainted with his assistant's interest in the missions, an interest that had become evident on several occasions before. Later, Pius IX said that he had looked forward to this journey "not in order to experience hitherto unknown lands but only to win for Christ as many souls as I could."[10]

Meeting Pietro Ostini as he was coming from some church function, Mastai told him of his desire. The prelate was by no means against it, and promised to mention it to Cardinal Consalvi, Secretary of State, and Cardinal Della Genga, Cardinal-Vicar of Rome. In the end, however, Ostini refused the mission which was to have been entrusted to him. A new Vicar Apostolic was appointed, namely, Msgr. Muzi, who until then had been auditor of the Vienna Nunciature.

This hiccup did not prejudice Don Mastai's hopes. Cardinal Della Genga invoked the help of Msgr. Caprano. The latter, who (as we have seen) was one of the young Mastai's first Roman protectors, had just been appointed secretary of the Congregation of *Propaganda Fide* (the Congregation in charge of missions). He was the man of the moment. He wrote a letter to Fr. Capaccini, *primo minutante* of the Secretariat of State, who had the task of suggesting names of ecclesiastics suitable to accompany Msgr. Muzi on his mission. He praised the candidate Mastai in these terms:

> It would be difficult to find a person more equipped with all the requisite qualities than this most respectable priest. He has a singular and solid piety, gentleness of character, an unusual prudence and sagacity, a great zeal that is matched by knowledge in abundance. Finally, he is young, only a little over thirty. To this I would add that he has the desire to serve God and be useful to his neighbor in the mission to unbelievers.

Msgr. Caprano did, however, make two reservations: there was his fragile health and the fact that he would be greatly missed at the *Tata Giovanni,* where he was appreciated by all.[11]

Don Mastai's candidature was successful. He was appointed "auditor" of the mission directed by Msgr. Muzi. Another ecclesiastic, Don Sallusti, would fulfill the role of secretary. On May 17, officially presenting the members of the mission in a letter to Chile's extraordinary envoy, Fr. Capaccini said this of the young "auditor":

> Count Mastai, canon of the Basilica of S. Maria in Via Lata, less than thirty-five years young, of angelic bearing and distinguished intellect. By birth and by his virtues he would have been able to proceed easily to the

---

[10] A sentiment included in the *Novae animadversiones* of the beatification process, cited by Polverari, I, 73, n.4.
[11] Letter of April 23, 1823, cited in Serafini, p.249.

Roman prelature; however, imbued with a truly evangelical spirit, he has preferred to set forth on the Mission to Chile as a simple subaltern.[12]

The Countess Mastai, on the other hand, was horrified at the prospect of such a long voyage. On May 18 she wrote to Cardinal Consalvi demanding that her son's nomination be annulled, arguing that his "strength was unequal" to the task. It was too late. His nomination had been notified to the Chilean representative the day before.

To prepare himself for this great voyage, in which everything was uncertain—including the possibility of being able to go and evangelize the pagans (for this was not the Mission's official aim)—Don Mastai once again underwent the Spiritual Exercises with the Jesuits of Sant'Andrea al Quirinale.

On July 3, 1823, the three members of the Mission left Rome for Genoa, where they were to embark on board the *Héloise.* Don Mastai would not see Rome again until 18 months later, in November 1825. Beginning in Florence, on July 8, he kept a log of his journey. He kept it up day in, day out, and this enabled him, on his return to Rome, to write a *Breve relazione del viaggio fatto al Chile,* amounting to more than three hundred manuscript pages.[13] In Genoa the three travelers met Cienfuegos, who accompanied them to Chile.

The departure was delayed as a result of financial difficulties encountered by the ship's owners and by the bad news received from Rome, where the Pope had had a serious fall. His death could put a question-mark over the entire Mission. Msgr. Muzi and Don Mastai took the opportunity of this delay to go to Turin, which at that time was the capital of the Kingdom of Piedmont-Sardinia. They had a mutual friend there, Antonio Tosti, who had been the Holy See's *chargé d'affaires* at the Court for the past year. No doubt Mastai had known him in Rome, of which he was a native, in connection with some of the good works in which he had been involved.[14] They spent a few days in Turin and then returned to Genoa. They learned Spanish to pass the time.

Finally, on August 23, they heard the news of Pius VII's death, which had taken place three days earlier. This created a further delay. The Mission would have to be confirmed by the future pope. Msgr. Muzi and Don Mastai went to present themselves to the Archbishop of Genoa, Msgr. Lambruschini, who offered them hospitality in his palace.

On October 1, they learned that Cardinal Della Genga had been elected pope on September 28 and had taken the name of Leo XII. The interest he had taken in the Mission some months earlier and the part he had played in nominating Don Mastai were sure indications that the

---

[12]   Letter to Canon Cienfuegos, cited in Fuentes, *Escritos menores*, p.88.
[13]   Cf. Calm, *El Chile de Pio IX.*
[14]   Falconi, *Il giovane Mastai*, p.778, n.26.

Mission would be confirmed. Without waiting for this confirmation, the Mission left Genoa on October 5 on board the *Héloise*.

The sea voyage to Argentina took three months. Then there was the overland journey to Chile, which took a further two months. The voyage was not without event. The first storm overtook the vessel near the island of Majorca. At Las Palmas those on board were first quarantined, and then finally arrested by the local authorities who were involved in the recent rebellion against Ferdinand VII.[15] They were released after some days.

After crossing the Strait of Gibraltar at the end of October, the vessel was rocked so violently by wind and wave that Don Mastai was not able to say Mass on All Saints' Day, nor on the day after. In the latitude of the Canaries the vessel was attacked by Colombian pirates who rifled everything, ill-treating the passengers, before letting the ship go. Not only did these events add a discordant note to the crossing; as far as Don Mastai was concerned, they also prompted reflections of a moral and spiritual nature. Towards the end of the voyage he wrote a résumé, which has come down to us, containing his resolutions in twelve points; here are some of them:

1. Reflect upon God and have recourse to Him when faced with the unexpected.
2. Maintain a Christian firmness and *sang-froid* [coolness under fire].
8. Mortify your feelings.
9. See Jesus Christ in all things, and so be victorious.
12. Continue to ask for a knowledge of self and the strength to improve.[16]

Finally, after a violent storm which affected the passengers very badly as they approached the coast of South America, the ship landed in Montevideo on January 1, 1824. He then continued his journey to Buenos Aires. The enthusiastic welcome the foreign travelers were given by the Argentine children reminded Don Mastai of how St. Francis Xavier too had been received by children in some of his missions.

Msgr. Muzi had begun administering the sacrament of Confirmation in a chapel, but another confirmation ceremony that had been arranged for the following day had to take place in the residence of the Apostolic Visitor because the (Freemasonic) government had forbidden Confirmation to be given without its authorization. There were other administrative annoyances which cast a cloud over the stay in Buenos Aires. In the end the Mission was able to pursue its journey to Santiago de Chile in several horse-drawn carriages.

---

[15] In July 1822 the Spanish liberals had begun a revolt against the absolute monarch, Ferdinand VII. In April 1823 Louis XVIII had sent an expeditionary corps to assist Ferdinand VII. At the end of the summer of 1823 the whole of the Iberian peninsula had been brought under control, except for certain Balearic islands.

[16] Memorandum of December 17, 1823, not reported by Mastai in his *"Relazione."* Published by Serafini, p.270.

On the way, in the town of Rosario, which had not seen a bishop for many years, Msgr. Muzi, assisted by Don Mastai, conferred the sacrament of Confirmation to a multitude of children. Then they had to cross the pampa, not without a certain fear of the Indians, who had the reputation of attacking travelers or isolated habitations.

At San Luis they had to halt for a week because one of the convoy carriages, the one carrying Cienfuegos, had broken down. "When the Vicar Apostolic was seen to arrive and stay in San Luis," Don Mastai wrote, "it had the effect of a mission." Once again Msgr. Muzi conferred the sacrament of Confirmation. Next they had to cross the Andean Cordillera on mule-back. "At every step we came across corpses and bones of mules and horses," wrote Don Mastai, no doubt with some exaggeration. He also records that at the narrowest and most sheer places "I kept my eyes closed, letting myself be guided by the mule I was riding and reciting ejaculatory prayers."

A journey of this sort, at this period, took a toll of one's physical and nervous constitution. It was a relief when the Mission arrived in Santiago, safe and sound, on March 6.

The political situation had changed. O'Higgins, who had re-established relations with the Holy See and had initiated this Mission, had been overthrown by a *coup-d'état*. The new *Director Supremo,* General Freire, did not share the attitude of his predecessor. Right from the start he tried to curry favor with the Apostolic Visitor by bribery. The latter refused, strongly encouraged by Don Mastai. The Mission's beginning was not auspicious. After the receptions which took up the first days of their stay Don Mastai, faithful to his spiritual resolutions, made a retreat, before Easter, in the monastery of Dominican Recollects in Santiago.

This Dominican house was the only male religious house in the city still keeping the religious rule and community life. "When we arrived," Mastai wrote, "the religious orders were in a very decadent state. There was discord and division, particularly concerning the election of a provincial, which caused great scandal." On the other hand, "the secular clergy were greatly respected in the city, as were the seven convents of enclosed nuns." At that time Santiago had some thirty churches. The bishop, who had shown himself loyal to Spain during the revolution, had been exiled for three years.

We can see the state of mind in which the young "auditor" fulfilled his mission from several long letters which Mastai wrote to his family and friends (notably Cardinal Odescalchi and Canon Graziosi).[17] He was very interested in the religious life of the people and endeavored to understand

---

[17]   Published in Calm, *El Chile de Pio IX*, pp.127ff.

their traditions and mentality, and took an interest in the different aspects of daily life.

From the various extant documents it seems that Don Mastai energetically assisted the Apostolic Visitor, whose health was fragile. He exercised an authentic religious mission, making many visits to parishes, celebrating Mass and hearing confessions. He also agreed to be chaplain to a convent of Capuchin Clarisses. Nor, it is reported, did he refuse to act as sponsor at the Confirmation of a young Chilean, the son of a modest janitor.

The Apostolic Visitor and his auditor had the greatest difficulties with the civil authorities. Cienfuegos, through ambition, played a troublesome part here, which Mastai records on a number of occasions in his *relazione*. The Mission of Msgr. Muzi was to adjudicate the different disciplinary and canonical problems presented to the Church and to establish the groundwork of agreement with the civil authorities. In fact the new *Director,* who was liberal and anti-clerical, proved hostile to all serious negotiation and ultimately put forward unacceptable demands such as the abolition of several religious feasts, the nomination of bishops solely at the discretion of the civil authorities, and the *exequatur* (by which the civil authority reserved to itself the right to authorize or refuse, within its own territory, the publication of acts of the Holy See).

In the wake of a new political upheaval the existing constitution was abolished, and on September 23 the government ordered the forces of law and order to disperse the religious communities of the entire country and confiscate their goods. It went on to nominate new bishops, including Cienfuegos, who was nominated auxiliary bishop of Santiago, and ordered Msgr. Muzi to consecrate them. He refused, on the grounds that the norms fixed by the Pope had not been observed.

The Mission was in stalemate. On October 19 it left Santiago and traveled to the Pacific coast, to Valparaiso, to take ship. After passing Cape Horn without suffering any damage, but in snow and surrounded by whales, the ship arrived at Montevideo on December 4. The Mission stayed there for two months. Msgr. Muzi conducted several priestly ordinations. Don Mastai ardently wanted to remain in Montevideo, as he wrote, "particularly in order to devote myself to the spiritual welfare of the peasants." He asked for Msgr. Muzi's authorization. The latter refused. He was fearful lest Don Mastai should be exposed to danger, and it seemed better to him that the entire Mission should return to Rome to give the Pope an account of the work that had been done.

On February 18, 1825, the Mission left Montevideo to return at last to Italy. After staying for one day in Tangiers and for several weeks in Gibraltar, it reached Genoa on June 5.

After a fortnight's quarantine in the port along with the whole ship's company, Don Mastai went to spend some days with his family, and then returned to Rome.

Director of the Ospizio San Michele

Once Leo XII had been acquainted with the reports of the Mission to Chile and had assessed the zeal shown by the young auditor, he no doubt offered him some further diplomatic mission. In this way Don Mastai could have pursued a fine career in the service of the Holy See. He refused. The difficulties he had encountered in Santiago, as well as nostalgia, no doubt, regarding his former apostolate, moved him to prefer a ministry in Rome.

It was impossible for him to take up the direction of *Tata Giovanni* once more. When he had left for South America two years earlier, a new director had been appointed, Fr. Carlo Luigi Morichini. Don Mastai visited him several times and the two men were on friendly terms, but there was no question of replacing him.

Finally Leo XII appointed him "President" of the Apostolic Hospice of *San Michele a Ripa*. At that time this hospice was the most important caritative and social institution in Rome, directly responsible to the Pope. For a century the Sovereign Pontiffs had richly endowed it and guaranteed the finances essential to run it. A diplomat of the time describes it in these terms: "This vast establishment serves at the same time as an asylum, a school of arts and trades, a school of fine art, a hospital, and a house of refuge; it is a kind of city in itself, and just as difficult to administer as a provincial capital."[18] This is an exaggeration, but it is true that the institution was an impressive one. The hospice looked after some 1,200 people, who lived in separate buildings. There was an asylum for old men, a study and work center for abandoned children, a house of correction for young delinquents, and a refuge for "fallen" women. The huge building, which had been constructed in the Trastevere quarter at the beginning of the eighteenth century by the architect Carlo Fontana, now houses the Ministry of Cultural Property.

The appointment of Don Mastai to the presidency of such an imposing institution astonished many because his predecessors in this role had all been cardinals. It was interpreted as a mark of special favor on the part of Leo XII who, while he was still a cardinal, as we have seen, had done what he could to facilitate Mastai's journey to Chile. The Director of the Hospice was in regular contact with the highest dignitaries of the Church,

---

[18] Comte d'Ideville, *Pie IX: Sa vie, sa mort; souvenirs personnels* (Paris: Victor Palmé; Brussels: J. Albanel, 1878), pp.11-12.

and in particular with the Pope, who remained the work's chief benefactor.

When Don Mastai received the news of this appointment he believed that he was unworthy to carry out such a charge, not least since his predecessor had left the work in poor shape from an administrative and disciplinary point of view. In a letter which shows his genuine spirit of humility, he asked Leo XII to reconsider his decision, citing his weak intellectual gifts and poor memory—a result, he said, of his former illness. He was afraid of doing damage, by his incompetence, to an administration of such vast proportions.

The Pope did not reconsider. So Don Mastai dedicated himself energetically to his new charge. For twenty months he was an effective administrator, giving support to a declining institution.

He paid great attention to providing training and a trade for the hospice's young residents. Teachers and master-craftsmen came every day to teach the inmates the rudiments of their craft; Don Mastai wanted to diversify the curriculum offered and introduced new crafts at *San Michele*.

He also initiated what nowadays is called "participation." Until then, those who resided at the hospice and worked either outside or inside it, received no remuneration. The whole of what they earned was retained by the administration to pay for their keep, which meant that they received only thirty écus on leaving the hospice. Don Mastai decided that the establishment's apprentices and workmen would henceforth receive half of their work's earnings. This money would be lodged in a bank and would be available to them, with interest, when they eventually left the hospice.

He also found ways of obtaining subsidies from the ecclesiastical or civil authorities to improve the existing facilities. He was very solicitous for the many inmates, and wrote many letters of recommendation to help the youngest (of working age) to find employment, to defend their interests, or get them out of trouble. At his instigation a complete list of residents was drawn up, which enabled him to devote special attention to the most difficult cases.

Good educator that he was, at *San Michele* he adopted some of the disciplinary methods he had known ever since his youth at the college in Volterra. With the Pope's approval he appointed a *vigilatore* (a chief superintendent) from outside, someone "honest, proven, and active," who was well paid to ensure his loyalty and whose task was to see to it that the establishment's rules were adhered to. This *vigilatore* was assisted by a number of room prefects who were in charge of discipline. Don Mastai was also concerned to improve the quality and quantity of food served in the refectories.

He also took care concerning the spiritual life of the hospice residents. He made it his custom to explain the Gospel of the day every Sunday, and on major feasts he gave a homily.

The direction of *San Michele* did not occupy all of his time. Don Mastai continued to preach and to exercise his apostolate among young people. In the year 1826-27 he was confessor to the young boarders of the Scolopes Fathers' Nazzareno College. He also visited his former inmates at *Tata Giovanni*, giving them a spiritual conference. He also visited the Congregation *dei Sacconi* and the Pious Union of the Priests of Santa Galla.

As a preacher he was much sought after. The most important of his addresses at this time was a panegyric of the Immaculate Conception given in the Basilica of St. Mary Major on December 8, 1826. Here the future pope, who would be the promulgator of this doctrine, preached it with great enthusiasm, with very frequent references to the Bible. He also preached a triduum on the Sacred Heart—another devotion that had a special place in his affections.

A much sought-after preacher, President of the *Ospizio San Michele*— where he succeeded in putting both finances and discipline on a good footing—Don Mastai was summoned, less than two years after he had been appointed, to a higher charge: the episcopate.

We may well imagine that, in putting him at the head of a great institution in some difficulties, Leo XII had wanted to test his administrative ability. Don Mastai was hardly thirty-five when he was nominated Archbishop of Spoleto.

CHAPTER 4

BISHOP OF SPOLETO

It was on April 24,1827, that Don Mastai learned that he had been nominated Archbishop of Spoleto. The president of the *Ospizio San Michele* was extremely surprised by this promotion.

Once again his first reaction was to refuse. He felt incapable of bearing such a responsibility. He shared his apprehensions with his spiritual counselors. They persuaded him to accept, no doubt citing his success in the recent missions entrusted to him. To Msgr. Falconieri, who had been nominated Archbishop of Ravenna the previous year, Don Mastai wrote, with humility but not without humor: "The good God is really amusing Himself *in orbe terrarum,* wanting to raise such a miserable insect to so much honor."[1] It is clear from this same letter that Don Mastai had gone to the Pope to express his apprehensions: "I laid my difficulties before the Holy Father, and since then I have been at peace."

Then, on May 5, writing to Falconieri again, he expressed his fear of the "examination" which, at that time, future bishops had to undergo: "The examination will take place on the eighteenth, and we shall see how the Lord will chastise my pride. The consistory takes place on the 21st."[2]

This examination, sometimes presided over by the Pope surrounded by cardinals, theologians, and canonists, was a shorter or longer oral examination of the candidate, on religious questions. We know neither the questions put to Mastai nor the answers he made; but we do know that, more than ten years later, he still had an unpleasant memory of the event.[3]

However, Leo XII must have thought that the candidate had come out of this examination very honorably. At the consistory at which Mastai was officially appointed Archbishop of Spoleto, the Pope praised the new bishop: "He has fulfilled the charge of preacher, and currently he also carries out the function of the Director of this Apostolic Hospice; he has shown himself to be a distinguished canon of the collegiate church of Santa Maria in Via Lata. A man endowed with gravity, prudence, doctrine, probity, experience, and perfectly versed in the exercise of ecclesiastical functions."[4]

---

[1] Undated letter, published by Cittadini, *Lettere IV*, p.103.
[2] Letter of May 5, 1827, in *Lettere IV*, p.105.
[3] Letter of Msgr. Mastai to Cardinal Polidori, May 13, 1838, cited in Polverari, I, 89. Carlo Falconi exaggerated the importance of this test and Mastai's intellectual limitations (pp.618-21).
[4] D. Moroni, "Spoleto," in *Dizionario di erudizione storico-ecclesiastico* (1861), cited by Fernessole, I, 52.

Don Mastai had not looked for this honor. Several witnesses tell us that he only accepted it out of obedience, and that he was heartbroken to leave the *Ospizio San Michele*. Once he became pope he visited it several times and granted it subsidies.

To prepare himself for the ceremony of episcopal consecration Don Mastai made a six-day retreat with the Jesuits at Sant'Andrea del Quirinal. He stayed at the Novitiate from May 27 to June 1 and once again made the Spiritual Exercises. As usual, the notes he kept show the high spiritual tenor and the spirit of mortification which animated him. Here we can read the resolutions he made, which reveal, in counterpoint, the faults and imperfections of the exercitant:

> Do not be impatient with the poor and people who are obstructive, demanding, or troublesome. Ask from God the grace of deliverance from the temptation to sleep in the morning, particularly so that your meditation may be profitable…. In order to acquire humility you must become accustomed to go against your own will, during the day, even in things that are licit.[5]

On this occasion the Spiritual Exercises were not only a method of spiritual introspection; they also had to be a preparation for the fullness of the priesthood which the episcopate is. Thus among the retreat notes we find a three-page meditation on the vocation of a bishop, the "Church's bridegroom." Here Don Mastai takes as his model in the episcopate one Gregorio Barbarigo, Bishop of Bergamo at the end of the sixteenth century, who eventually became a cardinal and was canonized by John XXIII. Msgr. Barbarigo left to posterity his *Rules* for the benefit of future bishops.

Don Mastai also drew up a daily timetable to be followed in his new functions. As it should, this timetable sets aside a significant period of time throughout the day for liturgical and spiritual offices: "Vocal prayer and meditation" at 6:30, Mass at 7, second Mass (of "thanksgiving") at 7:30, recitation of the Hours at different times of the day, and Rosary after the daily walk.

Spoleto

On June 3, 1827, on the Feast of Pentecost, in the church of San Pietro in Vincoli, Don Mastai received episcopal consecration from the hands of Cardinal Francesco Saverio Castiglione (who would become pope less than two years later, taking the name Pius VIII), assisted by Msgr. Piatti, Archbishop of Trebizond, and Msgr. Sinibaldi, Archbishop of Damietta. This same day, in order to place his new departure from Rome under di-

---

[5] Cited by Fernessole, I, 53.

vine protection, he became a member of the pilgrims' Archconfraternity of the Most Holy Trinity.[6]

Even before reaching his city, Msgr. Mastai wrote a pastoral letter to his faithful. Then he arrived in Spoleto.[7]

At that time Spoleto was a small but ancient Umbrian city, belonging to the Papal States. Among its illustrious sons it counted martyrs (Saint Britius, Saint Sabinus, and Saint Martial) and a pope, Urban VIII.

The see had only been vacant since February 24, but Msgr. Mastai's predecessor, Msgr. Mario de Baroni Ancaiani, had died after a long illness, during which his diocese had been left to its own devices. The population's moral state had declined steeply and the archbishopric's coffers were empty. Msgr. Mastai himself had to defray the costs of his consecration and subsequent installation. To do this he sold a small property of his and took a loan guaranteed by his brother Gabriele.

It is appropriate to mention that at this time he acquired two ecclesiastical benefices which made supplementary funds available to him. In April 1827 he entered into possession of the Ercolani prelature, in Parma, and in February of the following year he was provided with the benefice of the chapel of San Giorgio and San Antonio in the cathedral of Senigallia.

On July 1, 1827, Msgr. Mastai officially took possession of his cathedral. His first sermon made a favorable impression on the faithful. His youthful and active person contrasted with that of his predecessor, who had been rendered feeble by great age and a partial paralysis. The task awaiting the new bishop was immense.

One of the first things he had to do was find a secretary. He chose Canon Giuseppe Stella, from Nocera. In a letter to Cardinal Polidori he described him as "good, pious, exemplary, but obstinate and punctilious."[8]

Two months after his installation in Spoleto, Msgr. Mastai asked the pope for permission to reserve the Holy Eucharist in the private chapel of his episcopal palace, which was some distance from the cathedral. He was looking forward to be able to adore the Blessed Sacrament in his residence and at leisure. The Sacred Congregation of Rites did not grant him this permission, no doubt for fear of theft or sacrilege on the part of strangers. At all events, Msgr. Mastai went to the cathedral every day to make a visit to the Blessed Sacrament.

---

[6] Serafini, p.415.

[7] On this episcopate, in addition to Serafini, Fernessole, and Polverari, an important study has been produced by Msgr. Ottorino Pietro Alberti: "L'episcopato di G. M. Mastai-Ferretti a Spoleto," *Atti del II. Convegno*, pp.116-172. This study has been republished in the collected volume entitled *Pio IX Arcivescovo di Spoleto* (Florence: Vallecchi, 1980).

[8] Letter of December 28, 1838, cited in Serafini, p.840.

In several letters to Leo XII the new bishop gave an account of his government of the diocese. It was a question of taking things in hand again, in a systematic, patient, and energetic way. His diocese had about 45,000 faithful in 172 parishes. Initially, in order to get a good idea of the condition of his diocese, he carried out many pastoral visitations. It took him four years to visit all the parishes. In December 1831, at the end of this long pastoral visitation of the diocese, he wrote a detailed *relazione* to the Holy See.

Even today many villages and localities, including some situated in mountainous regions, hard of access, have kept commemorative plaques of their bishop's visit. He did not restrict his visits to his clergy and parishioners, not hesitating to visit poor isolated dwellings scattered in what is sometimes called the "Apennine Desert."

When visiting a remote mountain village he wrote, not without humor, to Msgr. Polidori: "Pray for me, tormented in these rugged mountains, taking water and wind in quantity."[9]

On many occasions he had to rally a clergy that was morally dissipated and give them an example of how to preach, administer the sacraments, and give catechism. In the first period of his episcopate he had St. Charles Borromeo's *Advice to Confessors* distributed to his clergy.

In his parish visitations he was at pains to reorganize the confraternities and the very many charitable works, and have the isolated oratories restored. He interrogated the children on the catechism, but also on their secular knowledge. He delighted in reciting the Rosary with the faithful at the conclusion of the pastoral visitation.

In addition to pastoral visitation, his time was taken up with personal correspondence and gatherings of priests in the cathedral. Many of Msgr. Mastai's addresses and homilies to his priests have come down to us; they deal with the "examination of conscience," obedience, the duties of state, attention to study, modesty, and "the exceptional dignity of the priest and the greatness of his power."

He was equally concerned on behalf of future priests. He asked the Jesuit Fathers who were in charge of the town's college to come and teach in the seminary alongside the secular priests. Also, Msgr. Mastai frequently gave spiritual conferences to the seminarians; from 1831 he did this every week. There were not many seminarians when Msgr. Mastai arrived, but their number grew rapidly. At the end of 1831, in a report to the Holy See, he mentions the figure of sixty-five students. He was vigilant in admitting to sacred orders only candidates who were worthy and certain to persevere; to that end he obtained all necessary information on each candidate presented to him. On several occasions he refused candidates;

---

[9] Letter of May 28, 1831, cited in Serafini, p.433.

he also gave financial assistance to others who did not have the means to pay the required fees.

The new bishop also set himself to reform the religious communities where necessary. In his very first month after arriving he had to give much attention to a convent dedicated to the Infant Jesus, where there was unrest and discontent. He entrusted the town's Jesuit Fathers with the task of taking the convent in hand, and he himself drew up a new rule for it.[10] He was devoted to the task of reviving the religious spirit, and he did this by giving instructions and exhortations on the occasion of canonical visitations or by letters. He also used the occasion of the solemn adoption of the habit or the profession of vows for the same purpose. On February 13, 1830, for example, during his first canonical visitation of the convent of Palazzo, he exhorted the nuns in these terms: "It cannot have escaped you that the state of a religious is not a state of inaction and coldness but, on the contrary, a state of hard work and fervor."[11]

Msgr. Mastai often insisted on respect for the religious rules proper to each congregation or institute, and also on the necessity of conventual liturgical life and an assiduous practice of mental prayer. Towards this aspect of religious life, and the mystical graces which could flow from it, Msgr. Mastai always adopted an attitude of prudence, but not hostility. He would show the same attitude when he became pope.

During his Spoleto episcopate there was one nun in particular, of the convent of Santa Chiara de Montefalco, Sr. Chiara Teresa del S. Cuore di Maria,[12] to whom he gave spiritual direction. He visited her several times and wrote many letters to her. He taught her simplicity, humility, charity towards her neighbor, and confidence in God. "What the Lord demands of you," he wrote to her on November 28, 1831, "is first of all humility, distrust of self, spiritual joy, and an equal charity for all the Sisters, even when you believe that you have been slighted." To the same nun, who aspired to the mystical life and wanted to plunge into the works of St. John of the Cross, Msgr. Mastai replied, without any prevarication: "No; that nourishment is not for your teeth."[13]

He was also concerned for the civil population of the diocese. The great inequality of conditions put him in contact with very different social strata. In his preaching he addressed everyone and he showed a great facility in this area. His talents as a preacher caused him to leave the dio-

---

[10] Letter cited by Alberti, "L'episcopata di G. M. Mastai-Ferreti," p.167, n.67.
[11] Cited by Fernessole, I, 59.
[12] This woman, originally from Ancona, was under Don Mastai's spiritual direction from 1825. When he became Bishop of Spoleto, she asked to become a religious in a convent of his diocese. Msgr. Mastai enabled her to enter the Poor Clares of Montefalco.
[13] Letters cited by Fernessole, I, 60.

cese on several occasions, to deliver panegyrics or conferences in Rome or
Senigallia.

A permanent feature of his apostolate was his concern for the poorest. On November 8, 1829, under the patronage of the Virgin Mary, he
opened a hospice for orphans. During the day the children were sent to
various establishments to learn a trade, and the Jesuits, whose church was
close by, gave them religious instruction.

The Revolution of 1831

Pius VIII, who had succeeded Leo XII less than two years previously,
died on November 30, 1830. The Conclave to elect a successor to Pius
VIII was a long one.

The Carbonari, an Italian secret society linked to Freemasonry, ex-
ploited this situation to attempt an insurrection in Rome.[14] The objective
of the Carbonari was the unification of Italy and the creation of a republic.
Two prominent Carbonari whose names have come down to posterity
were Giuseppe Mazzini, the future head of the revolutionary movement
Giovane Italia ("Young Italy"), and Louis-Napoleon Bonaparte, nephew
of Napoleon I. Mazzini, who at that time was exiled to France, took no
part in the attempted rebellion, but Louis-Napoleon Bonaparte took an
active part in it. It took place in December 1830, but came to nothing.

In February 1831, when Cardinal Cappelari had been elected pope
and took the name of Gregory XVI, other troubles, fomented by the Carbonari, erupted in the Papal States, in Bologna, and in the Duchy of Parma, whose prince was expelled. The insurrection extended to the whole
of the Romagna, the Marches, and Umbria (where Spoleto was located).
In Bologna a provisional government was put in place, presided over by a
liberal lawyer, Giovanni Vicini; on February 8 it declared that the pope's
temporal power over the city and province was "dissolved, *de facto* and *de
jure*, for ever."

Gregory XVI, while trying all the time to preserve the Eternal City
from upheaval (he arranged for arms to be bought abroad and established
a Civic Guard in Rome), tried to calm things down by reducing taxes. He
lowered customs duty and the tax on salt and gave an amnesty to seventy
political prisoners who had been sentenced for crimes against the state.
All these measures were insufficient to satisfy the passions that had been
inflamed. The Ancona garrison surrendered to the insurgents, and Cardinal Benvenuti, who had been sent by the Pope as legate, was arrested and
imprisoned.

---

[14] On the general aspects of this Italian revolution of 1831, cf. Salvatorelli, *Histoire de
l'Italie*, pp.466ff.

In Spoleto, on February 23, a "provisional government" of four members (of whom two were lawyers) succeeded in seizing power, ejecting the civil authorities appointed by the Pope.

Gregory XVI then decided to ask for military aid from Austria. Austria would have intervened in any case, because it feared the spread of revolution to Lombardy, which it had controlled for more than a century. In March the Austrian troops crossed the Po, re-established the Duchess of Parma and the Duke of Modena in their Duchy, and then, at the end of the month, liberated Bologna. Some revolutionary troops commanded by General Sercognani turned south and entered Umbria.

Spoleto was at the very heart of this attempt at revolution. In the initial days of the rising Msgr. Mastai, in a letter to the Secretariat of State, showed himself in favor of a swift intervention of the papal troops: "... all the (revolutionary) forces of Perugia, Foligno, Spoleto, and Terni together hardly amount to 500 men. Without uniforms, not properly commanded, lacking in courage, it is certain that they will not impress anyone.... Either the papal troops are resolved to fight and victory is assured, or the papal troops are utterly corrupt, in which case I shall put the matter into the Lord's hands and hold my peace."[15] In this same letter he also says that "Louis Bonaparte's son is in Spoleto in the hope of recruiting many young men, but so far he has not found many inclined to follow him." One month later, however, at the approach of Sercognani's troops, the situation had become worrying. Msgr. Mastai was not aware of the recapture of Bologna and surrender of the revolutionary government, which was signed on March 26.

That very day he decided that it would be prudent to leave Spoleto, particularly since the Civic Guard, which had been set up in his city, had embraced the revolution. He took refuge in the Capuchin convent of Leonessa, a city in his diocese which, territorially, did not belong to the Papal States but was dependent on the Kingdom of Naples. It was there he received a despatch from Cardinal Benvenuti, who had been liberated from Ancona, telling him of the collapse of the revolutionary government and appointing him, by order of Gregory XVI, Extraordinary Apostolic Delegate for the provinces of Spoleto and Rieti, with the task of re-establishing the Pope's temporal power there.

Msgr. Mastai was back in Spoleto by the evening of March 29. He was given a very warm welcome: the evidence is that the major part of the population had remained loyal to the papal government. The following day he appointed a commission to help him in his function as Apostolic Delegate, and had a public proclamation read out appealing for calm.

---

[15] Letter of February 24, 1831, cited by Alberti, "L'episcopata di G. M. Mastai-Ferreti," p.139.

He succeeded in disarming three hundred revolutionaries who had taken refuge in the city and issued them with safe-conducts.

On March 31, three thousand revolutionaries arrived in Spoleto. They were talking of organizing a guerrilla campaign against the Austrian troops who were advancing in the region, and people were afraid that the little city would be engulfed in fire and blood. Here again Msgr. Mastai succeeded in getting them to lay down their arms and leave the city, giving passports to those who wanted them and distributing food to them.[16] In this way, before the arrival of the Austrian troops, Msgr. Mastai had managed to bring peace to his city without the spilling of blood.

The beatification process reports that, when a commander of the Austrian garrison finally presented him with a list of citizens suspected of complicity in the rebellion, the Archbishop of Spoleto had replied: "When the wolf intends to devour the sheep, he does not tell the shepherd," and tore up the list.[17]

Another anecdote was reported by several witnesses at the beatification process. According to this, Louis-Napoleon himself was rescued by Msgr. Mastai, who furnished him and his mother, Queen Hortense, with an English passport and a gift of two hundred écus.[18] This story, which is reported by the first biographers of Pius IX and more recent authors, would seem to explain why, once he had become President of the French Republic and then Emperor of the French, Louis-Napoleon Bonaparte, in order in some way to repay his debt, sent an expeditionary force on two occasions to assure the safety of the pope who had at one time been his protector.

While Louis-Napoleon Bonaparte's presence at Spoleto is attested by Msgr. Mastai's letter, already cited, the anecdote in its final form seems rather contrived. Pius IX himself denied it to two different people, to the Jesuit Fr. Ballerini and to Count Resia, who was the first director of the papal railways.[19]

In this episode of the revolution of 1831, Msgr. Mastai acted neither out of cowardice, as certain authors have claimed, nor out of sympathy for liberal ideas, as others have maintained. Most of all he tried not to add further misfortune to the upheavals which were already serious. Not for a moment did he doubt the legitimacy of the popes' temporal power over these provinces. According to the terms of an entreaty he addressed to the Sovereign Pontiff on April 5, 1831, he saw himself as a "man of peace and

---

[16] Letter of April 1, 1831, to Cardinal Bernetti, Secretary of State, cited by Alberti, *ibid.*, p.141. Cf. also *Summarium* §2928.

[17] *Summarium* §2278.

[18] *Summarium* §§1412, 1722, 2029.

[19] Ballerini's testimony is cited in *Summarium* §2660, and the testimony of Count Résie, director of the papal railways, is reported by the diplomat d'Ideville.

a mediator."[20] The purpose of this entreaty was to obtain pardon from Gregory XVI for his Spoleto "sheep" *(mie pecorelle)*, *i.e.*, the public representatives who had gone over to the insurrection. Gregory XVI acceded to his request.

This tentative revolution of 1831 was the harbinger of other upheavals which would agitate the Papal States sporadically in the following years, finally leading to the revolution of 1848.

Throughout his entire pontificate Gregory XVI had to face political and religious opposition, which rarely attracted public attention and came from the most diverse quarters. His main opposition came from those who contested the Pope's politics. They reproached the Pope with being one of the last absolute sovereigns in Europe, *i.e.* holding on to the three powers (executive, legislative, and judiciary), and having a government composed entirely of ecclesiastics.

The more moderate opponents of Gregory XVI demanded reforms, notably the participation of laymen in government and the introduction of a consultative or legislative assembly. The most radical, particularly the clandestine association *Giovane Italia* (Young Italy), created by Mazzini in Marseilles after the failure of the 1831 revolution, actually sought the abolition of the popes' temporal power, the unification of Italy, and the inauguration of a republic.

After the 1831 revolution the more moderate elements were encouraged by the great European powers, who urged the Pope to reform his politics. Some months after the upheavals, France, aiming to neutralize the Austrian influence in Italy, organized an international conference in Rome attended by representatives from England, Austria, Prussia, and Russia. On May 21 this conference presented a *memorandum* to Gregory XVI which wished to see various reforms: the admission of laymen to the administrative and judiciary functions, the amelioration of the judiciary system, the creation of elected municipal and provincial councils having real administrative power, the creation of an independent assembly to control the budget of the Papal States, and the establishment of a Council of State to elaborate laws and judge those which were contentious.

Nowadays historians recognize that the picture his enemies have painted, of an obtuse and reactionary Gregory XVI, is a caricature. In the months following the *memorandum* the Pope and his Secretary of State, Bernetti, acted on some of the recommendations of the European powers. Several edicts created local and provincial councils. (They were not, indeed, elected; two-thirds were chosen from the landowners and the remaining third from the liberal professions.) The judiciary system was reformed and a central finance committee was set up. Furthermore, laymen

---

[20] Letter to Cardinal Pacca, Dean of the Sacred College, begging him to present his plea to Gregory XVI, cited in Polverari I, 103.

could now have access to certain administrative responsibilities, in post and telegraphs, customs, and preliminary tribunals. On the other hand, Gregory XVI did not institute any consultative assembly, nor did he admit laymen to government, nor did he completely laicize the administration. Those things the Pope had not granted caused people to forget what he *had* granted. There was no abatement of criticism of him, particularly since he was unable to put an end to certain very real abuses which a certain kind of popular literature took pleasure in denouncing. The sonnets of G. G. Belli are the most famous illustration of this. In these years, Belli was the author of thousands of sonnets which circulated behind closed doors, being copied and recopied many times; they were evidence of an anti-clerical state of mind which was spreading throughout the population of the Papal States. In his (often humorous) sonnets, Belli criticized "favoritism, the preoccupation with spying, the lethargy and confusion of the legislative apparatus, the abuses of power on the part of the magistrature, the state of the finances...."[21]

Msgr. Mastai's correspondence shows that some of these criticisms were shared by certain ecclesiastical dignitaries. He himself also criticized the indolence and disorder of the bureaucracy, the abuses of power, and the inadequacy of the police. He observes, and deplores, that "many are ashamed to be the Pope's subjects, and many are indifferent on that score."[22] Some years later, as Bishop of Imola, we see him writing to the Secretariat of State with some very concrete suggestions of reforms, without abandoning his complete loyalty to Gregory XVI and without in any way questioning the pope's temporal power.

The Temptation to Give Up

Some months after these events had come to an end, an exhausted Msgr. Mastai felt a great weariness and requested to be relieved of his see. In a memorandum of November 1831 to his friend Cardinal Odescalchi, who had become Prefect of the Congregation of Bishops, he asked, writing of himself in the third person, to be discharged from his functions. Arguing that he was still affected by the consequences of the epilepsy he had suffered from 1809 to 1818, "consequences," he wrote, "which prevent him applying himself as he would wish to the execution of his duties,"[23] he said that he hoped to "live in seclusion, far from the tumult of affairs." Then, in presenting his Christmas good wishes to the Sovereign Pontiff at the end of November (as was the custom then in the Papal States), he repeated his request to Gregory XVI. Once again he put forward his "weakness," his "inexperience of sacred studies," his "lack of the charisms

---

[21] Martina, I, 51.
[22] Letter cited in Serafini, p.1404.
[23] Text reproduced by Alberti, "L'episcopata di G. M. Mastai-Ferreti," pp.142-43.

which the Apostle requires of a bishop," and "the fragile health which has afflicted me for several years."[24] The written replies to these two letters have not come down to us, but we can imagine that Odescalchi, who knew him well, counselled a "wait and see" policy.

After the revolutionary attempt of 1831, another dramatic event took place on January 13 the following year, putting the Archbishop of Spoleto to the test. Three towns in his diocese, Bevagna, Trevi, and Montefalco, as well as other localities, were devastated by an earthquake. In Bevagna three-quarters of the dwellings were destroyed. Two thousand people found themselves without a roof over their heads at the depth of the winter.

Msgr. Mastai visited all the localities affected by the earthquake. He distributed financial aid and established on-the-spot connections to facilitate aid from the civil authorities and the Holy See. In Bevagna, at his own expense, he had wooden barracks constructed to house those with no shelter. He sent out a circular letter appealing to the generosity of all the faithful of his diocese. Gregory XVI sent an initial contribution of 5,000 écus, and collections were made in several neighboring provincial dioceses for the diocese of Spoleto. The pope set up commissions of public assistance in the most affected areas, naming the Archbishop of Spoleto as president.

The last months of Msgr. Mastai's episcopate in this diocese were mainly spent in organizing the distribution of assistance, restoring the public buildings, and financing the reconstruction of homes.

However, a natural disaster of this kind called not only for material solidarity. In Msgr. Mastai's view, good people should see it as a heavenly warning, and the wicked should see it as a "merited punishment" visited upon them by God.[25] He requested the Jesuit Fathers to come and preach courses of spiritual exercises in several towns of his diocese.

A few days after the earthquake he himself went to Trevi for the feast of the town's patron saint. Trevi was one of the towns where the destruction had been greatest. The archbishop preached in the town square and concluded his exhortation with a fervent prayer: "Lord, if you require a victim to satisfy your justice, I beg you spare the flock and strike the shepherd."[26]

---

[24] Letter cited in *ibid.,* pp.143-44.
[25] The expression was used by Msgr. Mastai, prophetically, some days before the earthquake, in a letter to a Roman correspondent; the letter is cited in Serafini, p.529.
[26] Cited in Alberti, "L'episcopata di G. M. Mastai-Ferreti," p.147.

CHAPTER 5

BISHOP AND
CARDINAL OF IMOLA

Gregory XVI had been very pleased with the way in which Msgr. Mastai had brought peace to Spoleto and Umbria after the 1831 revolution. No doubt he also thought that a change of post would be the best remedy for the weariness of which his bishop had been complaining.

On November 19, 1831, the Archbishop of Spoleto received a letter from the Pope announcing his transfer to the bishopric of Imola. This was by no means a punishment; it was a promotion. This is clear from the fact that the diocese of Imola had a much larger population than that of Spoleto—it was one of the most important dioceses of the Romagna; traditionally, a cardinal's hat was attached to its bishop. In the past, two bishops of Imola had become pope: Cardinal Chigi, who, as pope, took the name Alexander VII in 1655, and Cardinal Chiaramonte, who became Pius VII in 1800.

As a sign of particular favor, Gregory XVI announced the news to Msgr. Mastai, not through the intermediary of the Curial service, but by a personal letter. Furthermore, unlike his preceding appointments, this translation to the diocese of Imola did not throw Msgr. Mastai into a state of anxiety. He immediately replied to the Pope in a letter completely imbued with obedience. He saw this appointment as a "decree of the divine will" and submitted himself to it as the Church's faithful servant: "... otherwise I would betray the regard with which Your Holiness has deigned to favor me....I shall keep silent concerning the apprehension which I feel about the increased difficulties and the heavier burden you have deigned to impose on me."[1]

His appointment was not made public until December 17. For the reasons we have seen, although Msgr. Mastai was moving from an archbishopric to a bishopric, his appointment was understood as a promotion. On the other hand, it was a difficult diocese. The Romagna had been one of the most ardent hotbeds of the 1831 revolution, and there was still much agitation abroad there. The former bishop of the diocese, Cardinal Giacomo Giustiniani, had had to flee the city during the upheavals of the previous year; he had taken refuge in Rome, and begged the Pope to relieve him of this see. Gregory XVI had hesitated for almost two years, and

---

[1]   Letter of November 19, 1832, cited in Fernessole, I, 74.

then, finally, he appointed Msgr. Mastai in the hope that he would prove to be just such a "man of peace and a mediator" as he had been in Spoleto. In Spoleto many of the clergy and faithful regretted his departure. Letters were sent to the Pope urging him to reconsider his decision—but in vain.

Msgr. Mastai wrote a pastoral letter to the clergy and faithful of Imola for December 25, but he did not reach his new diocese until the night of the February 8-9, 1833.[2] After leaving Spoleto he wanted to visit the sanctuary of Our Lady of Loreto and venerate the Virgin there; then he went to Senigallia to see his mother and celebrate a pontifical Mass at the request of the bishop of the town. His solemn entry into the cathedral of Imola and the ceremony of enthronement took place on February 13 in the presence of a great crowd. His reputation had preceded him. Count Giuseppe Alberghetti, Imola's representative in Rome, had written to the city's *gonfaloniere*, telling him of Msgr. Mastai's appointment. He presented him in these terms: "He is well known and respected by all for his holiness, gentleness, prudence, and moderation."[3]

Imola was situated in the north of the Papal States, in the Romagna. Administratively it belonged to the Legation of Ravenna. Politically, like the whole of the Romagna, it exhibited three different currents of thought: 1) The "Austrian" party, which favored the extension of Austrian rule over all the Legations. 2) The "papal" or "sanfedist" party (which defended the pope and the "holy faith"), which not only sought to preserve the pope's temporal authority in these territories, but also favored the domination of the clergy in social and political areas. 3) The "liberal" party, which wanted to see the end of the pope's temporal power or, at least, wide reforms in all areas.

At that time the term "liberal" included a great diversity of political doctrines and programs. On the one hand there were the "Mazzinians" of *Giovane Italia* (Young Italy), who wanted the unification of Italy and a republic. At the other end of the spectrum there were those who were beginning to dream of a kind of Italian confederation that would maintain and unite all the existing monarchies and principalities of the peninsula.

Msgr. Mastai did not support any of these three parties, in spite of what has been said by some of his contemporaries who, when he was elected to the Sovereign Pontificate, presented him as a "liberal." Some months after he arrived in Imola, in a letter to his friend and neighbor Cardinal Falconieri, Archbishop of Ravenna, he gave a very apt description of his "golden mean" approach: "I detest and abominate, in the very marrow of my bones, the liberals' ideas and actions; but I have no sympathy, either, for the fanaticism of the so-called 'papalist' party. The golden mean, the

---

2   In addition to Serafini and Polverari, cf. Mino Martelli, "Pastoralità di G. M. Mastai-Ferretti Vescovo e Cardinale di Imola (1832-1846)," *Atti del II. Convegno*, pp.173ff.
3   Letter cited in Polverari, I, 111.

Christian golden mean—and not the diabolical golden mean which is fashionable today—is the path I would like to follow, with the Lord's help. But shall I succeed in this?"[4]

Reform of the Clergy

The religious state of the diocese was deplorable. The revolutionary agitation of 1831 and 1832 and the two years' vacancy of the episcopal see had had a lowering effect on the moral life of the population, and the clergy themselves were inadequate in many ways. Parish priests were addicted to gambling, hunting, or smuggling operations with nearby Tuscany; others frequented the theaters or did not wear clerical attire. Many canons habitually dispensed themselves from their choir office.

Msgr. Mastai did not delay in reforming the clergy. He imposed strict "constitutions" on the canons of the cathedral and of other collegiate churches. In drawing up these constitutions he consulted various chapters, notably those of Osimo and Our Lady of Loreto, and found inspiration in the rules these institutions observed.

In order to maintain regular contact with his clergy he periodically sent out circulars which were both religious and administrative in substance. Msgr. Mastai insisted that his priests wear the soutane; he forbade all commercial activity and all frequenting of gambling halls; and he urged that their servants "of the opposite sex should be at least forty years old."

These orders were not followed equally everywhere, particularly in the most isolated parts of the diocese. Even ten years after his arrival Msgr. Mastai, in a circular letter to his vicars forane, was still complaining that some parish priests, "especially in the mountainous region" of the diocese, were "real wolves who, far from exercising the function of shepherds, were the scandal and ruin of the flock, a pain and embarrassment to the good people, and a continual source of heartache to those of their confreres who are zealous and exemplary...." He laid down precise rules for all:

1. It is forbidden for all parish priests, priests, and clerics to wear... any kind of secular dress in public.
2. The aforementioned should see that they have in their possession no prohibited weapons of any kind, nor should they carry them.
3. Meetings to discuss cases of conscience are expressly recommended....
4. ...make sure that parish priests reside constantly in their respective presbyteries, explain the holy Gospel, teach Christian doctrine, and make sure that the people are aware of the vigils and feasts....[5]

These disciplinary instructions were accompanied by exhortations to deepen their spiritual lives. Msgr. Mastai recommended to his clergy to cultivate the regular practice of prayer, weekly confession, reading of the

---

[4] Letter of June 3, 1833, cited by Martina, I, 52.
[5] Circular letter of August 22, 1843, cited in Fernessole, I, 77-78 and in Martelli, "Pastoralità," p.182.

Bible and the lives of the saints, "all those practices which help us to maintain the ecclesiastical spirit and to obtain from God the graces we all need to combat spiritual enemies."

Furthermore, on April 7, 1834, he inaugurated a large house of twenty-seven rooms where the priests could spend a few days following the Spiritual Exercises. A former convent, near to the sanctuary of the Madonna del Piratello and the town cemetery, had been refurbished to receive the priests twice a year, in spring and autumn.

In a pastoral letter to his clergy, dated March 1 of that same year, he gave a detailed account of the method and spirit of the Spiritual Exercises and of the benefit which the priests could draw from them, both for their personal sanctification and for the exercise of their ministry. Msgr. Mastai had asked the general superior of the Jesuits in Rome to send him a priest to conduct these Exercises.

He himself regularly went on retreat to Piratello, alone or together with some priests. A deposition at the beatification process indicates that he liked to spend the night "in a room that he himself had had painted in the form of a grotto or catacomb, with a little niche containing skulls and bones."[6] We should not see this as evidence of a taste for the morbid; rather, it shows Mastai's constant concern (to which we have already referred) to prepare for a good death and to pray for the departed. In fact, the Roman confraternity of the *Sacconi,* of which he was a member, used regularly to meet in the necropolis of the chapel of San Theodoro. May Msgr. Mastai have wanted to recreate, here in Imola, a place that was spiritually dear to him?

He took some personal notes during the first retreat organized at Piratello, and these have come down to us. They reveal the defects and inclinations he wished to correct, and also show the high tone of his soul:

> Make war on your self-love and never speak of yourself and personal things, let alone cultivate them and take pleasure in them. Be diligent in rising for meditation. Cut short your recreation after meals....Have great patience and never be overcome by motions of anger. Speak of everyone with charity and be persuaded that you are worse than the others. Recover your former diligence in writing, as an aid to memory. Cultivate a great union with God, especially in recitation of the divine office.[7]

These Piratello retreats, alone or surrounded by his priests, were of great importance for his episcopate at Imola. There can be no doubt that they were a spiritual support in the trials he had to undergo there. The Jesuit preachers he invited to Imola were of a high caliber. After 1838, when his friend Cardinal Odescalchi had surrendered his cardinalate and his

---

6   *Summarium* §2969.
7   Serafini, pp.697-98.

position as prefect of the Congregation of Bishops and Regulars in order to become a simple Jesuit—before dying in the odor of sanctity—Msgr. Mastai asked him, on several occasions, to preach the Spiritual Exercises at Piratello.

In order to improve the doctrinal formation of his priests, Msgr. Mastai created a Biblical Academy where, every month on a Thursday, a conference on the Holy Scriptures was given to the clergy. He also set up conferences of moral theology to deepen the clergy's grasp of questions in this delicate area and help them resolve the most difficult "cases." However, this reform of his diocesan clergy was neither easy nor quick.

As in Spoleto, Msgr. Mastai was anxious to give his diocese good priests. When he arrived, the seminary was occupied by Austrian troops. The seminarians had found a precarious and uncomfortable refuge in the smaller rooms of the episcopal palace. Even before he went to Imola, Msgr. Mastai had written to the Secretary of State, Cardinal Bernetti, asking him to build a barracks for the occupying soldiers so that the seminary could be returned to its occupants. In the end he succeeded in negotiating an agreement with the commander of the Austrian troops: they would evacuate the seminary and install themselves in a former Dominican convent.

In September the seminarians took up residence again in their seminary, and in November the new bishop was in a position to inaugurate the academic year. He was careful to restore the seminary in the spirit of the Council of Trent, obliging all the students to live as boarders. He himself paid the fees for the less well-off clerical students, and at the same time he did not hesitate to exclude those seminarians who did not seem to be made for priestly life. He followed the progress of all the candidates up to the priesthood, and was present at the examinations. In order to improve the formation of future priests he introduced two subjects which, up to now, had not been taught there: a course in liturgy began in 1838, and a course in Sacred Scripture began in 1843.

Similarly, he watched over the wholesome expansion of religious communities in his diocese. In Lugo there was a convent of Canonesses of St. Augustine which was in dire straits; in a letter to the vicar forane of Lugo he complained that these nuns, mostly very old, contented themselves with "saying the Rosary and nothing else…. The indispensable remedy is to bring in a religious who not only wears the habit, but also has a head."[8]

Soon he appointed a new superior, who had a particular devotion to the Sacred Heart, Sr. Maria Annunziata Andreucci. He had known her while he was Bishop of Spoleto. At that time she belonged to a convent of Poor Clares of Trevi and was under his direction. We have many letters of

---

[8] Letter cited by Martelli, "Pastoralità," p.184. The final word-play is difficult to translate: *"non solo la tonaca ma anche la testa."*

spiritual direction from Msgr. Mastai to Sr. Maria Annunziata, and they show that he was a wise priest in this area also.

Once Sr. Maria Annunziata had obtained permission to leave the Poor Clares for the convent at Lugo, Msgr. Mastai had the convent's statutes changed, giving the nuns a new name which better expressed their vocation: they became the nuns of Perpetual Adoration of the Sacred Heart of Jesus. He visited them often. The convent sprang into life again and the nuns strongly increased in numbers, even if Sr. Maria Annunziata died prematurely, in 1842, in the odor of sanctity. The particular vocation of this new institute is noteworthy: it reflects Msgr. Mastai's longstanding devotion to the Sacred Heart.

Msgr. Mastai, in addition to the spiritual direction he gave by letter to several nuns in his diocese, gave spiritual conferences in the convents on various occasions. His reputation in the direction of nuns was such that in 1841 the Congregation of Bishops and Regulars named him Apostolic Visitor to a convent of Dominican nuns in Fognano, in the neighboring diocese of Faenza.

The convent housed sixty nuns, who ran a girls' school of eighty-seven pupils. This convent was going through a profound crisis.

On his first visit, Msgr. Mastai spent five whole days, *i.e.*, ten hours a day, listening to the nuns' grievances and interviewing them one by one. He exercised this office as Apostolic Visitor for five years, until he was elevated to the pontificate.[9] There he became acquainted with a mystical soul, Mother Rosa Teresa Brenti. She had received the stigmata since 1819, and chose him as her spiritual confidant.

They continued to write to each other even after Msgr. Mastai had become pope.[10] In scandalous writings which appeared in the 1860's Mother Brenti was calumniated and presented as the pope's mistress.

Other, traditional ways of reforming his clergy and diocese were the pastoral visitations and the missions lasting several days. One by one he visited all the parishes of his diocese from June 1833 to December 1834; he was commencing a second round of visitations when he was summoned to the Sovereign Pontificate.

As for the missions, they were often entrusted to three or four Jesuit Fathers who spent a few days preaching, hearing confessions and organizing ceremonies for the entire city.

In Imola itself, the last mission had been preached in 1815. During Msgr. Mastai's episcopate there were two: one in 1836 (on the occasion of the centenary celebrations for the miraculous painting, the *Salus Infirmo-*

---

[9]   Martelli, *ibid.*, p.185.
[10] Information provided by Joachim Bouflet, author of *Encyclopédie des phénomènes extraordinaires de la vie mystique* (1st vol. Paris: F.-X. Guibert, 1992).

rum, to which we shall return) and the other during Lent, 1846, on the tenth anniversary of the previous mission.

When the first mission took place, there were such crowds that the preachers had to leave the churches and preach in the open air. Msgr. Mastai invited his friend Cardinal Falconieri to give the concluding sermon at the Sunday communion.

It was the attraction he felt towards evangelizing missions which had led him to Chile, and this attraction had not left him. In Imola in 1839 he carried out the canonical erection in his diocese of the Association for the Propagation of the Faith, which had been initiated in Lyons in 1822 by a laywoman, Pauline Jaricot. The aim of this association was to organize the collection of funds for the missions. A magazine entitled *Annals of the Propagation of the Faith* made missionaries' reports available to a wide public and gave information about the progress of missions. Msgr. Mastai was the first Italian bishop to introduce this association into his diocese; he issued a pastoral letter to promote it.

One should mention, in addition to his pastoral concerns, the spiritual help he gave to prisoners and those condemned to death. In 1835 he himself set the example by going to Lugo for the guillotining of two assassins. The presence of a bishop at the side of criminals in prison, and then at the foot of the guillotine, scandalized certain respectable people. Msgr. Mastai made it possible for these men to die as Christians, but he was profoundly affected by their execution. He wrote to Falconieri: "For the first time, I have seen the guillotine: I still have this image before me, and I think that for many a year I shall not forget the sight I witnessed."[11]

It is important, also, to point out the special place he kept, in his apostolate, for the cult of Mary.

In 1836 he wanted to celebrate, with all appropriate solemnity, the centenary of a miraculous painting of the Virgin, venerated under the title *Salus Infirmorum.* On Thursday May 12 the picture was solemnly brought from the church of the Servites of Mary, where it was kept, to the cathedral. On Friday the picture was carried from monastery to monastery and offered to the devotion of the different religious orders and the faithful. On Sunday May 15, the centenary day, after a pontifical Mass celebrated in the cathedral by the bishop, the miraculous image was returned to the church of the Servites of Mary.

The success of these grand Marian ceremonies, as well as his long-standing devotion to the Immaculate Conception, prompted Msgr. Mastai, some months later, to institute a solemn procession between the church of St. Francis, which housed a painting of the Immaculate Conception, and the cathedral. Henceforward, every December 8, the bishop

---

[11] Letter of July 21, 1835, cited in Martelli, "Pastoralità," p.189.

would come to the chapel and the painting would be carried to the cathedral with great pomp, with all the town's clergy and faithful attending.
There it would be venerated by a *triduum*.

A Prudent Administrator

Did Msgr. Mastai manage his diocese well? In financial terms we can
probably say no. The diocesan income was not enough for the charitable
works that he created or continued, nor, most of all, for the private acts of
charity in which he was very open-handed. Here is one example among
many:

> One day a poor old woman managed to get into the prelate's study,
> threw herself on her knees, and begged alms of him. The bishop had
> only just emptied his purse; he hadn't a single *bajoccho* in his drawer.
> Nonetheless, he couldn't send this unfortunate woman away with noth-
> ing. "Take this plate," said the good prelate, giving her a silver plate bear-
> ing his coat-of-arms. "Take it quickly, and go to the pawnbroker's, and I
> will get it back when I have the money." In the evening his steward, upset
> and concerned, announced to his master that a plate had disappeared and
> that they would have to search for the thief, who had to be in the house.
> Then he noticed that the bishop was laughing at him; he needed to look
> for the thief no longer, and instead delivered a veritable sermon to the
> "victim" of this theft.[12]

This anecdote, so much in the style of hagiography, is confirmed by
other sources. Many witnesses report other acts of charity on the part of
Msgr. Mastai. When he left Imola for the Holy See, he left debts behind
him which he had to repay once he had become pope. Among the charitable works he reformed, for instance, there was a girls' orphanage which
he entrusted to the care of the Sisters of Charity. He incorporated two
other institutions into this orphanage: a free school for girls and a girls'
boarding school.

In July 1836 he set up the *Opera di S. Pier Crisologo* (Institution of
St. Peter Chrysologus), named after the church to which it was attached.
This institution, which reminds us of the *Ospizio Tata Giovanni*, was entrusted to the Oratorians. It was for abandoned boys. On feast days they
were given religious instruction, and during the week they were placed
with craftsmen or farmers to learn a trade. Msgr. Mastai erected similar
establishments in other towns of his diocese, including Lugo and Casola
Valsenio.

Another work he founded should be mentioned here. It was a hostel
for "fallen women," which he put into the care of the Congregation of
the Good Shepherd of Angers, which sent four nuns to look after it, of
whom two were French. He also established a pawnbroker's shop, a *monte*

---

[12] Saint-Hermel, *Pie IX,* pp.40-41.

frumentario (to make food and provisions available) and the *Società di S. Terenzio* (Society of St. Terence), which provided the poor with home medical care.

If he was a manager who could not balance his books, at Imola he was an administrator praised by all, including his liberal adversaries. Of course, although Imola belonged to the Papal States, the bishop was not in administrative and political charge of the diocese; very often, however, he was obliged to act as intermediary between the population and the Roman and local authorities representing the pope. He urged the upkeep of the bridges and dikes, which were frequently damaged by the flooding of rivers. He kept an eye on the mills and the organization of markets, to make sure they operated effectively. Many hospitals in various towns of the diocese came into being as a result of his support, and he was also instrumental in obtaining a new road to link Imola and Bologna (a project which was completed when he was pope). It should also be noted that, to combat the practice of usury, he supported the setting-up of savings banks; the attempt failed at Imola, but in 1842, in Lugo, the town's first banking establishment came into being.

As a good administrator he was at pains to show no partisan preference for any of the factions which were striving to influence public opinion in Imola. He had regular meetings with Imola's ecclesiastics and prominent citizens to study "the best ways of promoting the city's material well-being."[13]

It was in circumstances such as these that he was led to make the acquaintance of liberals, notably Count Pasolini. We have already quoted one of Msgr. Mastai's letters to his friend Cardinal Falconieri in which he asserted that he wanted to adhere to the "Christian golden mean." This attempt to find the "Christian golden mean" led, in the summer of 1834, to his being accused of liberalism.

One of those who denounced the Bishop to the Secretariat of State was the Imola city magistrate, Cesare Codronchi, one of the most prominent figures of the "Austrian party." In particular he accused Msgr. Mastai of being hostile to a police corps, the Pontifical Volunteers, which had been created by Cardinal Bernetti, the Secretary of State. The latter charged one of Mastai's friends, Cardinal Polidori, to inform the Bishop of Imola of the accusations that had been made against him and show him the supporting evidence.

During the summer Msgr. Mastai wrote several letters to Cardinal Polidori and Cardinal Bernetti refuting these accusations. These letters are very frank and straightforward, showing that, faced with lies and errors

---

[13] *Summarium* §1725.

(from whatever quarter), Msgr. Mastai would not compromise. We see this strength of soul in many acts of his future pontificate.

On the question of the Pontifical Volunteers, Msgr. Mastai wrote to their founder, Cardinal Bernetti. Far from engaging in expressions of polite approval, he was not afraid to say that "some of them [have been] guided by passion and fury." He went on: "I have always believed it my duty to urge the Volunteers to maintain their dignity, not to engage in abuses of power, and to give a good example at all times, as is appropriate for a body of men whose task is to keep order and serve the Vicar of Jesus Christ."[14]

Cardinal Bernetti's views were not far removed from those of Msgr. Mastai. In 1836, however, he was replaced at the Secretariat of State by Cardinal Luigi Lambruschini. The latter was clearly more inclined to defend law and order at all costs and to uphold the Austrian way of looking at things.

While the accusation of "liberalism" pursued Msgr. Mastai for a long time, even up to the first years of his pontificate, the progress of his career shows that Gregory XVI never attached any credence to it.

Cardinal

Since 1836 there had been a rumor that Msgr. Mastai was going to be appointed nuncio in Paris. Finally, in 1838, in a more official manner, he was sounded out about this post, it being made clear that he would have enough leisure to retain the bishopric of Imola as well. No doubt the pope thought that the "man of peace" and "mediator" of 1831 and the reforming Bishop of Imola would be the very man for the situation in Louis-Philippe's France.

In religious matters France at this time was in a paradoxical situation. On the one hand it was experiencing a profound religious rebirth. For instance, the number of priestly ordinations had grown considerably within fifteen years, increasing from 715 in 1814 to 1,400 in 1821, and reaching 2,350 in 1829.[15] On the other hand, in public opinion there was an equally large increase in anti-clericalism and liberalism, particularly since the revolution of 1830.

It can be doubted whether, at that time, Msgr. Mastai had an accurate view of the French situation; it seems that the first point was more in his mind than the second. At all events, in a letter to Cardinal Polidori, he put forward the various reasons which dissuaded him from accepting such a post. There was his inadequate mastery of the French language; his defective memory, which sometimes let him down "even in impor-

---

[14] Letter of July 28, 1834, cited by Fernessole, I, 95.
[15] Adrien Dansette, *Histoire religieuse de la France contemporaine* (Paris: Flammarion, 1948), I, 256.

tant matters"; the superiority of the French clergy against whom, he felt, he would cut a poor figure; and finally his fear that "a different climate" would cause the reappearance of the epileptic attacks from which he had suffered in his youth.[16]

We can imagine that the most serious reason for his refusal was that he would have to be absent from his diocese for many months, and that his program of religious restoration would suffer as a result. In the end Gregory XVI offered the nunciature to another prelate, but some months later, in March 1839, the Secretary of State proposed Msgr. Mastai's name for the nunciature in Naples.

Once again Msgr. Mastai took avoiding action. When one of his secretaries, Msgr. Sbarretti, observed that in refusing a nunciature again, he had forfeited *"il Cappello"* (the cardinal's hat), he replied, "That means little to me."[17]

Should we see these offers of prestigious nunciatures, not as promotions, but as a flattering way of removing from the Romagna a bishop whom Secretary of State Lambruschini thought too moderate? Perhaps.

In the event, Gregory XVI maintained confidence in the Bishop of Imola and proved Msgr. Sbarretti's prediction wrong. At a consistory on December 23, 1839, he named Msgr. Mastai cardinal *in petto.* The enthronement ceremony did not take place until December 14 of the following year.

When the Pope expressed his intention of creating Msgr. Mastai a cardinal, Cardinal Lambruschini is said to have protested, "the Mastai are all liberal, even the cats!" If the story is true, it shows that the rumor put about five years earlier was still going the rounds; but it also shows that it had so little credibility that Gregory XVI, a thorough-going anti-liberal pope, did not take it seriously: he ignored his Secretary of State's objection and created the Bishop of Imola cardinal.

Mastai himself tried initially to decline the honor given to him. A letter from him to Cardinal Falconieri indicates that he only accepted the cardinal's hat on the direction of the Jesuit Fr. Seguir, who was conducting the Spiritual Exercises for the Imola clergy.

Reformer

The beginning of the 1840's in Italy saw a multiplication of publications of various tendencies, all issuing a twofold call: for the reform of the pontifical government and for Italian unity.

The most celebrated of them was the work of Fr. Vincenzo Gioberti who, from exile, published his *Del primato morale e civile degli Italiani*

---

[16] Letter of May 18, 1838, cited by Fernessole, I, 90.
[17] *Summarium* §1843.

(On the moral and civil primacy of the Italians). In this work, which aroused great enthusiasm among certain Italians (80,000 copies were sold, which was an enormous quantity for the period), Gioberti summoned Italy to be reborn and take up her ancient civilizing mission. The first step in this rebirth would have to be the country's return to a political unity. The different existing Italian states would constitute a federation around the pope; he was the only principle capable of uniting the Italians, who had long been separated from one another and were jealous of their different traditions and casts of mind. The King of Piedmont-Sardinia would be the armed champion of this federation of states. Each state would keep a part of its sovereignty, but introduce the reforms essential to this unity, notably the election of a consultative assembly and the granting of press freedom.

In a second edition of his book, Gioberti inserted "prolegomena" in which he violently attacked the Jesuits, whom he accused of being one of the principal obstacles, by the education they gave to all the sons of the noble and landed classes, to Italy's political and religious unity.

The following year the Piedmont historian Cesare Balbo, published a work entitled *Le speranze d'Italia* (Italy's hopes), which became very popular. In it, he rejected Giobert's neo-Guelf solution, which he criticized as having reduced religion to a function of society and politics. As a good liberal, Balbo thought that the Catholic religion should be kept above politics and that the spiritual and temporal realms should be absolutely independent of one another. Balbo was a partisan of Italian unity and wanted neither the "papal primacy" (like Gioberti) nor recourse to violence and arms (like the revolutionaries); instead, he urged his readers to wait for the right time and prepare people's minds for the changes which would come about sooner or later.

Was Msgr. Mastai seduced by the ideas of these two authors? This was the verdict of Count Pasolini which we have already mentioned. According to him, he himself was instrumental in bringing the works of Gioberti and Balbo to the notice of the Bishop of Imola. Count Pasolini's son has even claimed that, when going to attend the Conclave in 1846, Msgr. Mastai took these two books with him "to give them to the new pope"—a sign of the importance he attached to them.[18]

These stories, which were spread abroad even in the earliest days of the pontificate, helped to substantiate the notion of a pope who, for some years, had been under the sway of liberal ideas. In reality, the accounts given by the Pasolinis, father and son, are highly exaggerated; they are propaganda in favor of national and liberal ideas. Nationalist and liberal partisans were trying to claim the pope's authority in support of their aims.

---

[18] Giuseppe Pasolini, *Memorie raccolte da suo Figlio* (Turin: 1887), pp.52ff, cited in Aubert, p.15.

It is clear that in Imola, in a Romagna which was being agitated by liberal and revolutionary ideas and movements, Msgr. Mastai was already acquainted with the works of Gioberti and Balbo. He may not have read them, but at least he knew the main ideas behind them, for these writings were frequently discussed among the prominent citizens of the region.

What is most important for us is to ascertain his personal view of these ideas. Several sources enable us to say that he did not share them.

In a letter to a Jesuit correspondent, Fr. Ferrara, in connection with Gioberti's book, Msgr. Mastai stigmatizes the "classic errors of this poor ecclesiastic."[19] For the historian, this severe verdict has more value than the one-sided comments of third parties. If we wish to know the real thought of the future pope at this time, and his judgment on the temporal policies of Gregory XVI, we can have recourse to a memorandum he wrote in September 1845 to Msgr. Rioberti, *sostituto* at the Secretariat of State for Internal Affairs.

This lengthy document had already been drawn up when new upheavals took place in the Romagna. On September 27, insurgents easily managed to seize the town of Rimini, but remained masters of it only for some days. They had published a *Manifesto of the Populaces of the Roman State to the Princes and Peoples of Europe,* which demanded the admission of laymen to upper levels of administration, the election of municipal councils by citizens, and the creation of a Council of State from members of provincial councils.

Thus Msgr. Mastai's memorandum was written at a time of turmoil, even if Imola, some distance away from Rimini, had not been touched by these troubles—which, indeed, were quickly brought under control. It should be explained, lest we distort the sense of his remarks, that the Bishop of Imola did not take part publicly in the ongoing debates at the time.

The memorandum had no doubt been prepared some months ago, and was intended solely for the eyes of the Secretariat of State. The public knew nothing of it. Msgr. Mastai wished only to submit various suggestions of reforms to those who had charge of the Papal State.

Like any reform program, this memorandum is critical towards the existing administration and does not fail to denounce many abuses. However, it is in no way linked to the theories of Gioberti and Balbo. It is both more modest (it is very soberly entitled *Thoughts on the Public Administration of the Papal State*) and very pragmatic, divided into fifty-eight paragraphs of greater or lesser length.[20]

---

[19] Letter of April 15, 1846, cited in Serafini, p.126.
[20] The text was fully published for the first time in the *Elenchus Scriptorum* of the beatification process. After this, Serafini and Polverari reproduced it in its entirety.

It is immediately apparent how many issues of the temporal order, calling for administrative reform, are intertwined here with issues of the moral order, which call for other, very concrete, measures. In accordance with Catholic doctrine, Msgr. Mastai did not separate the two realms: it is through religion that social and political problems find their solutions.

We need not list the fifty-eight paragraphs or suggestions one by one; it is enough to indicate the most important points. In financial matters, as a way of overcoming the present "humiliating" position (§1) he suggests a general tax reform, which would see the tax rate fixed by law (§13) and prohibit townships from fixing their own rate (§45). He also called for a revision of the very strict system of censorship. While he did not question the basic principle of censorship, he suggested that it should be entrusted to a "college of revisors" (§2). As regards the very high number of political and criminal prisoners in the Papal States (20,000 prisoners for 2.5 million inhabitants), he suggested that, first of all, a "charitable union" should be set up, such as existed in Milan or Vienna, to look after prisoners on their release, so that they should not be left to their fate (§7 and §8). Further on he suggested the proclamation of a "moderate" amnesty for political prisoners and exiles. "The multiplicity of political exiles multiplies the channels of revolution" (§48).

In the different areas of administration he urged a better choice of men: "The State tribunals need a better caliber of men: perhaps they should be better paid" (§9); the governors are "timid, lacking in expertise, and incapable of upholding the honor of their post. To say nothing of the corruption and ignorance of certain chancellors and their deputies" (§9), who also should be better paid (§37).

The nobility, landowners, and men of talent are kept aloof from public affairs, whereas they could usefully represent their provinces at Rome and form a Consultative Council (§12). Of course one would have to make sure that, if these greater responsibilities were entrusted to laymen, it would not "undermine the foundations of government" (§15). The "indigenous troop" (*i.e.*, natives of the Papal States, unlike the Swiss Guards) is "another scourge of the State" as a result of its lack of military training and the corruption of its superior officers (§11). It should be better employed, for instance, as an auxiliary arm to the police, and be better paid (§25).

Public instruction lacks a "unity of direction"; the Congregation of Studies should prescribe the authors to be studied in all schools: "At the present time there is a misuse of the study of philosophy," Msgr. Mastai stresses. The light of philosophy is inadequate; it must be subordinated to a sound theology (§16). The university faculties grant diplomas too easily (§17 and §52). Every university should have a "school of religion" and provide the students with a "philosophical catechism" to ward off "the continual assaults of unbelievers" and "the tyrannical domination of indifferentism" (§17). Courses in "Christian doctrine" should be obligatory in all colleges and schools (§47).

The Bishop of Imola also proposed that a prize should be endowed to reward the writers of dramatic works "in order to eliminate the indecency and immorality of current works" (§37).

Fr. Martina, author of the most voluminous study of the pontificate of Pius IX, gave a very severe judgment on this text, written less than a year before his election as pope: "These *Pensieri* denounce the abuses that have entered the system, but do not call it in question. Their author shows himself to be a man of good will, desiring peace and the public good, but he is neither discerning, nor profound, and he is often even simplistic in his solutions."[21]

To us this verdict seems unjust. Yes, the *Pensieri* of the Cardinal of Imola are presented in some disorder and contain repetitions. But they should be taken for what they are: not as the manifesto for government of a *papabile* cardinal preparing himself for an imminent papal election, but as a series of very concrete and precise observations and suggestions, drawn up by the bishop of a diocese situated in a province in upheaval, anxious lest the situation should continue to fester.

Furthermore, these *Pensieri* are a collection of observations and suggestions which their author, as a private person, had already formulated in various letters in the preceding months and years. They should not be regarded as a response to the contemporary situation in the Romagna. Their origin is to be sought earlier.

By contrast, there is a direct link between the troubles of the Romagna and the little book published by Massimo D'Azeglio a few months later, in March 1846: *Degli ultimi casi di Romagna* (Recent events in Romagna). This book, like those of Gioberti and Balbo, was a great success. It caused its author to be expelled from the Grand Duchy of Tuscany, but the work continued to be propagated clandestinely in Florence and elsewhere.

D'Azeglio condemned both the attempt at revolution in Rimini the previous year and the policies of Gregory XVI. He put his hope in the government of Charles Albert, King of Piedmont-Sardinia, whom he regarded as a moderate, and in a liberal pope. His praise of Cardinal Gizzi made quite a stir at the time. Gizzi, Apostolic Legate in Forli, opposed the political trials in the wake of the Rimini insurrection being conducted by the "Special Mixed Commission," a kind of extraordinary tribunal which had recently been set up and was detested in the Romagna for the severity of the sentences it handed down.[22]

---

[21] Martina, I, 55.
[22] Stefano Gizzi, *Il Cardinale Tommaso Pasquale Gizzi* (Amministrazione provinciale di Frosinone, 1993), pp.149-50.

Nonetheless, Cardinal Gizzi was not a liberal. D'Azeglio did not present him as such, but praised "his humanity," "his nobility of heart," and his "temperate mode of acting."

Ultimately, D'Azeglio wanted the future pope fundamentally to reform his States; to reign, but no longer govern personally; to make the transition from an absolutist regime to a representative regime founded on a constitution; and to leave the direction of public affairs to laymen.

We know that the future Pius IX read this new work of the liberals and judged it severely: "Among many lies and barefaced calumnies," he wrote to Fr. Luigi Taparelli D'Azeglio (Massimo's brother and one of those working for a renewal of Thomism),

> he says some true things. He is not irreligious, for he says nothing against religion and proclaims himself to be a Catholic. Only he is stirred up by the Italian fever, and if his friends who think like him were to follow his advice, we would have one good thing and one bad thing. The good would be that there would be no more of the rioting and sedition which he condemns; the bad would be that we would have a profusion of writings criticizing, condemning, and protesting against the government.[23]

Msgr. Mastai suffered from the partisan passions which were rending the Romagna. True, the revolutionaries were odious to him, and he judged them more severely than common criminals;[24] but the "fanatics" on the other side, the "papalists," filled him with "disgust."[25] As for the repression inflicted on the political opposition, he found it excessive.

Some months after he had been elected pope, he wrote to his friend Falconieri: "Imola is peaceful at the moment, but 200 prisoners are a very dangerous commodity in a little city guarded by a single company of Swiss Guards."[26]

It would be a big mistake, however, to judge the Cardinal of Imola as a weakling. Another letter of this period shows this clearly. It is addressed to Cardinal Secretary of State Lambruschini, and in it Cardinal Mastai insists that a commission be "publicly set up without any political hue" with the task of judging, as a matter of urgency, the perpetrators of crimes committed under cover of political action.[27]

The man who was to be elected pope in June 1846 was, therefore, a man well informed on the political situation of the Papal States and someone of well-settled views.

---

23 Letter of April 19, 1846, in Pietro Pirri, *Carteggio del P. Luigi Taparelli d'Azeglio* (Turin: 1922), p.182, cited by Martina, I, 56-57.
24 If the latter are protected by "a single legion of demons," the former are protected "by all hell": letter of May 21, 1845, cited in Martelli, "Pastoralità," p.189.
25 Letter of September 12, 1834, cited in *ibid.*, p.191.
26 Letter of September 27, 1845, cited in *ibid.*, p.194.
27 Letter of September 17, 1845, cited in Fernessole, I, 96.

Gregory XVI died on June 1, 1846. When the Cardinal learned the news, at four in the morning, he was practicing the Spiritual Exercises at Piratello, surrounded by some of his priests. On June 6 he proceeded to priestly ordinations and celebrated a funeral office for the deceased pope in the cathedral crypt. The same day he wrote to the Sister Superior of the convent of Perpetual Adoration of the Sacred Heart, in Lugo: "Pray to the Lord more than ever, that he will deign to give his Church a pontiff able to bear the heavy load in these difficult times...."[28]

---

[28] Letter cited in Martelli, "Pastoralità," p.194.

CHAPTER 6

SOVEREIGN PONTIFF

That month, June 1846, the names of many *papabili* were circulating, including that of Mastai. The latter's election was not a felicitous surprise, as some historians have maintained. As early as 1842 the Austrian ambassador to Rome mentioned his name as one of the *papabili*. When the news of Gregory XVI's death became known and people began to think of probable successors, several ambassadors—of France, Naples, and Piedmont—in their diplomatic dispatches to their minister, referred to Mastai as a possible or even a probable pope. Nonetheless, the election of Cardinal Mastai was not a foregone conclusion.

The Conclave

Cardinal Mastai, accompanied by his secretary, Canon Stella, and his vice-majordomo, Badalleli, left Imola on June 6 or 7. At one stage of the journey he stayed at a convent in Rimini. The beatification process records that a nun told him that he would soon be pope and would not return to his episcopal see of Imola.[1] The unnamed nun has been identified as Sr. Maria Maddalena della Ss.Trinità (1821-87), who was called "the Saint of Rimini." This nun, who bore the stigmata, was several times received in audience by Pius IX, from 1860 onwards, in connection with a religious foundation she hoped to establish in the Romagna. Her beatification cause has been introduced. The Pope held her in the highest esteem.[2]

During his journey to Rome, Cardinal Mastai stopped at another convent, in Nocera Umbra, to celebrate Mass. After he had left, a mystical soul (whose beatification cause has also been introduced) called Sr. Maria Agnese Steiner told her confessor: "I have seen the new pope." The priest is supposed to have said to her, "It's impossible. Cardinal Mastai is too young."[3]

Decades earlier another prophecy is said to have been made concerning this election by Pius VII during his exile at Fontainebleau. He is supposed to have announced in a written document that one of his successors in the episcopate at Imola would be elected pope and take the name Pius. The document is said to have been given to Pius IX, who had it authenticated and granted a pension for life to the donor.[4] It seems, however, that these documents have not come to light in the Vatican Archives.

---

[1] *Summarium* §283.
[2] Identification and information provided by Joachim Bouflet.
[3] *Summarium* §768.
[4] *Summarium* §388.

On June 12, Cardinal Mastai arrived in Rome and resided at the Palazzo Filippani. The informal meetings of cardinals had already commenced. On June 8, Basso, the Sardinian vice-consul in Rome, informed his government that "several cardinals have frequently been to see Cardinal Polidori. Lambruschini, Altieri, Brignole, Amat, and others have had long discussions at his residence."[5] It would be a mistake to see these meetings with Polidori, a long-standing friend of Cardinal Mastai, as some kind of conspiracy in favor of the Bishop of Imola. In fact, some of those who attended these meetings would be rival candidates. Rather, the meetings were simply to facilitate an exchange of views on the Church's needs and the various possible candidates.

Public opinion was divided as to who should be the successor to Gregory XVI. Some revolutionaries, joined by liberals, circulated petitions in several towns of the Papal States and in the Legations, calling for the future pope to commit himself to political reforms along the lines of the 1831 *Memorandum* and to grant an amnesty. Petitions of this kind circulated in Orsino, Ancona, Forli, and Bologna.

These petitions did not mention names; many cardinals, on the contrary, were in favor of the Romans. The more liberal of them championed Cardinal Gizzi, nicknamed "pope D'Azeglio," referring to the work of Massimo D'Azeglio, already cited, which sang his praises. Among the common people the old Cardinal Micara, a Capuchin friar and a well-known preacher, was the favorite—but his age (he was an octogenarian and the Dean of the Sacred College) and his precarious health deprived him of any serious chance of being elected. Other cardinals' names circulated among the faithful: Angelo Mai, Mezzofanti, Falconieri (Mastai's friend, the Archbishop of Ravenna); the name of the Bishop of Imola was little known by the Romans. At the heart of the Sacred College a certain number of cardinals favored continuity with the previous pontificate and considered that the election of Cardinal Lambruschini would assure stability and maintain good relations with Austria. (Their opponents called them *zelanti,* or the "intransigent.")

A different current of thought wanted to see a less intransigent pope, someone not from the Vatican bureaucracy but from a diocese. They wanted a pope who was from the Papal States and was acquainted with the difficulties there, and who was also well-informed about the problems of the Church in other lands. That is how the name of Mastai became current, whereas that of Gizzi, who had been given a high profile by D'Azeglio's little book, seemed too much imbued with the spirit and the disputes of the present time.

---

5   Letter cited in Martina, I, 89.

The Conclave opened on Sunday, June 14, not in the Vatican but in the Quirinal (a custom that had become established since the death of Pius VII), in the presence of fifty cardinals.

There were sixty-two members of the Sacred College, but Gregory XVI, in a Bull of 1844, had adopted a new rule of succession: at the pope's death, if the cardinals present judged it necessary, the Conclave could open immediately, without waiting for the cardinals from remoter regions to arrive, provided that the traditional law (which required two-thirds of the votes for an election) was respected. So the cardinals entered the Conclave without waiting for the arrival of all the foreign cardinals, who represented only a minority of the Sacred College. (Of the sixty-two cardinals, fifty-four were Italians.) It was clear that only an Italian could possibly be elected. The three French cardinals, La Tour d'Auvergne, Bonald, and Bernet, had received a "Note containing instructions to be followed in the case of a Conclave" from Guizot, the head of the French government. This long "note" of twelve pages, written in an elevated tone, did not, of course, instruct the cardinals how to vote, nor did it attempt to exclude any particular *papabile* candidate. It deemed it sufficient to sketch the portrait of an "ideal" pope. It will be noted that certain of these ideal features could easily have been applied to Cardinal Mastai:

> The sincerest piety, the liveliest faith, the most edifying morals, the highest degree of theological science—these are, no doubt, the prime virtues, the dominant qualities which one would desire to see on the Chair of St. Peter. At the same time, however, the Head of the Church needs to possess, on the one hand, the necessary illumination to carry out the spiritual and temporal administration committed to him for the common good of the faithful and for that of his own people in particular; on the other hand, he needs to have that lofty character and high view of things, that knowledge of men and affairs, that understanding of modern times, that mixture of firmness and moderation which are more indispensable than ever for the government of people's hearts and minds.[6]

Guizot did not explicitly mention the name of Mastai. Yet this name was not unknown to the European governments. In 1842 Lützow, Austrian ambassador to Rome, had written to his government that Cardinal Mastai would be an acceptable candidate for those who believe that the next pope should be "neither friar nor foreigner."[7]

As the Conclave approached, other diplomats informed their governments of the probability that Mastai would be elected. On June 3, the

---

[6] "Note" of June 8, 1846, Archives du Ministère des Affaires Etrangères, Paris, "Correspondance Politique," Rome 986, ff. 187-192; hereafter, A.M.A.E., C.P., Rome.

[7] The sentiment against a "brother" was a clear allusion to Gregory XVI, who was a member of the Camaldolese Order. The sentiment against a "stranger" expressed the hope that the next pope would be a native of the Papal States.

Sardinian vice-consul, and on June 4 the Neapolitan ambassador, thought that the Bishop of Imola would be the next pope because he enjoyed a good reputation in his diocese and had shown a conciliatory spirit in difficult times.[8]

However, other names were also being discussed. This raised the prospect of a long Conclave and a large number of ballots. In the event, only four ballots were needed, and the Conclave, properly speaking, lasted for only forty-eight hours. Whereas the pontificate of Pius IX would last for nearly thirty-two years (the longest in the Church's history), the Conclave which elected him was one of the shortest. Its brevity was in marked contrast to the conclaves which had resulted in the election of his predecessors: Pius VIII had been elected at the end of a conclave of eighteen days, Leo XII after a conclave of thirty-six days, and Gregory XVI after a conclave of fifteen days.

Two ballots took place on June 15, and two more the following day. According to various sources, which sometimes differ in detail,[9] we can present the results of these four ballots as follows:

	15 June		16 June	
	1st ballot	2nd ballot	3rd ballot	4th ballot
Lambruschini	15	13	11	10
Mastai	13	17	27	36
Falconieri	4	7	4	4
Oppizoni	3	7	-	-
De Angelis	3	5	4	5
Gizzi	2	2	2	1

This shows that, at the first ballot, two cardinals, the Secretary of State and the Bishop of Imola, attracted a large number of votes, whereas Cardinal Mastai was the only one to show a steady and significant progression.

We also know that, right from the first ballot, Cardinal Polidori, who can be regarded as having been one of Giovanni Maria Mastai's spiritual teachers during his time as a young priest, and Cardinal Bernetti, the former Secretary of State of Gregory XVI, came forward as the "grand electors" of the Bishop of Imola, i.e., they called on others to vote for him.

Certain historians also see it as significant that, on the evening of the first day of the Conclave, after two ballots, Cardinal Falconieri (another

---

[8]   Diplomatic dispatches cited by Martina, I, 85.
[9]   Fernessole, I, 119; Martina I, 92-93.

friend of Cardinal Mastai) asked his supporters to give their votes to the Bishop of Imola. If this is true, it is also the case that his recommendation was not followed to any great extent, since votes for Falconieri persisted until the end. It is also clear that little weight was attached to Cardinal Gizzi, the candidate of the liberals and of D'Azeglio.

For a long time some historians have wanted to stress the importance of the veto of the Emperor of Austria-Hungary against Cardinal Mastai, who was judged hostile to Austrian interests in Italy.[10] The veto could not take effect because the Austrian cardinal who bore it arrived at the Conclave too late to participate in the voting.[11]

An Austrian historian has firmly established that, at this election of 1846, Austria-Hungary did indeed wish to use its right of veto, not against Cardinal Mastai but against Cardinal Bernetti, who was felt to be too much a Francophile.[12] It was Cardinal Gaysruck, Archbishop of Milan (which was an Austrian possession at that time), who had been charged with the task of delivering this Austrian veto. He could not carry this out, since he did not arrive in Rome until June 19, i.e., two days after the election result was proclaimed.

On the evening of June 16, at the fourth ballot, Cardinal Mastai received the number of votes necessary to become pope: 36 votes were cast in his favor as against only 10 for Lambruschini. The two-thirds majority, as canonically required, had been reached.

There is a tradition, repeated by several historians, that Mastai, who was one of the three scrutineers who had to sort and count the ballot-papers, fainted when he realized that he was going to win.[13] The fact is that when he saw that there were already twenty-seven ballot-papers bearing his name, Cardinal Mastai requested to be replaced as a scrutineer. He was replaced by Cardinal Serracassano. Nine further ballot-papers bore his name. It is probable that the interruption of the counting of votes, which is well attested in the archive documents relating to the Conclave, was subsequently embellished and seen as the result of the newly-elected pope's being overcome with humility and emotion. The reality is more straightforward: out of modesty, Cardinal Mastai doubtless did not want to have to announce a result which, clearly, was going to be in his own favor. He preferred to hand over this task to someone else. There was no

[10] The Emperor of Austria, the King of Spain, and the King of France still enjoyed the privilege of opposing the election to the sovereign pontificate of any cardinal they judged to be hostile to their interests.
[11] T. Ortolan, "Conclave," *Dictionnaire de Théologie Catholique*, III, 707-727. The *Summarium* §236 also reports this failed veto against Mastai.
[12] F. Engel Jonas, *Österreich und Vatikan* (Graz and Vienna: 1958), cited by Martina, I, 87.
[13] Other versions of the incident speak of Cardinal Lambruschini fainting in fury on seeing the tiara escape him.

fainting-fit, and the testimony of one of the cardinals present, Cardinal Fieschi, one of the scrutineers, shows on the contrary that the Bishop of Imola remained perfectly calm as he accepted without hesitation the heavy charge laid upon him.[14] The tradition goes that he immediately said that he wished to take the name of Pius IX in memory of, and in gratitude to, Pius VII, to whom he owed his priesthood and whom he had succeeded as Bishop of Imola.

The canonical act which registers his election is dated June 16, at a quarter to midnight. Given the lateness of the hour, the pontifical election was not announced to the population until 9 o'clock the next morning.

His first letter, that very evening, was to his three brothers, Gabriele, Giuseppe, and Gaetano, who had stayed in Senigallia. This letter reveals the state of mind of the newly-elected pope:

> ...God most blessed, who humiliates and exalts, has willed to elevate my wretchedness to the most sublime dignity on earth. May His most holy will be ever done! I am aware of the immense gravity of such a charge, and equally I know my own poverty—not to say the veritable nothingness of my spirit. Pray, and have others pray for me.[15]

It is noteworthy that, in this same letter, he did not try to prevent the festivities which the municipality was not slow to organize in his honor. In fact, he asked that "the sum to be spent should be used entirely for projects of benefit to the city." Similarly, in 1840, he had not refused to finance the popular festivities in Imola in honor of his elevation to the cardinalate. When an adviser suggested to him that the money would be better spent on the poor, the new cardinal had pointed out that it was the poorest people who took part in these festivities and enjoyed them.

On the morning of June 17, from the balcony of the Quirinal, Cardinal Tommaso Riario Sforza announced the name of the new pope to the crowd which was waiting below on the Piazza Monte Cavallo.

Neither his name nor his silhouette was familiar to the Roman population. Certain contemporary witnesses report that, initially, the name of the newly-elected pope was received without enthusiasm. There had been a rumor, the day before, that Cardinal Gizzi had been elected; those who were expecting him to appear were disappointed. However, when Pius IX came out on to the balcony, his youth (he was only fifty-four), his comely,

---

[14] At the beatification process, Cardinal Nocella would state that, according to his confidential informants, the new pope slept uninterruptedly on the night after the election, cf. *Summarium* §13. Another deposition states that Cardinal Mastai had brought with him to the Conclave, as spiritual reading, a manual of devotion on the Sacred Heart by the Jesuit Father Carlo Borgo, *Summarium* §111.

[15] Letter published in "Lettere do Pio ai familiari," *Pio IX nel primo centenario della sua morte* (Vatican City: Editrice la Postulazione della causa di Pio IX/Libreria Editrice Vaticana, 1978), p.45; hereafter, *Pio IX nel primo centenario*.

oval face, his splendidly full figure, and his pleasant voice won over the assembled crowd.

In the days that followed, some journalists reminded their readers that in his youth Mastai had proved to be a zealous and committed director of the *Tata Giovanni* Orphanage, and then of the *Ospizio San Michele*. This added to his budding popularity. At the same time the rumor began to spread—an unfounded rumor, as we have seen—that the new pope was a "liberal."

A. de Broglie, the secretary of the Roman embassy, reported the story which then spread throughout the city. When the first stage-coach from Rome arrived at Civita-Vecchia after the papal election, people inquired of the first passenger to get down what the new pope's name was. In his enthusiasm, what he came out with was, *"Il papa è fatto e liberale, coglione!"* (the pope elected is a liberal, you blockhead!).

Reformers of all tendencies began to dream that the pope so greatly desired by D'Azeglio had arrived. Those in the know, however, made no mistake about it: Pius IX would not be a liberal pope. Not in the area of religious doctrine, nor in political matters either.

Metternich, who had been so fearful that the cardinal elected would be a partisan of Italian unity and in favor of war against Austria, expressed his contentment to his ambassador to Rome on June 26. The election of Pius IX, he wrote, gave him "a satisfaction that was as lively as it was legitimate." Pellegrino Rossi, the French ambassador to Rome, told Guizot that he had met two cardinals "who must be foremost in the thoughts of the Holy Father. They have assured me quite positively that the amnesty and the railways will be agreed to immediately. If this happens, I regard the peace of the provinces as guaranteed."[16]

Another diplomat, Auguste de Liedekerke, Minister of the Netherlands at Rome, wrote a report to his government presenting the newly-elected pope as "full of gentleness and modesty" and "endowed with excellent judgment."

He also thought that Pius IX would be able to impart "a good and wise direction" to temporal affairs and "keep this kindness of his within proper limits…for, in public life, kindness can easily degenerate into weakness and hence nourish grave abuses."[17]

All these diplomats knew the new pope, at least by name and reputation, and were very accurate in their estimate of him. None of them imagined that the man elected by the Conclave was a liberal. Subsequent history has shown that his apparent kind-heartedness could at times hide an unshakable determination.

---

[16] Dispatch of June 17, 1846, A.M.A.E., C.P., Rome 986, f.197.
[17] Dispatch of June 19, 1846, cited in Martina, I, 95.

The day after Pius IX's death, Charles de Mazade sketched a portrait which deserves to be kept in mind:

> Pius IX in no way resembled those secular-minded popes of times past, who were so calculating in their politics. He was of the race of true pontiffs: simple, sincere, and brave, with an absolute sincerity of faith which went as far as mysticism, but which, at the same time, he could imbue with urbanity and grace. Meeting him, one could not avoid being struck by this mixture of stirring piety, witty good humor, and penetrating acumen which imparted such an expressive originality to his physiognomy.
>
> He had the gaiety that comes from a clear conscience; and it was a kind of open-heartedness, much more than ambitious planning, that enabled him to carry out the most striking acts, the boldest ventures of his reign.
>
> ...His words had a gentle and fine irony which disconcerted even the most grave personages.[18]

Mazade the liberal, and an opponent of the pope's temporal power, painted a very faithful portrait, corroborated by others who knew the pope closely: Pius IX was a pope filled with a great sense of the supernatural, which dictated all his activity—what Mazade called his "absolute sincerity of faith." But he was not a cold person, impenetrable or tormented: his outbursts of anger, his humor, and his delight in irony are well known.

The Pope of the Amnesty

The new pope's coronation took place on June 21. The day before, Pius IX had ordered alms to be distributed to the poor of Rome and all the objects in the city's pawn-shop to be returned to their owners, he himself paying the sums due. Most people were impatiently waiting to see the first decisions he would take in the temporal sphere. The rumor was going around that on the day of his coronation he would announce two important concessions: the railways and the amnesty.

Naturally, the construction of railways in the Papal States would benefit commerce and industry; for the liberals and revolutionaries, however, it symbolized that modernity which the pontificate ought to embrace. As for the amnesty of political prisoners, while it would show the new pope's desire for conciliation, to the liberals and revolutionaries it would also symbolize a break with the disgraced regime of Gregory XVI.

The Pope was well aware of the false interpretations to which his first decisions could give rise, and for that reason he decided not to do anything in a hurry. The coronation ceremony took place without any spectacular announcement being made.

---

[18] "Chronique de la Quinzaine," *Revue des Deux-Mondes,* March 1, 1878, p.957.

Pius IX was anxious first of all to have the advice of the cardinals who were most well-versed in political matters. On June 30, he created a consultative commission composed of six cardinals with the task of examining, together with him, the most urgent questions. He chose his predecessor's two former Secretaries of State (Bernetti and Lambruschini) and cardinals Mattei, Macchi, Gizzi, and Amat; a young prelate, Msgr. Corboli Bussi, who would exercise a great influence on Pius IX in the months and years to come, acted as secretary.[19]

It will be noted how, in this first consultative organ, Pius IX deliberately mixed people who were reputed to be "reactionaries" and "liberals." It emerges clearly from the decisions taken that, as regards temporal affairs, Pius IX was concerned to do two things: to pacify the turbulent by conducting a reform of the administration of the Papal States, while at the same time not allowing liberal ideas to triumph. By considering only the measures he took towards pacification and reform, some of his contemporaries, followed by some historians, encouraged the legend of the "liberal" pope who was subsequently to turn his back on his former ideas.

The reality is different. Pius IX showed himself both generous and prudent in his first decisions. When he was Bishop of Imola, as we have seen, he had already suggested that Gregory XVI should introduce certain reforms in the government and administration of the Papal States. What more natural than that, once he had become pope, he should try to carry out these same suggestions?

The Conclave had been an opportunity for several cities of the Papal States and Legations to send in, to the cardinals there assembled, public letters containing requests and demands for reforms. Pius IX took account of these in his first decisions, even if there was no question of satisfying all the requests that had been formulated.

Accordingly, dated June 10, *i.e.*, four days after the Conclave opened, members of Roman civil society had written a letter to the cardinals which contained a detailed list of the hoped-for reforms:

- A representative municipal body in Rome, composed of those who best preserve and promote the Roman people.
- Civil and criminal laws to be appropriate to modern life; crimes against the State to be examined and punished in ordinary tribunals; the jurisdiction of ecclesiastical tribunals no longer to apply to laymen.

---

[19] G. Martina: "He was more than a very efficient executor of the Pope's directives: he was one of his main inspirations. Between him and his sovereign there developed not only a profound and reciprocal regard, but also a real cordiality that recalls the intimate communion of feeling between Pius X and Cardinal Merry del Val" (I, 115). Msgr. Corboli Bussi died prematurely in 1850 at the age of thirty-seven.

- A general and full amnesty for existing political prisoners.
- The establishment of a Supreme Council of State residing in Rome.
- Civilian, military and judiciary posts and dignities to be open to laymen.
- A Civic Guard; foreign militias to be withdrawn.
- The clergy to be withdrawn from public education and its administration, except for religious instruction.
- Press censorship to be restricted to moral and religious matters.
- The provision of railways, and all the other social improvements which are associated with the progress of the other civilized people of Europe.[20]

We can see that the hoped-for reforms contained things that were acceptable (such as the introduction of railways), but also things that were completely unacceptable to the head of the Church, particularly the laicization of education.

The commission of cardinals met for the first time on July 1 in the presence of the Pope. Three questions were examined (a sign, if one were needed, that the agenda was fixed by the Pope, not left to the initiative of the cardinal consultors): the reform of the Secretariat of State, with the aim of defining more clearly the particular competence of each of its departments; the building of railway lines; and the amnesty.

There was more dispute concerning the last two of these, particularly on the part of Cardinal Lambruschini. He insisted that the building of railways would endanger the security of the State by making it all too easy for people to move about; it would also mean that local industries would be forced into greater competition with the industries of other states. Others raised the question of the financial cost of such a project.

Lambruschini declared that he was equally reluctant to the granting of an amnesty to political prisoners: it could seem to give encouragement to the revolutionaries and call the preceding pontificate into question. Others, like Cardinal Gizzi, thought, on the contrary, that a conciliatory measure such as this would help to calm people down. Certain cardinals underlined the necessity of requiring the amnestied prisoners to give an oath of loyalty and retract their former errors.

There can be no doubt that Pius IX had already decided to grant an amnesty. This had been one element in the suggestions he addressed to the Secretariat of State in 1845. It will be remembered, however, that he thought that such an amnesty would have to be "moderate." Granted the

---

[20] Letter published in Fernessole, I, 118.

principle of an amnesty, it would be very important to weigh the terms in which the decree would be published, so that neither party could misinterpret the reasons behind it.

On July 8, a second meeting of the commission of cardinals was convened, and discussed the modalities of the amnesty. It was agreed that the following would be excluded from it: clerics, government employees, all those who had exercised public office, and common criminals. A declaration of loyalty to the Sovereign Pontiff would be demanded of those who were to be released from prison or authorized to go into exile.

Other matters were raised, requiring longer examination: the equilibrium of public finances, the struggle against corruption in the administration, the reorganization of the army, the establishment of centers of education and welfare for young people out of work. Again, we see that the Pope was submitting for scrutiny certain suggestions he had already made in former years when he was in Imola.

On July 15, the amnesty decree was proposed to the commission of cardinals. The text had been prepared by Msgr. Corboli Bussi. Even the decree's terms show clearly that, in this situation, the Pope was not acting in weakness, nor as a demagogue, but with generosity and realism. He expressed his compassion for the political prisoners, who were "young and inexperienced, and who, drawn into the arena of political unrest by foolish illusions, seemed more victims of seduction than seducers themselves." He also uttered his "conviction that it was possible to extend pardon without endangering public order"; the decree went on to show clearly that he had no intention of renouncing his sovereignty, nor of tolerating further unrest in the future.

Indeed, he went on:

> We are pleased to hope that those who shall benefit from Our clemency will at all times respect Our rights and their own honor. We are still confident that Our pardon will bring peace to hearts and put an end to the civil discord which is always either the cause or the effect of political passion. This will vindicate the bond of peace which, in God's design, should unite the sons of the same father. If Our hopes prove to be disappointed in part, We shall remember, albeit with bitter pain, that, while clemency is the sweetest prerogative of sovereignty, its first duty is justice.[21]

Articles 1 and 2 of the decree stipulated, as a condition of the amnesty, that those who benefited from it should make a written declaration, both expressing their recognition of Pius IX as their "legitimate sovereign" and committing themselves "not only to refrain from abusing, in any way and at any time, the grace granted to them, but also to fulfil all their duties as good and faithful subjects."

---

[21] Text of the decree in Fernessole, I, 133-34.

Dated July 16, the decree was published in Rome on the evening of the 17th. Writers differ as to the range of application of this amnesty. Some, like Fernessole, speak of some 1,500 political prisoners (condemned or accused) being released. Martina, having consulted various different archives, gives the more modest figure of about 400 prisoners released and 269 exiles permitted to return to Rome once they had signed the required declaration.[22] More than 100 other exiles, obedient to the command of Mazzini, who was in exile in London, refused to sign the formula of submission; however, a certain number were able to return to their country all the same, the most celebrated being the liberal Terenzio Mamiani, who had links with Gioberti, and who subsequently would be one of Pius IX's ministers.

This amnesty, so wide in its application, was welcomed with great enthusiasm by the population. From the morning until the evening of the 17th there were many demonstrations of joy in the streets, and great torch-lit gatherings were organized on the principal squares of Rome and around the Quirinal Palace, where the pope habitually resided. This lasted for several weeks and was imitated in the main cities of the Papal States.

The famous poet, Gabriele Rossetti, wrote a song which was soon on everyone's lips. Its refrain was: "Long live Italy, long live Pius IX, long live the union, long live liberty." Rossini composed a "People's hymn to Pius IX" which was played for the first time hardly a week after the proclamation of the amnesty. Some time later a triumphal arch, of wood and cardboard, was erected in the Pope's honor on the Piazza del Populo.[23]

Newly born boys were given the name Pio and girls were called Pia. Portraits of the Pope holding the amnesty decree in his hands were printed and distributed in Rome, but also throughout Italy and even in foreign countries, notably in France, where the press had unanimously celebrated the amnesty. The Bibliothèque Nationale in Paris possesses a number of examples of these portraits that were printed for widespread distribution, and the Pius IX Museum in Senigallia exhibits a neckerchief of the period on which the complete text of the amnesty decree is reproduced.

Louis Veuillot who, among the lay publicists, would be an indefatigable defender of Pius IX during his entire pontificate, noted: "Nothing, perhaps, will ever equal the hosannas of the first days of this reign which, apart from rare intervals, was nothing but one long tempest....It was as if a spell of affection had been cast over the world."[24]

---

[22] Martina, I, 100, n.5.

[23] All these festivities were recalled in an exhibition organized in 1987 in Rome at the Museum of Folklore: "Rome 1846-49: From the Reform of Pius IX to the Roman Republic," reviewed in *L'Osservatore Romano,* February 28, 1987.

[24] L. Veuillot, *Pie IX,* Oeuvres Complètes (Paris: Lethielleux, 1929), X, 391.

With historical hindsight it can be said that the amnesty "was the start of a collective delirium on the part of public opinion, partly spontaneous and partly artificially engendered, which reached its conclusion in the European revolution of 1848."[25] While it was itself measured and prudent, and contained a warning, it was presented by the liberals and revolutionaries in a different light: it was hailed as a beginning, and even as the promise of wider reforms, and as the dawn of a new era. Committees were set up to engineer demonstrations of enthusiasm, which soon became opportunities for manipulating public opinion and a way of intimidating the new pontifical authority.

First Measures

The nomination of a Secretary of State is one of the most eagerly-awaited acts of any new Sovereign Pontiff. Even if the Secretary of State is first and foremost the executive officer of pontifical policy, he can sometimes contribute to it or impart a certain quality to it as a result of his temperament and influence. Furthermore, by choosing this or that man as his key political executive, the pope indicates more or less clearly, to the ecclesiastical hierarchy as a whole, the direction he intends his pontificate to take. There was great anticipation, therefore, regarding Pius IX's choice.

It was not until August 8 that he nominated Cardinal Gizzi as Secretary of State. The latter, as we have seen, had the reputation of being a liberal. There was no substance to this reputation.[26] The civil and ecclesiastical authorities of the Papal States would soon discover this.

On August 24, with the Pope's agreement, he sent a circular letter to the provincial authorities and local magistrates requiring them to put an end to the demonstrations in favor of the amnesty. These expressions of enthusiasm had taken a disturbing, triumphalist tone and had given rise to repeated incidents. He warned people explicitly against "certain theories and tendencies towards which His Holiness himself is completely opposed."[27]

A circular of the same tone would be sent on October 8.

Soon, in February 1847, in a letter to the nuncio in Vienna who was ordered to communicate its contents to Metternich, Cardinal Gizzi explained the policies being followed. In it he distinguished between the legitimate material progress which should be envisaged (various reforms, the improvement of commerce, industry, agriculture, the construction of

[25] Martina, I, 101.
[26] Mario de Camillis, "Gizzi Pasquale Tommaso," *Enciclopedia Cattolica* (Città del Vaticano: 1951), VI, 863-864, and Gizzi, *Il Cardinale Gizzi*.
[27] Circular of August 24, 1846, cited in Gizzi, *op. cit.*, pp.174-75.

railways) and the unacceptable constitutional demands being made by the liberals.

Practical measures followed one another as the weeks and months went by. A "Consultative Commission on Railways" was set up, composed of clerics and laymen, with the task of studying how this new means of transport should be introduced into the Papal States. On November 7, a "Notification" was published, announcing the building of five railway lines. Finally, in spite of the fact that the revolution of 1848 caused the studies and the work itself to be interrupted, a first line was inaugurated in 1856 between Rome and Frascati. Other lines would be constructed in due course.

Other measures adopted by Pius IX in the first period of his pontificate added to his popularity: he lowered the price of bread and salt, ordered projects to be undertaken which would provide work for the unemployed, opened a mine, and instituted night schools and Sunday schools for apprentices and workmen.

However useful such practical measures were, they were not the thoroughgoing reforms that were called for in the areas of administration, justice, finance, the police, and the army. It has been said that "Pius IX did not have a very clear idea of the reforms that should be adopted" and that he dithered in some of his major political decisions.[28] This assessment seems unjust. His *Pensieri* of 1845 clearly show that their author had a sharp awareness of the abuses and inadequacies in the administration of the Papal States. Once he was pope, he was confronted with a series of problems which sometimes amounted to veritable dilemmas. Thus, speaking to the French ambassador to Rome of the weaknesses and evils which encumbered his administration, the Pope referred to "the obstacles he encountered most of all from people who should have been bound to help and support him," admitting that "unfortunately we have multiplied posts and jobs too much, with the result that the positions are poorly recompensed and carried out by men who are both lacking in ability and badly paid; it was hard to deprive them of their employment, and it was ruinous for the treasury to pension them all off."[29]

It is wrong to reproach Pius IX, in 1846-47, with not having "a very clear idea of the reforms that should be adopted." Rather, we should consider the method he adopted in the very first weeks of his pontificate: not to take any decision in a hurry, and first to gather advice from competent persons. A prelate who knew him for thirty years, Msgr. Tizzani, Bishop of Terni, judged with great insight when he said, at the very dawn of the

[28] Martina, I, 119.
[29] Dispatch from Rossi to Guizot, December 18, 1846, A.M.A.E., C.P., Rome 986, ff.330-31.

pontificate: "We have a new pope, Pius IX, who is loved by all. He is a man of peace, and will give us a long and fine pontificate."[30]

Qui Pluribus

In studying the first period of the pontificate, so rich in decisions of all kinds, we risk putting the Sovereign Pontiff himself in second place. It would be a grave error, however, and would falsify our understanding of his pontificate, if we left his spiritual life and his religious concerns in the shade.

Ever since his early years as a priest, as we have seen, Pius IX had eagerly attended spiritual retreats and frequented various pious confraternities. He had always dedicated significant time to his priestly obligations and to prayer. As a bishop, in Spoleto and then in Imola, he always tried to make sure that his new responsibilities did not obstruct his spiritual life. He acted no differently once he had become pope. We can say, without getting involved in hagiographical legend, that he always put his spiritual life first. The process of beatification contains very many testimonies illustrating this fact.

A short while after his election, Pius IX renewed his consecration to the Blessed Virgin Mary.[31] Despite the crushing weight of his office, the many anxieties and the various grave issues he had to face, his priority was to reserve a significant space of time every day for prayer. In addition to Mass and breviary, which he executed with one or other of his private secretaries, he made a daily visit to the Blessed Sacrament, reserved in a chapel just above his room. In this chapel, which he called *Mio Paradisetto,* he placed several relics which were dear to him.[32]

He made a practice of daily mental prayer.[33] Fr. Huguet, who spent time in Rome and learned confidential details from the Pope's secretaries, gave this account of the Pope's daily routine, even while Pius IX was still alive:

> The Holy Father goes early to his chapel....Pope Pius IX celebrates the Mass in a slow and holy manner; his august features are often bathed in tears as he holds in his consecrated hands the hidden God whose Vicar he is. He usually says Mass at half-past seven, and then, by way of thanksgiving, attends a second Mass celebrated by one of his chaplains; then, on his knees, with one of the prelates of his household, he recites part of the breviary, and then returns to his room. As day declines, a time indicated by the sound of the *Angelus* and called the *Ave Maria,* the Pope recites the

---

[30] Letter of Msgr. Vincenzo Tizzani to Cesare di Castelbarco, July 18, 1846, cited by G. Radice, "Pio il grande dal carteggio letterario col Conte Cesare di Castelbarco (1846-56)," in *Pio IX nel primo centenario*, p.306.

[31] *Summarium* §391.

[32] *Summarium* §§257-258.

[33] *Summarium* §2096-2097.

Angelic Salutation together with his household, adding a *De Profundis* for those of the faithful of the entire world who have died during the day. The Holy Father spends three hours every day in adoration before Our Lord. It is thence that he draws so much light and help for the governing of the Church.[34]

Allowing for a certain pious exaggeration and the style of the period, this nonetheless gives us a fairly accurate picture of the Pope's private religious life. We can complement it with other significant features. Before taking his meal, he frequently used to read, or have read to him, a selection of texts from St. Francis de Sales, and he often recommended this work.[35] This was his practice at least for a certain period. We can be sure that it was this love of St. Francis de Sales—which was communicated to him by Cardinal Polidori—that led Pius IX to proclaim him a Doctor of the Church in 1877. This special attachment to the author of the *Introduction to the Devout Life* was also evident after his death when, in one of his prayer-books, a special little picture was found: in it, he himself had put together tiny portraits of the saints who were dear to him: the Blessed Virgin; the apostles Peter and Paul; St. John; St. Catherine, virgin and martyr; St. Philip Neri; St. Louis Gonzaga; and St. Francis de Sales.[36]

The first encyclical Pius IX published can be considered both as the key of his pontificate and as a true revelation of his personality. Dated November 9, 1846, the encyclical *Qui Pluribus* introduces, in embryo, the great doctrinal documents of the pontificate, namely, the encyclical *Quanta Cura*, the Syllabus, and the two Constitutions to be defined at the First Vatican Council.

This encyclical, which was prepared to a large extent by Cardinal Lambruschini, should have destroyed the myth of the "liberal" pope once and for all, but this myth persisted for a further two years. The legend began to fade only after Pius IX had rejected the idea of a war against Austria and subsequently refused to yield to the Roman revolution. At that time there were many who would accuse the Pope of casting aside his earlier convictions.

Appearing at the dawn of Pius IX's pontificate, however, *Qui Pluribus* was a solemn revelation of the Pope's mind and of the religious direction to be taken by his pontificate. It was also a severe doctrinal warning.

---

[34] Letter in R. P. Huguet, *L'Esprit de Pie IX* (Lyons-Paris: Félix Girard, 1866), pp.4-5.

[35] *Summarium* §3. Cardinal Nocella, reporting this fact, speaks of "Giussada." Bogliolo has established that it was, in fact, "Gessaga" (p.155, n.11). Carlo Antonio Gessaga, director of the Sisters of the Visitation in Rome, was the author, in the 1750's, of a work entitled *Motivi o sieno Avvertimenti cavati dalle Opere di S. Francesco di Sales per ciascum giorno dell'anno*. The work was re-edited in 1857 under the title *S. Francesco di Sales. Diario sacro estratto dalla sua vita e dalle sue opere*. This is doubtless the edition used by Pius IX.

[36] *Summarium* §76.

Even today some historians are astonished at the encyclical's grave tone: "There is, no doubt, a certain contrast between the moderation and human warmth of which Pius IX gives evidence in his personal contacts and the sour, pessimistic tone, lacking any ray of light, of *Qui Pluribus*; this difference corresponds to a real struggle in the pope's soul."[37] In our view there was no "struggle" whatsoever "in the pope's soul." The encyclical was not a thunderbolt out of a clear sky; it in no way contradicts the administrative and political reforms which had been begun. The liberals expressed their disappointment that it seemed remote from current political preoccupations and contained no announcement of reforms.

The reason for this was that it was on a different level: it was essentially dealing with concerns of a religious nature. In temporal affairs Pius IX could show himself to be a conciliator and reformer provided that this did not call into question his temporal sovereignty nor endanger the independence of the Papal States; but on the religious level, for him, there could be no question of any compromise whatsoever.

The advance of irreligion in society, in Italy and elsewhere, and the development of erroneous philosophical and theological doctrines—even in the Church herself—called for a struggle of a doctrinal order in order to defend a faith in danger and to elicit a spiritual awakening among the faithful and clergy. For Pius IX, moreover, any temporal reform of society was doomed to failure if it did not rest on a solid religious base.

The tone of this encyclical, in our view, is neither "sour" nor lacking in the "light" of hope. Indeed, his judgment of the situation is severe: "In this deplorable century a ferocious and implacable war has been declared on Catholicism."[38] The Pope goes on to point out the different "enemies of our religion," recalling the condemnations which his predecessors had already issued against some of them.

First of all there are the rationalists, those who dare "to teach loudly and publicly that the august mysteries of our religion are errors and human inventions" and who regard reason and faith as mutually opposed. Pius IX refutes this opposition, in what will be one of the constant doctrinal concerns of his pontificate: "Although faith is above reason, there can never be any opposition, any real contradiction, between them, because both come from God himself, the sole source of immutable and eternal truth. It follows that they should support each other, right reason demonstrating, supporting and defending the truth of faith, and faith cleansing reason from all errors, illuminating, confirming and completing it by the knowledge of divine things."

---

[37] Martina, I, 1219.

[38] Full Latin and French text in *Encycliques et documents en français et en latin*, ed. Fr. Raulx, 2 vols. (L. Guérin, 1865), I, 51-84; hereafter, *Encycliques*.

He also refers to the secret societies that "have emerged from the
shadows for the ruin of religion and the ruin of states." Pius IX recalls the
condemnations of Freemasonry, beginning with those of Clement XII,
and reaffirms them. He also follows the line of Gregory XVI in condemning the "perfidious Bible societies which take up the ancient schemes of
the heretics and unceasingly disseminate vast numbers of cheap copies of
the books of the Scriptures, translated—contrary to the Church's most
holy rules—into all the vulgar languages and often explained in a perverse
sense."

In what would be another recurrent doctrinal theme of his pontificate
the Pope also sounds a warning note against "that appalling system of
indifference towards all religion" which supposes "that men can obtain
eternal salvation in any religion whatsoever." Finally—and this is significant—two years before the publication of the *Manifesto of the Commu-
nist Party* by Karl Marx and Friedrich Engels, Pius IX was the first pope
to condemn "the execrable doctrine called communism, which is totally
contrary to the natural law itself and could not be implemented without
fundamentally overturning the totality of rights and interests, property,
and society itself."

In this encyclical, Pius IX does not content himself with giving a grim
diagnosis. He also indicates the most appropriate ways of building a dike
against "this general deluge of errors" and "this frenetic licence in thought,
discussion and writing." He summons the bishops to defend the faith by
untiring preaching and by forming a zealous and serious clergy:

> Therefore, as you are well aware, you must take the utmost care, as the
> Apostle commands, not to impose hands on anyone in haste. Consecrate
> with Holy Orders and promote to the performance of the sacred mysteries
> only those who have been carefully examined and who are virtuous and
> wise. They can consequently benefit and ornament your dioceses. These
> are men who avoid everything which is forbidden to clerics, devoting
> their time instead to reading, exhorting, and teaching....

The provision of a good formation for clerics, as well as the reform
of the religious orders, would be one of the major preoccupations of the
first years of his pontificate. As we shall see, one year after his election Pius
IX published a very important encyclical, *Ubi Primum Arcano,* addressed
to the superiors of religious orders.[39] It contained solemn warnings and
heralded a reform of which we shall speak later.

---

[39] Text in *Annales ecclésiastiques de 1846 à 1866,* ed. Joseph Chantrel (Paris: Gaume &
Cie, 1887) I, 7-10; hereafter *Annales I.*

The Universal Church

The turbulent political situation in Rome and the huge political re-forms set in train by Pius IX must not cause us to forget the Pope's other concerns for the rest of the Church. Results achieved with certain great powers hitherto hostile to the Church seemed to presage a happy tomor-row.

First of all there was the signing—against all hope—of a concordat with Russia. The vast Russian Empire included six or seven million Ro-man Catholics, mostly foreigners: Poles (since the Partition of Poland be-tween Russia, Prussia, and Austria at the end of the eighteenth century), Lithuanians, and Latvians. There were also about two million Catholics of the Byzantine Rite (also called "Uniates") in certain regions, particularly in Ukraine and Belorussia.

After the Polish revolution of 1831 (which failed, and which Greg-ory XVI had condemned), the Uniate Catholics were forcibly integrated into the Orthodox Church and their "Union" with Rome was officially abolished in 1837.[40] However, a private visit to Italy on the part of Tsar Nicholas I led to a meeting with Gregory XVI on December 13, 1845, which in turn sowed the seeds of a concordat.[41] When Pius IX became pope some months later, he approved this project; official negotiations began in November 1846.

On the Holy See's side the negotiators were Cardinal Lambruschini, assisted by Msgr. Corboli Bussi. There were twenty-seven sessions of dis-cussions, and on August 3, 1847, the concordat was officially approved by the two parties and ratified by the Pope the following August 24.

Various positive elements were satisfactory to the Church. As well as the maintaining of all the Polish dioceses, there was the re-establish-ment or creation of seven dioceses in the Empire's other Catholic regions. Each diocese was provided with a seminary, and a Catholic Ecclesiastical Academy—corresponding to a faculty of theology—was set up in St. Pe-tersburg. The pope would choose the bishops from lists drawn up by the Russian government. If we remind ourselves that all the episcopal sees but one were vacant, this concordat was a success.

Some serious problems were left unsolved, however. Notably there was the question of mixed marriages and the suppression of the Ukrainian Uniate Church. In the years to come the Russian Empire—which had never published this concordat officially—would violate its previsions on several occasions.

---

[40] Wolodymyr Kosyk, *L'Ukraine et les Ukrainiens* (Paris: Publications de l'Est européen, 1993), p.116.

[41] Aubert, p.22, and Giovanni Krajcar, "Pio IX e la Russia," *Atti del II. Convegno*, pp.347-60.

A happier story was the re-establishment of relations with Turkey.[42] On the suggestion of a Neapolitan priest residing in Constantinople, Sultan Abdulmecit I agreed to re-establish official relations with the Holy See. At the beginning of 1847 he ordered the Turkish ambassador to Vienna to go to Rome in order to assure Pius IX that the sultan "desired to live in friendship" with him and that he "would protect the Christians living in his vast estates," *i.e.*, the whole of the eastern Mediterranean littoral. The visit of a diplomat of the Sublime Porte—the first for three and a half centuries—did not go unnoticed. This unexpected rapprochement enabled Pius IX, the following October 4, to announce the re-establishment of a Latin Patriarchate in Jerusalem and the nomination of an Italian, Msgr. Valerga, to this see. This was not an arbitrary creation but the re-establishment of a patriarchate that had disappeared in 1291 following the destruction of the Latin Kingdom of Jerusalem. There was also "the Holy See's desire to guarantee Catholic rights of access to the Holy Places, which are directly threatened by the aggressive conduct of the Greek Orthodox clergy."[43] In 1852 the Sultan also signed a *firman* dividing the guardianship of the Holy Places between Greeks, Armenians, and Latins.

In connection with the ongoing re-establishment of the Latin Patriarchate we should note the publication, on January 6, 1848, of an encyclical entitled *In Suprema Petri*.[44] It was addressed to "Christians of the East," *i.e.*, both to Catholics of different rites and to non-Catholics. Speaking to Oriental Catholic bishops, of non-Latin rites, Pius IX praised their "particular Catholic liturgies" and undertook to keep them "intact." Addressing Oriental Christians who "hold aloof from communion with the See of Peter," the Pope first recalled the fundamentals of the doctrine of papal primacy and then appealed to them to return to the bosom of the Catholic Church. He assured priests and bishops who would return to the bosom of the Catholic Church that "their rank and their dignities" would be preserved.

It has been stressed by some that this call to unity "had no effect."[45] In reality this summary verdict masks a number of positive consequences that are far from being negligible. It is true that, at that time, there was no conversion to Catholicism on the part of the Eastern non-Catholic hierarchies, and that there were strident rebuttals of the encyclical. Nonetheless, the latter did "prompt an exchange of theological writings between

---

[42] Aubert, p.21; Pierre Médebielle, "Pie IX et la restauration du Patriarcat latin de Jérusalem," *Pio IX nel primo centenario*, pp.76-92; and Jean-Pierre Valognes, *Vie et mort des Chrétiens d'Orient: Des origines à nos jours* (Paris: Fayard, 1994, pp.505-6, 570 [hereafter *Chrétiens d'Orient*].

[43] Valognes, *op. cit.*, p.505.

[44] Text in *Annales I*, 19-23.

[45] Aubert, p.22.

Catholicism and Orthodoxy on the topic of the re-establishment of full communion between Christians."

Moreover there was a patent re-awakening of Oriental non-Latin Catholics. In 1849, for example, the Greek-Catholic Church held a provincial council in Jerusalem, presided over by the Patriarch of Antioch. Finally, supported by the link with the Latin Patriarchate of Jerusalem, the number of Latin Catholics in the Holy Land grew from 4,000 to 40,000 within a few decades.

After Russia and the Holy Land, a third country was of particular concern to Pius IX prior to the revolution which expelled him from Rome, namely, Switzerland.[46] In certain Swiss cantons, beginning in the last years of the pontificate of Gregory XVI, there had been an increase in actions hostile to the Catholic Church, instigated by "liberalism's extreme wing, influenced by proscribed émigrés from Germany, Italy, or Poland, vassals of Freemasonry."[47] There had been the illegal closing of convents and, most important of all, in 1844 and 1845 the Canton of Lucerne (where the Jesuits had just set up a house) fell victim to veritable punitive expeditions led by armed bands who were tolerated by the neighboring cantonal authorities. On December 11, 1845, at the instigation of the lawyer Constantin Siegwart-Müller, the seven Catholic cantons—Lucerne, Uri, Schwyz, Unterwalden, Zug, Fribourg, Valais—decided to form a "separate alliance" (*Sonderbund*) to preserve their sovereignty and maintain the principle of a confessional state.

On July 20, 1847, the Federal Diet, where the radicals were in the majority, declared the *Sonderbund* illegal and demanded its dissolution. The following September 3, it ordered the expulsion of the Jesuits from the Canton of Lucerne, accusing them of being behind the Catholic resistance. The Catholic cantons refused to yield. The twelve other cantons raised an army of 50,000 men, commanded by General Dufour. On November 4, the Diet ordered that submission be enforced.

This was civil war. The population of the Catholic cantons was only one-fifth of the size of the other cantons together. The *Sonderbund* hoped for aid from neighboring Catholic powers, Austria and France. The latter proposed a collective mediation by the five European Great Powers, but Great Britain deliberately "delayed its reply to allow the Swiss federal troops to occupy all the cantons of the *Sonderbund*."[48] When the note from the five European Great Powers was sent, on November 30, 1847, the last Catholic canton had surrendered the day before.

---

[46] Fernand Mourret, *Histoire générale de l'Église*, Vol. VIII: *L'Église contemporaine* (Paris: Bloud & Gay, 1922), 426-29; Aubert, pp.22-24; Victor Conzemius, *Philip Anton von Segesser* (Paris: Beauchesne, 1991), pp.41-56.

[47] Aubert, p.23.

[48] Guy Antonetti, *Louis Philippe* (Paris: Fayard, 1994), p.892.

In three weeks the troops of the *Sonderbund* had been crushed and the radicals were able to impose their policy, namely, expulsion of all the religious and the installation of liberal governments in the Catholic cantons. Some months later a new constitution was adopted, accentuating the federal character of the state and reducing the power of the cantons. In August 1848, the five cantons making up the diocese of Geneva and Lausanne saw the imposition of a convention making episcopal nominations entirely subject to the state; among other things, it also provided for an oath of allegiance to the constitution and the laws of the cantons. Msgr. Marilley, Bishop of Geneva and Lausanne, protested in a letter dated September 14. On the 30th of the same month, through his Secretary of State, Pius IX also protested. The government responded by arresting Msgr. Marilley on October 25, and by putting him under house-arrest. It then exiled him to France. Not until 1856 was he able to return to Fribourg.

CHAPTER 7

FROM REFORM TO REVOLUTION

While there was an alternation of successes and failures in the life of the Catholic Church abroad, the situation in Rome continued to be equally delicate.

Eighteen forty-seven was the year when Pius IX accomplished the most important administrative and political reforms in his States. The previous November a manifesto had announced new practical measures, in particular the enlargement of the commission in charge of reforming the civil and criminal codes. Liberals and moderates, however, were expecting reforms on a grand scale: freedom of the press, the establishment of a real government including laymen, and the creation of a representative assembly.

The expectation and even impatience felt by one section of public opinion, in Rome and abroad, is well illustrated by a letter from the French Minister for Foreign Affairs, Guizot, to his ambassador in Rome, Rossi. This report is all the more interesting since it acknowledges that the pope's options were strictly limited; also, it emerges that the French minister was well informed by his representative in Rome. The latter, in fact, regularly had long audiences with the Sovereign Pontiff.

As regards the promises of reform made by Pius IX, Guizot observes:

> We have no doubt that he is firmly resolved to keep them. We can sincerely sympathize with him as to all the difficulties which beset him: there is the ill will and opposition of those who will always think he is doing too much and going too fast (although he is proceeding with reserve and maturity); there is the inexperience of those men who are most inclined to help him; and from a different angle there is the deplorable composition of the administrative personnel. Still, our view is that it is time, finally, for action to match promises, and that the moment has come to implement some reforms.[1]

One of the great reforms anticipated was the introduction of press freedom. The existing censorship was threefold: religious, material, and political. Its purpose was to make sure that newspapers and books, whatever matter they were dealing with, did not inflict harm on "right belief, good morals, and public order." It operated prior to publication, of

---

[1] Letter from Guizot to Rossi, January 23, 1847, A.M.A.E., C.P., Rome 986, f.14.

course, and could lead to the work or newspaper being banned. It had the effect of making all everyday journalism practically impossible. The only newspaper in existence, the *Diario di Roma,* carried a wealth of official news and scientific articles, but did not publish commentaries on current affairs.[2] Nonetheless, the pontifical state was not a totalitarian state in which every printing-shop was under surveillance and where every frontier was hermetically sealed. Books printed in Rome without authorization, or elsewhere in Italy, could be obtained clandestinely.

So at the beginning of 1847 Pius IX, without completely abrogating this censorship, judged it advantageous to grant a wider freedom to the press and publishers.

Just before the decree was to be made public, the Pope wrote a letter to Cardinal Amat, Legate in Bologna. In it he justified the step by explaining that, while this kind of press freedom was certainly "quite dangerous," it was limited in scope and would help to diminish the number of dangerous writings.[3] Events would soon disappoint these somewhat naïve hopes on the Pope's part.

The edict, dated March 15, 1847, and drawn up by Msgr. Corboli Bussi following the Pope's directives, granted a greater freedom for the printing of all writings relating to science, literature, the arts, history, and public administration. On the other hand, writings on religion and government remained strictly controlled. In particular, all writings that "directly or indirectly" stirred up hatred against the government were liable to be banned.

Furthermore, three months previously, as an initiative of the director-general of the police, Msgr. Marini, a sort of official journal had been launched, entitled *Il Contemporaneo,* with the aim of informing public opinion of the government's views and taking issue with the many clandestine publications which criticized the policies it followed.[4]

The French ambassador wrote to his Minister as follows, commenting on the decree on press freedom: "It is a small thing in itself. But here it means a great deal. I think the censors will be quite indulgent and there will be a great increase in publications. It has to be said that the liberals find it insufficient. They have even described it as a return to the system of Gregory XVI."[5]

In fact, far from calming people down, press freedom of this kind worked in favor of the expression of the most contrary and most passion-

2   Gizzi, *Il Cardinale Gizzi,* p.186.
3   Letter to Cardinal Amat of March 13, 1847, in G. Maioli, *Pio IX da Vescovo a Pontefice, Lettere al card. Luigi Amat* (Modena: 1949), p.111; cited by Martina, I, 124-25.
4   When he was still Bishop of Imola, Pius IX had already suggested the launching of a journal of this kind in his *Pensieri* addressed to the Secretary of State, §§29, 30, 51.
5   A.M.A.E., C.P., Rome 986, ff.39v-40.

ately-held opinions. Some months after the edict was published, Cardinal Gizzi had to order the expulsion from Rome of thirteen suspects and the seizure of clandestine newspapers sold "under the counter" in the city's cafés. Some authorized newspapers were also seized for having published articles or manifestos hostile to the policies conducted by the pontifical government.

Agitation was organized by a dozen "circles," which could be compared to the "clubs" existing in Paris during the 1789 Revolution.

The three most important Roman circles were the "circle of business," which was fairly moderate; the "Roman circle," which included a number of great names of the nobility like Michelangelo Gaetani and recruited a number of partisans with "national" ideas, *i.e.*, those in favor of a war "of independence" to liberate Italy from all Austrian presence; and, finally, the most extreme, so-called "popular circle" directed by Angelo Brunetti (nicknamed "Ciceruacchio"), who would prove to be a skilful agitator. This circle was "national" and revolutionary: it favored Italian unity and was hostile to the pope's temporal power.

The "circles" operated through meetings or demonstrations, and by distributing printed material, with or without authorization. The governor of Rome, Msgr. Grassellini, tolerated this ever-growing agitation. At this time Pius IX was at a crossroads. He had committed himself to certain reforms, but had no intention of calling into question either his temporal power or the underlying principles of Christian politics. Certain people in his entourage feared that the concessions made were already excessive. Cardinal Gizzi, in particular, urged more energetic measures against the public demonstrations which, while applauding Pius IX, reviled the Secretariat of State and constituted a constant threat. He wished the majority of those amnestied to be banished far from Rome.[6]

Gizzi, however, was in poor health. In February he had to stay in bed for several weeks because of attacks of gout. On April 4 he offered his resignation to Pius IX, who refused to accept it.

At the same time certain currents of public opinion began raising the stakes and tried to obtain still more reforms from the Pope. Pius IX cannot be reproached with having acted in too much of a hurry. All the reforms already undertaken and those which would be carried out in the following months had been preceded by lengthy preparation.

To a large extent the Pope took account of divergent views, and up to 1848 the decrees or instructions promulgated put in place institutions with clearly limited scope. Each time, however, the liberals and revolutionaries regarded them as the first steps towards radical upheavals—which Pius IX certainly did not wish. When there was delay in the announcement of the

---

[6] Gizzi, *Il Cardinale Gizzi*, p.201.

promised reforms, well-organized demonstrations showed the Pope the impatience and discontent of his "subjects."

So, for instance, when, on March 25, 1847, Pius IX went to the church of Santa Maria sopra Minerva to celebrate the Feast of the Annunciation, he was received by a crowd manipulated by the "popular circle," shouting "*Viva Pio Nono solo*" (Long live Pius IX alone), "Down with Gizzi!" and "Courage, Holy Father, the people are with you."

In the space of a few months several important institutions were put in place. On June 12, a *motu proprio* created a real Council of Ministers in which the responsibilities of each one were better defined, but the Secretary of State remained the pivot of government: he was in charge of the Ministry of the Interior and the Ministry of Foreign Affairs. The other ministers (of Industry and Commerce, of Public Works, of Justice, of War, of Finance) were all cardinals or prelates.

Those who were calling for the entry of laymen into government were not satisfied. Ten days later Gizzi had to publish a circular letter in which, listing the reforms that had already been granted and confirming that other improvements in public administration were to be implemented, he ordered the Romans to cease their demonstrations. We know that at this time he was already preparing to invoke Austrian military intervention in case of trouble. The situation became very worrying. At the end of June Ambassador Rossi, a good observer, wrote to his minister: "A lot of satires are going the rounds. Speech is getting more and more free and critical in the cafés and at gatherings, and passions are becoming inflamed."[7]

Some days later, giving an account of an interview with Pius IX, he explained: "The Holy Father acknowledged that the situation had become serious and that it was a matter of urgency to calm public opinion by some prompt and satisfactory measures; he told me that his intentions were always the same, and that the public did not sufficiently take account of the obstacles he had to overcome."[8]

On July 5, by edict, a Civic Guard was created, composed of citizens aged twenty-one to sixty, in imitation of the National Guard that had existed in France since the beginning of the Revolution in 1789. This Civic Guard was commanded by a layman, Prince Rospigliosi.

Cardinal Gizzi, hostile to this Civic Guard, which seemed to him to be a source of problems, once more offered his resignation to the Pope. This time Pius IX accepted it and replaced him at the Secretariat of State by Cardinal Gabriele Ferretti, who was his cousin and Legate at Pesaro. Rossi describes Ferretti as "popular, active, effervescent, prompt to act once he has understood what is to be done."[9] The new Secretary of State

---

[7]   Dispatch of June 28, 1847, A.M.A.E., C.P., Rome 987, f.78.
[8]   *Ibid.*
[9]   *Ibid.*, f.105v.

carried out the reforms that had been set in train, not without some clum-
siness due to excessive haste. He also had to face the first serious external
crisis of the pontificate.

Threats from Austria

At the beginning of July 1847, the rumor of a plot was going around
Rome. This plot was no doubt inspired by those whom the liberals and
revolutionaries called the "Gregorianists," *i.e.*, those who looked back
with nostalgia to the pontificate of Gregory XVI and were hostile to the
reforms being implemented. The governor of Rome and director of the
police, Msgr. Grassellini, and several pontifical officials were implicated in
this plot, which was directed against the liberals. The conspirators would
have been acting in league with Austria, which was inclined to intervene
militarily in the Papal States to put an end to the worrying agitation.
Certain foreign newspapers, in particular *The Times,* gave credence to the
idea of a plot and accused Austria. In fact, the only agitator found to be
in the pay of Austria was Virginio Alpi, and no large-scale operation had
been in preparation.[10]

After the revolution of 1848, Pius IX, drawing up a clear-sighted summary of these troubled years in his famous allocution of April 20, 1849,
denied that there had been any real conspiracy. At the time, however, the
rumor was used by the liberals and revolutionaries to cry treason. Ferretti,
the Secretary of State, believed he was doing the right thing in removing
the unjustly-accused governor of Rome, Msgr. Grassellini, and replacing
him by Msgr. Morandi.

This incident added to the turmoil in Rome and the surrounding
countryside and gave impetus to the press, which—whether authorized or
not—published more and more articles hostile to Austria. What is more,
the supposed "plot" was to go into operation on July 17. That same day
860 Austrian soldiers crossed the Po and established themselves in Ferrara.

Ever since the Treaty of Vienna Austria had the right, for its own security, to maintain troops in the Ferrara citadel and in two municipal barracks. The city, however, was entirely under the sovereignty of the Papal
States; the Pope was represented there by a legate, Cardinal Luigi Ciacchi.
The introduction of additional troops into the city, and not only in the
citadel and barracks, constituted a clear external interference and was contrary to the articles of the Treaty of Vienna.

Pius IX had been faced with a *fait accompli*. The Austrians were acting
on their own initiative and had not notified the Legate of Ferrara until the

---

[10]   Martina, I, 143-145.

evening before they were to enter the Papal States. Their arrival provoked certain incidents.

The "national" party immediately stirred people up against this "invasion," and there was growing turmoil in Rome and in the other Italian states. There were many demonstrations against the Austrian presence, and there were calls for the Civic Guard to avenge the insult. Historians today agree that, in these circumstances, Pius IX succeeded in calming things down and preventing the situation getting worse. He was supported in this by a number of liberals, particularly Massimo D'Azeglio, who published a pamphlet entitled *Protesta per i casi di Ferrara* appealing for conciliation and a unity centered on the figure of Pius IX.[11]

The Pope showed himself both firm and prudent. First of all, the Legate of Ferrara and then the Secretary of State protested against the deployment of Austrian troops in Ferrara.

On August 16, Pius IX summoned a congregation of cardinals to decide what attitude to take towards Austria. The idea of recalling the Vienna nuncio was rejected because a gesture of this kind could be interpreted as a severing of diplomatic relations, which in turn could seem to give encouragement to those who were bent on coming to blows with the Austrians. The preferred course of action was a twofold diplomatic initiative directed at both Vienna and the other Italian states.

It was decided that a "customs league" would be proposed to the other Italian states, with the aim of improving commercial relations between them and strengthening their mutual links. The idea was not new; it had already been implemented in 1834 in the German states in the form of the *Zollverein*. It was also in harmony with Italian foreign policy as desired by Pius IX: not a political unity, which he completely rejected, wishing to preserve the complete sovereignty of the Papal States, but the establishment of good neighborly relations which would be of economic profit to each region. This had been the spirit behind the signing, one month before this meeting, of a treaty of trade and navigation between Piedmont-Sardinia and the Papal States.

The project of a "customs league" did not spring to life spontaneously in August 1847, but the events in Ferrara furnished the opportunity to implement it. Msgr. Corboli Bussi, who had just been appointed secretary of the Congregation of Extraordinary Ecclesiastical Affairs, was charged with presenting the project to the different Italian governments. In August he went to Florence and Turin.

At the same time diplomatic dispatches were exchanged between Rome and Vienna with the aim of coming to a peaceful solution of the Ferrara question.

---

[11]   The text of this pamphlet was "revised and approved by Pius IX himself," writes Martina, I, 48.

As for the extremist elements, they dreamed of conducting a war of "liberation" against Austria.

On November 8, Mazzini, from his exile in London, published an open letter *A Pio IX, Pontefice Massimo,* in which he urged the Pope to put himself at the head of the movement for Italian unity.

Garibaldi also offered his services to the Pope to throw out the Austrians. The King of Piedmont-Sardinia, Charles Albert, also felt that, at last, he had the pretext to make war on the hereditary enemy. Pius IX, while defending the rights and the honor of the Papal States, had no desire whatsoever for a war. On September 12, he wrote to Ferdinand, Emperor of Austria, officially requesting him to contain his troops within the Ferrara citadel. The Pope did not align himself with the extremist positions of the "national" movement, but called for a strict observance of the Treaty of Vienna.

At first Ferdinand refused, citing the growing upheavals and the anti-Austrian conspiracies in Italy. Next, meetings were arranged in Rome and Milan between Austrian representatives and the Secretary of State or his envoys. Finally, on December 16, Austria yielded and ordered its troops to return to the Ferrara citadel and the appointed barracks.

Pius IX's patience had won out, but the myth of the "liberal" pope had gained strength: for the liberals and revolutionaries, he was not only a reformer but the champion in the struggle against Austria.

This interpretation of the Ferrara incident was highly exaggerated. Some months later, when war broke out between the Kingdom of Piedmont-Sardinia and Austria, we shall see Pius IX refuse to involve the Papal States in the conflict and join in the "anti-Austrian crusade."

To understand Pius IX's real position on the notions of Italian independence—which he did not confuse with the cause of Italian unity, something he rejected—we must remember what he declared to the Austrian ambassador some months before the Ferrara incident: "As an Italian, I cannot blame them; as a sovereign, I desire good relations with my neighbor Austria; as pope, I beg God for peace between nations. But, above all, I must do my duty."[12]

War Approaches

The Ferrara affair did nothing to slow down the reforms in train. On October 2, by a *motu proprio,* a Municipal Council was set up in Rome. This "deliberative council" (Pius IX's expression) included one senator, eight counselors, and a hundred members. The first members would be nominated by the Pope and the others would be co-opted; they would

---

[12] Pius IX to the Austrian ambassador to Rome, April 12, 1847, cited by Martina, I, 152.

then elect the senator-president. The first senator-president was Prince Corsini.

It was not a body elected by universal suffrage (something that the more radical spirits immediately criticized), but nonetheless this Municipal Council or Senate allowed Rome, after many centuries, to rediscover a way of representing its population which had already existed in antiquity. The event was celebrated with joyous demonstrations.

Once again Pius IX showed himself to be the boldest of Italian sovereigns. After his edict on the press at the beginning of the year, the Grand Duchy of Tuscany and the Kingdom of Piedmont-Sardinia too had allowed a certain degree of press freedom; the two kingdoms were again obliged to follow the concession that the Pope had granted in his estates.

Ten days later, on October 14, by another *motu proprio,* a Council of State was instituted. Presided over by a cardinal legate—the first was Cardinal Antonelli—it was composed of twenty-four counselors nominated by the Pope from a list of candidates. (Each province had been invited to send in three names.) The project had been in preparation for several months and had been constantly demanded by various quarters.

The most radical elements welcomed even the *motu proprio* and endeavored to use it, quite improperly, for their own propaganda. It had been stipulated that this Council of State was a representative and consultative assembly. Some people wanted to see this as only the first step towards an elected and legislative assembly. Such an idea went far beyond both what the Pope had said and what was in his mind.

On November 15, before holding their first session, the members of the Council of State were received by the Pope. He addressed them in memorable terms, as the French ambassador to Rome reported: "The Holy Father seemed very animated in his discourse…insisting very strongly on the two essential points, which were the purely consultative role of the new assembly and his government's firm resolve to resist the agitators. He is even said to have uttered the word *ingratitude,* which is not, however, found in the printed text."[13] The word is appropriate if we remember the part to be played in coming months by certain men to whom Pius IX had entrusted important responsibilities in the new institutions.

The first day of 1848 began under evil omens. Ciceruacchio presented himself at the Quirinal at the head of a delegation of Roman interest groups to give the Pope a list of twenty-four demands. They included: that the Papal States should be given a liberal constitution; that lay ministers should be brought into the government; that the press should have complete freedom; and that the Jesuits should be expelled.

They were received by the Secretary of State who, having read their demands, flew into a rage and cried: "You scoundrels! You'll never be sat-

---

[13] Dispatch of November 18, 1847, A.M.A.E., C.P., Rome 987, ff.205-9.

isfied, will you? You are insatiable!"[14] The incident immediately precipitated a noisy demonstration, calmed by Pius IX when he received Senator Corsini. However, external events would eventually draw Pius IX into a maelstrom from which he could extract himself only by fleeing to Gaeta.

In Milan, on January 3, incidents involving "patriots" and Austrian troops caused several deaths and a good many wounded. This same month, in the Kingdom of Naples, an insurrection spread from Sicily, calling for a "constitution" and "freedom." Soon all the Italian states, including Rome, experienced demonstrations which were organized to demand war against Austria and the setting-up of constitutional governments. This twofold demand united demonstrators who in other ways did not share the same political ideas. Ambassador Rossi, reporting to his minister, properly draws a distinction between "radicals" and "nationals"; further distinctions could also be drawn.

In the Papal States the "radicals" (Ciceruacchio, Sterbini, Galletti, Prince Canino) had adopted the theories of the exiled Mazzini and showed themselves partisans of Italian unification and the inauguration of a republic—which implied the overthrow, by violence if necessary, of papal power. The "nationals" (D'Azeglio, Mamiani, Minghetti) were more moderate and not hostile to the papacy; they favored the introduction of a constitutional regime, but also looked forward to the departure of the Austrians and dreamed of some kind of Italian unity, at least in the form of a confederation. Some of the latter had been received by the Pope in preceding months; faced with the events of the beginning of 1848, Pius IX would bring some of them into his government.

In January army minister Cardinal Massimo died, giving Pius IX the opportunity of introducing a layman into the government for the first time, in the person of General Pompeo Gabrielli. On January 21, Cardinal Ferretti, who was sick and in a state of depression and had been at cross-purposes with Pius IX, handed in his resignation. On February 7, the Pope replaced him at the Secretariat of State by Cardinal Bofondi, who until then had functioned as Legate of Ravenna. In eighteen months there had been three Secretaries of State, which did not help the Pope conduct his policies.

The day after this nomination, a new demonstration was organized beneath the Quirinal balcony. It was led by Senator Corsini and Ciceruacchio, and was accompanied by cries of "Down with the ecclesiastical ministries!" and "Long live Italy!"

On February 10, in a proclamation "To the Romans," Pius IX announced that he was going to increase the number of laymen in ministries; he said that he was ready to grant whatever would contribute to

---

[14] Polverari, I, 185.

the public good, but he also warned the agitators, declaring that he was determined to "resist all violent disorder with the force of the existing institutions" and also "those demands which are in conformity with neither (my) duties nor your happiness." He denounced equally those who were stirring up "the peoples of Italy with the appalling prospect of a foreign war, encouraged and prepared by internal conspiracies or the malevolent inertia of governors." If such a war were to take place, however, the Pope would know that he could count on all the faithful: "If We, the supreme head and pontiff of the most holy Catholic religion, were to be unjustly attacked, would We not have countless sons to defend the Father's house and support the center of Catholic unity? It is a great gift from heaven, among so many other marks of predilection for Italy, that scarcely three millions of Our subjects have two hundred million brothers in every nation and speaking every language." The proclamation concluded with the following invocation: "Bless Italy, O Great God, and ever preserve in her this most precious of all gifts, the faith!"[15]

As far as this papal intervention was concerned, the most fanatical Romans and the other Italian "patriots" took no more from it that the final blessing of Italy. They interpreted it as bolstering the cause of Italian unity and encouraging a holy crusade against Austria. This was a complete travesty of what the Pope actually said. He had been speaking as a spiritual leader, not as a temporal sovereign. Pius IX blessed Italy on several subsequent occasions—even after the King of Italy had taken his states away. In doing this he was blessing, not the institutions or a regime, but a country and its inhabitants.

The "patriots" took no account of the calls for calm and the warnings contained in this proclamation. Nor did they pay any attention to the term "internal conspiracies," which revealed Pius IX's perspicacity. The Pope was well aware that, under the pretext of Italian independence and unity, some men (the heirs of the Carbonari, Freemasonry) were following another agenda, namely, to strip him of his temporal sovereignty and laicize Italian institutions and society. After the revolution Pius IX several times denounced those who were plotting to "corrupt the heart" of Italy.

On February 12, as he had promised two days earlier, he established a new government containing four laymen: Pasolini, Sturbinetti, Gaetani, and Gabrielli.

In the eyes of the most fanatical, however, external events had already rendered this new concession obsolete. Quite apart from the revolution which overturned the monarchy of Louis-Philippe in France (February 24) and the government of Metternich in Austria (March 13), it should be borne in mind that there was a "constitutional revolution" which caught fire in the different Italian states one by one: on February 10, Ferdinand

---

[15] Complete text of the manifesto in Polverari, I, 186-87.

II granted a constitution to the Kingdom of Naples; on February 15, Leopold II did likewise in the Grand Duchy of Tuscany; and on March 4, Charles Albert did the same in the Kingdom of Piedmont-Sardinia.

Although in fact it had been in preparation for one month by a commission of cardinals which included Cardinal Antonelli and in which Msgr. Corboli Bussi played a significant role, the "Fundamental Statute" granted by Pius IX on March 14 was seen as being but the tardy imitation of the constitutions already granted in the neighboring realms. The "Fundamental Statute for the Temporal Government of the States of the Church" transferred the Papal States from an absolute regime in which executive power did not depend on any other power, to a constitutional regime. Two chambers were created: a Supreme Council composed of ecclesiastics and laymen, and an elected Chamber of Deputies which would be responsible for voting for laws, but whose deliberations would be subject to the pope's approval. These new powers, as will be seen, were significantly restricted. Pius IX, both a spiritual head and a temporal sovereign, could not allow a laicist assembly to decide, on its own, concerning legislation to be applied in his States.

This "Fundamental Statute" was announced four days after one of its architects, Cardinal Antonelli, had become Secretary of State, replacing Cardinal Bofondi, a distinguished canon lawyer but ill-suited to public affairs. Antonelli had also established a new, predominantly lay government, containing six laymen for three ecclesiastics.

Cardinal Antonelli stayed at his post for almost thirty years, apart from a brief interruption, exercising a political artistry that earned him the name "the Italian Richelieu."[16]

Giacomo Martina has given a very just definition of his personality and the complement (and sometimes the antithesis) it provided to that of Pius IX: "A deacon, not a priest, a believer, faithful to his duties without ever being devout or pious (the accusations touching his private life are without foundation), cold, reserved, capable of duplicity, attached to his family, eager to accumulate a substantial patrimony, he was the perfect antithesis of Pius IX, who was sometimes too effusive, sincere, incapable of dissimulation, very pious, and profoundly devout. The Cardinal's skill in economics and politics—in short, the complementarity of these two men, explains how this close collaboration lasted for twenty-eight years."[17]

Initially Cardinal Antonelli only stayed a fortnight at the Secretariat of State and in the presidency of the Council of Ministers; then he prudently withdrew into the immediate background (though remaining a

---

[16] Cf. Carlo Falconi, *Il Cardinale Antonelli* (Milan: Arnoldo Mondadori Editore, 1993); hereafter, *Antonelli*.

[17] G. Martina, "Pie IX," *Dictionnaire historique de la papauté,* under the direction of Philippe Levillain (Paris: Fayard, 1994), p.1345.

man of great influence) and waited for the hour of his official return to strike.

Demands for war against the "barbarians" increased, and in March 1848, Venice and Milan, the two principal cities of Northern Italy belonging to Austria, experienced insurrections against the occupying power. First the King of Piedmont-Sardinia dithered, but finally, on March 24, he declared war on Austria. Immediately, throughout all the Italian states, volunteers began to be organized and sent on to reinforce the Sardinian troops.

In Rome, on the eve of the official declaration of war, a huge meeting organized by the most enthusiastic "patriots" had been held at the Coliseum, in favor of war against Austria. Two religious had spoken at the meeting, Fr. Gavazzi and Fr. Dumaine, a Frenchman; this was a sign that some of the clergy were linked to the most extreme wings.

The same day a first contingent of volunteers had left Rome. Pius IX had authorized these enrollments—which would have gone ahead even without his authorization—but when the first volunteers came to ask the Pope to bless their standards, he had refused, expressly ordering them only to "protect the frontier" and not to cross it.[18] Then, with Cardinal Antonelli, he tried to organize the masses of volunteers coming from all the Papal States, often members of the Civic Guard. Two army groups were made: one of about 7,000 men drawn from the regular troops, under the command of General Durando; and the other, of more than 10,000 volunteers, commanded by General Ferrari. While the former were fairly well equipped, both groups were inexperienced in the arts of war. Their only mission was to defend the frontiers; in no case were they to attack Austria or rush in to help the Lombards and Venetians.

Following this logic of defense, Pius IX, once he had consulted the cardinals of the Congregation of Extraordinary Affairs, suggested that the different Italian states should constitute a "Defense League." All accepted, apart from Piedmont-Sardinia, which would have preferred a common military engagement against Austria and the establishment of a council of war under its presidency—which Pius IX absolutely rejected.

Some of his entourage, notably Msgr. Corboli Bussi, were inclined towards a war with Austria. We should also mention the arguments of Fr. Rosmini, the philosopher and theologian to whom, some months later, the Pope gave audience on a number of occasions. Rosmini too was a partisan of the "war of independence." The Pope should embark upon war not only because it would be a "just" war, but also because it would be of "great national benefit."[19]

---

[18] Martina, I, 230.
[19] Cited in Polverari, I, 193.

In the wake of a declaration issued on March 30, it seemed that the party in favor of war had won the Pope over. In the preceding days the Piedmontese had gained victories against the Austrians in Lombardy and Venetia, and the Pope, in a proclamation largely inspired by Msgr. Corboli Bussi, declared that "the events that have succeeded one another so rapidly these last two months are not a human work"; he believed that "one should adore the hidden designs of Providence at work in them."

Even if the enemy was not named, the anti-Austrian tone of this proclamation seemed to be an invocation of blessing upon the "war of independence." Hardly had he arrived in Bologna, on April 5, General Durando published an "order of the day to the corps of operations," in fact drawn up by D'Azeglio, which called in the Pope's name for "the extermination of the enemies of God and of Italy" and for war against Austria up to the very borders of Piedmont.

Pius IX was betrayed, but initially his reaction was weak. Dated April 10, the *Gazzetta di Roma*, the government's official organ, published a government communiqué: "An order of the day to soldiers in Bologna, dated April 5, expresses ideas and sentiments as if they had been dictated by the mouth of His Holiness: whenever the Pope wishes to make his sentiments known, he speaks himself and never by the mouth of any subordinate." At the same time General Durando was called to account for his conduct. The latter, persisting in his disobedience to the Pope's orders, sent his troops across the Po on April 21. De facto the papal troops found themselves engaged in war.

The situation was a dramatic one. Austria had expelled the Redemptorists from Vienna in retaliation. There were fears that the war would stir up hostility against the Holy See among all the German-speaking peoples, or even that a schism would result. The majority of the Pope's ministers were pressing him to commit himself officially with regard to the war, since the cardinals were divided. Although an extraordinary commission of cardinals, convoked by the Pope on April 17, had rejected the idea of war, Cardinal Antonelli, Secretary of State and president of the Council of Ministers, adopted a hesitant or even ambivalent attitude.[20]

On April 25 Pius IX admitted his predicament to a diplomat: "My authority is getting weaker every day. I have no more than a nominal power in temporal affairs. And these men, whose fanatical patriotism knows no restraint, want me to declare war, when I am the leader of a religion that knows only peace and concord! So be it: I shall protest; and Europe will learn of the violence to which I have been subjected. If people keep

---

[20] Martina, I, 240-241. Polverari gives an analysis more favorable to Antonelli (I, 198-199).

demanding of me things that are repugnant to my conscience, I shall retire to a monastery to weep over unhappy Rome."[21]

The signaled protest was issued on April 29 in an allocution to the Consistory which dispersed all equivocation once and for all. After listing all the temporal reforms he had granted since the beginning of his pontificate, Pius IX protested against the malicious way in which his acts and words had been interpreted, and declared that it was "impossible for him to desire war." To show that it was his spiritual duty that inspired his conduct he added: "Faithful to the obligations of Our supreme apostolate, We embrace all countries, all peoples, all nations, in an equal sentiment of paternal love."

This allocution provoked consternation among the interventionists. The diplomatic representatives of Piedmont, Tuscany, Naples, Milan, and Venice demanded an audience with the Pope to make their protests. In Rome, in the most radical circles, people were crying "treason." For the first time it was not only the Pope's collaborators and the cardinals who were attacked, but Pius IX himself.

Cardinal Antonelli resigned from his twofold office as Secretary of State and president of the Council of Ministers, and the entire government followed him. Antonelli's resignation should not be seen as a disapproval of the allocution of April 29, contrary to what certain historians have said, but as a clear change of policy.[22] For him, in agreement with Pius IX, it was a case of disengaging himself from internal political issues and breaking with the liberals; this was in order to safeguard his liberty and authority in external affairs and to hold himself in reserve for the future. Unlike previous Secretaries of State who had resigned, he was not returned to specifically religious duties; instead the Pope made him responsible for the Congregation for Extraordinary External Affairs.

As for Pius IX, he had to continue to negotiate with the existing political forces in Rome and take account of the war situation that had been imposed on him. He summoned Count Terenzio Mamiani to form a government. Mamiani had been one of those amnestied in 1846, in spite of his refusal to take the required oath of fidelity, but he was regarded as a moderate. Even if, officially, the Secretary of State always presided over the government, now, for the first time, the government was in fact headed by a layman. What is more, the Secretary of State's authority had been eroded by successive changes of incumbent: Cardinal Orioli, Antonelli's successor, stayed at his post for only a month. In June he was succeeded by Cardinal Soglia.[23]

---

[21] Words reported by Auguste de Liedekerke, plenipotentiary minister of the Low Countries to Rome, cited in Aubert, p.31.

[22] Convincing analyses in Falconi, *Antonelli*, pp.172-73 and in Polverari, I, 198-99.

[23] Carlo Grillantini, "Il Cardinale Giovanni Soglia Ceroni," *Pio IX*, No. 1 (1974), pp.144-56.

In parallel to this the Pope made praiseworthy efforts to bring peace back to Italy. On May 3, he wrote to the Emperor of Austria, Ferdinand I, urging him to stop the war and withdraw his troops from Venetia and Lombardy. At the same time he wrote a letter to King Charles Albert to get him involved in negotiations with Austria. Then, on May 27, he sent a mediator, Msgr. Morichini, to Austria.[24] The Austrians, however, were already having success in the reconquest of Venetia and Lombardy, and were not disposed to stop the fighting, which would have deprived them of victory. Soon Piedmont-Sardinia was compelled to sign an armistice.

Austria profited from this to occupy the north of the Papal States. In August, through the intermediary of his Secretary of State, Soglia, Pius IX issued a firm protest and called for the departure of the Austrian troops.[25]

This setback with regard to Austria did nothing to alter the political facts in the Papal States. The crusade against the "barbarians" could no longer appear in the order of the day, but the strivings towards a unitary state had not faded away. Moderate elements like Msgr. Corboli Bussi and Rosmini still dreamed of an "Italian Confederation" in which each of the States would renounce part of its sovereignty in favor of a federal Diet. The most radical elements kept stirring up passions against Pius IX, who, ever since his April allocution, had been judged a traitor to the Italian cause. Not having defeated Austria, these radicals were hoping to overthrow the pontifical power. In September a rumor spread that an insurrection was imminent, with the aim of proclaiming a republic.

In a report to his government the Wurtemberg consul-general in Rome told how this threat had been temporarily avoided: Pius IX "intended to take the initative against the fanatics, in particular Sterbini, Prince Canino, Count Mariani, Dr. Pantaleoni, and others....The minister of police, Galletti, was the first to show himself reluctant to take measures against the liberals, and finally the entire ministry resigned."[26]

It was under these circumstances that Pellegrino Rossi was summoned to set up a new government. The former French ambassador to Rome under Louis-Philippe had not left the Eternal City after the revolution of February 1848 deprived him of his post. While ambassador he had very frequently been received by Pius IX and had had long conversations

---

[24] Msgr. Morichini, who had succeeded him, with considerable success, as head of the *Ospizio Tata Giovanni* many years earlier, enjoyed the Pope's full confidence. Pius IX summoned him after the loss of Msgr. Corboli Bussi, who, in the wake of the allocution of April 29, no longer wished to carry out any official mission.

[25] Letter of Soglia, dated August 8, 1848, cited in Grillantini, *op. cit.*, p.152.

[26] Report of Karl von Kolb, September 18, 1848, cited by F. Leoni, "L'uccisione di Pellegrino Rossi nella relazione dei diplomatici stranieri a Roma," *Pio IX nel primo centenario*, p.264. The fact that Galletti was a Freemason, and his subsequent conduct, may suggest that he was linked to the conspirators.

with him which went beyond the usual level of diplomatic relations. In summoning him at this difficult hour, the Pope was hoping to break with the politics of waiting and negotiating which he had pursued since Cardinal Antonelli's departure. The cessation of hostilities with Austria made it possible to return to coherent internal policies. In the new government established on September 16 under the nominal presidency of Cardinal Secretary of State Soglia, Rossi occupied the key posts of Minister of the Interior and of Finance; soon he would become chief of police as well. He was a man of experience with very clearly defined objectives: to defend "the rights of the sovereign and of the nation" within the limits of the Fundamental Statute, and to "assure…public order" and advance the "prosperity" of all.[27]

Some of his noteworthy first initiatives were the imposition of a new tax on the goods of the clergy to remedy the grave financial crisis being experienced in the Papal States, and the construction of telegraphic lines between Rome, Bologna, and Ferrara in order to facilitate communications between the capital and the Legations and speed up the measures necessary to maintain public order. In his negotiations with the courts of Turin, Naples, and Florence, Rossi was also concerned to lay the foundations for an Italian Confederation. This project differed from that of Corboli Bussi and Rosmini in that each of the States would keep its authority intact: it would simply be a case of harmonizing its administration and economy with those of its confederate allies.

Revolution

This work was brutally interrupted by Rossi's assassination on November 15. It was the day of the opening session of the Chamber of Deputies. The minister was to put forward in detail his program of government. When he got down from his carriage he was greeted with jeers and whistles. In the resulting *melée*, which the forces of order did nothing to control, he was stabbed in the body and the aorta. Five minutes later he was dead. What gave great scandal to the diplomats present—they immediately left the hall—the president of the Chamber, Sturbinetti, went ahead and opened the session as if nothing had happened.

It turns out that the assassination of the man in whom Pius IX had placed all his hopes was not something out of the blue. There had clearly been a plot. For a long time liberal historians had the effrontery to suggest that "Rossi's assassination was very probably the work of the clerical party."[28]

---

[27] *Gazzetta di Roma,* September 22, 1848, cited in Martina, I, 281.
[28] Diego Soria, *Histoire générale de l'Italie de 1815 à 1850* (Nîmes: 1860), I, 503.

In fact, many years later, Sante Costantini and Luigi Grandoni were sentenced to death as the main authors of the assassination; Ruggero Colonello and Bernardino Facciotti, as accomplices, were condemned to the galleys for life; and twenty-five year prison sentences were handed down to Francesco Costantini, Filippo Facciotti, and Innocenzo Zappacori. All these men were more or less associated with Sterbini's "Popular Circle"; most important of all, they were all Freemasons.

It was said that Pellegrino Rossi had once belonged to the Freemasons. Was he assassinated by his "brothers" for having betrayed the cause? Were the orders given by Sterbini, president of the Popular Circle and the author of an article very hostile to Rossi a few days before the crime? This is what the Belgian *chargé d'affaires* in Rome suggested, the day after the assassination, in a report to his government: "It is being said that, at a dinner recently organized in Florence, attended by the Tuscan ministers Montanelli and Guerrazzi and the Roman deputies Sterbini and Canino, it had been decided to get rid of Count Rossi."[29]

As in every revolution, abomination knew no bounds. A French diplomat serving in Rome some years later, kept an account of what took place on the evening of November 15:

> The National Guard, the very police who had allowed the crime to be committed, permitted its apotheosis to be organized publicly. Meanwhile Fr. Vaure, Rossi's most faithful friend and adviser, had the body secretly transported to the crypt of a chapel; but they came and stole it, to carry it to Rome in a triumphal procession. The horde of assassins, having fraternized with the troops, spread out into all the streets, terrorizing the cowardly people into festooning and decorating the route. The wretches bellowed a slogan invented by Sterbini: "Blessed be the dagger, the sacred dagger that struck the weakling down!" The whole evening the bloody weapon, decorated with flowers and attached to the Italian tricolor, was paraded around; it was set up in a café so that the Romans could venerate it; one could even see fanatics jostling to kiss the hand that had struck the blows: "Oh, *la santa mano!*" Furthermore, so that the glorification of the crime should be complete, the hideous trophy was carried to Rossi's house and borne aloft to the height of the second floor, before the eyes of the victim's widow and children, as they did in former times with the head of the Princess de Lamballe.[30]

Next day the revolutionaries organized a demonstration outside the Quirinal Palace, demanding from the Pope a new government, elections to a Constituent Assembly, the recommencement of the war against Austria, and the removal of the Swiss Guards. While the demonstrators were

---

[29] Report of Emile de Meester de Ravenstein, dated November 16, 1848, cited by Leoni, "L'uccisione di Pellegrino Rossi," pp.272-73. In a letter to the *Journal des Débats*, published May 13, 1851, Sterbini denied that he was responsible for the assassination.

[30] Ideville, *Pie IX*, pp.33-34.

fraternizing with the Civic Guard and a canon was being aimed at the Palace, the Secretary of State, in order to avoid worse trouble, agreed to receive a delegation of the demonstrators. Then he communicated the list of demands to Pius IX. In order to gain time, the latter declared that he would consider the demands made. During this first demonstration a prelate, Msgr. Palma, Secretary of Briefs, was killed by a bullet when he appeared at a window of the Palace.

Pius IX found himself alone, surrounded only by a few soldiers who had remained loyal, some prelates, and diplomats. In the days which followed Rossi's assassination the cardinals fled Rome one after the other; at the Quirinal the Roman nobility—which owed everything to the Sovereign Pontiffs—was notable for its absence.

The Popular Circle formed a "permanent public safety committee," which went to Pius IX on the 17th. Under threats, the Pope allowed the formation of a government under Msgr. Muzzarelli (who, in spite of his title, was not a priest but a canon lawyer of the Rota and a liberal by inclination), including the most extreme elements: Galletti at the Interior Ministry, Sterbini at Commerce and Public Works.

From this date Pius IX no longer had any hope of settling the situation himself. For the present he contented himself with assembling the diplomats of the Great Powers and protesting to them against the violence that had been done to him. Something that happened on the 17th prompted him to conceive the idea of the flight from Rome as the best solution for the good of the Church.

That day he received a small parcel, sent by Msgr. Chatrouse, Bishop of Valence.[31] As we have seen, it was in this town that Pius VI died in 1799, after being taken prisoner by French revolutionaries. Throughout his entire flight, Pius VI had been able to keep the Blessed Eucharist with him in a little pyx. It was this pyx that Msgr. Chatrouse had sent to Pius IX. The Pope saw this as a sign of Providence as to what he should do.

Secretly he prepared to flee Rome, with the complicity of some diplomats and loyal officers. All was organized by Count Benedetto Filippiani, who had been closely associated with the future Pius IX ever since the 1820's and who, the day after the election, had become the Pope's *scalco segreto*.[32]

On the evening of November 24, the Duc d'Harcourt, French ambassador to Rome, went to the Quirinal to be received in audience by the Pope. He was introduced and, following a plan prepared in advance, he helped Pius IX to divest himself of his white papal robes and put on the simple black soutane of a priest. Then the Sovereign Pontiff left the Quiri-

---

[31] Detailed testimony in *Summarium* §402, pp.118-19.
[32] There is a lengthy deposition from his daughter, Giulia Filippani, who became a nun, in the beatification process (*Summarium* §§401-28).

nal on foot, with Filippiani, by a secret door, and went to the carriage of the Bavarian ambassador, Count Spaur, which was waiting for him some distance away. When the Duc d'Harcourt came out from his supposed "audience" with the Pope, he told the personnel not to disturb the Sovereign Pontiff, as the latter had retired to his private apartments. So it was not until the next day that the revolutionaries learned of the Pope's flight; by that time he was already far away, on the territory of Naples. On the 25th he arrived at the little port of Gaeta, some forty-three miles north of Naples. There the Pope, incognito, had taken a room in the *Giardinetto* tavern while he awaited the King of Naples, who had been informed of his arrival.

Several countries, especially France, were hoping that the Sovereign Pontiff would seek refuge with them. In the end Pius IX remained on Neapolitan soil, at Gaeta and then at Portici. This exile was to last for almost eighteen months.

Should we see this as the turning-point of the pontificate? Should we see Pius IX now rejecting his former reforming ideas and moving in a "reactionary" direction? This is the version maintained by the liberals who initially put their hopes in him. Thus, the day after the Pope's death, the historian Charles de Mazade, summing up the Pope's reign, wrote:

> From this moment everything changes. This is the beginning of uninterrupted reaction. The liberal pope of 1846 returns to the rigidity of the priest and pontiff....There are two parts to his life, striving against and contradicting each other, and the pontiff in the wake of the revolutions seems to be doing penance for the liberal impulses of the pope of 1847.[33]

The facts, it seems to us, show this verdict to be mistaken. Pius IX did not change his overall principles on temporal politics before or after his exile. He continued to defend the sovereignty of the Papal States and to be hostile to the separation of Church and State. Nor did he change anything in the broad lines of his doctrinal and pastoral action. No doubt his Neapolitan exile gave him an opportunity to examine his conscience and to make new resolutions, but all was in continuity with a pontificate that, in outline, was already clearly drawn.

A number of publications concerning the apparition of the Virgin Mary at La Salette on September 19, 1846—that is, a few months after Pius IX's election to the sovereign pontificate—suggest that this flight from Rome was the beginning of the fulfillment of the "secrets" revealed to the two little seers, Melanie and Maximin. Without entering into the details of a very controversial question, we can say that, if the first part of the message given that day by the Virgin—a message calling for pen-

---

[33] Charles de Mazade, "Chronique de la Quinzaine," *Revue des Deux Mondes,* March 14, 1878, pp.955-956.

ance, prayer, and sanctification of Sunday, and threatening divine punishments—was acknowledged to be of supernatural origin by the Bishop of
Grenoble in 1851, the other part of the message was not.

In 1851, Pius IX read a first version of the "secrets," but testimonies
disagree as to the importance he attached to them. One version, much
longer and very apocalyptic in tone, was written down by Melanie in
1878 and published the following year, *i.e.*, after the Pope's death. The
version read by Pius IX in 1851 has not been discovered in the Vatican
Archives; hence the contradictory hypotheses. Fr. Jean Stern, in his highly
documented study,[34] thinks that the secrets received in 1846 only concerned the seers themselves. Fernand Corteville[35] considers that the secret
revealed to Melanie in 1846 should be interpreted as a prophecy of the
troubled reign of Pius IX and the promise of further chastisements.

---

[34] *La Salette: Documents authentiques,* 3 vol. (Vol. I: D.D.B., 1980; Vols.II and III: Cerf,
1984 & 1991).
[35] Fernand Corteville, in *Pie IX, le P. Pierre Semenenko et les défenseurs du Message de N-D
de La Salette,* distributed by Téqui, 1987.

CHAPTER 8

THE POPE IN EXILE

As soon as he had been informed of the Pope's arrival on Neapolitan soil, Ferdinand II went to Gaeta with the Queen, the Crown Prince, and a number of troops. It was an honor for him to receive Pius IX; as a sovereign he had a reputation for genuine piety, and he attached a certain mystical significance to the honor accorded to him. For the seventeen months of the Pope's exile there were close links between the two sovereigns.

Ferdinand II arranged for Pius IX to be installed in the little royal fortress of Gaeta. He would have preferred the Pope to reside in Naples or Portici, in more prestigious palaces, but the Sovereign Pontiff, in agreement with Cardinal Antonelli, who had by now arrived, judged it better to stay in Gaeta: the little town was nearer to Rome, and he did not wish to seem to be under political influence from the Kingdom of Naples.

On November 27, two days after his arrival, Pius IX addressed a *motu proprio* to the Romans. In this text, which he took a long time to prepare, the Pope explained to his subjects that he had been obliged to flee Rome in order to preserve his independence. He invoked the divine pardon on those who had gone astray in good faith, and refused to ascribe "any validity" to the government of November 16, which had been extorted from him by "unheard-of violence." He also announced the creation of a "provisional governmental Commission" to manage Rome's public affairs in his absence, presided over by Cardinal Castracane and consisting of Msgr. Roberti, the Princes Barberini and Roviano, the Marquis Bevilaqua and Ricci, and General Zucchi.

No doubt Pius IX had few illusions about this Commission's scope for action. In any case it could not be set up, since several of its members had already fled Rome. At least, however, the *motu proprio* showed his determination to break all links with the liberals and revolutionaries who had become masters of the Eternal City. They in turn, of course, paid no attention to the pontifical exhortations and did not recognize the authority of the provisional Commission.

In December the deputies present in Rome elected a provisional junta of three men to rule the State. This junta made a decree, dated December 29, announcing the election on the following January 21, by universal suffrage, of a constituent assembly. The break between Gaeta and Rome was now fixed and irremediable.

On December 4, the Pope had officially summoned Europe's Catholic nations to assist him in regaining his temporal power. Even before this appeal, France had declared her readiness, in a vote of the legislative Assembly, to send troops to the Pope's aid. It was only the purely political hostility of Louis-Napoleon Bonaparte, elected President of the Republic on December 10, that caused this expedition to be adjourned. In the end, some months later, the Prince-President thought better of it, and General Oudinot's troops liberated Rome.

Return to the Spiritual

It would be a mistake to suggest that temporal affairs took second place in the Pope's mind during his Gaeta exile. His determination to recover his sovereignty over the Papal States remained intact, and the presence at his side of Cardinal Antonelli guaranteed that the question was closely followed day by day. We have seen that Antonelli had stayed in the background after resigning from the Secretariat of State in April 1848; here in Gaeta he regained a high-profile role. On December 6 he was officially appointed Pro-Secretary of State, a lesser title than that which was his formerly, no doubt to soothe the susceptibilities of Cardinal Soglia, who had not resigned. Everyone understood, all the same, that Cardinal Antonelli had been reinstated in all his prerogatives as Pius IX's "right arm."[1]

While politics never forfeited its claims during this Neapolitan exile, circumstances did make the issues less acute. At Gaeta the papal court, and most of all the pontifical administration, were only partially reconstituted. Though some twenty-five cardinals and fifteen diplomats had joined the Pope by the end of December 1848, the essential personnel of the dicasteries and the temporal administration remained in Rome. The management of the affairs of all orders was suspended or greatly slowed down.

By the force of events, but also no doubt out of interior necessity, Pius IX found himself freer than in the previous two years to dedicate himself to properly spiritual matters. His first appearance outside the Gaeta fortress was on November 28, when he solemnly proceeded to the sanctuary of the Holy Trinity, which was not far away. In the presence of the royal family of Naples he celebrated Mass and then, before giving Benediction of the Blessed Sacrament, he uttered this prayer, kneeling and with much emotion:

> Eternal God, our august Father and Lord, behold at Thy feet Thy Vicar who, though unworthy, pleads with all his soul that Thou wouldst pour upon him, from the lofty height of the throne where Thou sittest in

---

[1] He officially regained his title of Secretary of State on March 18, 1852.

glory, Thy ample benediction. O great God, direct his steps, sanctify his intentions, guide his mind, govern his actions; in this place to which Thou hast brought him in Thine admirable providence, or in whatever part of Thy sheepfold he may find himself, may he be a worthy instrument of Thy glory and of the glory of Thy Church, which is suffering—alas!—the blows of her enemies!

If, in order to appease Thine anger, so justly aroused by so many iniquities committed by words, by the press, by deeds, the very life of Thy most insignificant servant may be a holocaust agreeable to Thy heart, then he dedicates it to Thee from this moment on: Thou hast given it to him; to Thee alone it belongs to take it away whenever it pleases Thee. But, O God our Creator, may Thy glory triumph, may Thy Church be victorious! Sustain the good, support the weak, and may Thine almighty arm awaken those who are at present sunk in the shades and shadows of death.

Bless the cardinals and the entire episcopate of the world, so that, along the gentle paths of Thy law, they all may accomplish the salutary work of sanctifying the nations. Then we may hope not only to be saved, in this our mortal pilgrimage, from the ambushes of the wicked and the traps of the tempter, but also to set our feet within the refuge of eternal peace. *Ut hic et in aeternum, te auxiliante, salvi et liberi esse mereamur.*[2]

There was nothing spontaneous about this long prayer. The Pope had worked at it in the first days after his arrival. It reflects, in a moving way, the state of Pius IX's soul at a particularly tragic time for him and for the Church. He was the third pope, within half a century, to be compelled to leave Rome. He had no idea how long this exile would last, nor to what it would lead (as the prayer says, "in this place…or in whatever part of Thy sheepfold he may find himself"). The prayer is remarkable for his expressed readiness to make the sacrifice of his life in reparation for all the "iniquities" committed, and his care for the universal Church.

This solemn religious ceremony at Gaeta was the first of many pilgrimages to various sanctuaries in the Kingdom of Naples. The exile pope became a pilgrim pope, with a threefold motivation: penitence for his own sins and inadequacies, reparation for the errors and calamities which had struck Italy in the past year, and also, no doubt, his personal devotion and the desire to turn to God.[3]

From his residence at Gaeta, and later at Portici, Pius IX made many visits to different shrines. On February 10, 1849, he went to the great Marian shrine of Monte Civita, which is the guardian of a very ancient icon attributed to St. Luke, which had been brought from Constantinople at the time of the iconoclastic persecution. He also visited the church of the Annunziata in Gaeta, which has, in a chapel called the "golden grotto,"

[2] Cited in Huguet, *L'Esprit de Pie IX*, pp.10-11.
[3] Polverari devoted a whole chapter to these exile pilgrimages (II, 34-48. There is also much information in Rosario F. Esposito, "Nell'esilio napoletano Pio IX maturo la proclamazione," *L'Osservatore Romano*, December 7, 1973.

a painting representing the Immaculate Conception, executed by a Jesuit painter, Fr. Scipione Pulzone. Pius IX prayed in front of this painting. On September 6, he went to the cathedral of Naples and visited the famous chapel of St. Januarius. Three days later, in the same city, he visited the church of the Gesù Vecchio, making his devotions in a little chapel dedicated to the Immaculate Virgin. There Pius IX recited the Litanies of the Virgin and three *Aves*, leaving behind him a note with these words: "Pius IX puts himself under the protection of Mary Immaculate."

Among many other visits to shrines and convents, we should note in particular the double pilgrimage of October 8 in the environs of Naples. At Nocera de Pagani Pius IX went to pray at the tomb of St. Alphonsus de Liguori.[4] Then he visited the tomb of Gregory VII in the cathedral of Salerno; this was a particularly moving pilgrimage because this great pope of reform and restoration, who was canonized by the Church, died in exile in this city in 1085.

On several occasions during these pilgrimages there were devotions to the Mother of God under the title of the Immaculate Conception. Pius IX had a particularly fervent attachment to this title. We have already referred to his devotion to this belief which, while it had not yet become a dogma of faith, was widely held in the Church. In the early stages of his pontificate, in 1847, an eminent Jesuit theologian, Fr. Perrone, had published a memorandum entitled "Can the Immaculate Conception of the Blessed Virgin Mary Be Made the Object of a Dogmatic Definition?" and his reply was in the affirmative. The memorandum attracted considerable attention and the Pope had written to the author expressing his satisfaction.

Then, in June 1848, at the height of the pre-revolutionary upheavals, Pius IX had summoned a commission of twenty theologians to study the question once more. At the time this commission had been kept secret. It was during his Neapolitan exile that the Pope officially took the decision to set in motion the procedure that would lead to the proclamation of this new dogma.

For several months he had been receiving requests along these lines from religious congregations and bishops. He was still in Rome when, in September 1848, he had received from the King of Naples a petition from forty Neapolitan bishops calling for the proclamation of the dogma of the Immaculate Conception. Then, in Gaeta the following December, he received a new petition from Ferdinand II signed by fifteen other bishops.

---

4   The works of Alphonsus Liguori (1696-1787) in the fields of moral, ascetical, and dogmatic theology went through many new editions in the nineteenth century and exercised a considerable influence in the struggle against Jansenist rigorism. He was canonized by Gregory XVI in 1839 and proclaimed a Doctor of the Church by Pius IX in 1871.

On December 16, *i.e.*, less than a month after his arrival in Gaeta, Pius IX created a commission of cardinals to examine whether it was opportune to make this dogmatic definition. This commission, composed of eight cardinals, two bishops, and six theologians, met for a preliminary session in Naples on December 22.[5]

The ten members present all expressed their views on the legitimacy and opportuneness of such a definition, but they also asked for the commission's members to be increased in number, and for the bishops of the whole world to be consulted. Pius IX would follow this recommendation.

We must also mention the parallel influence exercised on Pius IX by a mystical soul, Sr. Maria Luisa Ascione (1799-1875), who had received a number of revelations. Msgr. Stella, secretary to Pius IX, had known her since 1842. She lived in a Naples convent. Pius IX met her during his stay in Gaeta. She would be present in Rome when the dogma was defined. Her beatification cause has been introduced.[6] On February 2, 1849, having celebrated the Mass of the Feast of the Purification of the Virgin in the cathedral of Gaeta, Pius IX read out the encyclical *Ubi Primum,* addressed to the bishops of the entire world.[7] He required the bishops to "send word as promptly as possible regarding the devotion practiced by your clergy and faithful towards the Conception of the Immaculate Virgin, and as to their desire to see the Apostolic See issue a decree in this matter," and to give their own "wishes" and "sentiments" on the subject. He had already established that the clergy of Rome, in reciting the Breviary, could say the canonical office in honor of the Immaculate Conception; here and now he granted liberty to all bishops to have this office said by their diocesan clergy.

This request, along with subsequent studies, led to the solemn proclamation of the new Marian dogma in 1854.

It is not insignificant that the process leading to this striking result originated during the Gaeta exile. Faced with the ills the Church had suffered in 1848, the Pope sought succor in the Blessed Virgin Mary. He says so explicitly in his encyclical:

> The hope to which we entrust ourselves is this, that the Blessed Virgin, who has been elevated by the greatness of her merits above all the choirs of angels to the very throne of God (St. Gregory), who has shattered the ancient serpent's head beneath the foot of her virtue, and who, placed

---

5   Bernardo Giuliani, "Gli atti di Pio IX per la definizione dommatica dell'Immacolata Concezione," *L'Osservatore Romano*, December 8, 1988.
6   Cf. Giuseppe M. Besutti, "Pio IX e la Serva di Dio Maria Luisa Ascione, fondatrice delle Suore di Maria SS. Addolorata," *Pio IX nel primo centenario*, pp.120-36. I received other information from Joachim Bouflet.
7   Complete text in *Annales I*, 69-71.

between Christ and the Church (St. Bernard), full of grace and sweetness, has always rescued the Christian people from the greatest calamities
and from the traps and attacks of all its enemies, saving it from ruin,
now also will deign, having pity on us in that immense tenderness which
habitually flows from her maternal heart, to remove from us, through the
instant and all-powerful protection she wields from heaven, the grievous
and lamentable misfortunes, the cruel anxieties, the pain and want from
which we are suffering; that she may deflect the scourges of the divine
anger which afflict us because of our sins, calm and dissipate the frightful
tempest of ills by which the Church is assailed on all sides, to the immense
sadness of our souls, and finally change our mourning into joy.

Examination of Conscience

Pius IX was continually worried by news coming from Rome. Learn-
ing of the supreme junta's announcement that it was going to organize
elections to a constituent assembly, he reacted on January 1, 1849, by
issuing the *motu proprio Da Questa Pacifica Stazione,* denouncing such
elections as an "act of rebellion and a sacrilegious outrage" and threatening
with excommunication any subjects of his States who took part in them.
His warning was heeded in part since, despite pressure from the "circles,"
only a third of the potential electorate went to the ballot box.[8]

The two hundred elected deputies, apart from some notable exceptions, had a majority in favor of the new power. On February 9, this
Assembly adopted a decree, in four articles, declaring that the Pope had
"forfeited, *de facto* and *de jure*, the temporal government of the Roman
State" and proclaiming the "Roman Republic." Soon Mazzini was granted
Roman citizenship and chosen as one of the triumvirate directing the new
republic.

Pius IX again made a solemn protest to the diplomatic corps present
in Gaeta, and on February 18, a diplomatic note from Cardinal Antonelli
was made public: it was addressed to the governments of France, Austria,
Spain, and Naples, and asked for their military assistance to re-establish
the rights of the Sovereign Pontiff.

The Roman Republic was not content merely to usurp the pope's
temporal power. In the 138 days of its existence it allowed anarchy to take
over and, in spite of some appearances of religiosity (such as the celebration of a *Te Deum* in St. Peter's Basilica the day after the proclamation of
the Republic), it led to violently anti-clerical policies. In imitation of the

---

8   Martina, on the contrary, believes that this electoral participation was "notable for
    the period" (I, 328). However, if we compare this with the result of the French
    elections under the Revolution of 1798 or that of 1848, this favorable view cannot be
    maintained. Rather, we would be inclined to say that Pius IX was right when he said:
    "The vast majority of the Roman people and other pontifical subjects have remained
    faithfully attached to Us," allocution of April 20, 1849, in *Encycliques*, I, 129.

acts of the French Revolution it proclaimed that all the Church's assets and all the ecclesiastical properties were "national assets." Many monasteries and convents were occupied by troops. Much destruction and profanation had to be tolerated. Many priests and religious were arrested, some of them were assassinated, and Cardinal De Angelis was imprisoned in the citadel of Ancona.

Many were the troubles endured in the provinces too. There was pillaging, arbitrary arrest, and assassination. At Senigallia the Pope's family was maltreated: his elder brother Giuseppe was arrested, and his sister Virginia and his nephew Filippo Giraldi were taken hostage, along with other persons of the town, and brought to Ancona.

To what extent was Pius IX responsible for the ills that rained upon the Papal States in 1848 and 1849? Historians have given different and contradictory answers to this question. What is remarkable is that he himself asked this very question and wished to make a kind of public examination of conscience during a very long allocution he gave in a consistory at Gaeta on April 20, 1849.[9] This allocution is simultaneously an account of the work he had carried out in the temporal domain since his elevation to the pontificate, a justification against certain accusations made against him, and a detailed analysis of the revolutionary process; it refers to many facts that should be taken into consideration by historians.

Pius IX recalls that the concessions made (amnesty, press freedom, *etc.*) "failed to produce the fruits we had desired, nor could they even take root, because these skillful artisans (the revolutionaries) only used them to prompt further agitation." He acknowledges that the Civic Guard was "proposed and established with such haste that it was impossible to give it a regular form and discipline." He also stigmatized the treachery of some of his ministers and also, in January 1849, of the general of the Swiss Guards.[10]

The allocution also contains a justification of the papacy's temporal power: "It was by a singular design of divine Providence that, when the Roman Empire was divided into several kingdoms and divers powers, the Roman Pontiff, to whom Our Lord Jesus Christ entrusted the government and direction of the whole Church, should have a civil power. Doubtless this was in order that, in governing the Church and protecting her unity, he could enjoy the necessary plenitude of freedom for accomplishing his apostolic ministry. For it is evident to all that the Christian

---

[9] Allocution *Quibus Quantisque,* in *Encycliques,* I, 109-154.
[10] "Once again We ordered Our Swiss troops to come to Rome; We were not obeyed, and their commanding officer, in the event, failed in his duty and did not act honorably." At the time, in response to this accusation on the Pope's part, Swiss newspapers laid the responsibility on the papal envoy to Bologna, Msgr. Bedini, and the Army Minister, Zucchi; cf. Polverari, II, 27.

peoples, nations, and kingdoms would never have full confidence in and complete obedience to the Roman Pontiff if he were seen to be subject to the domination of a prince of a foreign jurisdiction and thus deprived of his liberty."

Even if this allocution did not express it in clear terms, Pius IX, from this time on, was no longer disposed to maintain the Fundamental Statute which had made the Papal States a constitutional regime. Several detailed witnesses attest that, henceforth, the Pope declared himself to be "anti-constitutional."

In a letter to Cardinal Dupont, Archbishop of Bourges, dated June 10, he clearly expressed the reasons for this resolve: parliamentary government involves "the weakness of those who profess to favor civil order"; "freedom of opinion and of the press, freedom of association, *etc.*, are intrinsically evil and tend to destroy both religion and public order. How, in conscience, could the Pope admit them?"[11]

Pius IX, as we have seen, accepted freedom of the press and a constitutional government in his States only in tandem with important formal restrictions which, he hoped, would limit its negative effects.

On the basis of his experience he henceforth rejected these two principles of the modern democracies. Nor is it any wonder that, on June 6, 1849, he sanctioned a fourfold condemnation issued by the Congregation of the Index the previous May 30.

These were the forbidden books placed on the Index: *The Constitution according to Social Justice* and *The Five Wounds of the Holy Church*, by Rosmini; *The Modern Jesuit*, by Gioberti; and the *Funeral Discourse on the Vienna Dead, given on 29 November 1848*, by Ventura. These three ecclesiastical authors had exercised great influence during the fatal year that had elapsed.

It was not surprising that Gioberti's work was condemned; he was very hostile to the Jesuits. Fr. Ventura, in spite of his affirmations,[12] never had any profound influence on Pius IX, and his "Discourse" commemorating those who died in the Austrian revolution and comparing them to martyrs for the faith, was bound to be condemned.

---

[11] Letter cited in Martina, I, 365.
[12] On February 26, 1848, in a letter to Cardinal Lambruschini, he claimed: "I alone put ideas of political reform into the mind of Pius [IX], at a time when he himself thought of nothing but administrative reforms. I can say, without vanity, that I have the merit of having contributed, together with Pius IX, more than any other Italian to the resurgence [*risorgimento*] of Italy" (cited by Martina, I, 119, n.44).
[13] Cf. Fr. Giovanni Pusinieri, "Notice biographique," in Antonio Rosmini, *Anthologie philosophique*, ed. Emmanuel Vitte (Lyons: 1954), pp.55-71; Gianfranco Radice, "Pio IX e la condanna de 'Le cinque piaghe della Chiesa' di Antonio Rosmini," *Pio IX*, No. 2 (1972), pp.207-294; Alfredo Valle, "Il Cristianesimo è la storia dell'amore," *L'Osservatore Romano*, June 4, 1982; and Falconi, *Antonelli*, pp.179ff.

With Rosmini the issue was more complex.[13] Pius IX had consulted Fr. Rosmini on several occasions, in Rome from August 1848 on, and then in Gaeta in 1849. Pius IX had a high regard for him, nominating him a consultor of the Congregation of the Index and of the Holy Office; he had even asked him to prepare for office as a cardinal. However, it had come to the notice of the cardinals of the aforementioned Congregations that certain of Rosmini's recent works, with which Pius IX was not yet familiar, contained heterodox propositions. Consequently Pius IX suspended the official announcement of his elevation to the cardinalate and ordered the suspect books to be examined in more depth. Hence the two titles condemned in June 1849.

The two books did indeed contain ideas of which Pius IX could not approve. In his *Constitution* Rosmini expressed himself opposed to the principle of a "state religion" and said that he was in favor of religious liberty and the election of bishops by clergy and people. In his *Five Wounds* Rosmini summoned the Church to recover the five attributes she had lost: unity, truth, charity, liberty and poverty. When Rosmini heard the news of the condemnation, he immediately wrote to the Master of the Sacred Apostolic Palace expressing his full submission.[14]

The Reconquest of Rome

The Pope's appeal to Europe's Catholic nations to re-establish him in his rights was heard. Each of the countries addressed (France, Spain, Austria, and the Kingdom of Naples) sent an official representative to Gaeta.

Several meetings of this international conference (March 30, April 14 and 15, 1849) failed to yield a result. But the decisive defeat of the Piedmontese at Novara (March 23), which led to Charles Albert's abdication in favor of his son, Victor Emmanuel II, followed by the occupation of Parma (April 6) and Florence (April 12) by the Austrians, prompted France not to let Austria alone restore the Pope to his States. On April 22, under the command of General Oudinot, an army corps of 9,000 men left Marseilles, arriving in Civita Vecchia on the 25th. Next, a Spanish expeditionary force of 6,000 men, commanded by General Fernando Fernandez de Cordoba, disembarked on May 27.

The Roman Republic was of a mind to resist. It recruited volunteers throughout Italy and even abroad, notably two hundred Poles who had fled their country after the failure of the revolution the previous year. Garibaldi and his Italian Legion arrived in Rome with all haste. The first

---

[14] The Rosmini affair went through further vicissitudes: in 1854 the Congregation of the Index, effectively presided over by Pius IX, published a decree declaring that "Antonii Rosmini-Servati *opera omnia...esse dimittenda,*" i.e., "are acquitted"; but in 1888, under Leo XIII, a new decree was published condemning forty propositions drawn from several of his works.

encounter between French and "Roman" troops took place under the walls of the Eternal City on April 30, allotting a defeat to the former.

Louis Napoleon then sent a mediator in the person of Ferdinand de Lesseps. Shortly after his arrival the latter hastily concluded an armistice, recognized the Roman Republic, and assured it of France's protection! This was diametrically opposed to the Pope's appeal and the wishes of the French deputies, who had finally approved the sending of an expedition-ary force. The French change of direction was all the more unfortunate since the Neapolitans had already liberated the south of the Papal States and were approaching Albano, and the Austrians were re-establishing the pontifical authorities in the Bologna and Ancona Legations.

General Oudinot contested the armistice concluded by Lesseps, and finally, on May 25, the French government denounced this agreement. Lesseps was recalled to Paris and replaced by Claude de Corcelle, whose mission was to achieve his original goal. Fighting resumed on June 3, and lasted for almost a month. On June 30, Mazzini left Rome; Garibaldi left on July 2; on July 3, General Oudinot entered the liberated city. A provi-sional administration was put in place under the authority of General de Rostolan, who was named governor of the city. The same day Oudinot sent a messenger to Pius IX with the keys of Rome and a letter announc-ing the end of hostilities.

The Pope's temporal power was declared officially restored on July 15, and a *Te Deum* was celebrated in St. Peter's by Cardinal Castracane. On the 17th, in an address to the Romans, Pius IX rejoiced in the event and appointed a commission of three cardinals (Altieri, Vannicelli Ca-sone, and della Genga Sermattei) to administer the city until his return. On August 1, these three cardinals published a manifesto expressing their gratitude to the "Christian troops" who had facilitated Rome's liberation and announced the creation of a commission of inquiry with the task of carrying out a purge of the administration.

Louis Napoleon was greatly displeased by this manifesto, seeing in it an "insult to our flag" (because the French troops had not been specifically mentioned) and an attempt "to stifle Italian liberty." He recalled General Oudinot to France, transferring his responsibilities to Rostolan. Then, on August 18, he replied to the three cardinals' manifesto by a letter to Colonel Ney, one of his aides-de-camp in Rome, who was charged with transmitting orders to Rostolan.[15] In it the Prince-President was in fact dictating the terms for the Pope's return to his States: "I sum up thus," he wrote, "the pope's temporal duties: a general amnesty, secularization of the administration, the implementation of the Napoleonic code, and a liberal government."

---

[15] Letter published in Saint-Hermel, *Pie IX*, pp.195-96.

This letter, which was made public, went against the Pope's political instincts. Coming after the "Lesseps incident," this "Ney incident" showed the ambiguous side of the French intervention and the dangers it could present. Future evasions on the part of Napoleon III would show that these fears were well founded.

Pius IX did not accept that his actions should be dictated by the president of the French Republic. In an important *motu proprio* dated September 12, he set forth the new institutions he intended to give his States.[16] Having again thanked the "valiant armies of the Catholic powers" who had liberated the Romans from "tyranny"—once again without making explicit reference to France—he outlined, in six articles, the institutional bases necessary "to console the good, who have so well merited Our benevolence and Our special attention, and to discountenance the evil and blind, who took advantage of Our concessions to overthrow the social order": he would create a Council of State to give "its views on legislative projects before they are submitted to the sovereign's sanction"; he would create a State Assembly for Finances which would examine the State's expenditure and give its opinion "on the imposition of new taxes or the reducing of existing taxes"; he would confirm the provincial councils, whose "councilors will be chosen by Us from lists presented by the local councils"; a commission would be set up to introduce reforms and improvements in "civil, criminal, and administrative legislation."

Finally, "always inclined to clemency and pardon," the Pope granted a new amnesty for "those wayward men who have been drawn into treason and revolt by the seductions, hesitation, and—perhaps—weakness of others."[17] It should be noted that while, faithful to the lessons and experience of 1847-48, Pius IX did not re-establish a constitutional system and parliamentary government, he continued to grant a certain degree of representation and a consultative voice. Certain historians are wrong, therefore, to see this as "an absolute and centralized government."[18] What is more, Pius IX did not turn his back on such "reforms" and "improvements" as seemed still necessary to him to assure the prosperity of his States.

Pius IX did not immediately return to the Papal States which had been restored to him. On September 4, he had left Gaeta to take up residence in the royal palace of Portici, in the Bay of Naples, where apart-

---

[16] Complete text in *Annales I*, 84-85.
[17] A public order simultaneously excluded the following from the benefit of amnesty: the members of the Constituent Assembly elected in January 1849, the ministers and military who had participated in setting up the Republic, and the common law prisoners.
[18] The expression used by Martina, I, 392, to refer to the new institutions.

ments had been prepared for him by Ferdinand II. He remained there for
seven months, until April 1850.

In fact, Rome was not yet ready to receive him. The administration
was utterly disorganized and the finances were in a pitiable state. People
were afraid that new upheavals would take place, and indeed, several serious incidents arose in the capital and provinces in subsequent months.
Ultimately, Pius IX feared that he might find himself subject to pressure
from the French occupying authorities.

The finances of the Papal States, which had already shown a struc-
tural deficit prior to the revolution, had been made worse by the Roman
Republic. It had spent recklessly, gone into debt, and issued money prodi-
gally, creating a paper currency which, like the *assignats,* the paper money
at the time of the French Revolution, had quickly been devalued.

France was approached to find the necessary sums to refloat the papal
exchequer. Msgr. Fornari, nuncio in Paris, was instructed to consult the
representatives of high finance who might be ready to lend the required
sums. It was the Rothschilds, who had been among the Holy See's bankers
since 1831, who made the most attractive offers.[19] They made their loan
conditional on an improvement in the lot of the Jews of Rome: the ghetto
where, traditionally, the Jews were confined, should disappear, and Jews
should be allowed to appear as witnesses before Roman tribunals. In the
end this stipulation was not specifically mentioned in the loan contract
signed in Paris in January 1850.

As a result, Pius IX was able to wipe out the debts left behind by the
Roman Republic, withdraw the paper money from circulation by buying
it back from those who had it, and reimburse the loans authorized by the
foreigners.

This is also the place to mention that it was during his exile at Gaeta,
and thanks to the Rothschild loan, that Pius IX promoted the creation
of a journal which was to become one of the most famous religious journals of the nineteenth and twentieth centuries: the *Civiltà Cattolica.*[20] The
Jesuit Fr. Curci, who had envisioned a review of Catholic studies that
would use the means of the press to do battle against increasing irreligion,
submitted his project to Cardinal Antonelli in December 1849. The latter showed himself very interested. Fr. Roothan, the Jesuit General, was
hardly in favor of it, but Pius IX, once he had been informed of the project, gave it much attention, and in January 1850 insisted that the journal
should come out as soon as possible. He advanced the necessary money to

---

[19]   Falconi, *Il Cardinale Antonelli*, pp.233-236, 65, and Herbert R. Lottman, *La Dynastie
        Rothschild* (Seuil, 1995), p.58.
[20]   L. Merklen, "Civiltà Cattolica," *Catholicisme* (Letouzey & Ané, 1950), II, col.1153-
        54; Martina, I, 424-34; Piolanti, *Pio IX e la rinascita del tomismo*, pp.36-37; Falconi,
        Il giovane Mastai, pp.245ff.

cover the initial issues. Fr. Curci gathered together several collaborators, who were all Jesuits: Fr. Bresciani; Fr. Taparelli D'Azeglio, a lawyer; Fr. Piancini, professor of mathematics; Fr. Liberatore, a philosopher; Fr. Piccirillo, a professor of physics. The purpose of the journal was to provide a Catholic response to modern errors in all the spheres of knowledge. In addition, through the labors of Frs. Taparelli D'Azeglio, Curci, Liberatore, and Cornoldi, it was instrumental in the renewal of Thomism in the second half of the nineteenth century.

On March 3, Fr. Curci was able to send out 120,000 prospectuses, announcing the journal's program to the whole of Italy; the first number appeared on April 6, 1850. Initially it was published in Naples and then, some months later, in Rome.

During the pontificate of Pius IX it came out every fortnight and was one of the pontiff's warmest supporters. Very often, where sensitive subjects were broached, it published articles inspired by the Pope himself.

Return to Rome

The signing of the financial contract with the Rothschilds coincided with the announcement, at the beginning of February, that the French troops would be considerably reduced, from 80,000 to 10,000 men. Pius IX could think about returning to Rome.

France's extraordinary envoy in Rome sent a report to his minister describing the situation in the Eternal City in these terms: "The party opposing the Pope's return is strong and numerous. The clergy are hostile to the Holy Father; they do not forgive him for having compromised the papacy with his concessions and displays of weakness; twice already they have made overtures suggesting that he should agree to retire to a monastery.... The cardinals are at the head of this party."[21]

It may have been the case with a number of clergy and prelates, but to suggest that this hostility was general among the clergy and cardinals is extremely exaggerated. The affectionate welcome Pius IX received all the way along the route of his return shows that the predominant feeling was quite different.

On April 4, Pius IX left Portici. The King of Naples and his court accompanied him to the frontier. The journey lasted several days. At Velletri the Pope was received by representatives of the three great Roman basilicas (St. John Lateran, St. Peter's in the Vatican, St. Mary Major's) and by the French extraordinary envoy, General Baraguey d'Hilliers. The latter had been advised by his Minister for Foreign Affairs that there was a

---

[21] Dispatch of Baraguay d'Hilliers to the minister, February 5, 1850, A.M.A.E., C.P., Rome 994, ff.76-77.

conspiracy against the Pope, planned abroad by Mazzini.[22] Special security measures had been taken.

The reports of Baraguey d'Hilliers to his minister describing the course of the journey speak of the very favorable welcome Pius IX was given at Genzano, Albano, and Rome.[23] Having arrived in Rome on April 12, the Pope received the homage of the cardinals, the diplomatic corps, and the municipal Commission in St. John Lateran. Simultaneously 101 cannon rounds were fired from the Castel Sant'Angelo, where the papal flag was hoisted.

Next, the Pope went from St. John Lateran to St. Peter's, surrounded by an enthusiastic crowd. In the evening, for three days, the city witnessed illuminations recalling the auspicious hours of 1846. These popular festivities were repeated every year on April 12, even after the 1870 annexation. On April 15, Pius IX officially received the diplomatic corps, reinstated in its entirety in Rome once more; and he went to visit and thank the French soldiers who were being looked after at the hospital of St. Andrew at the Quirinal. (He did the same the following day at the hospitals of St. Dominic and St. Sixtus.)

In subsequent months the institutions announced in the allocution of September 12, 1849, were gradually put in place. As Alberto Polverari has rightly observed, this 1850 institutional reorganization "represents a change in relation to the constitution of 1848, and at the same time a continuity with regard to the original program set forth in the Bishop of Imola's *Pensieri*."[24]

On September 12, 1850, an edict of Cardinal Antonelli created a Council of State, a consultative organ which we have already described; a further edict reorganized the government. The latter, presided over by the Secretary of State, who was responsible for the Holy See's relations with foreign governments, was composed of five ministries: the Interior, Grace and Justice, Finance, Commerce (including agriculture, industry, fine arts, and public works), and Armies. These five ministries could be entrusted to laymen.

On October 28, the Council of State for Finances was created. It was presided over by the Secretary of State and was composed of twenty members appointed by the Pope from a list proposed by the provincial councils and five other members chosen by the Apostolic Chamber.

On November 22, a new edict implemented an administrative reorganization of the twenty-one provinces of the Papal States, dividing them into four Legations and Rome. The Bologna Legation included the provinces of Ferrara, Forli, and Ravenna; the Legation of Urbino and Pesaro

---

[22] Telegram, April 7, 1850, A.M.A.E., C.P., Rome 994, ff.155 & 157-58.
[23] Dispatches of April 12 & 13, 1850, A.M.A.E., C.P., Rome 994.
[24] Polverari, II, 69.

had the provinces of Macerata and Loreto, Ancona, Fermo, Ascoli, and Camerino; the Legation of Perugia included the provinces of Spoleto and Rieti; the Legation of Velletri had the provinces of Frosinone and Benevento; and Rome included the provinces of Viterbo, Civita Vecchia, and Orvieto.

Each province was administered by a council composed of members chosen by the Pope from lists drawn up by the local councils.

On November 24, finally, a last edict laid down the composition and competence of the local councils. Depending on the number of inhabitants of a locality, the council would consist of ten to thirty-six councilors; two-thirds of these would be elected by the landowners who paid the heaviest taxes, the merchants, teachers, and artists; each local council would also include one or two ecclesiastics appointed by the bishop. These councils would be responsible for all questions of local administration (commerce, taxes, hygiene, and public order).

All these institutions made the papal regime unique among the great European states. It was neither parliamentary (like France or England) nor autocratic (like Russia); it rejected absolutely the principle of popular sovereignty, while conceding a real representation of the population through consultative organs. After the somersaults of 1848, the papal regime was rediscovering its nature as an absolute monarchy; absolute, in the sense that it was independent of any other power, but not depending merely on the good pleasure of the prince. These institutions functioned until the collapse of the Papal States in 1870.

CHAPTER 9

RESISTANCE AND RENEWAL

The most striking act of the years after the Pope's re-establishment in his States was the proclamation of the dogma of the Immaculate Conception in 1854. All the same, while Pius IX closely followed the consultations and studies which eventually led to this solemn act, there were other important questions which preoccupied him; these were to be the subject of significant declarations and decisions in the early 1850's.

Laicization in Piedmont-Sardinia

In spite of defeat in the struggle against Austria, the new King of Piedmont-Sardinia, Victor Emmanuel II, had not given up presenting himself as the champion of an independent Italy. His objective remained to "liberate" Lombardy and Venetia from Austrian tutelage, but from the 1850's, under the influence of personalities such as Cavour, he pursued a more ambitious goal: "To put Piedmont at the head of the Italian national movement and constitute at least a kingdom of Upper Italy."[1]

In parallel with this, he wished to reduce the Church's influence in state and society. Concordats signed between the Holy See and the Kingdom of Piedmont-Sardinia in 1828, and then in 1841, had confirmed certain particular rights of the Church and, most importantly of all, had guaranteed her independence:

> The possession of considerable goods and property, which continued to grow as a result of gifts and legacies (authorized from sixteen years upwards); the maintenance of the tithe-system in Sardinia; the right, on the part of bishops with inadequate resources, to impose supplementary charges on people within their diocese; legal sanctions against those who did not respect the Sunday rest or offended religion in whatsoever manner; legal recognition exclusively of religious marriage, the clergy being responsible for keeping the civil marriage registers; a relaxation of the penal code in favor of priests and religious; finally, privilege granted to the ecclesiastical forum, according to which the episcopal curias alone were competent in cases of outrages against religion, tithes, marriages and all matters in which a cleric was implicated.[2]

The liberals and anti-clericals saw this as a raft of "privileges," inherited from the *ancien régime*, which must be abolished in order to promote the liberty of all and reduce the Church's influence in society. On her part,

---

[1]   Salvatorelli, *Histoire de l'Italie*, p.500.
[2]   Aubert, p.76.

the Church, in fidelity to the traditional doctrine of the non-separation of Church and State, regarded these as means guaranteed by law for the accomplishment of her mission and the preservation of her independence. This gave rise to a conflict which would not cease until the end of Pius IX's pontificate.

Ever since 1848, under pressure from the left wing of its Chamber of Deputies and in order to save face after the failure against Austria, the government of Piedmont-Sardinia had decided to implement a program of laicization that would restrict the Church's action in society.[3] The Jesuits were expelled from the kingdom in August 1848, and the following October a law on education had the effect of putting all education under State control. From now on the appointment of teachers, professors and directors of Catholic schools, and even the choice of chaplains, was under the government's control. Pius IX had protested, but his difficult situation in his own States meant that his protest carried little weight.

The following year Victor Emmanuel II had sent Count Siccardi to Portici with the task of obtaining from the Pope the resignation or dismissal of two bishops (including Msgr. Fransoni, the Archbishop of Turin) who were felt to be too hostile to the government, and the abolition of ecclesiastical courts. Pius IX regarded this as calling the concordat into question, and since Count Siccardi refused to substantiate the accusations against the two bishops, the discussions were fruitless. The Pope, however, fearing the evil consequences which might flow from decisions taken unilaterally by the government of Piedmont-Sardinia, entrusted Msgr. Charvaz, who had once been Victor Emmanuel II's teacher, with a conciliatory mission to Turin.[4] The Pope was even ready to envisage the negotiation of a new concordat. This mission was a failure, however. In one of his reports, Msgr. Charvaz justly underlined Victor Emmanuel's weakness: "This sovereign, whose intentions would be generally good, seems to be under some illusion about the dangers threatening the Church and the monarchy in his States. I observe that he is totally dependent on his ministers, who succeed in quashing his best ideas. He makes promises and means well, but his hands are tied...." This observation is even more relevant to the coming years, whether as regards the policy of laicization or that aiming to unify Italy.

Pius IX was still at Portici when he received information about a draft law proposed by Siccardi, who had become minister of Justice. The purpose of this law was to withdraw clerical immunity, abolish the right of ecclesiastical sanctuary, limit the number of religious holy days, and de-

---

3 Pius IX mentioned all the stages of this policy, and his reactions, in an allocution given in a consistory of November 1, 1850, in *Encycliques*, I, 217-33.
4 Martina, I, 445-46, gives details of the Siccardi and Charvaz missions.

prive the Church of the faculty of acquiring goods. Another draft law was proposed authorizing civil marriage.

Cardinal Antonelli was instructed to protest against these proposals in a letter of February 9, 1850, to the Holy See's *chargé d'affaires* in Turin. This letter had no effect since Siccardi's law was promulgated on April 9, while Pius IX was on his way back to Rome. This constituted a unilateral breaking of the concordat. The nuncio in Turin was recalled and diplomatic relations between the Holy See and Piedmont-Sardinia—which had become the Kingdom of Italy—were not normalized until 1929, after the signing of the Lateran Accords!

The violation of the concordat was followed in May by the arrest of Msgr. Fransoni, accused of having denounced a law which would have resulted, in fact, in the confiscation of ecclesiastical goods. He was brought to the Turin citadel and, in September, was condemned to exile; the archdiocesan property was sequestrated. The situation was serious.

At the end of the year Piedmont-Sardinia sent Count Manfredo Bertone di Sambuy to Rome with an ambiguous mission: he was to restore good relations with the Holy See but without yielding with regard to the adopted laws. In a letter to Pius IX dated November 2, accrediting Sambuy's mission, Victor Emmanuel II requested "forgetfulness of the past, and a blessing for the present and the future."[5]

Pius IX replied on December 13:

> Forgetfulness of the past. With all my heart, but in an appropriate manner....A blessing for the present. An abundant blessing, with my whole heart; but there are certain of your subjects who cannot possibly participate in this blessing....A blessing for the future. God is my witness of the prayers I make for Piedmont; frequently, even, I offer the sacrifice of the altar for Your Majesty, his august family, and all his subjects....But at the same time, at the last session of the Chamber, I see ministers, acting in the person of Your Majesty, again expressing ideas which give me little hope that the Lord's blessing will reach them.

In this reply, showing Pius IX's temperament, full of generosity but not without firm determination, he made it clear that he would remain vigilant in the face of the current of laicism which was dominating the parliament and government of Piedmont-Sardinia.[6] In fact, following years would see the Turin government pursue policies hostile to the Church,

---

[5]   Letter of Victor-Emmanuel II and Pius IX's response, cited in F. Della Rocca, "Pio IX e Cavour," *Pio IX nel primo centenario*, p.387.

[6]   On August 22, 1851, the apostolic letter *Ad Apostolicae Sedis Fastigium* (*Encycliques,* I, 243-254) condemned two works of canon law by Jean-Népomucène Nuytz, *Cours de droit ecclésiastique* and *Traité sur le droit ecclésiastique,* which expressed a laicist political theory by saying that the Church has no power to compel, that civil law must prevail over ecclesiastical law, that the primacy of the Bishop of Rome is only circumstantial, that marriage is a simple civil contract, *etc.*

always using the same tactics: "Present the Holy See with a *fait accompli* and demand, purely and simply, that it accept it."[7] This is what happened with the draft law on civil marriage presented to the Chamber of Deputies on June 12, 1852. While civil marriage remained optional, the validity of even religious marriage was entirely dependent on its being recognized by a civil jurisdiction.

On July 2 Pius IX protested against this draft law which imperilled the Catholic doctrine of marriage by reducing it to the level of a simple civil contract. This draft law "is not Catholic," Pius IX clearly told Victor Emmanuel; and in a new letter dated September 19 he reaffirmed the sacramental character of marriage and the Church's exclusive right to define its validity: "Let the civil power look after the civil effects resulting from marriage, but let the Church take care of regulating its validity between Christians. The civil law, in regulating the civil effects, must take as its point of departure the validity or non-validity of marriage as the Church shall have determined it, for this matter is beyond its sphere of competence."[8]

In this same letter to the sovereign of Piedmont-Sardinia we find the request which recurs frequently when Pius IX addresses heads of state: "We beg you also to rein in the press, which does not cease to vomit blasphemy and propagate immorality. Innumerable are the sins engendered by licence in speaking and writing."

Was Pius IX's protest heard—for once—or should it be seen as some kind of political maneuver? At any rate, in December the law on marriage adopted by the Chamber of Deputies was rejected by the majority of the Senate of Piedmont-Sardinia. One month later, however, Cavour, who had been a minister several times up to then, had become President of the Council. He remained at the head of the government of Piedmont-Sardinia until his death, conducting a policy more and more hostile to the Church, with the support of the anti-clerical left. As Roger Aubert has noted:

> His family relations with Protestants of the "Free Church" founded by Vinet in Suisse Romande, and subsequently his contacts with French liberal Catholics, had made Cavour a skillful exponent of the phrase "A free Church in a free State" and an enemy of concordats, which seemed to him to infringe the Church's full liberty and suppose that the Church is a "perfect society" like the State, negotiating with the latter for shared influence over a common territory; whereas, for him, since the spiritual and the temporal belonged to utterly distinct domains, it was important clearly to separate the civil and political competences from the religious.[9]

---

[7] Martina, I, 449.

[8] Letter of Pius IX to Victor Emmanuel II, September 19, 1852, published—under the erroneous date of September 9—in *Encycliques*, I, 271-83.

[9] Aubert, pp.79-80.

Cavour's ideas on the separation of Church and State ran clean contrary to Catholic doctrine and had no chance of attracting the agreement of Pius IX. The latter, prepared to renegotiate a concordat with Piedmont-Sardinia, had to face the truth that, under the influence of Cavour, Victor Emmanuel II was moving further and further from the possibility of conciliation.

Piedmont-Sardinia's laicist policy was further aggravated in May 1855 as a result of the "law of the convents," which withdrew all juridical recognition from religious congregations except those dedicated to preaching, teaching, and the care of the sick. This law brought about the closing of more than six hundred monasteries and convents, mostly those of contemplative orders. Their goods were confiscated and their members were obliged to disperse.

Pius IX who, the preceding January, had demanded that Cavour's government should give up this project, reacted with severity to the announcement of the vote and the promulgation of the law. In a consistory allocution on July 26 he pronounced a major excommunication against "all those in Piedmont who have had the temerity to propose, approve, and sanction these measures, these laws against the Church and the rights of the Holy See" and against "all those who have given them order, support, counsel, adherence, and made themselves the executors of their wishes."[10]

The policy of laicization implemented in Piedmont-Sardinia was the result of the coming-to-power of liberal and anti-clerical persons intent on breaking "the alliance of Throne and Altar." This was not an isolated case. Other countries in Europe, and Latin American countries formerly tied to Europe, experienced similar changes. In the pontificate of Gregory XVI, for instance, the Republic of New Granada (today Colombia) had been the first of the young republics emerging from the Spanish colonial domain to be recognized by the Holy See. As in many newly-independent countries of Spanish America, the new power was influenced predominantly by Freemasonry and successively adopted laws aiming to laicize state and society and reduce the Church's influence: ecclesiastical immunity was at an end, tithes were abolished, and all religious denominations were authorized.

In May 1851, three laws were introduced to further aggravate the Church's situation in New Granada: the Jesuits were expelled and every religious order which professed "passive obedience" was forbidden; ecclesiastical courts were suppressed and the appointment of parish priests was exercised by "parish assemblies," not the bishop. Many clerics protested against these laws. Many were arrested and imprisoned. The vicar-general

---

[10] Text of the allocution of July 26, 1855, in *Encycliques*, I, 335-42.

of the capital, Santa Fe de Bogotà, was incarcerated and his archbishop, Msgr. de Mosquera, was expelled from his diocese, all the property of the archbishopric being placed in sequestration.

This threefold law and its consequences provoked a solemn protest on the part of the Pope in a consistory on September 27, 1852.[11] In this allocution Pius IX denounced the principles of liberty of opinion and religious liberty, which had been written into the infant republic's constitution, as the root of all the evils: "It grants full and complete liberty to all to publish their ideas, even those opinions that are most monstrous, and simultaneously grants them the liberty to profess any religion they please, either in private or in public."

Pius IX's policy in his relations with States and regimes of whatever hue was constant from the beginning of his pontificate to its end: the doctrine which aims to separate Church and State is erroneous. The State does not enjoy unlimited rights, and the Church possesses rights of her own which do not depend on the civil authority. The latter, in governing and in elaborating laws, must act in conformity with natural law.[12] Like his predecessors, Pius IX endeavored to sign concordats with the newly-independent states or with older countries where conflicts had arisen between Church and State. In the view of Pius IX this was the surest way of guaranteeing the Church's rights. After negotiations that were sometimes difficult, concordats were signed in these years with the Grand Duchy of Tuscany, Spain, and Bolivia (1851); Costa Rica and Guatemala (1852); and Austria (1855). We shall return to the latter case later, since it has considerable symbolic value.[13]

Reform of Religious Life

These concordats often proved favorable to the renewal of religious life, even if, as in the case of Spain, for instance, the hostility of liberals and radicals would soon put a question-mark, at least in part, over the accord achieved. Good relations with the State, and a Christian State, were not enough to enable the Church to fulfill her mission. At the same time, therefore, Pius IX dedicated himself to promoting a renewal in the

---

[11] *Encycliques*, I, 285-306.

[12] These principles, along with others, would be set forth, in a lapidary and negative manner, in the famous Syllabus of 1864.

[13] Concordats did not always have beneficial consequences. Thus, in Spain, the application of the concordat brought about the disappearance of faculties of canon law and theology, since the teaching of these subjects was reserved to seminaries. This has a deleterious effect on the intellectual formation of the Spanish clergy. Leo XIII responded to this situation by establishing ten pontifical universities in Spain between 1896 and 1897. Cf. Vicente Carcel Orte, "Le cardinal Mercier et les études ecclésiastiques en Espagne," *Revue d'Histoire Ecclésiastique,* January-June 1995, pp.104-12.

whole Church through other means. Ever since his first encyclical, as we have seen, the Pope had exhorted the bishops to show themselves in their preaching to be true defenders of the faith in the face of the "general deluge of errors" and the "unbridled licence in ideas, discussions, and writings." He had also called them to be vigilant with regard to the formation and discipline of the clergy.

The renewal of the religious orders was another objective adopted by Pius IX from the early days of his pontificate. He had begun to implement this prior to his Gaeta exile, and carried it forward in the 1850's. This vast reform of the religious orders is one of the least known aspects of Pius IX's work.

During the decades of the Enlightenment and the French Revolution, many monasteries and convents had been closed all over Europe; certain religious orders had even disappeared entirely. In the first half of the nineteenth century, however, the religious houses had filled again. But by the beginning of Pius IX's pontificate, in many cases, "religious institutes were in considerable crisis, essentially due to inadequate selection and theological preparation of candidates; the failure to observe life in common; internal dissensions arising from political, regional, or family causes; and the favoritism which paralyzed the action of superiors by protecting intolerant and rebellious subjects."[14]

From the very first months of his pontificate Pius IX determined to get to the roots of this situation and remedy it. Until then, religious were under the aegis of two different congregations: the Congregation of Bishops and Regulars and the Congregation of Regular Discipline. This led to rivalry in the distribution of responsibilities. On October 7, 1846, a new congregation was created, the Congregation for the Statute of Regulars, with the specific purpose of proposing to the Sovereign Pontiff measures for promoting a renewal of the discipline of religious and of conventual life.[15]

Even if many cardinals were members of this Congregation (notably Cardinal Polidori, who was very close to Pius IX), the Pope reserved the presidency to himself, showing the importance he attached to the work it would have to do. Msgr. Andrea Bizzarri, who was already assessor at the Congregation of Bishops and Regulars, was appointed secretary of this new Congregation. He would be its inspiration and very active executive.[16] Shortly after his appointment he presented a long report on the reform of religious life, suggesting a series of measures to promote a better

---

[14] Martina, I, 507.
[15] For a detailed study of this question, based on many archive documents, see Paolo Gavazzi, "Pio IX e la Riforma degli Ordini Religiosi (1846-1857)," *Atti del II.Convegno*, pp.203-42.
[16] Dom Guéranger would complain that he was all-powerful. Cf. Dom L. Robert, *Dom Guéranger chez Pie IX* (Association des Amis de Solesmes, 1960).

observance of the rule in convents and monasteries. These were: modifications in the admission to the novitiate and religious profession, a better
selection process for candidates, the obligation of common life on all right
from the beginning of the novitiate (and for other religious, a "prudent introduction to common life"); the constitutions of religious orders should
be revised and brought up to date, and there should be a greater participation of religious in the pastoral activities of dioceses.

Msgr. Bizzarri's report was accepted by Pius IX, who also followed his
advice in addressing all religious superiors in an encyclical. Clothed in the
pontifical authority, a solemn exhortation of this kind would have more
effect than the Congregation circulars which, in the past—under the pontificate of Pius VII, in particular—had called for a renewal. The encyclical
Ubi Primum, dated June 17, 1847, was addressed to "all generals, abbots,
provincials, and other superiors of religious orders," but it was also communicated to all bishops.[17]

Pius IX informed them of his determination to "strengthen whatever
may be weak, heal what may be sick, restore what may be broken, bring
back whatever may have gone astray, lift up what may have fallen down,
and thus to instill new life everywhere and cause moral integrity, holiness of life, observance of regular discipline, sacred letters, and, above all,
sacred science, and the laws proper to each order, to flourish and prosper
from day to day." He announced the creation of a Congregation entirely
dedicated to "restoring religious discipline" and required all religious superiors to "take part in this great work" by showing prudence in the admission of novices, forming them with care ("the stability and splendor of
each consecrated family depends entirely on their perfect formation"), and
working with the bishops and secular clergy "in building up the Body of
Christ." Accompanying the Encyclical was a Brief inviting all the address-
ees to make their suggestions regarding the reform being undertaken.

Three main requests emerge from the replies received from the religious superiors and bishops from the entire world: greater strictness in the
admission to the novitiate and religious profession; a gradual re-introduc-
tion of common life in all monasteries and convents; and the opportunity,
in all religious orders, to take simple vows prior to making solemn profession. The Congregation was encouraged by these initial steps and was able
to pursue its work.

Soon it presented to the Pope two decrees, which were approved on
December 29, 1847. The first, *Romani Pontifices,* bound all convents and
monasteries not to admit any candidates to the religious life unless they
presented letters testimonial from the bishop of their diocese of origin.
The second decree, *Regulari Disciplina*, stipulated that the admission and

---

[17] Text in *Annales I*, 7-10.

formation of novices no longer depended solely on the local superior but should be under the inspection of provincial and general superiors as well.

The 1848 revolution in Rome put a heavy brake on the activity of the Congregation for the Statute of Regulars. After Pius IX returned from exile it was able to pursue its work in a sustained manner, and Pius IX encouraged it. On January 12, 1851, addressing all the general superiors of religious orders meeting in Rome, he energetically invited them to cooperate with the current reform and scrupulously to apply, in their establishments, the constitutions proper to their order. The general superiors were well aware of the need for a general restoration. In their name, Fr. Venanzio de Celano, Minister General of the Franciscan Friars Minor, asked the Pope to intervene again directly by issuing a circular letter or Brief.

Pius IX acceded to their request and on April 12 the same year a circular prepared by the Congregation required all superiors of novitiates to impose "perfect common life" in their convent or monastery; all superiors of religious houses of study to impose "the perfect observance of the constitutions"; and all superiors, without distinction, to re-introduce the *deposito* (that is, the controlled operation of a common exchequer) and no longer to allow the practice of individual payments, which had led to much abuse.

The provisions of this circular could not be implemented without overcoming certain obstacles. Thus Fr. Jandel, vicar-general of the Dominican Order, was confronted with the opposition of all the Italian provinces of his order. It required the threat of his resignation and the Pope's intervention fully to reintroduce the strict observance in the Dominican houses of Italy.[18]

The reform of the religious orders continued steadily, all the more so since, from 1852 onwards, Msgr. Bizzarri combined his responsibilities as secretary of the Congregation for the Statute of Regulars with those of secretary of the Congregation of Bishops and Regulars. A considerable influence was also exercised by the Capuchin Fr. Giusto de Camerino, a consultor of the Congregation since its inception. He was created cardinal in 1853.

Pius IX closely followed the work of the Congregation's commissions, and intervened personally by communicating with superiors of convents and monasteries, with general superiors, or by more solemn acts. On March 5, 1854, for instance, addressing general superiors of orders who had been summoned to Rome again, he told them of his resolution to introduce a period of simple vows prior to solemn profession in all religious orders. At this stage it was not an obligation but an authorization, and the

---

[18] Cf. pp. 287-306 of the "Memorandum" he drew up, published in Bernard Bonvin, *Lacordaire Jandel* (Paris: Cerf, 1989).

Pope wished to know the views of the superiors of orders. Finally, three years later, the circular *Nemina Latet* stipulated that there should be one year for the novitiate and three years in simple vows prior to religious profession; general superiors would have the power to prolong the novitiate until the age of twenty-five.

Without going into the history of all the religious orders it is possible to affirm that this restoration of religious discipline had good results in the long term. For example, the Dominican Order, which had eleven provinces in 1844, had twenty-five in 1872;[19] there were 5,209 Jesuits in 1853 and 11,480 in 1884.[20]

However, success differed depending on the region concerned:

> The reforming efforts inspired or encouraged by Pius IX quickly produced good results in the centralized orders, but they met with great inertia in the abbeys of central and southern Europe, which had remained very independent. In the countries of the south, furthermore, religious life had undergone severe trials in the Spanish revolutions and as a result of the Piedmont secularization, which had spread to all Italy after 1860. In western Europe, by contrast, as in North America, quite remarkable progress was made, both in the number of religious and in the quality of religious life, and there the congregations became an essential factor in the flowering of works and the intensity of spiritual life.[21]

We can add that the efforts of Pius IX and the Congregation were supported by religious men and women of great determination. Often they had been placed at the head of their orders by Pius IX himself, who was not afraid, when necessary, to override the canonical rules of appointment. Thus, in 1850, the Pope showed his preference for Fr. Venanzio de Celano as Minister General of the Friars Minor, ignoring the negative advice of the outgoing Minister General whose term of office had expired. Also in 1850, fearing that an Italian would be elected, Pius IX decided to suppress the general chapter which was to appoint the new Master General of the Dominicans. As "vicar-general of the Order *ad beneplacitum Sanctae Sedis*" he appointed Fr. Jandel, associated with Fr. Lacordaire, who had re-introduced the Dominican Order into France.

In 1855, Pius IX intervened in the Dominican Order again, imposing Fr. Jandel as Master General irrespective of the constitutions of the Order, which laid down that the Master General would be elected by all the superiors. The Pope had done the same with the Augustinians in 1850, first appointing a vicar-general, Fr. Giuseppe Palermo da Salemi, and then giving him the title of General the following year. In 1853, on the other hand, he allowed the Company of Jesus to designate a new Superior, Fr.

---

[19] Bonvin, *Lacordaire Jandel*, p.133.
[20] Aubert, p.458.
[21] *Ibid.*, p.457.

Pierre Beckx, according to its constitutions; no doubt because at that time the Jesuits were a very flourishing order where the constitutions were respected.

Among other interventions of Pius IX we should also note his appointment, in 1850, of Dom Casaretto as Abbot of the famous Benedictine monastery of Subiaco, in order to re-establish the observance there. Dom Casaretto would be involved in the creation of a new Benedictine congregation, the Congregation of Subiaco. It was due to the Pope's urgent insistence that, two years later, the ancient congregation of Monte Cassino returned to the observance of common life, the enclosure, and the practice of mental prayer. Nor should we forget the close links between Pius IX and Dom Guéranger, the restorer of the Benedictine Order in France and founder of the Congregation of Solesmes. Quite apart from questions concerning the Roman liturgy, the Pope consulted Dom Guéranger on various doctrinal matters.[22]

The Secular Clergy

The secular clergy were just as much the object of the Pope's special attention as the regular clergy. Here again the 1846 encyclical had been the broad manifesto, setting forth what should be the bishops' concern for their clergy. Pius IX wrote:

> You cannot be too zealous in your efforts to render your clergy outstanding in the gravity of their conduct, in purity of life, and in holiness and knowledge; you must keep a strict observance of the ecclesiastical discipline established by the sacred canons, and to instill new vigor into it wherever it has fallen away....Do not be too hasty, as the Apostle teaches, to lay hands on any man: you should initiate into sacred orders and entrust with sacred functions only those who, after precise and rigorous tests, seem to you to be adorned with all the virtues, recommend themselves by their wisdom, are apt to serve and bring honor to your dioceses and hold aloof from all that is forbidden to clerics, and apply themselves to study, preaching, and instruction....[23]

In the case of the religious orders, the formation of the clergy and good ecclesiastical discipline depended on the restoration of a rule applying to the whole world and the appointment of a superior general having authority over all the order's houses. This could not be the case with the secular clergy. For them, the chief authority was the bishop of the diocese. This meant that the quality of the clergy was dependent in part on the bishop's own zeal and ecclesiastical spirit.

---

[22] Cf. Dom Delatte, *Dom Guéranger, abbé de Solesmes* (Solesmes: 1984), revised and augmented edition; Dom Cuthbert Johnson, *Dom Guéranger et le Renouveau liturgique* (Paris: Téqui, 1988).
[23] *Encycliques,* I, 69.

A significant feature of the pontificate of Pius IX was that he encouraged the holding of local councils and the constitution of regular episcopal assemblies to reinforce the cohesion of the bishops of the same country and to facilitate common measures and decisions. In this he was entirely faithful to the Council of Trent, which, in its canons, had prescribed that "every three years" councils were to be held in each ecclesiastical province "to regulate conduct, correct excesses, settle disputes, and all the other things permitted by the sacred canons."[24] It is sometimes said that Pius IX encouraged provincial councils (which would be very large in number, in all the continents) in order to obstruct the holding of national councils, which he regarded as dangerous. The accusation is unfounded. Quite apart from the constitution of annual plenary episcopal assemblies (such as that of the German bishops, beginning in 1848), he allowed the Irish Church (in 1850 and 1875) and the American Church (in 1852) to meet in national councils. On the other hand it is true that in 1849 he had rejected the request of thirty French bishops for a national council, doubtless because he feared a resurgence of Gallicanism.[25]

Throughout his pontificate Pius IX, having taken stock of the reports submitted to him, did not hesitate to admonish bishops who showed themselves ineffective in the formation of their clergy and unable to enforce respect for Church discipline. Thus in 1853 he sent a very severe circular to seven bishops of the Grand Duchy of Tuscany: "The clergy do not have the ecclesiastical spirit, and from different Tuscan priests who have come to Rome in recent times I have learned, to my great sorrow, that a part of this clergy, through ignorance and immorality, far from edifying, actually gives great scandal and brings ruin on the work of God—to which it is called and which it has the obligation of upholding, defending, and propagating...."[26]

Along the same lines we should mention one of his most memorable initiatives, namely, the foundation in Rome of the *Pontificio Seminario Pio.* There already existed a Roman seminary for the clergy of Rome. While he was still in exile, Pius IX had had the idea of founding another seminary in the Eternal City which would receive the best candidates from the dioceses of the Papal States. It was placed under the protection of the Immaculate Virgin and St. Pius V (hence its name, the "Pius Seminary") and could accommodate a maximum of seventy students. Each of the sixty-nine dioceses of the Papal States could send one seminarian, but the Diocese of Senigallia (Pius IX's home diocese) had the privilege of sending two.

---

[24] Council of Trent, Session XXIV, Canon II, in *Les Conciles Ecuméniques* (Paris: Cerf, 1994), Pt. II, II, 1547.

[25] Delatte, *Dom Guéranger*, p.440.

[26] Circular of November 25, 1853, cited in Martina, II, 247.

The aim of this seminary was to train good priests in solid doctrine, who would not remain in Rome after their ordination but return to their diocese of origin as model priests. This seminary opened its doors in October 1853. It is significant that Pius IX chose a Dominican as its director: Fr. Francesco Gaude, the procurator-general of his Order, a convinced Thomist. When he left his post two years later, having been elevated to the cardinalate, Pius IX appointed another Dominican in his place, Fr. Giovanni Tommaso Tosa. Fr. Tosa was also a Thomist and the author of several treatises in dogmatic theology inspired by Aquinas.[27] These appointments are only two illustrations of different initiatives undertaken by Pius IX to promote the revival of Thomism.

This same month, October 1853, by an Apostolic Letter *Ad Piam Doctamque* the Pope laid down the rule and program of studies to be applied in the new seminary, but also in the other seminaries already existing in Rome.[28] The first two years were taken up with philosophy and the four following years with theology, followed by a further three years of civil and canon law. The study of Sacred Scripture, Church history, Greek, and Hebrew were also obligatory. The Pope intended that these norms, laid down for the Roman seminaries, should also be applied to the diocesan seminaries, or at least be the inspiration behind their curriculum.

Pius IX gave special encouragement to the founding of foreign seminaries in Rome. In the sixteenth and seventeenth centuries, since Protestantism had caused seminaries to close in many countries, seminaries had been founded in the Eternal City to provide for the future priests of these countries. Colleges for the Germans, Hungarians, English, Poles, Scots, and Irish had been established.

Under the pontificate of Pius IX there were further foundations of foreign seminaries, but this time it was done for different reasons. It was no longer a question of providing for the continuance of a Catholic clergy which could not be trained in the country of origin, but of assembling chosen candidates in the capital of Christendom to give them a formation in the "Roman" spirit.

This is very evident in the foundation of the French Seminary, one of the first foreign seminaries created under the pontificate of Pius IX. The project originated with a number of ultramontane bishops: Cardinal Gousset, Archbishop of Rheims; Msgr. Parisis, Bishop of Arras; and Msgr. Pie, Bishop of Poitiers. They asked the Congregation of the Holy Spirit to create a seminary in Rome where they could send "some of their subjects, in the hope of accelerating the movement in France towards the pure doctrines of the Roman Church and towards the closest possible union

---

[27] Piolanti, *Pio IX e la rinascita del tomismo*, pp.42-43.
[28] *Annales I*, 152, and Polverari, II, 97.

with the Holy See."[29] The French Seminary was founded in 1853, with
Fr. Lannurien as its first superior. A good number of its students would
become bishops in the years to come.

The same idea was behind the founding of the Latin American College in 1858, and the North American College in 1859. The first was due
to the initiative of a Chilean priest, Msgr. Eyzaguirre, encouraged by Pius
IX—who also gave material assistance.[30]

The second, by contrast, was a strictly Roman enterprise.[31] In 1853,
Pius IX had entrusted Msgr. Gaetano Bedini with a mission to the Catholics of the United States. It was he who suggested the creation of an
American seminary in Rome. The bishops of the United States were very
reticent, but the Congregation of Propaganda, supported by the Pope,
turned a blind eye to this and gave the necessary authorizations.

Re-establishment of the Hierarchy

The re-establishment of the episcopal hierarchy in England and the
Netherlands was one of the major events in the early 1850's. In both
countries the Church had been a victim of the Protestant Reformation
in the sixteenth century: the episcopal hierarchy had been officially proscribed. At the beginning of the nineteenth century the Catholics of these
countries, who were numerous but not a majority, existed as in a mission
territory, without canonically organized dioceses. It was Pius IX's determination, quite as much as the circumstances obtaining at the time, that allowed him to remedy a situation that placed English and Dutch Catholics
in a condition of inferiority.

In England, in 1829, the government had passed an "Emancipation
Act" which accorded Catholics their basic civil rights after several centuries in which they had been treated as pariahs. Some highly educated
people succeeded in raising the profile of Catholicism and giving it a hearing, notably Nicholas Wiseman, who had been trained in Rome and who,
in London in 1836, delivered his "Lectures on the Principal Doctrines
and Practices of the Catholic Church." That same year he founded the
Dublin Review.

Two other facts were favorable to the increase in the number of Catholics in England. In the years 1845-50 Ireland experienced a terrible fam-
ine due to a disease affecting the potato crop, which was the staple diet
of the Irish population at that time. The population dropped from eight

---

[29] Letter of the Superior General of the Congregation of the Holy Spirit introducing the
    future superior of the French Seminary to Cardinal Fransoni, cited by Joseph Lécuyer,
    "Le Père Lannurien," *Libermann 1802-1852* (various) (Paris: Cerf, 1988), p.771.
[30] In 1867 the Latin-American College became the *Collegio Pio Latino Americano* in
    gratitude for the financial aid that Pius IX had given it.
[31] Polverari, II, 97-101.

ITALY (1815-48)

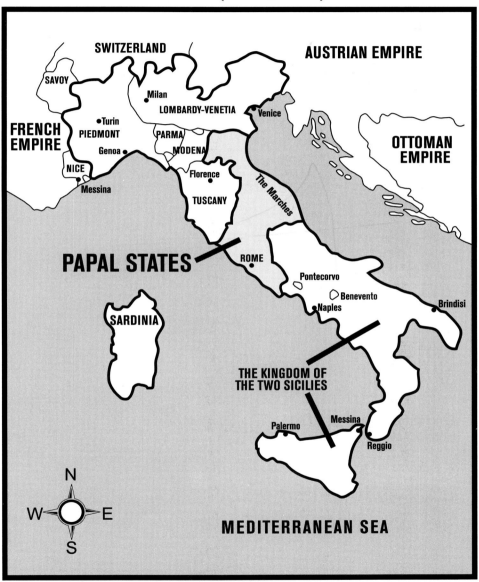

COUNT GIROLAMO MASTAI-FERRETTI, PIUS IX'S FATHER (1750-1833)

Scion of a noble family that had taken root in the port city of Senigallia, near Ancona, Italy, in the sixteenth century. He had five daughters and four sons, of which the future Pius IX would be the last.

CATERINA SOLAZZI, PIUS IX'S MOTHER

She attended Mass daily at the church of St. Martino and instilled in the future Pius IX a great devotion to Our Lady.

PIUS IX'S CRIB

The future Pius IX was born May 13, 1792. On the day of his birth, he was consecrated to the Virgin Mary by his mother. He had a special lifelong devotion to Our Lady of Loreto, whose shrine was only thirty miles from his birthplace. Once he had become Pope, one of his first acts was to renew his consecration to Our Lady.

THE FONT WHERE PIUS IX WAS BAPTIZED

Giovanni Maria was baptized on the day he was born in the Cathedral of St. Peter in Senigallia by his uncle Andrea. He was given seven Christian names, but custom was to be called by the first two.

THE FUTURE POPE PIUS IX AT AGE EIGHTEEN (1810)
Although he had already started his clerical studies, the Napoleonic upheavals forced him to abandon the cassock and return to Senigallia. He would resume his studies in 1814.

POPE PIUS IX (c.1860's)

POPE PIUS IX'S PRIVATE TRAIN ARRIVES AT VELLETRI (1863)

Velletri is one of the 120 sections of the province of Rome approximately 20 miles from the city of Rome. This predates the current Vatican railroad, which came into existence only as a result of the Lateran Treaty of 1929.

POPE PIUS IX GIVES A BLESSING TO PILGRIMS ASSEMBLED IN ST. PETER'S SQUARE (1869)

POPE PIUS IX AND HIS BROTHERS

Of Pius IX's eight brothers and sisters, the three eldest were the
boys pictured in this family cameo. From left to right: Gabriele,
Giuseppe, Gaetano. The family's fourth child was a girl who died
within a year, followed by the birth of four more girls, and then
Giovanni Maria. His papal crest is in the center of this memento.

POPE PIUS IX (1877)
This is one of the last known pictures of the Pope.
When this was taken, he would only have a year left before died.

ST. PETER'S SQUARE DURING THE REIGN OF POPE PIUS IX

FIRST VATICAN COUNCIL (1869-70)

A drawing of one of the sessions of the First Vatican Council, which defined
the dogmas of Papal Primacy and Papal Infallibility. It was suspended by the
invasion of Rome in 1870 and was never formally closed.

CARDINAL GIUSEPPE ANDREA BIZZARI (1802-77)

One of the presidents of the First Vatican Council, he was appointed head of the Congregation of Bishops and Regular Clergy in 1846 by Pope Pius IX. In addition, he played a prominent role in the Congregation for the Statue of Regulars. Dom Gueranger once complained that he was "all-powerful" in this capacity.

CARDINAL FILIPPO DE ANGELIS (1792-1877)

Cardinal de Angelis was the chief presiding cardinal of the First Vatican Council. In addition, he was Papal Nuncio to Switzerland and Portugal for a time.

CARDINAL LUIGI BILIO (1826-84)

Cardinal Bilio, a professor of theology, philosophy and canon law, was one of Pius IX's advisers. The Syllabus of Errors (1864) owes its formulation particularly to him. He would become the President of the Commission on Faith at the First Vatican Council.

CARDINAL LOUIS-EDOUARD-DÉSIRÉ PIE (1815-80)

Cardinal Pie was only Bishop of Chartres during the reign of Pius IX, yet he was already well-known for his uncompromising opposition to modernity and his prolific writing and speaking. Napoleon III once told him that it was not yet time for the rights of the Church, to which Cardinal Pie responded, "Sire, since the time has not come for Christ to reign, then the time has not come for government to last."

IGNATIUS VON SENESTREY (1858-1906)

Bishop of Regensburg in Germany, he was one of the most stringent defenders of papal infallibility at the First Vatican Council.

CARDINAL FILIPPO MARIA GUIDI (1815-79)

A Dominican cardinal, he was the first Latin-Rite prelate to challenge the doctrine of papal infallibility on the Council floor.

BARON WILHELM EMMANUEL VON KETTELER (1811-77)
Bishop of Mainz in Germany, one of the most prolific writers on contemporary social and economic questions. His 1864 book *The Labor Question and Christianity* formed the background to Pope Leo XIII's famous encyclical *Rerum Novarum*.

CARDINAL GIACOMO ANTONELLI (1806-76)
Secretary of State under Pope Pius IX. Arranged the Holy Father's flight to Gaeta and "was practically the temporal ruler of Rome until 1870, being charged by Pius IX with the care of public interests, that the Pontiff might devote himself more exclusively to his spiritual duties." (*Catholic Encyclopedia*)

FELIX ANTOINE PHILIBERT DUPANLOUP (1802-78)

Ordained at the age of twenty-three and consecrated a bishop in 1849 for Orléans. The *Catholic Encyclopedia* calls him "one of the ablest bishops of his day," receiving "numerous papal Briefs of encouragement and episcopal letters of approval from all parts of the world."

CARDINAL NICHOLAS PATRICK WISEMAN (1802-65)

The first Archbishop of Westminster after Pius IX's restoration of the hierarchy in England. When he began his work in England, there were 500 Catholic priests; when he finished, there were 1,500. The number of converts during the fifteen years (1850-65) he was Archbishop of Westminster had increased tenfold, and fifty-five monasteries had come into being.

CARDINAL HENRY EDWARD MANNING (1808-92)

Successor of Cardinal Wiseman as Archbishop of Westminster. He received several votes in the conclave that elected Pope Leo XIII and wrote much in defense of the decrees of the First Vatican Council.

CARDINAL JOHN HENRY NEWMAN (1801-90)

"Cardinal-Deacon of St. George in Velabro, divine, philosopher, man of letters, leader of the Tractarian Movement, and the most illustrious of English converts to the Church." (*Catholic Encyclopedia*)

JOHANN JOSEPH IGNAZ VON DÖLLINGER (1799-1890)

A German historian and priest who worked with Cardinal Wiseman in an attempt to strengthen Catholicism in England through the German clergy. He did not accept the First Vatican Council's definition of infallibility, was excommunicated, and became one of the founders of the schismatic "Old Catholic Church."

LOUIS VEUILLOT (1813-83)

One of the most brilliant of the Catholic counter-revolutionaries, he ran several journals, including *L'Univers*. Pius IX himself defended the journal when it came under attack by some of the French bishops. According to the *Catholic Encyclopedia*, his rule of conduct was: "Avoid factions of all kinds; we belong only to our Church and our country."

FÉLICITÉ ROBERT DE LAMENNAIS (1782-1854)

A French priest who founded a religious congregation for young intellectual clergy. Pope Gregory XVI's encyclical *Mirari Vos* is essentially directed against Lamennais's liberal ideas which were being spread primarily through *L'Avenir*, his magazine. Chief among his ideas was a false notion of freedom, which was popularized in clichés like "A free Church in a free State." He died unreconciled to the Church.

FR. JEAN-BAPTISTE LACORDAIRE, O.P. (1802-61)
A liberal Dominican Father who was "the greatest pulpit orator of the nineteenth century" according to the *Catholic Encyclopedia*. Collaborated with Félicité de Lamennais's journal *L'Avenir*.

THE COMTE DE MONTALEMBERT (1810-70)
Named *Civis Romanus* under Pius IX in 1850 for his efforts to secure freedom for Catholic education in France. Nevertheless, he was at odds with characters such as Cardinal Pie and Louis Veuillot for his defense of religious liberty and his association with Lamennais and Lacordaire.

GIUSEPPE GARIBALDI (1807-82)

Known as "the hero of two worlds" for his military campaigns in South America and Europe, he fought in the *Risorgimento* for Italian unity. Attempted to attack the Papal States in 1862 but was prohibited by fellow Italian soldiers from achieving success. He remains one of Italy's national heroes.

COUNT CAMILLO BENSO DI CAVOUR (1810-61)

Founder of the *Risorgimento* and Prime Minister of Piedmont-Sardinia. He lived to see the foundation of the Kingdom of Italy, but died before Venetia and Rome completed his territorial goals.

DIPLOMATIC CHESS

This cartoon appeared in a contemporary newspaper during the *Kulturkampf* of Otto von Bismarck. As Bismarck and Pius IX play on the chessboard of Europe, note that the Pope's chesspieces are labeled "Encyclical" and "Syllabus," both references to the weapons used by the Holy Father.

OTTO VON BISMARCK (1815-98)

One of the most famous European statesmen of the nineteenth century. Duke of Lauenberg, Prime Minister of Prussia from 1862-90, and Chancellor of the German Empire from 1871 onwards, he sought the unification of Germany. His attempts to minimize the influence of Catholics in his realm through the *Kulturkampf* put him at odds with Pope Pius IX.

KING VICTOR EMMANUEL II (1820-78)

In 1861, he became the first king of Italy (as a united nation), an office he held until his death. He was the public face of the *Risorgimento*, and fought a long battle with Pius IX over the seizure of the Papal States in 1870.

POPE PIUS IX IN THE ANTECHAMBER (1862)

The antechamber was behind the throne room at the Vatican. The clergy in this picture, such as Secretary of State Cardinal Antonelli (circled), would have waited here as the Holy Father gave audiences.

PIUS IX WITH FRANCESCO II (APRIL, 1862)

Francesco was the King of the Two Sicilies and much opposed to
Italian unification although a cousin of Victor Emmanuel. He fled
to Paris with his wife after Rome fell, and died in Austria in 1894.

THE CHARETTE BROTHERS

The members of this
family volunteered for the
papal army and distinguished
themselves in battle (1861).

GENERAL CHRISTOPHER LEON DE LA MORICIÈRE

La Moricière was placed in charge of the papal troops on April 1, 1860. Although a commanding and inspiring leader, he was forced to surrender later that year after his troops were forced out of the Ancona citadel.

PAPAL OFFICERS

These men display the Medal of Castelfidardo (1861). Castelfidardo was the site of the defeat of the papal forces ("Zouaves") in the fall of 1860.

PAPAL VOLUNTEER SOLDIERS RECEIVE
A BLESSING FROM POPE PIUS IX (1866)
This photograph was taken at Rocca di Papa, an area in the province of Rome.

PAPAL SOLDIERS AT THE CASTLE OF MENTANA (1867)
Contrary to the defeat at Castelfidardo, Mentana was the occasion
of victory for the papal army. Here papal troops defeated
Garibaldi's forces, which surrendered November 4, 1867.

HERMANN KANZLER (1827-88)

Kanzler replaced Msgr. de Mérode in October 1865 at the department of Ministry of War. When Italian troops finally entered the city of Rome (see picture below), Kanzler was one of the generals of the papal army.

THE INVASION OF ROME (SEPT. 20, 1870)

Italian troops invaded Rome, ending Holy Mother Church's temporal power. Although outnumbered, the papal troops fought valiantly but without hope of success. Afterwards Pius IX was known as "prisoner of the Vatican." This was the occasion of Victor Emmanuel II declaring himself king of Italy.

THE TOMB OF POPE PIUS IX

Pope Pius IX died February 7, 1878, and was buried in St. Peter's Basilica. In 1881, with the funeral convoy under threat of attack by revolutionaries, his body was moved to the Basilica of St. Lawrence Outside the Walls.

On April 4, 2000, "a delegation of bishops and monsignors in full regalia arrived at Rome's Basilica of St. Lawrence Outside the Walls. They descended to the sixth-century cathedral's crypt and were led to a white stone tomb. A casket was opened for them. At this point, wrote Monsignor Carlo Liberati of the Vatican's Congregation for the Causes of Saints, 'there was a moment of profound and intense commotion.' The body within, that of nineteenth-century Pope Pius IX, was 'almost perfectly conserved'" (*Time*, Sept. 4, 2000).

The April 2000 exhumation was preparatory for Pius IX's beatification. His body was transferred to a clear crystal casket (above) to encourage Catholics to venerate his remains. He was jointly beatified with Pope John XXIII by Pope John Paul II on September 3, 2000.

to five million: hundreds of thousands of Irish people died of starvation and typhus, and hundreds of thousands more emigrated, primarily to the United States, England, and Wales.

This sudden influx of Irish Catholics came in addition to the movement of conversion which was penetrating the Anglican Church. The most eminent figure of what was called the "Oxford Movement" was the Anglican clergyman John Henry Newman, who converted in 1845.[32] Subsequently he was received by Pius IX in Rome; the latter encouraged him to establish, in England, a Congregation of priests directly inspired by the Oratory of St. Philip Neri.[33] Several Protestant clergymen would enter this Congregation. Newman's conversion was preceded by that of three of his friends, but it was estimated that "more than three hundred conversions resulted from Newman's, and this movement would not cease henceforth."[34]

The English Church had been reduced to the level of a "mission," governed by eight vicars apostolic, but by the middle of the nineteenth century England had 700,000 Catholics in a population of 18 million, the churches and clergy were too few, and the "mission" status was an anachronism. The vicars apostolic judged it appropriate for a regular hierarchy to be established in England: resident bishops would have more authority over faithful and clergy, who were sometimes embroiled in division, and could pursue more effectively the great movement of apostolate and conversion which had been going on for some decades. In 1847 they commissioned their most influential member, Wiseman, to take up negotiations with Rome.[35] The announcement of the decision was delayed by objections made by certain English Catholics, supported by an English prelate of the Curia, Cardinal Acton, and, most of all, by the Revolution of 1848 and the Pope's Neapolitan exile.

Finally, on September 29, 1850, by the apostolic letter *Universalis Ecclesiae Regendae,* Pius IX re-established the episcopal hierarchy in England by instituting an archdiocese (at Westminster) and eight dioceses. On the 30th, Wiseman was created cardinal in a secret consistory and, shortly thereafter, Archbishop of Westminster. On October 7, the new

---

[32] He gave the following reasons for his conversion: "It is based on my study of the history of the early Church. I believe that the Church of Rome is in all points the continuation of the early Church....'They differ in doctrine and discipline as a child differs from the adult, not otherwise. I see no middle way between denying Christianity and embracing the Church of Rome," Letter to Richard Westmacoo, July 11, 1845, published in Cardinal Newman, *Choix de lettres* (Paris: Téqui, 1990), p.101.

[33] Letter to Mrs. Bodwen, February 21 & 23, 1847, in Newman, pp.112-13.

[34] Mourret, *Histoire génénerale de l'Eglise,* VIII, 230.

[35] The re-establishment of the hierarchy in England is discussed by Mourret, *op. cit.,* VIII, 432-36; Aubert, pp.70-71; Martina, I, 463-65.

cardinal addressed a pastoral letter to the English faithful expressing his great joy: "The great work is accomplished," he wrote; "Catholic England has once again found her orbit in the religious firmament, from whence her light had long vanished."

The Pope's decision and Wiseman's triumphalism were not well received by English Protestant opinion. The *Times* spoke of "the impudence of Pius IX" and the Prime Minister, Lord Russell, denounced "the Pope's aggression against English Protestantism." Effigies of Pius IX and Wiseman were burned in the streets of London. Back in England, Wiseman succeeded in calming public opinion by issuing an eloquent *Appeal to the English People* and giving a series of lectures.

One consequence of this agitation was to hasten the conversion to Catholicism of an Anglican clergyman who was to become one of the eminent figures of English Catholicism: Henry Manning. He was converted in 1850, and from 1854 he was Cardinal Wiseman's very effective auxiliary at Westminster. Pius IX, to show his support and admiration for English Catholicism which, according to a phrase of Newman's, was experiencing a "second spring," conferred the cardinal's hat on Manning. Manning would be the fervent defender of the Ultramontane cause in England and, at the First Vatican Council, an ardent defender of papal infallibility.

The re-establishment of the Catholic hierarchy in the Netherlands was undertaken for the same reasons, but took place in entirely different circumstances. Here Catholics represented a third of the population, *i.e.*, more than a million faithful.[36] They were found primarily in the two southern provinces of Limburg and North Brabant; in the other provinces they were a minority. While the Catholics were governed only by vicars apostolic, the Jansenists, who had set up a parallel Church at the beginning of the eighteenth century, possessed two dioceses even though they were a hundred times smaller in numbers. A concordat signed between the Holy See and the Dutch government in 1827 had envisaged the creation of two dioceses, Amsterdam and 's-Hertogenbosch. However, this had remained a dead letter. On the basis of the liberalizing revision of the constitution by King William II in 1848, Dutch Catholics campaigned for more liberties.

In part, the new constitution granted their wish since, for the first time in the country's history, it was recognized that "all religious groups are equal before the law" and that "every religious society may regulate its own internal affairs." In the eyes of many Catholics and the majority of the clergy, the re-establishment of dioceses in the Netherlands was seen

---

[36] The question is discussed, on the basis of Dutch studies, in Aubert, pp.63-67, and on the basis of Archives of the Holy See in Martina, II, 693-98.

to be the normal extension of this legal emancipation. The head of the Belgian Catholics, Cardinal Sterckx, Archbishop of Malines, supported this request in Rome.

Some authorities in the Curia showed themselves hesitant: recalling the Jansenist crisis which had found strong support in these regions in the seventeenth and eighteenth centuries, they were afraid that local bishops would prove too independent. The Pope, however, acceded to the request. As in the preceding case of England, Pius IX showed himself to be determined, and even bold. Looking forward to a complete restoration of the Dutch episcopal hierarchy, he did not hesitate to denounce the 1827 concordat, considering it to be nugatory on the grounds that it had never been applied. After fruitless attempts to negotiate with the government, the Congregation of Propaganda and Pius IX took the decision to act unilaterally. On March 4, 1853, the Pope signed the apostolic letter *Ex Qua Die* erecting an archbishopric in Utrecht and four other dioceses. This constituted an explicit gesture of continuity with Dutch Catholicism's historic past, the ancient metropolitan See of Utrecht, founded by St. Willibrord, regaining its primacy, in spite of the fact that Catholics there were in very small numbers.

The following month bishops were designated for the new dioceses. The decision was very ill received by the Dutch Protestants and the Jansenists. This wave of protests against the Roman decision and against the government—which was accused of being weak—has gone into history as the "April Movement": there were public meetings, press articles, preaching against Catholicism in the Protestant churches, petitions to the King and Parliament with a view to preventing the erection of dioceses. In Utrecht, the capital of Dutch Jansenism and a hotbed of Protestantism, the petition received 200,000 signatures.

In September, however, having hesitated for some time, the Dutch government officially recognized the new bishops. It had obtained some concessions: the diocesan bishops would take an oath of fidelity to the King, and the Bishops of Utrecht and of Haarlem would not reside permanently in their cities. The restoration of the Catholic hierarchy in the Netherlands opened a new era in the history of the Dutch Church. Many Dutchmen would be found among the papal soldiery.

CHAPTER 10

THE POPE OF THE IMMACULATE CONCEPTION

The year 1854 was one of the happiest of Pius IX's pontificate: it saw the proclamation of the dogma of the Immaculate Conception. No doubt, there were worrying signs. A number of states were hindering the Church's mission by failing to respect the concordats that had been signed or by adopting hostile legislation or administrative orders. On the eve of this year, which was to be so important in the history of Catholic dogma and piety, Pius IX gave an allocution in which he reviewed the "cruel misfortunes" which were afflicting the Church in different countries: the German Grand Duchy of Baden, Haïti, Piedmont-Sardinia.[1]

In the Kingdom of Piedmont-Sardinia the Pope deplored the laicist policies we have already discussed.

In Haïti, the pretensions of the new political authorities, totally lacking in experience, under the Emperor Faustin I, as well as the negligence and immorality of a large portion of the indigenous clergy ("who could not suffer being exhorted to a stricter manner of life, and one worthy of the sacred ministry") had compelled the Holy See's representative to leave the island. Some years later, however, following a change of government and regime, the situation would settle down and it would be possible to sign a worthwhile concordat with the Holy See.

The incidents occurring in the Grand Duchy of Baden, which the Pope so deplored, were but the beginnings of a much wider movement. In December 1853 Pius IX was faced with the refusal of four German Rhineland States (The Grand Duchy of Hessen-Darmstadt, the Duchy of Nassau, the Kingdom of Wurtemberg, and the Grand Duchy of Baden) to grant what the Catholic bishops of this ecclesiastical province had collectively requested, namely, liberty to create seminaries and Catholic schools, and unfettered administration of the Church's property.

After their respective governments had rejected their requests, Msgr. Ketteler, Bishop of Mainz, and Msgr. Vicari, Archbishop of Freiburg, protested and decided to ignore the administrative ban. The Baden government tried to intimidate the faithful by proceeding to arrest people, including members of the clergy.

---

[1]   Allocution *In Apostolicae Sedis Fastigio*, December 19, 1853, in *Annales I*, 153-56.

This explains the public encouragement given by Pius IX in the allocution to which we have referred: "Rejoicing in and justly praising this admirable constancy in supporting the Church's cause, We exhort Our venerable brother the Archbishop of Freiburg and his courageous brothers in office not to let themselves be dismayed, but to draw new strength from the virtue of the Lord, who has promised to be with His Church through all time, and who has prepared palm and crown for those who fight the good fight."

A few months after this papal encouragement, the affair became embittered under the influence of Bismarck. The latter, who had become head of the Prussian government some years before, was conducting a policy aiming to unify the different German states under the domination of Prussia. For him, "Catholicism is synonymous with Prussia's enemy."[2]

At the Diet of Frankfurt, in the first months of 1854, Bismarck succeeded in imposing his views on other German States: the Catholic movement was a menace, and no demonstration should be tolerated if it were hostile to the civil authorities. Furthermore, on May 19 of this year, measures were taken against the Archbishop of Freiburg: Msgr. Vicari, accused of having incited people to disobedience, was placed under house arrest and forbidden to communicate with his clergy.

At the same time, Bismarck broke off the negotiations for a concordat between Prussia and the Holy See. Although concordats continued to be made with some small German states in the following years, and although German Protestantism's great battle with Catholicism did not take place for nearly two decades, these events of 1854 can really be seen as a kind of distant prelude to the *Kulturkampf*.

In pronouncing the dogmatic definition of the Immaculate Conception of the Virgin on December 8 that year, Pius IX was conscious of the temporal context of such a definition. He was not simply giving the sanction of his authority to a very ancient belief that was now an article of faith, but also equipping the Church with an additional weapon. In the spiritual warfare he and the whole Church had to wage against philosophical and theological errors, against laicism and anti-clericalism, the invocation of the Virgin Mary was a powerful aid.

In the Bull containing the dogmatic definition, Pius IX explicitly put his trust in the Mother of God, that she would remove "all obstacles" and vanquish "all errors":

> We repose Our entire and absolute confidence in the certainty of Our hopes: namely, the Blessed Virgin who, utterly beautiful and immaculate, has crushed the venomous head of the cruel serpent and brought salvation to the world. She who is the praise of prophets and apostles, the honor of

[2] Letter from Bismarck to Leopold von Gerlach, January 20, 1854, cited in Mourret, *Histoire générale de l'Eglise*, VIII, 411.

martyrs, the joy and crown of all the saints; she who is the sure refuge and invincible helper of all that are in peril, the world's all-powerful mediatrix and conciliatrix with her unique Son, the glory, splendor, and safeguard of the holy Church, has always destroyed all heresies; she has snatched away faithful peoples and nations from the greatest calamities and from ills of all kinds, and has delivered Us from the innumerable perils that have assailed Us.

By her powerful patronage the Blessed Virgin will ensure that, all obstacles being removed, all errors conquered, the Holy Catholic Church, our Mother, will grow stronger and flourish more and more every day among all peoples and all countries, reigning from one sea to the other, from river-banks to the earth's extremities, fully enjoying peace, tranquillity, and liberty, so that the guilty may obtain pardon, the sick a remedy, the weak strength of soul, the down-hearted consolation, and those in peril succor; so that all who are in error, seeing the darkness of their minds dispersed, may return to the path of truth and justice, where there is only one flock and one shepherd.[3]

Towards the Definition

We saw how, in exile in Gaeta, Pius IX had officially initiated the process leading to the dogmatic definition of the Immaculate Conception of the Virgin Mary. After having taken the advice of a first commission of cardinals and theologians on the opportuneness and legitimacy of such a dogmatic definition, he had issued the Encyclical *Ubi Primum,* in which he asked the advice of the bishops of the entire world. The result of this first major consultation of the worldwide episcopate is well known.[4] The replies sent in to Rome were published in ten volumes: of 593 bishops who replied to the Pope in writing, only 8 thought that a belief of this kind could not be defined theologically (one of these was Msgr. Sibour, Archbishop of Paris) and 2 were unsure. More numerous were those who, while they accorded faith to this belief, thought its dogmatic definition inopportune (35 bishops, including Cardinal Pecci, Archbishop of Perugia, the future Leo XIII) or were uncertain about it (48 bishops).

Thus, the vast majority of bishops were in favor of the dogma being proclaimed. There is nothing surprising in this quasi-unanimity. In fact, the belief that, from her conception, the Virgin Mary was preserved from all sin, is very ancient. It is expressed in the liturgy first and foremost. The East has celebrated the Immaculate Conception ever since the eighth century.[5] In the West, in Rome, and in many European monasteries, this

---

3   Complete text of the Bull *Ineffabilis Deus* in *Annales I,* 172-80.
4   Bernardo Giuliani, "La definizione dogmatica," *L'Osservatore Romano,* December 5, 1873, and "Gli atti di Pio IX per la definizione dommatica dell'Immacolata Concezione," *L'Osservatore Romano,* December 8, 1888.
5   Gerardo Cardaropoli, "L'elaborazione teologica," *L'Osservatore Romano,* December 7, 1973.

celebration is attested a little later, c.750-800, even if the traditional date of the feast, December 8, was not fixed until the end of the eleventh century, in England.[6]

While this belief did subsequently encounter some opposition from certain great doctors of the Church, such as St. Bernard and St. Thomas Aquinas, it had illustrious defenders in the whole of Christendom. The Franciscan Order was one of these from its very beginning. In 1477 Sixtus IV, a Franciscan pope, approved the composition of an Office and Mass in honor of the Immaculate Conception. Twenty years later Robert Gaguin, Minister General of the Trinitarian Order, caused the Sorbonne's eighty-two doctors in theology to resolve that "no one henceforth shall be registered at the University unless he takes an oath to believe and defend the Immaculate Conception."[7] In 1617, Paul V prohibited those opposed to the Immaculate Conception from defending their theories publicly. Five years later Gregory XV extended this prohibition to private discussions also.

Finally, some decades before Pius IX's dogmatic definition, something happened to throw supernatural light on this belief. In 1830, a nun of the Sisters of Charity, Catherine Labouré, witnessed three apparitions of the Virgin Mary.[8] On the second occasion, November 7, the Virgin Mary appeared crushing a snake under her feet. She was carrying a golden globe of the earth surmounted by a little cross, and rays of light streamed from her hands. She was surrounded by an inscription which read, "O Mary, conceived without sin, pray for us who have recourse to Thee." Some moments later Catherine Labouré saw the reverse side of this image, showing the letter M surmounted by a little cross and, at the bottom, the Hearts of Jesus and Mary. Then the Virgin said, "A medal must be struck according to this pattern, and those who wear the indulgenced medal and devoutly say this brief prayer will enjoy the very special protection of the Mother of God."

When the apparitions had come to an end the Archbishop of Paris, Msgr. de Quélen, gave authorization for the medal to be struck according to the Virgin's demand, although he did not prejudge the nature of the vision. The first medals were struck in June 1832. Under the invocation of the Virgin "conceived without sin," many miracles of healing and of conversion were reported. When Catherine Labouré died in 1876 one billion Miraculous Medals had been distributed to all countries.

---

[6]   Dom Bernard Billet, "Culte et dévotion à la Vierge Marie dans l'ordre monastique aux VIII.-IX. siècles," *Esprit et Vie*, May 11, 1972, pp.299-303.

[7]   Charles Molette, "Une enquête sur la devotion à Marie en France dans les Congrégations féminines aux XVII. et XVIII. s.," *De Cultu mariano saeculis XVII et XVIII* (Rome: Pontificia Academia Mariana Internationalis, 1988), VI, 264-65.

[8]   René Laurentin, *Vie authentique de Catherine Labouré*, 2 vols. (Paris: Desclée De Brouwer, 1980).

Thus, Pius IX's proclamation of the dogma is framed by two apparitions of the Virgin that expressly recall the article of faith: the apparition of "Mary conceived without sin" in Paris in 1830, followed by the apparition of "The Immaculate Conception" in Lourdes in 1858.

The practically unanimous response of the bishops of the whole world had strengthened Pius IX in his determination finally to define a belief that was so universally held. Yet, showing a constant trait of character, he was not over-hasty in taking action. It was six years and six months between the institution of the first consultative theological commission and the Bull containing the dogmatic definition. No less than four different commissions, of cardinals and theologians, examined the question from three points of view: Could the belief be defined? Would such a definition be opportune? And what should be the terms of the definition?[9]

A draft definition had been drawn up in 1850, at the Pope's request, by the Jesuit Fr. Giovanni Perrone. This first text was submitted to sixteen theological consultors; seven further versions followed. Pius IX was convinced of the revealed character of the doctrine of the Immaculate Conception because it had been an object of faith in the universal Church for many centuries. However, he also wanted the definition to give a precise answer to the theological objections of the doctrine's opponents.

For a long time these objections had been of two kinds.[10] Firstly, there is no explicit statement in the New Testament that the Virgin Mary was exempt from original sin. Secondly, to accord an individual privilege of this kind to the Virgin Mary is to contradict the doctrine that says that the universality of the salvation brought by Jesus Christ corresponds to a universality of human sin since Adam.

Dom Guéranger played an important role in this preparatory work. The restorer of the Abbey of Solesmes was valued by Pius IX as one of the most enthusiastic advocates of a return, on the part of the French dioceses, to the Roman liturgy. He asked him to study the question. In April 1850 Dom Guéranger completed an important *Memorandum on the Immaculate Conception,* which the Pope greatly appreciated.[11] Then, at the end of 1851, Pius IX summoned Dom Guéranger to Rome.[12] He had decided to appoint him consultor of the Congregation of Rites, but also consultor of the Congregation of the Index, because he had a high regard for his intellectual qualities and doctrinal soundness.

[9] Giuliani, "Gli atti di Pio IX."
[10] Cardaropoli, "L'elaborazione teologica."
[11] Delatte, *Dom Guéranger*, p.456.
[12] An account of this long stay is given in Robert, *Dom Guéranger chez Pie IX.* For the draft cf. Dom Georges Frénaud, "Dom Guéranger et le projet de bulle *Quemadmodum Ecclesia*," *Virgo Immaculata* (Rome: Academia Mariana Internationalis, 1956), II, 337-86.

During his stay in Rome Dom Guéranger was received in audience by the Pope on several occasions and was asked to assist in various doctrinal tasks. He was asked to revise his *Memorandum* and then, in January 1852, he was entrusted with the task of writing the Bull containing the dogmatic definition. As we have seen, Fr. Perrone, and subsequently Fr. Passaglia, another Jesuit, had already produced drafts that were assessed as unsatisfactory. This time a Benedictine was undertaking the task. He worked together with his immediate predecessor, and on January 30, a new draft Bull was presented to the Pope. Pius IX was satisfied with the text as a whole, but required a good number of emendations. Ultimately, on February 27, he asked for the entire draft to be recast. What he now wanted was that the Bull giving the dogmatic definition should include a solemn condemnation of the great contemporary theological and philosophical errors. An article had appeared in the *Civiltà Cattolica,* suggesting that the proclamation of the dogma should be linked to a condemnation of errors.

Dom Guéranger was received by the Pope on 29th. He strongly voiced his opposition to such a project and suggested that two separate texts should be composed. He was unaware that it was the Pope himself who had worked together with the Jesuits on the article in the *Civiltà Cattolica.* Pius IX explained to Dom Guéranger that he greatly wished to "link the proclamation of the privilege of the Immaculate Conception with another proclamation, namely, the power of the One who has overthrown all heresies: *Gaude, Maria Virgo: cunctas haereses SOLA interemisti in universo mundo!*" Then he told him that he had had "a kind of interior movement" for some days, impelling him to link the two proclamations. Dom Guéranger bowed in submission.

Finally, after the Abbot of Solesmes had left Rome, his idea of separating the two things by composing two different constitutions was taken up. The solemn condemnation of errors was postponed (this would be the Syllabus, ten years to the day after the proclamation of the dogma of the Immaculate Conception), and work got under way on a new draft of the dogmatic definition. The Bull's definitive text was not ready until four days before the solemn definition, and after Pius IX had intervened personally to have certain expressions corrected.

The Proclamation

It was Pius IX's wish that this proclamation should be made with arresting solemnity, in the presence of the biggest possible number of bishops, in order clearly to manifest the assent of the universal Church. On December 8, 1854, fifty-three cardinals, forty-three archbishops, and ninety-nine bishops took part in the impressive ceremony of proclama-

tion. It was the first time since the Council of Trent in the sixteenth century that so many bishops coming from different continents were assembled
around the pope. Several times, in the years to come, Pius IX would repeat
these assemblies of the world's episcopate around the pontifical throne, to
illustrate the authority of the Sovereign Pontiff and re-affirm the Church's
unity.

The proclamation of the new dogma took place during a solemn
Mass celebrated in St. Peter's Basilica in the presence of 50,000 faithful.
After the Gospel had been read, the *Veni Creator* was sung to invoke the
Holy Spirit's assistance, and then, not without emotion, the Pope read the
defining Decree:

> ...We, by the authority of our Lord Jesus Christ, of the blessed Apos-
> tles Peter and Paul, and by Our own authority declare, pronounce, and
> define that the doctrine which holds that the Most Blessed Virgin Mary
> from the first moment of her conception was, by the singular grace and
> privilege of Almighty God, in view of the merits of Christ Jesus the Savior
> of the human race, preserved immune from all stain of original sin, is
> revealed by God and is therefore firmly and constantly to be believed by
> all the faithful.
>
> Wherefore, if any persons shall dare to think, which God forbid, oth-
> erwise than has been defined by Us, let them clearly know that they are
> condemned by their own judgment, that they have suffered shipwreck to
> their faith and fallen from the unity of the Church, that they thenceforth
> subject themselves *ipso facto* to the penalties provided by law if they shall
> dare to express their views in speech or writing or in any other way.[13]

Those present observed how, in reading this decree, Pius IX seemed
very moved. Three years later he himself referred to this occasion when
speaking to a group of nuns:

> When I began to read the dogmatic decree I felt that my voice could
> not make itself heard by the immense crowd filling the Vatican Basilica;
> but when I got to the formula of definition, God gave such strength and
> supernatural vigor to his Vicar's voice that it resounded throughout the
> entire Basilica. As for me, I was so profoundly impressed by such divine
> assistance that I had to break off for a while in order to give free rein to
> my tears. Furthermore, while God was proclaiming the dogma by the
> mouth of his Vicar, God himself gave my mind such a clear and extensive
> understanding of the incomparable purity of the Most Holy Virgin...that
> no language could describe it. My soul remained flooded with ineffable
> delights that are not of this world, and which can only be found in heav-
> en....[14]

---

[13] Original Latin text in H. Denzinger–A. Schönmetzer, *Enchiridion Symbolorum,
Definitionum et Declarationum de Rebus Fidei et Morum*, 36th ed. (Freiburg: Herder,
1976), pp.561-62; hereafter, Denzinger-Schönmetzer.
[14] *Summarium* §79.

Immediately following the reading of the dogmatic Decree, Pius IX
authorized the publication of the Bull *Ineffabilis Deus,* which took up the
dogmatic definition and provided it with very thorough theological arguments.

On the evening of that memorable day Rome was lit up with the
customary illuminations for very special occasions. "The city is literally a
city of light," one witness reported:

> There is not a balcony, not a window, not a garret without its lights.
> The city's great arteries, the Corso, the Via Papale, Ripetto, are so many
> rivers of light; the public squares, the monuments and churches are all
> illuminated. The Capitol sparkles, and, in the name of the people of
> Rome, open-air bands salute the triumph of the Queen of Heaven, who
> is also the Queen of the Church and of Rome. Everywhere there are pic-
> tures and images of Mary, inscriptions in her honor; everywhere one sees
> the watchword: *Maria, sine labe originali concepta.* An immense crowd
> streams through the city; the entire population is in the streets, on the
> squares, and most of all at St. Peter's, its dome raising a sparkling diadem
> over the city.[15]

Soon a huge column would be erected on the Piazza d'Espagna to
commemorate this dogmatic proclamation. Four colossal statues of Mo-
ses, David, Ezekiel, and Isaiah surround the pedestal, which is adorned
with two bas-reliefs, one representing Joseph, asleep, being instructed by
an angel concerning the mystery of the Incarnation, and the other representing Pius IX in the act of proclaiming the dogma of the Immaculate
Conception. Elsewhere in the world other monuments would be erected
in honor of the event: churches would be dedicated to the Immaculate;
there would be statues (*e.g.,* the immense statue of the Virgin erected on
the top of the Puy mountains) and commemorative plaques.

Some months later, on April 12, 1855, something very dramatic occurred that struck Pius IX as a supernatural confirmation of the Immaculate's almighty power: while he was receiving the homage of the 110
seminarians of the College of Propaganda Fidei in the Monastery of St.
Agnes, the floor of the hall where everyone was assembled gave way,
throwing many cardinals and prelates and a score or two of young clerics
into the resulting chasm. Pius IX invoked the Madonna, crying out, "Immaculate Virgin, come to their aid!" Against all hope and in spite of the
entangled mass of beams and stones under which some of them had been
trapped, all were found to be safe and sound, apart from a few who had
slight wounds. The Pope immediately went to the nearby basilica to sing a
thanksgiving *Te Deum.* Subsequently he would often refer to this episode
as an authentic miracle.[16]

---

[15] Huguet, *L'Esprit de Pie IX,* p.45.
[16] Cf. *Summarium,* §81, and Polverari, II, 129-31.

It is worth noting that those who had been opposed to the definition of the dogma no longer raised objections once the proclamation had
been made. Among the twenty French bishops who were present in Rome
on December 8 was Msgr. Sibour; on returning to Paris he took measures against those Gallican theologians who obstinately refused to accept
the new dogma.[17] As for Döllinger and other Munich theologians, they
only made their opposition public after the First Vatican Council had
produced the definition of a new dogma, Papal Infallibility, which they
likewise rejected.

Finally it should be pointed out that this dogmatic proclamation by
Pius IX was given heavenly confirmation, as it were, four years later, by the
apparition of the Virgin Mary at Lourdes.[18] In the year 1858, the Virgin
Mary appeared nineteen times to an illiterate adolescent girl, Bernadette
Soubirous. It was only at her fourteenth apparition, on March 25, that
the "Lady," as Bernadette called her, revealed her identity. She said, in
the patois of Lourdes: *"Que soy era Immaculada Councepciou"* (I am the
Immaculate Conception). Bernadette did not know this term, and could
not have invented it. For the parish priest, Fr. Peyramale, it was this specifically dogmatic title (though in an unusual formulation) that assured
him that it was really the Virgin Mary who was appearing to Bernadette.
After rigorous investigation Msgr. Laurence, Bishop of Tarbes, published
an official letter affirming the supernatural character of the apparitions
that had taken place in Lourdes.

Shadows and Lights

Pius IX wanted to take the opportunity of the presence of so many
bishops, who had come to Rome from all over the world, to draw attention to certain errors that needed to be countered. Instead of the solemn
condemnation he had originally envisaged, he gave an important allocution, *Singulari Quadam,* which in many points is reminiscent of his
first encyclical.[19] It was delivered in a consistory on December 9 in the
presence of the cardinals and some 150 bishops currently in Rome. Here
the Pope said that the Church's main enemies where "those belonging to
secret societies which, in league with one another by a criminal pact, stop
at nothing in their attempts to overthrow and destroy the Church and
the State, even going so far as to despise and violate all rights." The Pope
went on to detail the three main grave errors which must be combated:

---

[17] Dom Delatte reports: "The Sovereign Pontiff had taken a little malicious revenge
against the Archbishop of Paris, Msgr. Sibour, giving him the signal honor of holding
a candlestick during the pontifical Mass..." (p.554).

[18] In addition to the many works by René Laurentin, cf. Anne Bernet, *Bernadette
Soubirous* (Paris: Perrin, 1994).

[19] Complete Latin-French text in *Annales I*, 307-26.

the governments which want to subordinate the Church to the State, the authors who want to subordinate religion to reason, and, finally, the view that all religions lead to salvation.

On this last point Pius IX recalled the Church's teaching and the meaning to be given to the traditional dictum "Outside the Church no salvation":

> The Faith commands us to hold that outside the Apostolic Roman Church no one can be saved. She is the sole Ark of salvation, and anyone who has not entered her will perish in the waters of the Flood. On the other hand it is equally to be held as certain that ignorance of the true religion, if it is invincible, is not culpable in God's eyes. But who will dare to assume the right to set out the limits of such an ignorance, taking account of the different conditions of peoples, countries, minds, and the infinite multiplicity of human affairs?

The allocution also contains more openly positive assessments: "Generally, the perversity of unbelievers inspires others with horror; the human mind has a certain tendency to seek religion and faith," and the Pope noted "a kind of progress towards the truth." Considering the decades yet to come and the "progress" that would be made by unbelief and materialism and also by the growing number of rationalistic critics of Christianity, we can regard Pius IX as being exaggeratedly optimistic here.

Nonetheless, certain facts seemed to justify the Pope's stance. Even if, in the Kingdom of Piedmont-Sardinia, 1855 was marked by the famous "Law on the Convents" to which we have already referred, which showed that Cavour was intending to pursue his policy of laicization and secularization, hostile to the Church,[20] other events gave the Pope some comfort, for instance, the signing of a concordat with Austria, which took place on August 18 that year.

Ever since the eighteenth century the Habsburg Empire had been noted for its policy of subordinating the Church to the State (called "Josephism" after the name of the Emperor Joseph II who had instigated it). This policy had resulted, from 1780 onwards, in the closing of certain religious houses, the introduction of civil marriage, and the subjection of the Church to State administration. Franz-Joseph, Emperor since 1848, had decided to break with this policy. In 1853 he agreed to negotiations being opened with the Holy See.

Pius IX was gladdened by this positive state of mind on the part of the Emperor, and he wanted the Austrian concordat to be a model con-

---

[20] During the parliamentary debate on this law, Victor Emmanuel II was visited by successive calamities: January 1855 saw the deaths of his mother, Maria Teresa, and his wife, Maria-Adelaide; in February his brother Ferdinando died, and then his last-born son. Catholics saw in this a divine protest against the law, which was finally adopted on May 29.

cordat, faithful, in its content, to the demands of Catholic teaching. The Redemptorist Fr. Rauscher, the Emperor's former teacher, was the soul of these negotiations. His appointment as Archbishop of Vienna in 1853 seemed to predict a satisfactory understanding between the two parties. Indeed, after two-and-a-half years of negotiations, on August 18, 1855, a few months after Pius IX's optimistic hopes at the consistory to which we have referred, the concordat signed between Rome and Austria brought him complete satisfaction, since it recognized "the great principles put forward by the Ultramontane school, namely, the pope's primacy of jurisdiction and the autonomous character of ecclesiastical law, which was acknowledged to have legal force; it underlined the Church's distinctly privileged position in the State, confirming, among other things, the bishops' superintendence of education at all levels, declaring ecclesiastical tribunals to be exclusively competent in all matrimonial cases, and restricting the rights of non-Catholics to a fairly considerable degree."[21]

This concordat freed the Austrian Church from governmental bureaucracy and permitted a new expansion of Catholic life. The day after the signing, Rauscher was elevated to the cardinalate; until his death in 1875 he would be the dominant figure of the Austrian episcopate.

In the wake of this concordat, on March 17, 1856, the Pope wrote an encyclical to the Austrian bishops at their general assembly, exhorting them to pastoral vigilance.[22] He encouraged them to meet in provincial councils to deal with local church affairs, and in diocesan synods to promote the zeal of their clergy, create minor seminaries, organize conferences on theology and liturgy in order to spread wholesome teaching among the priests, and undertake episcopal visitations to keep their parishes up to the mark. Finally he reminded the bishops of their duty to inform the Congregation of the Council through diocesan reports. Pius IX regularly reminded the bishops of the entire world of these obligations.

The Pope also wished to put the bishops on their guard against two evils which, he wrote, "could justly be considered to be the source of all others," namely, indifference in religious matters and indifferentism. Indifference in religious matters means "that people completely neglect all duty to God...our holy religion is utterly put aside; the very foundations of law, justice, and virtue are shaken and almost entirely overthrown." Indifferentism "turns those who embrace it away from truth and renders them hostile to the practice of the true faith and forgetful of their salvation. Those imbued with it teach contradictory principles, they have no settled doctrine and will not admit there to be any difference between the most divergent creeds; they live in peace with all creeds and claim that all

---

[21] Aubert, p.133.
[22] *Singulari Quidem,* Latin-French text in *Encycliques,* I, 352-385.

of them, from whatever religion they are drawn, lead to the gate of eternal life."

Austria was subject to the intellectual influence of Germany, where liberal and rationalistic tendencies were developing among certain Catholics. So Pius IX devoted a lengthy section of his encyclical to warning against this other source of evil, "the fruit of pride, making a show of reason and calling itself rationalism." He pointed out what was the correct relationship between reason and faith. "Certainly, the Church does not blame the eagerness that wishes to know the truth, for it is God Himself who has put the passion for truth into the heart of man." However, "the foundation of faith is not reason, but authority." The Pope concluded with a fine eulogy of progress, conceived in a Catholic spirit:

> Nor should we conclude that, in the Church of Christ, religion makes no progress. It certainly does, and considerable progress at that. It is necessary, however, that this be genuine progress and not alteration of the faith. As the centuries and ages unfold, therefore, you must promote the energetic growth, the greatest possible growth of understanding, knowledge, and wisdom on the part of all and each, and of the whole Church. People should come to see more clearly what, heretofore, they believed without seeing. Posterity should consider itself fortunate to understand what antiquity venerated by faith alone. The precious stones of dogma should be polished, faithfully adapted, prudently displayed; their striking grace and beauty should be increased, albeit without changing anything, *i.e.*, without changing anything as regards dogma, as regards meaning and ideas, by varying the form and not the foundation.

In this sense, the proclamation of the dogma of the Immaculate Conception had constituted real "progress." Pius IX's entire pontificate shows that he was not an enemy of intellectual "progress." While he himself had not had a solid Thomistic formation as a young man, he fostered the rebirth of Thomism and Scholastic studies by a multitude of initiatives and well-chosen appointments. Pius IX wrote a laudatory letter to a French pioneer of this renewal, Fr. Frédéric Lebreton, author of the *Petite somme théologique de saint Thomas à l'usage des ecclésiastiques et des gens du monde* (Little Summa of St.Thomas for ecclesiastics and people living in the world), in which he spoke of St.Thomas Aquinas and the Scholastic method as the best "remedy for the sickness" of rationalism and erroneous religious opinions.[23]

---

[23] Letter of April 30, 1864, cited in Piolanti, *Pio IX e la rinascita del tomismo*, p.57, which contains very many other facts and documents. Msgr. Piolanti shows that, contrary to a widely-held opinion, the renewal of Thomism did not begin under the pontificate of Leo XIII.

CHAPTER 11

PIUS IX AND ITALY

While Pius IX was rejoicing in the dogmatic proclamation of the Immaculate Conception and in the concordat signed with Austria, the temporal affairs of the great European Powers were taking a direction that would lead to the loss of a major part of the Papal States.

In 1853 France and England had concluded an agreement to support the Ottoman Empire, which was on a collision course with Russia. On March 27, 1854, after war had broken out between these two latter countries, France and England declared war on Russia.[1] This "Eastern" or "Crimean War" would be to the advantage of the plans of Piedmont-Sardinia. To curry favor with Napoleon III, Piedmont-Sardinia also joined in the war against the Empire of the Tsars. The central event of this war was the long siege of Sebastopol, the most important Russian military port on the Black Sea. This lasted from October 1854 to September 1855.

The war concluded with the taking of Sebastopol, the mediation of Austria, and the advent of a new Tsar in Russia, Alexander II. The Congress of Paris was held from February 15 to April 8, 1856, with the purpose of concluding a peace treaty between the belligerent powers. Represented at the Congress were England, Austria, France, Piedmont-Sardinia, Prussia, Russia, and Turkey.

At the request of Cavour, representing Piedmont-Sardinia, however, there was also discussion of the situation of the Papal States and the Kingdom of Naples. What would henceforth be known as the "Italian question" was raised at an international diplomatic meeting for the first time. As one chronicler wrote, "This was the harbinger of the grave events which were to unfold later, bringing about one of the Church's greatest trials."[2]

The Italian Question

The Congress had met solely to sign a peace treaty. No questions except those of the Crimean War should have been raised. Furthermore, at the end of its March 18 session the Congress affirmed that none of the contracting Powers had "the right to interfere, collectively or individually, in the relations between a sovereign and his subjects."

---

[1] Alain Plessis, *Nouvelle Histoire de la France contemporaine*, IX, "De la fête impériale au mur des Fédérés 1852-1871" (Paris: Éditions du Seuil, 1973), 187-89.

[2] Joseph Chantrel, *Annales I*, 204.

This affirmation of the principle of non-interference could not satisfy Cavour, who was determined to indict the Papal States and the Kingdom of Naples. In Italy he carried out a program of subversive activities to discredit what he regarded as the reactionary governments of the Pope and the King of Naples. He covertly supported the Italian National Society, which had been founded by an exile, La Farina, to promote an Italian unity centered on Victor Emmanuel II. "By means of tracts and secret meetings this new organization succeeded in undermining the authority of the governments of central and southern Italy; in the Marches and the Romagna, in particular, it quickly supplanted Mazzini's republican doctrines by rallying all the liberals, radicals, and moderates to its standard."[3]

Cavour also used the Congress of Paris as a platform to promote his project of Italian unity. On March 27, he sent a verbal note to Count Waleski, the French Minister of Foreign Affairs and Napoleon III's representative at the Congress, and to Lord Clarendon, one of the two English representatives.[4] In this note he suggested that the Legations—"the provinces situated between the Po, the Adriatic, and the Apennines"—should be separated, administratively and politically, from the Papal States. These provinces, "still subject to the lofty domination of the Holy See," said Cavour, "would be completely secularized and reorganized, in administrative, judiciary, military, and financial matters, in a way totally distinct and independent from the rest of the State."

Adopting a solution such as this meant the start of the dismembering of the Papal States; the aim—even if Cavour did not say so explicitly—was to attach the Legations to Piedmont-Sardinia.

This verbal communication, which only came to light later, was not an official document. Cavour's aim in propagating it was to put pressure on the French and English representatives so that the Italian question would be officially raised at the Congress.

This is what happened at the historic session of April 8.[5] The English representative declared that "the administration of the Roman Estates presents certain inconveniences which could give rise to dangers that the Congress has a right to confront," and he recommended the Pope to "secularize the government and organize an administrative system that is in harmony with the spirit of the century and seeks to promote the happiness of the people." Cavour could be satisfied with this, and contented himself, in the customary diplomatic language, with "bringing to Europe's attention an abnormal state of affairs resulting from the indefinite occupation of a large part of Italy by Austrian troops."

---

[3] Aubert, p.83.
[4] Complete text of the note in *Annales I*, 209-12.
[5] Complete text of the session in *Annales I*, 204-07.

When the protocol of this session of April 8 was made public it was
saluted by *Il Risorgimento,* Cavour's newspaper, as "the spark of an irre-
sistible conflagration"; Lamartine saw it as "a declaration of war under a
signing of peace."[6] It stirred up the Catholics of all Europe, heavy as it was
with threats to the pope's temporal power. It is true, as was observed at the
time, that the Russian and Austrian representatives had explicitly refused
to touch on the Italian question during their interventions at this sitting,
but Piedmont-Sardinia had been officially supported in its ambitions, for
the first time, by England. France, effectively exercising the presidency
of the Congress, had covered the declarations of the representatives of
these two countries with the mantle of its own authority. As Louis Veuillot
would say in the wake of the Congress, "they had no official consequences,
but the signal had been given."[7]

It is interesting to compare these English and Piedmontese accusations against the Papal States with a long diplomatic document, the "Rayneval Memorandum," which gives a precise description of the Papal States
at this very time. A little more than a month after the famous session of
April 8, Count Rayneval, Envoy Extraordinary and subsequently French
Ambassador to Rome since 1850, wrote a long report to his Minister of
Foreign Affairs, Count Waleski. For the historian, this is an important
document, frequently plundered and rarely cited. It presents a nuanced
and non-partisan picture.[8]

In it, Count Rayneval first of all answers an accusation frequently
made at the time by those hostile to the pope's temporal power, namely,
that the Papal States are a theocracy ruled by priests. It is often said, writes
Rayneval, that "three thousand priests" are employed in the administration of the Papal States: in fact, fewer than two hundred ecclesiastics are
in State service (and this figure includes the prelates who are not priests).
It will be remembered that the English and Piedmontese representatives
at the Congress of Paris had called for the secularization of the pontifical
administration. Rayneval, without making any explicit mention of this
demand, nonetheless concludes that "the secularization called for as a
remedy is nothing but a pretext for introducing foreign operations and attacking the pontifical government." The institutions put in place in 1850

---

6 Cited by Msgr. Dupanloup, *Lettre à M. le Vte de La Guéronnière* (Paris: Charles
   Douniol, 1861), p.17; hereafter, *Lettre à La Guéronnière.*
7 Veuillot, *Pie IX*, Oeuvres Complètes, X, 399.
8 Full text of the dispatch, dated May 14, 1856, in *Annales I*, 216-229. This
   memorandum, mentioned in a few lines in Aubert, p.83, is passed over in silence
   by Martina. Aubert suggests that the Rayneval Memorandum was "perhaps" drawn
   up at the request of Cardinal Antonelli, Secretary of State. The latter's most recent
   biographer thinks that "proof is still missing" regarding any such request (Falconi,
   Antonelli, p.291).

(the Council of State, Council of Finances, and the provincial and local councils) are functioning satisfactorily, and laymen have a clearly preponderant role in them.

A further accusation was made against the pope, namely, that he had left his States in "a deplorable situation." Rayneval replies that the finances have been re-established, all the paper money issued during the Roman Republic has been withdrawn from circulation, the State budget is almost balanced, and the taxes paid in the Papal States are among the lowest in Europe (twenty-two francs a year compared to forty-five francs in France). Rayneval also stresses the fact that Pius IX has not shown himself to be an enemy of material progress; in this sense he can be regarded as a modern sovereign:

> A great number of roads have been opened, connecting different parts of the country; the port of Terracine has been enlarged; drainage work has been carried out in the Pontine Marshes. The marsh of Ostia is in the process of being drained and viaducts of considerable significance have been constructed in various places.
>
> Steam navigation has been introduced on the Tiber and, thanks to a good towing system, the port of Rome has been visited by a greater number of ships than heretofore. The city has been illuminated by gaslight, electric telegraphs have been established, and railway concessions have been allotted. The Frascati railway, which is to extend to Naples, will be in operation before long. Negotiations have been initiated for an important line linking Rome with Ancona and Bologna. The construction of the Civita-Vecchia Railway has been entrusted to a company which is to begin work immediately.
>
> Agriculture has also been encouraged by the government. Prizes have been instituted to encourage horticulture and the raising of stock. Finally, a commission composed of the main landowners is currently studying the problem—which to date has been unresolved—of draining the Roman campagna and getting people to live there.

At the same time, Rayneval does not gloss over the weaknesses of the Papal States. He describes the Roman people as "not inclined to work," shying away "in the face of fatigue, reluctant to use their energy and pecuniary resources in order to profit (as is done elsewhere) from the opportunities they are given." He goes on to present the pontifical government (not the personal governance of Pius IX, but his administration) as "suspicious, preoccupied with detail, hesitant, reluctant to accept responsibility; more examination goes on than decision-making. There is a predilection for evasion and compromise. There is a lack of energy, of activity, of initiative, of firm purpose—as is to be found in the nation itself."

Rayneval concluded his essentially positive portrayal of the situation in the Papal States by giving a warning: "Given the agitation which exists, in Italy, in people's minds, and the lively emotions prompted by the publication of protocols, it is impossible to banish a deep sense of anxiety with regard to the future of the Papacy. Unless action is taken, Europe will be confronted with this problem under a frightening aspect, connected as it is to the deepest and most fiery passions of the human heart."

This detailed memorandum, so much in contrast to the English and Piedmontese criticism, was unknown to the public until one year after the Congress of Paris, when it was published in several European newspapers.[9] We may suppose that its publication was the reason for Rayneval's recall to Paris and his replacement at the French Embassy in Rome by the Duc de Gramont. The latter was charged with the task of defending the policies of Napoleon III, who would be much more favorable to Piedmont-Sardinia in the future, as events would show.

Pius IX's Apostolic Journey

The protocol of April 8 did not fail to cause anxiety in the Holy See. The English and Piedmontese criticisms seemed unjustified. Furthermore, Pius IX charged a priest he respected and with whom he was in constant touch, Canon Giacomo Margotti, director of *L'Armonia,* the great Catholic newspaper of Turin, to draw up a defense of his pontificate.[10]

The work appeared at the beginning of 1857, some months after the Congress of Paris, entitled *Le vittorie della Chiesa sotto il pontificato di Pio IX.* In it, the author presented the past ten years of the pontificate of Pius IX as a succession of four victories. First of all, in the first two years, "Pius IX was victorious over the libertine hypocrisy"; then, in connection with the Gaeta exile and the return to Rome, the author spoke of "Pius IX victorious over demagogy"; the following years saw "Pius IX victorious over heresy," by re-establishing the episcopal hierarchies in England and Holland, by defeating "Josephism" in Austria, and by proclaiming the dogma of the Immaculate Conception in the face of the century's rationalism; finally there was "Pius IX victorious over diplomacy"—the felicitous government of the Papal States being a clear refutation of the criticisms put forward by the English and Piedmontese at the Congress of Paris.

This book, apologetic in tone, reaped great success in a few weeks. In the eyes of Cardinal Antonelli, however, it was not enough, on its own, to enlighten public opinion and the European diplomatic community as to the affection and loyalty felt towards their sovereign by the vast majority of subjects of the Papal States. He also suggested to the Pope that he should undertake a tour of his States. It would be an opportunity for Pius

---

[9] The positive view established here has been confirmed by serious historians, cf. Paulo Dalla Torre, "L'opera riformatrice e amministrative di Pio IX fra il 1850 e il 1870," *Pio IX,* XIV (1985), pp.114-64.

[10] Falconi, *Il giovane Mastai,* pp.292-93.

IX to meet his subjects and, in the face of Piedmont-Sardinia, to affirm his sovereign rights over the Legations; also, as Sovereign Pontiff, he could make a pastoral visitation of some of his dioceses.

The idea fell in with the Pope's wishes. Since the beginning of his pontificate he had wanted to return to the sanctuary of Our Lady of Loreto as a pilgrim, as he had done several times in his youth. From Loreto he could proceed to the Legations. Cardinal Antonelli prepared the journey. Roger Aubert, mentioning this journey in but a few lines, observes that "Antonelli planned everything in advance in minute detail. He prevented the municipalities from placing any administrative or political demands before the Pope by carefully vetting those to be admitted to his presence."[11] If we are to believe the existing accounts of the event, this statement is exaggerated. True, the Pope did not meet any of the revolutionaries or members of secret societies that were profoundly hostile to him and would never have paid him the homage due, but he did receive several liberal figures and in several places he listened to the requests presented to him regarding local issues. In any case, the Secretary of State's control of this journey was only relative, since he did not accompany the Pope. His responsibility was to look after the ongoing state business during the four months of the Pope's absence.

This official visit, in 1857, of a sovereign to his States, which was also a pastoral visitation on the part of the Sovereign Pontiff, proved a great success, and it would go into the history of the pontificate of Pius IX as the calm before the storm.

The Pope left Rome on May 4, having celebrated Mass in St. Peter's.[12] He was accompanied by Cardinal Macchi, Msgr. Berardi, *sostituto* at the Secretariat of State, and Msgr. Ferrari, prefect of ceremonies, and some other prelates and private secretaries.

The first important stage on the way was Viterbo where, in a ceremony which would be repeated in the other cities he visited, the civil welcome—with a presentation to the Pope of the keys of the city—was immediately followed by a religious ceremony, in this case, Eucharistic adoration in the cathedral; then there was a reception at the bishop's palace which began with the traditional kissing of the feet. Another custom that was respected on each occasion was the Pope's gift of certain precious sacred objects and a significant sum of money to be distributed to the poor. The party stayed overnight at Civita Castellana, where the joyful population came out, carrying lights through the town, ringing the bells and witnessing a display of fireworks. The same scenes were repeated in subsequent days at Narni, Terni, Spoleto, Foligno, Assisi, Perugia, Camerino, Tolentino, Macerata, and Recanati. On several occasions the Pope

---

[11] Aubert, p.84, n.1.
[12] *Annales I*, 282-86, and most importantly of all, Polverari, II, 136-179.

visited convents, schools, hospitals, and famous buildings; at Assisi he meditated at the tomb of St. Francis and that of St. Clare.[13]

The Pope arrived at Loreto on May 14, staying there for two days. This part of his journey was, no doubt, closest to his heart. He was returning as a pilgrim to the sanctuary where, in his youth, he had come to express his hopes of being cured and where he had asked for light regarding his priestly vocation. He knelt in the "Holy House" for long and silent prayer, and then he began the Litany of Our Lady of Loreto, to which the assembled crowd responded. He visited the Holy House twice during his stay, celebrating Mass there and himself giving Communion; he went a third time to visit the "Treasury" that houses innumerable precious objects, symbols of faith and gratitude left behind by pilgrims down the centuries. After visiting Fermo and Ascoli, Pius IX returned to Loreto on May 20. He desired to celebrate the Feast of the Ascension, May 21, in this sanctuary.

His journey proceeded via Osimo and Ancona. His visit to this latter city was a significant political event, since an important Austrian garrison was stationed in Ancona. At the Congress of Paris, France, England, and Piedmont-Sardinia had referred to this Austrian presence in the Papal States—in the wake of the 1848 revolution—as an "abnormal situation." Pius IX, by visiting the city's arsenal and fortress, wished to pay homage to the troops who had helped to restore to him his temporal sovereignty and guarantee the security of his States.

On May 26, the Pope arrived in his native town, staying three days there.[14] Right from the beginning of his pontificate he had endowed Senigallia with various institutions: a college (the *Ginnasio Pio*), whose direction he entrusted to the Jesuits, two churches, and a refuge for the sick and for abandoned children (the *Stabilimento Pio*). A month before his arrival in the town, by the bull *Gravissimas*, he had founded the *Opera Pia Mastai-Ferretti*, at his own expense, for the purpose of giving an annual scholarship to twelve seminarians of the town, as well as promoting many social enterprises.[15]

The municipality wished to honor its famous son who had become pope. There were decorations, music, illuminations: nothing was lacking to the Pope's welcome amid the acclamations of a large populace. On May 27, Pius IX celebrated Mass in the cathedral, at the altar where he had received his First Holy Communion practically half a century earlier. The following day he celebrated Mass at the church of St. Mary Magdalen,

---

[13] Which had been discovered seven years before.
[14] For additional details on the sources quoted cf. Angelo Mencucci, *Pio IX e Senigallia* (Senigallia: Editions Adriatica, 1987).
[15] Mario Gregori Ferri, *L'Opera Pia Mastai Ferretti: bilancio di un secolo* (Senigallia: Edizioni dell'Opera Pia Mastai Ferretti, 1992), pp.131-71.

where his parents were buried, and then he visited the nearby hospital, talking to the sick and distributing alms. In the evening he visited the port area to talk with the fishermen. During his stay in Senigallia he resided in his family's *palazzo*.

Having visited Fano and Pesaro, the Pope entered the Romagna, the Papal State most in turmoil, and where Austrian troops were present in the largest numbers. Rimini, Cesena, Forli, Faenza welcomed the Pope in their turn. In Faenza, according to contemporary witnesses, his welcome was initially cool. However, once the Pope had received the municipality's representatives, blessed the crowd on the steps of the cathedral, and visited the monastery of Santa Chiara, where religious from the town's different religious houses were assembled, the crowd's welcome gained in warmth. On June 6, he proceeded to Imola, where formerly he had been bishop. He stayed there three days, meeting many of the ecclesiastics and faithful whose pastor he had been. He called on many of the city's convents, including that of the Good Shepherd, which he had founded. He spent a long time there, making a kind of canonical visitation, inspecting all the buildings, even the kitchen, where he tasted the bread made by the Sisters. He celebrated Mass in the Marian sanctuary of the Piratello, for whose revival he had done so much in former times. Many were the memories of his long episcopate in Imola that he renewed on this occasion.

On June 9, he arrived at Bologna, staying there until August 19. This two-month stay in the chief city of the Romagna was punctuated by short visits to Modena, Ferrara, and Ravenna. It was not a holiday. It was a succession of receptions of various visitors, visits to religious houses, benevolent institutions, and schools; the Pope also gave many addresses in which, as a temporal sovereign visiting the most turbulent Legation of his realm, he reaffirmed his rights.

Mention should be made here of a more strictly pontifical act, which was performed in Bologna, namely, the condemnation of the theses of Anton Günther. Günther, an Austrian theologian and philosopher who was influential in the German-speaking countries, had seen his works put on the Index by a decree of the preceding January 8. By putting Günther's works on the Index, however, only a general condemnation was signaled; no specific propositions were cited. In a letter to Pius IX dated February 10, Günther submitted to the sentence.[16] However, a number of his disciples, professors of philosophy, of theology, of ecclesiastical history, or of

---

[16] Denzinger-Schönmetzer, p.564.

canon law in Vienna, Bonn, and Breslau, argued that the essentials of his theologico-philosophical system remained valid.[17]

So it was that, the following April 16, Msgr. Geissel, Archbishop of Cologne, wrote to the Pope complaining that Günther's errors continued to be propounded by some of his disciples. No doubt a reply to the Archbishop of Cologne had already been planned when Pius IX left Rome at the beginning of May; but it was essential to compose it in terms that were adequately precise if the errors attributed to Günther were to be refuted. It is conceivable that the definitive text was sent to the Pope en route. Pius IX did not want to delay making it public, lest the controversy should be blown out of proportion; secondly, it was an opportunity to issue an act of authority while he was on the territory of one of his Legations. So the brief *Eximiam Tuam* to the Archbishop of Cologne was dated "Bologna, June 15."[18] In it the Pope gave the reasons for Günther's condemnation: his system ended in rationalism, and he was professing errors concerning the Trinity and the Incarnation, and concerning the nature of the human being. Roger Aubert regards this 1857 condemnation as "the first great success of the Scholastic reaction."[19] Rather, it can be seen as a blow struck against a dangerous system of thought that was already widespread in university faculties in the German-speaking countries. As the same author goes on: "The more moderate submitted, but radicals like Baltzer, Knoodt, or his pupil Reinkens stiffened their resistance, thinking that their reputation as scholars was at stake; ultimately they left the Church. It was from them, subsequently, that the Old Catholics would acquire their most active members."[20]

It must be said that, while this condemnation made a great noise in Germany and Austria, it went unnoticed by the Pope's subjects, rejoicing to see their sovereign and enjoying the excitement on the occasion of his visit. During his stay in Bologna Pius IX received several princes: the Infant of Spain, King Louis of Bavaria, the Duchesses of Berry and Parma, the Duke of Modena, and the Grand Duke of Tuscany. The latter two

---

[17] Mourret sums him up thus: "In his *Introduction à la théologie spéculative*, which appeared in 1828, and in many other subsequent publications, he maintained that 'the reasonable soul is entirely distinct from the principle of corporal life and sense-consciousness'; he destroyed every link between the formulae of Catholic faith and the Aristotelianism of the Middle Ages; he encapsulated dogma within a new philosophical system he himself had created; he claimed to explain the mysteries of the Trinity as acts of consciousness on the part of the Divinity; he conceived the mystery of the Redemption as being a necessary consequence of the Creation..." (*Histoire générale de l'Eglise*, VIII, 90).

[18] Latin-French text in *Encycliques*, I, 405-13.

[19] Aubert, p.200.

[20] *Ibid.*, p.202.

sovereigns invited the Pope to visit their States, which were nearby. Pius IX promised to come.

Bologna was the stage for a second solemn pontifical act: on August 3, Pius IX held a consistory in the apostolic palace where he was residing. He performed four episcopal nominations for the dioceses of Tuscany. He also gave the pallium to the procurators of five foreign metropolitans (those of Toledo, Seville, Taragon, Valladolid, and Cashel) who had been made archbishops at earlier consistories. Here, in the capital of the Romagna, the Pope also visited many convents and monasteries, churches, hospitals, schools, and factories. Those who had predicted that he would have a stormy visit—threatening posters had been distributed among the population—were contradicted by events.

Back in Rome, Pius IX expressed his pleasure at the visit: "Wherever We went, all the people in every place, of all conditions and ages, thronged the route, vying to greet Us, giving such demonstrations of joy and filial devotion as they honored, in Our humble person, the Vicar of Jesus Christ on earth and expressed, as much as they could, the love they bear for their sovereign and the trust they bear towards him. On many occasions We could not restrain our tears."[21]

Having left Bologna, Pius IX kept his promise to visit the Grand Duchy of Tuscany. From August 17 to 31, he visited Florence, Pistoia, Prato, Pisa, Livorno, Lucca, Volterra, and Siena. One of the important events of this stay in Tuscany was the consecration of four bishops who had been nominated at the Bologna consistory, namely, the Archbishop of Florence and the Bishops of Volterra, Fiesole, and Montepulciano. He also visited the College of St. Michael in Volterra, where he had been to school.[22] He made this visit in the company of the Grand Duke, Leopold II. On August 27, the feast of St. Joseph Calasanz, founder of the Scolopes (Piarist) Fathers, he celebrated Mass in the church of his old college. Then he wanted to re-visit the places where he had lived. Passing the door of the Father Minister's parlor, he made a confidential remark (now well known) to the Grand Duke: "That's where I had my first epileptic attack. Everything seemed finished for me, but then, Providence...." Next, in an improvised throne-room, he received the homage of various people: first of all, four of his former fellow-students, then the school's religious teachers, and the pupils. He gave each of them either a medal or a ring.

On the following days he visited various churches of the city, the hospital, the prison, and different educational establishments. The municipality wanted to erect a commemorative monument as a reminder of this pontifical visit. The plans for it were presented to the Pope. Pius IX

---

21 Allocution *Cum Primum in Hanc Almam*, September 25, 1857, in *Annales I*, 283-86.
22 In addition to the sources already mentioned, there are additional details in Ausenda and Vilà Pilà, *Pio IX y las escuelas Pias*, pp.94-95.

requested that the monies already collected should be applied to a charitable establishment; the monument project was dropped.

On September 5, after visiting Pieve, Orvieto, and Viterbo, the Pope was on his way back to Rome. He gave a summary of this long journey in an allocution he delivered some weeks later at a consistory.[23] He expressed his satisfaction with the welcome he had been given. He also referred to the many interviews he had had with the civil authorities of the different towns visited:

> We had the joy of speaking from the warmth of Our paternal heart to all the magistrates of every locality and every rank, who presented Us with a number of particular requests and petitions related solely to special local needs and the interests of commerce. They laid their desires before Us with that respect and moderation which is appropriate in the Holy See's most loyal and devoted subjects. In many places, too, We immediately and gladly took prompt measures which seemed to Us most apt to re-awaken and promote religion and piety among the people, and also provide them with new temporal benefit and contribute to their well-being.

The Pope's journey, therefore, was not merely a succession of demonstrations of loyalty and formal meetings.

In a letter he wrote from Bologna to his brother Giuseppe, Pius IX spoke with greater precision: "In Ravenna and Lugo everything went not only well, but very well. As in Bologna, in Ravenna I had a long interview with the respective city authorities. None of them asked for anything they had no right to ask, and for my part I agreed to their requests, provided the treasury funds were sufficient to cover the expenses." The Pope added that the various requests that had been made to him would cost one and a half million écus[24]—no small figure if we realize that the total receipts for the Papal States for that year were twelve million écus. Thus we see that the Pope was attentive to the needs of the population of his States.

It has been suggested that, during this tour, Pius IX missed the opportunity of rallying "the moderates, who would have wanted only to unite their patriotism and liberalism with their Catholic faith and their devotion to the Roman pontiff."[25] This view is too general and is based on the writings of two liberals, Pasolini and Minghetti, whom Pius IX had met, respectively, in Imola and Bologna. It is clear that the liberalism of these two men could not have been reconciled with the policies the Pope was pursuing. Ever-present to his eyes, in Piedmont-Sardinia, were the disastrous results, for the Church, of a "liberal" policy; in addition there was his vivid memory of the 1848 revolution. He said to Minghetti, "The people are insatiable. What I have been through is far too painful."

---

[23] Allocution *Cum Primum in Hanc Almam*, September 25, 1857, *Annales I*, 283-286.
[24] Letter of July 29, 1857, cited in Polverari, II, 177.
[25] Aubert, p.84.

It should not be forgotten that the Pope only accepted the presence of Austrian troops in his States in order to guarantee public order—a task for which the meager papal retinue was inadequate. At the same time he was aware that, in many instances, the presence of these foreign troops was not taken kindly by the population. From Bologna, therefore, on June 18, he had written to Emperor Franz Joseph demanding that the Austrian troops garrisoned at Bologna and Ancona be reduced in number.

All these facts indicate that the 1857 tour was not a futile exercise. In one of his books Saint-Exupéry tells of a queen "who wanted to visit her subjects and find out whether they were pleased with her reign. To deceive her, her courtiers erected various pretty stage-sets and paid people to dance in them. Apart from the man who pulled the strings she actually saw nothing of her kingdom and did not know that, in the length and breadth of the countryside, there were those who were dying of hunger and cursing her."[26] The situation was very different in the case of Pius IX. Here there were no actors, there was no *papier mâché* scenery, nor were there peasants dying of hunger. Here it was a case of the Papal States, which enjoyed a statute that was unique in the history of the world, being exposed to the hostility of liberals and anti-clericals who regarded such a regime as anachronistic, and the expansionism of the kingdom of Piedmont-Sardinia which, under the energetic prompting of Cavour, was pursuing its ambition of unifying Italy.

From Orsini to Mortara

If 1857 had been dominated by this long apostolic journey, 1858 was the year in which Italy's destiny was at the mercy of the (then) secret agreement between Napoleon III and Cavour. It all started on January 14 with an attempt on the Emperor's life.[27] As he was going to the Opera, four Italian republicans, led by Orsini, a former member of the Constituent Assembly of the Roman Republic, threw bombs at the imperial cortege. Orsini, under the influence of an exiled French republican, believed that with Napoleon III dead, the Republic would be restored in France and would help Italy towards unity and towards becoming a republic too. The Emperor emerged unscathed from the assassination attempt, but 156 people were injured, more or less seriously, and eight of them died.

As well as intensifying the evolution towards a more authoritarian regime, Orsini's assassination attempt made Napoleon III determined to conduct policies more decidedly in favor of Piedmont-Sardinia. If France were to help Piedmont-Sardinia to throw the Austrians out of Italy, it would acquire the good graces of the partisans of Italian unity and also

---

[26] A. de Saint-Exupéry, *Terre des Hommes* (Gallimard) [English title: *Wind, Sand and Stars*].

[27] Louis Girard, *Napoléon III* (Paris: Fayard, 1989), pp.271-72.

of the French republicans who had so far been hostile to the Empire. Of course, Napoleon III reckoned to profit territorially from this military intervention in Italy. This was the purpose of the Plombières Accord. For some years Napoleon III and the Empress Eugénie had gone to take the waters in this spa in the Vosges Mountains. On July 21, Cavour discreetly made his way thither and had two long private discussions with the Emperor.[28] It was agreed that France would help Piedmont-Sardinia to expel the Austrians from the north of Italy. After the victory, Piedmont-Sardinia would annex the now liberated Lombardy and Venetia, but also Emilia and the Romagna, two regions of the Papal States. In exchange for its help, France would get Savoy and Nice which, in the wake of the 1815 Treaty of Vienna, had reverted to the sovereignty of the Kingdom of Piedmont-Sardinia.

The contents of this agreement remained secret. Cavour regarded the projected annexations as the first step towards Italy's complete unification. Napoleon III, however, had no intention of promoting a unified Italy at this time. True, in 1849 he had sent troops to re-establish the Pope in his temporal sovereignty, and now he had agreed to wrench part of the Papal States from him. He believed, however, that Italy could become a confederation and that the Pope, the head of the Papal States (even of a reduced Papal States) could give stability as president of this future Italian Confederation.

In many ways Napoleon III had the wool pulled over his eyes in this Plombières Accord. The skilful Cavour gave the impression that he would be content to create a kingdom of Northern Italy, whereas for a long time his real intention had been much broader. As for Napoleon III, he was lending his support to an enterprise that would have the immediate effect of handing Savoy and Nice to France; but this would alienate the sympathy of Catholics and break up the totality of the Papal States.

Under cover of a war of liberation against Austria, Piedmont-Sardinia was in fact preparing to attack and despoil the Papal States. Was it a coincidence that the "Mortara Affair" erupted a few months after the Plombières Accord? This affair, which was publicized by a Bologna newspaper on October 1, 1858, would feature in all the major European newspapers for some months. Liberals and anti-clericals saw it as an opportunity to lead a campaign against the Church's "obscurantism." In virtue of the many controversies it prompted, this "Mortara Affair" can be compared

---

[28] The only knowledge we have of their content is from the written account that Cavour made to Victor Emmanuel II, cf. Girard, *Napoléon III*, pp.280-81.

to the "Dreyfus Affair" which was to give France much anguish some decades later.[29]

Edgardo Levi-Mortara, son of a rich Jewish family of Bologna, born in 1851, fell gravely ill at the age of seventeen months. The family's Catholic servant, Anna Morisi, thinking that the child was near to death, decided to baptize him secretly herself, pouring water on him and pronouncing the sacramental words. Against all hope the child recovered, and the servant kept it a secret. In 1858 Edgardo's brother Aristide also fell seriously ill. One of Anna Morisi's friends said that she should baptize him. The servant refused, saying that she had already baptized Edgardo some years earlier, that he had recovered, and that since that time his parents had brought him up according to the Jewish law. She did not want a similar situation to arise in Aristide's case. The story became known to the Bologna ecclesiastical authorities, and, thinking the case too serious, they referred it to Rome.

The Congregation of the Inquisition, with the approval of Pius IX, decided to remove the young Edgardo from his family and bring him up as a Christian. This was June 24, 1858, and the boy would be seven next birthday.[30] Later Mortara spoke of the event: "The police took me to Rome and presented me to His Holiness Pius IX, who received me with the greatest kindness and declared himself to be my adoptive father, which, in effect, he was." The boy was entrusted to the Institute of Catechumens, which was administered by the congregation of the Sisters of the Sacred Heart.

His parents went to Rome to take him back; they were refused, but they were allowed to see him every day. The young Mortara himself declared that he did not wish to return to his parents, and they went back to Bologna. It was they, no doubt, who alerted the press to what they considered an "abduction." The Italian newspapers, followed by those of all Europe, seized on this unfortunate affair.

The fact is that, in acting in this way, Pius IX was only acting in accordance with the current canonical rules.[31] For centuries the Church had strictly forbidden the baptism of Jewish children without their parents' consent, except in two very precise circumstances: when a child had been abandoned by its parents, or if the child had been entrusted to the care of a Christian and was in imminent danger of death. In this second case, if

---

[29] *Civiltà Cattolica,* November 6, 1858, published a long article on this affair, translated in *Annales I,* 303ff. Mortara himself made a lengthy deposition, on this affair and other subjects, at the beatification process, *Summarium* §§1653-59. Cf. also the analysis of the affair in Martina, II, 31-35.

[30] Aubert, commenting on the affair in a few lines, mistakenly presents him as "a child of three" (p.87).

[31] They are quoted in a note by Mourret, *Histoire générale de l'Eglise,* VIII, 545.

the baptized child survived, it could be taken away from its family to protect it from apostasy. In order to avoid these dire circumstances the law of
the Papal States prohibited Jewish families from having Christian domestic servants, who might be inclined to baptize those in danger of death. In
employing Anne Morisi, therefore, the Mortara family had committed an
infraction against this wise measure.

In the case of the boy Mortara, furthermore, it should be stressed
that he was completely happy with his new position. Initially Pius IX had
considered placing him in a Jesuit college, but, given the rising tide of polemics, he was afraid that the Jesuits might again be exposed to the attacks
of the liberal and anti-clerical press. So, in December, he entrusted the
boy to a school run by the Canons Regular of the Lateran. Every month
the Pope paid the appropriate school fees and attentively followed his protégé's progress in his studies. Later, Mortara completed his novitiate with
the Canons Regular and was ordained priest.[32]

This Mortara Affair featured in the European press for several
months. In France, *L'Univers* was one of the very few newspapers to defend the Pope's decision. Louis Veuillot summoned Dom Guéranger to remind readers of the doctrine involved in the case. The Abbot of Solesmes
wrote:

> There are two distinct rights present here, that of the parents regard-
> ing their child's education, and the right of the child himself to enjoy the
> advantages obtained through his baptism and to be preserved from the
> peril resulting from any possible infraction of the duties incumbent upon
> him. As for these two rights, one belongs to the order of nature, and the
> other belongs to the supernatural order: both come from God. In this
> conflict, which has priority? The supernatural right, without any doubt.
> God cannot contradict Himself....[33]

The vast majority of the newspapers, however, denounced the
Church's "obsolete laws" and "theological law's oppression of the natural
law." As Louis Veuillot wrote, "This application of the law seemed cruel;
it seemed insulting to the generous spirit of the century, it was a crime
against nature and the final proof that the pontifical governance should be
swept from the world like the last spot of mire from the ages of barbarism.
The clamoring, or rather the bellowing, became universal."[34]

The Jewish community of Allesandria, in Piedmont-Sardinia, appealed to all the world's synagogues to protest publicly, and demanded

---

[32] "Mortara would be ordained priest by Msgr. Pie in 1875, for the community of
Notre-Dame de Beauchesne, in the diocese of Poitiers. In February of the same year
he would be present at the funeral of Dom Guéranger" (Delatte, *Dom Guéranger*,
p.904).
[33] Article of October 24, 1858, quoted in Dom Delatte, *Dom Guéranger*, p.634.
[34] Veuillot, *Pie IX*, Oeuvres Complètes, X, 399-400.

that governments should intervene diplomatically. France, through the intermediary of her ambassador in Rome, the Duke de Gramont, first sent a very severe note to Cardinal Antonelli, and then asked Pius IX himself to "give back" Mortara. The Pope replied that "in conscience" he could not allow "a Christian to be brought up in the Hebrew religion."

The Mortara Affair was, in many ways, an engine of war against the Church; it gave people the opportunity to denounce "the government of priests." Cavour, in private correspondence from this period, recognized this, not without a certain cynicism:

> The Emperor has been delighted with the Mortara Affair, as with everything that may compromise the Pope in the eyes of Europe and in the eyes of moderate Catholics. The more charges that can be made against him, the easier it will be to impose on him the sacrifices called for by the reorganization of Italy....We must make the most of all the Emperor's efforts to bring the Pope to follow a more reasonable political line...by insisting, with regret, that the Pope's conduct shows it to be absolutely impossible that he should keep the temporal power outside of the walls of Rome.[35]

The First Spoliations

The "reorganization of Italy" desired by Cavour began to be implemented from 1859 on. On January 1, at the traditional New Year's Day reception, Napoleon told the Austrian ambassador, "I am very sad that our relations with your government are not as friendly as heretofore."[36] This remark, which was not yet a threat, was noted.

On January 10, in his address for the opening of the parliament of Piedmont-Sardinia, Victor Emmanuel II declared: "While respecting the treaties, we are not insensible to the cry of suffering that reaches us from so many regions of Italy." This statement, agreed on in advance with the French Emperor,[37] provoked disquiet in Austria and a veritable delirium of jubilation among the partisans of Italian unity. These were the first steps leading to war.

On January 28, there was the official signing of the treaty of alliance between France and Piedmont-Sardinia, which envisaged the liberation of Lombardy and Venetia, the setting-up of a kingdom of Upper Italy based on Piedmont, and the ceding of Savoy and Nice to France. The other part of the Plombières Accord, namely the annexation of Emilia and the Romagna, to the Pope's detriment, was kept in the shadows. On January 30, in the grand tradition of royal marriages of convenience for political

---

[35] Letter from Cavour to Villamarina, November 25, 1858, cited in Martina, II, 35, n.54.
[36] Salvatorelli, *Histoire de l'Italie*, p.503.
[37] *Ibid.*, p.504, and Girard, *Napoléon III*, p.282.

interest, Prince Jerome, cousin of Napoleon III, married Princess Clotilde of Savoy, the daughter of Victor Emmanuel II.

On February 4, La Guéronnière, who was connected with the Emperor, published an unsigned pamphlet entitled *Napoléon III et l'Italie*. It was designed to prepare people's minds for war. In it La Guéronnière, whose text had been read and corrected by the Emperor, defended the principle of nationalities and urged a "federative union" in Italy. War in Italy "would have no other aim—whenever it might become necessary—but to obviate revolutions by affording the legitimate satisfaction of the needs of peoples."[38] The Kingdom of Piedmont-Sardinia was already enrolling volunteers into its army and concluding an agreement with Garibaldi so that he and his troops would take part in the "war of liberation."[39]

After England had made an attempt at mediation and Russia had proposed to host a congress to find a peaceful outcome, Austria addressed an ultimatum to Piedmont on April 23, demanding its unilateral disarmament. Piedmont refused, and the Austrian troops, from their bases in Lombardy, went into attack on the 29th.

On May 3, France declared war on Austria. Napoleon III made reassuring noises: "We have no intention of fomenting disorder in Italy, nor of dispossessing sovereigns, nor of breaking the power of the Holy Father—to whom, in any case, we restored his throne." Furthermore, his Minister of Religious Cults, Rouland, wrote a circular to all the French bishops, assuring them that the Emperor "wishes that the Supreme Head of the Church should be respected in all that concerns his rights as a temporal sovereign."[40]

The Pope was against this war. Two days prior to the beginning of hostilities he published an encyclical exhorting the parties to peace; in it he instructed all the bishops to organize public prayers in their dioceses, in order to obtain "the benefit of a constructive peace which is the fruit of salvation: peace with God, with themselves, and with other men."[41] Pius IX could not bless the troops of Piedmont-Sardinia since it had shown itself, in recent years, to be a persecutor of the Church; but he also refused to take Austria's part. At the beginning of May, when the Austrians put Ancona and its surrounding region in a state of siege, the Pope protested against this violation of the conventions regarding occupation.

The Austrians were hoping to crush Piedmont prior to the arrival of the French. They did not succeed in this, however, because their progress was retarded by deliberate flooding on the part of the Piedmontese peasants, who opened the sluice-gates of many irrigation canals on the

---

[38] Cited by Girard, *Napoléon III*, p.283.
[39] Garibaldi would soon be incorporated into the Sardinian army as a general.
[40] Declaration and circular cited by Msgr. Dupanloup, *Lettre à La Guéronnière*, p.11.
[41] Texts in *Annales I*, 331-32.

wide plain of the Po. Napoleon III arrived in Italy at the head of an army of 100,000 men. The Austrians were beaten successively at Montebello (May 20), Palestro (May 30-31), and Magenta (June 4). On June 8, Victor Emmanuel II and Napoleon III were able to enter Milan, the capital of Lombardy, as liberators. Meanwhile Garibaldi was occupying Como, Bergamo, and Brescia.

These French and Piedmontese victories were not without effect on the little principalities of central Italy. Part of the population of these States rose up in arms, skillfully manipulated by the secret patriotic societies; at the end of April the Grand Duke of Tuscany was forced to abandon Florence; and at the beginning of June, after the battle of Magenta, the Duchies of Modena and of Parma, whose princes had had to flee, proclaimed themselves annexed to the Kingdom of Piedmont-Sardinia.

The Papal States did not escape the enthusiasm that followed from these military victories. On June 12, in Bologna, a demonstration organized by the National Italian Society ejected the Pope's legate, Cardinal Milesi, and a governmental commission was put in place, which offered the city to Victor Emmanuel. On June 14, a provisional government was set up in Perugia, but the city was retaken on the 20th by the Swiss Guards.

The Austrian troops did not consider themselves beaten. Emperor Franz Joseph came in person to assume command of the troops. After a grim battle the French were victorious at Solferino (June 24). At that point Napoleon III judged it preferable to stop the war. On the one hand he was afraid that Prussia and the German Confederation would intervene on the Austrian side, and on the other he was aware that this war was not popular in France, particularly not among Catholics, who saw the Papal States once more a prey to revolutionary movements threatening Pius IX's temporal sovereignty.

To Piedmont's great displeasure, the two Emperors signed the peace preliminaries on July 11 at Villafranca. These preliminaries envisaged that Lombardy would be ceded to Napoleon III (who would then hand it on to Victor Emmanuel). Austria would keep Venetia, and the sovereigns of Tuscany and Modena would be re-established in their possessions.

This Villafranca agreement aroused the indignation of patriotic Italians. In protest, Cavour resigned from his post as head of the government. However, Napoleon III did not engage the military to re-establish the legitimate authorities in the Duchies and in the Romagna: the provisional, revolutionary governments there were maintained.

Catholic opinion was uneasy about the fate in store for the Papal States. There was alarm in France within a wide spectrum of people, from liberals like Montalembert to the most intransigent, like Veuillot. The

former, in a long article in the *Correspondant*,[42] saw himself as the spokesman of the majority of Catholics when he deplored Europe's "indifferent,
distracted, or complicit" attitude and stigmatized the volatile policies of
Napoleon III: "It was France that saved the Holy See's temporal independence in 1849, and it is France that has frittered it away in 1859." He also
said some fine things in defense of Pius IX:

> Of all the wrongs which the Italians have inflicted on other princes,
> is there a single one that can be justly imputed to Pius IX? Not one. Is he
> a tyrant? No. No one, even among his bitterest adversaries, would dare
> suggest such a thing. Is he in hiding? No. Is he a usurper? No. Is he a
> foreigner? No. He is the most Italian, the only completely Italian, prince
> of the Peninsula; he is far more Italian, at least as regards his origins, than
> this House of Savoy which is despoiling him in Italy's name. What, then,
> is his crime? He has one crime, only one: he is a priest. That is every-
> thing....The proud men of the Romagna...are no longer minded to obey
> the most ancient, the most venerable, and the most Italian sovereignty of
> all Europe, because this sovereign is a priest. That is the idea that drives
> them, that is what is in their minds; that is the way they understand the
> rights of man and the rights of a nation.

In all justice he observed: "Is there any man who seriously thinks that
reforms, of whatever kind, will satisfy or disarm a single one of the Holy
See's enemies, be they exterior or interior?" He concluded his reflections
by fearing that France might become "the Pilate of the papacy."

Montalembert's analysis was not unjust. Some time after his article
appeared, the official French position would shatter the Pope's last hopes.
A Congress was being talked about which would bring together the representatives of the Great European Powers with the aim of promoting a
definitive peace in Italy. With this Congress in mind, Pius IX wrote a personal letter to each of the sovereigns to be represented there. On December 2, he asked Napoleon III to intervene in his favor at the Congress so
that the territories conquered by Piedmont would be restored to him. The
French response was twofold. On December 22, an anonymous pamphlet
appeared (it was again, in fact, the work of La Guéronnière), entitled *Le
Pape et le Congrès*. In it, Napoleon III's semi-official spokesman, without
denying the legitimacy of the pope's temporal power, explained that Pius
IX would have to be content with a small piece of territory around Rome;
he would have to accept the loss of the major part of his States. Pius IX
described this pamphlet as an "outstanding monument to hypocrisy" and
a "base tissue of contradictions."[43] However, the author was only express-

---

[42] Dated October 25, 1859, reprinted as a pamphlet under the title *Pie IX et la France en
1849 et 1859* (Paris: J. Lecoffre & Cie, 1959).
[43] In his New Year address to the French troops in Rome, reproduced in *Annales I*,
pp.385-86. Several French bishops had already protested or were going to protest by
means of pamphlets, pastoral letters, or declarations.

ing the Emperor's own position. Napoleon III himself, on December 31, wrote to Pius IX inviting him to "make the sacrifice of his rebellious provinces."[44] The idea of a Congress was abandoned.

This French position, contradicting the official declarations made hitherto, permitted Cavour to return as head of the Piedmont government on January 21, 1860. On the basis of plebiscites organized in a climate that can be imagined only too well, he confirmed the annexation by Piedmont-Sardinia of the conquered territories: Tuscany, Parma, Modena, Romagna. On March 23, in exchange for his approval, Napoleon III was given Savoy and Nice.

Thus the Pope found himself robbed of the provinces in the north of his States. He had been abandoned by all the European Powers. On January 19, in the encyclical *Nullis Certe Verbis*,[45] he had explained that he could not sacrifice territories "which did not belong to the dynasty of any royal family, but belonged to all Catholics."[46] On March 26, in a very severe apostolic letter,[47] he denounced the tactics used by Piedmont-Sardinia to foment unrest in the Romagna and deprive him of this territory: "No fraud, no crime has been spared in goading the peoples of our pontifical realm into a criminal revolt. [Piedmont-Sardinia] has sent out emissaries on purpose, made money available, provided arms, conducted agitation through pamphlets and corrupt newspapers, and perpetrated all sorts of fraudulent practices; these things have been done even by those who were in Rome as its ambassadors."

He went on to pronounce a major excommunication of those who, whether by command or deed, "have taken part in the rebellion, usurpation, occupation, and criminal invasion of the aforesaid provinces of our States." Even if Victor Emmanuel II was not explicitly named, he was struck by this sentence in the highest degree. Pius IX ordered the text of this apostolic letter to be posted on the doors of the Basilicas of St. John Lateran and St. Peter's, the Apostolic Chancellery, on Monte Citorio, and at the entrance to the Campo di Fiori, so that everyone should take note.

The Papal Zouaves

This initial spoliation of the Papal States provoked a wave of protests in all the Catholic countries. Few and far between were those who re-

---

[44] Letter published in *Annales I*, p.384.
[45] *Annales I*, pp.388-90.
[46] After this encyclical was published by *L'Univers*, the Imperial government seized this as a pretext for suppressing the newspaper.
[47] *Cum Catholica Ecclesia*, Latin-French text in *Encycliques*, I, 415-431.

garded as legitimate the insurrection of the population of the Romagna, "under the regime of a former age," according to an expression used at the time by Msgr. Maret, a prominent liberal figure of the French clergy.[48] The vast majority of Catholics supported the papal cause. Petitions expressing support and fidelity to the Holy See were sent to Rome from different countries. Many bishops in France and in the whole of Europe intervened in various ways to defend the temporal sovereignty. Msgr. Dupanloup's work *La Souveraineté pontificale* aroused considerable notice; it quickly went into a third edition and won for its author a very complimentary letter from Pius IX.[49] On the initiative of the Austrian and German faithful, the St. Michael's Association was set up to provide material aid to the Pope and to pray for his intentions. In Belgium the *Denier de Saint-Pierre* (St. Peter's Pence) was founded to collect money for the Holy See; soon collections were extended to other countries, so that by 1870 considerable funds had been sent to the Pope.

In particular, these funds provided for the maintenance of the foreign troops (the famous "Papal Zouaves") which Pius IX decided to recruit in the first months of 1860. The existing papal troops were few in number—eleven battalions of six hundred men—and poorly equipped. France had kept some troops in Rome since 1849, but the policies adopted by Napoleon III in recent months made it uncertain whether there would be a French intervention in the case of a new attack.

Msgr. de Mérode, a former Belgian officer who had been in the service of Pius IX for ten years, suggested the recruiting of foreign volunteers to constitute a real defensive army for the Papal States. Secretary of State Antonelli showed himself hostile to this project; he feared that it would upset the foreign powers, particularly France. Pius IX went over his head. In February he appointed Msgr. de Mérode pro-Minister of Armed Forces and entrusted to him the task of recruiting adequate numbers of men. Msgr. de Mérode summoned a prestigious soldier, General de La Moricière, who had been imprisoned and then exiled for his hostility to the Second Empire. General de La Moricière arrived in Rome on April 1. Pius IX appointed him commander-in-chief of the existing troops. La Moricière presented the papal troops with a vibrant order of the day which concluded thus: "Like Islam in former times, the Revolution is today threatening Europe; and now, as then, the cause of the Papacy is the cause of civilization and of the world's freedom. Soldiers! Be confident; and be certain that God will sustain your courage and raise it to the level of the lofty cause he has entrusted to our arms."[50]

[48] Personal note of January 1860, cited by Aubert, p.89.
[49] "No one can be compared to you," wrote Pius IX. Cf. F. Lagrange, *Vie de Msgr. Dupanloup*, 3 vols. (Paris: Libr. Poussielgue Frères, 1884), II, 317-323.
[50] Cited in G. Cerbelaud-Salagnac, *Les Zouaves pontificaux* (Paris: France-Empire, 1963), p.18.

Some days later he appealed to Catholics of the entire world to send volunteers to Rome. In the following weeks there arrived Austrians, Belgians, Irishmen, Frenchmen (often the sons of legitimist families), and Italians too. The Austrians were present in particularly large numbers: 5,000 men; for the most part they were regular soldiers and officers whose departure had been organized by the Austrian government. There was a strong Irish contingent of 800 men, organized by themselves as the Battalion of St. Patrick. The French and Belgian volunteers, some 70 men, were organized in May into a company of Franco-Belgian Sharpshooters; as their effective size increased they became a battalion, and then, some months later, the battalion took the name under which it has gone down in history: the battalion of "Papal Zouaves."

These volunteers experienced their first large-scale battle at Castelfidardo. It was a disaster. In May there had been the Expedition of a Thousand, led by Garibaldi. Having left from Genoa, with the approval of Victor Emmanuel, Garibaldi and his thousand volunteers disembarked in Sicily to stir up the people there against their young sovereign, Francis II (aged twenty-three), who had succeeded his father, Ferdinand II, deceased the previous year. It was a hard struggle, and Garibaldi had to appeal for reinforcements before he succeeded, by the end of July, in making himself master of Sicily. In August he crossed the Strait of Messina to conquer the rest of the Kingdom of Naples. Under the pretext of preventing Garibaldi from marching on Rome, Cavour obtained Napoleon III's permission to occupy the Marches and Umbria, which were papal territories.

On September 7, he wrote a letter to Cardinal Antonelli in which he deplored "the formation and the existence of foreign mercenary troops in the service of the papal government"; "this foreign corps, which is insulting to the national sentiment and obstructs the manifestation of the people's wishes, will infallibly produce insurrections that will spread to the neighboring provinces." Accordingly he presented an ultimatum: the Pope must give "immediate order to disarm and dissolve these corps whose existence is a continual threat to Italy's tranquility."

On September 11, Cardinal Antonelli, in the Pope's name, rejected this ultimatum; but the very same day, before the negative reply had even reached Cavour, the Piedmontese troops crossed the frontier and occupied the Marches and Umbria.

On September 18, despite the great bravery shown by General de Pimodan, the papal troops were beaten at Castelfidardo. General de La Moricière, who had retreated with his troops to the Ancona citadel, sur-

---

[51] On all these military operations there is a long report from General La Moricière to Msgr. de Mérode, dated November 3, 1860, reproduced in Saint-Albin, *Histoire de Pie IX et de son pontificat*, II, 355-403. Cf. also the Marquis de Ségur, *Les Martyrs de Castelfidardo* (Paris: Tolra, 1891), which shows the spiritual sentiments of many of the combatants.

rendered on September 29 after the Sardinian fleet had bombarded the place.[51]

In the Marches and in Umbria a plebiscite was organized to ratify their incorporation into Piedmont-Sardinia. In the Kingdom of Naples hostilities lasted longer and did not come to an end until February 1861, with the capture of Gaeta. A sham referendum had already annexed the ancient kingdom to Piedmont-Sardinia, and the young King Francis II had taken refuge in Rome. Also, on March 17, Victor Emmanuel was in a position to be proclaimed "King of Italy." Rome remained the final objective. The "Italian" parliament voted on March 27 on the motion "That Rome, acclaimed as the capital by national opinion, should be re-united to Italy."

Henceforth all the provinces of the Peninsula were under the scepter of the new King of Italy, except Venetia—which the Austrians ceded in 1866, at the end of their war against Prussia and Italy—and Rome with its surrounding region, Latium. Cavour tried to obtain by negotiation what he had not been able to take by battle. In December 1860 he had instructed two of his close collaborators in Rome, Dr. Pantaleoni and the ex-Jesuit Passaglia, a renowned theologian, to present a memorandum to the Holy See.[52] The memorandum, officially drawn up by Pantaleoni, in fact perfectly reflected the mind of Cavour. The latter, faithful to his motto, "a free Church in a free State," suggested that the Pope should renounce his last temporal possessions; in exchange the Church would be guaranteed full liberty in the ecclesiastical sphere. It was stipulated that the Pope would be guaranteed the prerogatives of his sovereignty (particularly that of entering into diplomatic relations with the States) and his full authority over the clergy and bishops; that the Italian State would renounce its right to nominate bishops; that the Church would be free in her preaching, teaching, press, and associations; and that she would be able to count on the secular arm's intervention to ensure that her legislation and judgments in religious matters would be respected.

Pius IX was impressed by these assurances and agreed that discussions should take place. As the weeks went by, however, news coming from the annexed papal provinces showed that Cavour's government was still hostile to the Church: bishops were being arrested and exiled, convents were being closed, and ecclesiastical property was being confiscated. Pius IX and Cardinal Antonelli were convinced that Cavour, even if he were sincere in what he proposed, would not be able to resist pressure from the parties of the left who wanted to pursue anti-clerical policies. The unexpected death of Cavour on June 6, 1861, and his replacement at the

---

[52] On these negotiations (many points of which remain obscure) cf. Falconi, *Antonelli*, pp.388-95.

[53] Ricasoli drafted conciliation terms, in twelve articles, less generous than Cavour's, but he had to step down in March 1862.

head of the Italian government by Bettino Ricasoli, put an end to these negotiations for several years.[53]

CHAPTER 12

THE POPE OF THE SYLLABUS

Pius IX could not accept the spoliations carried out in 1859 and 1860. At the beginning of 1861, however, the vast majority of Catholics agreed with them. This was clearly seen when La Guéronnière, who had become a State Councillor, on February 15, published a third pamphlet entitled: *La France, Rome et l'Italie,* this time putting his name to his work. He reproached the Pope for failing to carry out the political reforms in the wake of the French intervention in 1849, regretted his ingratitude towards France, accused Catholics of having betrayed "the party of Order," and justified the policies of Napoleon III.

Msgr. Pie, Bishop of Poitiers, immediately answered this pamphlet with a pastoral letter "On the Subject of the Accusations Made against the Sovereign Pontiff and against the French Clergy."[1] He denounced the pamphlet's "lack of respect" and "failures of justice" and, drawing an analogy between the Pope's treatment and the Passion of Christ, he concluded with a clear allusion to Napoleon: "Herod, Caiphas, Judas, and the others had their part in the crime, but in the end it would have come to nothing without Pilate. Pilate could have saved Christ; and without Pilate Christ could not have been put to death....Wash your hands, Pilate; declare yourself innocent of the death of Christ." Msgr. Dupanloup, too, rejected the new pamphlet in a *Lettre à M. le Vte. de La Guéronnière* (Letter to the Viscount de La Guéronnière), in which he reminded his readers of the successive changes in French policy and pointed out the contradictions involved.[2]

Other bishops followed their lead in answering La Guéronnière. Louis Veuillot, who was having difficulty in bringing out *L'Univers* regularly, and had sought in vain for authorization to found a new newspaper, also published a pamphlet in reply to La Guéronnière. Entitled *Le Pape et la diplomatie,* it vigorously defended the pope's temporal rights: "Accepting insurrection in Bologna was equivalent to provoking it everywhere, ratifying it everywhere; it meant abdication. Accepting a laicist government for certain provinces was equivalent to condemning...papal governance everywhere and judging it incapable and unworthy; it meant abdication." Veuillot also developed an argument to which the more liberal Dupan-

---

[1] *Oeuvres de Msgr. l'Evêque de Poitiers* (Paris-Poitiers: H. Oudin, n.d.), IV, 145-65. This pastoral letter resulted in Msgr. Pie being held to be in contempt of the Council of State.

[2] Dupanloup, *Lettre à La Guéronnière.*

loup did not give any prominence: "No religion, whatever it may be, embraces only a part of man: it embraces the whole man. Morals, legislation,
the social and political life of all nations, at all times, have been nothing
other than the true mirror of their religious life." The Papal States made
it possible for Catholicism to "show itself to the eyes of the world in its
religious, social, and political totality." By "laying claim to Rome, revolutionary Italy is not only seeking a head for itself: it wants to decapitate
ancient Christian humanity."[3]

Here Veuillot was expressing an idea shared by Pius IX in all points.
All the Pope could do was to utter a *non possumus* to the very principle of
invasion and spoliation, as he would remind his hearers in a consistory allocution on March 18, 1861: the Holy See cannot "sanction the principle
that something taken unjustly and violently may be possessed in tranquillity by the unjust aggressor; this would be to establish the false maxim that
a successful injustice does not detract from the sanctity of the law."[4]

However, Pius IX did not reduce the spoliation of part of his States
to a question of violated sovereignty. The events of these last ten years had
shown that the partisans of Italian unity were not hoping simply to unify
the States of the Peninsula politically: they intended to establish a society
founded on new principles, namely, secularization and the separation of
Church and State. Pius IX had already denounced these principles in the
past. In the 1860's he would renew and amplify these condemnations of
"modern civilization," and his Syllabus would be their pedal point, as it
were.

The anti-clerical policy of the Kingdom of Italy was not an isolated
case. Other countries, by more or less violent tactics, were frustrating the
Church's action and attempting to subordinate it to the State. At the start
of 1861 one country, Mexico, where the revolutionary Benito Juarez had
just triumphed, set the example with a bloody persecution that was to
last for many years. Portugal was taking measures to disperse the religious
congregations and confiscate their goods. Many more examples could be
given.

Furthermore, in the aforementioned allocution Pius IX went beyond
the Italian case to express his opposition to "modern civilization":

> On the one hand this modern civilization is eager to show favor to
> every non-Catholic cult, fails to remove unbelievers from public posts,
> and opens Catholic schools to their children; and on the other hand it
> makes savage attacks on religious communities and the institutes founded
> to provide Catholic schools, on ecclesiastical persons of every rank, even
> those invested with the highest dignities (many of whom are today suffer-
> ing the anxieties of exile or imprisonment), and on the distinguished lay-

---

[3] Louis Veuillot, *Le Pape et la diplomatie* (Paris: Gaume Frères & J. Duprey, 1861).
[4] Allocution *Jamdudum Cernimus*, in *Encycliques*, I, 473-90.

men who, out of devotion to Our person and this Holy See, courageously defend the cause of religion and justice.

This civilization squanders its subsidies on non-Catholic institutions and persons, and at the same time it despoils the Catholic Church of her legitimate possessions, trying in every way, and with increasing zeal, to weaken her salutary influence. It grants free rein to those who, by the spoken or written word, attack the Church and the men devoted to her cause; it inspires, entertains, and foments licence; it also shows itself full of moderation and reserve in the matter of repressing the violent and odious attacks against those who publish good writings, while it treats the latter with extreme severity if it believes that, to whatever small degree, they have overstepped the bounds of moderation. Could the Roman Pontiff ever hold out the hand of friendship to such a civilization?

Rallying to the Chair of Peter

The following June saw the foundation of *L'Osservatore Romano*, which was intended to become, in some way, the pope's own newspaper. Its foundation testified to the will to defend the Church using "modern" weapons, *i.e.*, a combative daily press, without yielding to the principles of "modern civilization." Originally *L'Osservatore Romano* was not the property of the Holy See—it was Leo XIII who bought it up in 1890—but from its very first issue, July 1, 1861, it was the faithful interpreter of the pope's thought. Its first chief editor was the Marquis Augusto Baviera. A native of Senigallia, he had moved to Rome after the annexation of the Marches by Piedmont-Sardinia.

Pius IX also wished to strengthen the Holy See's links with the bishops and the faithful. Faced with the Italian situation, faced with erroneous doctrines that were being spread in various domains, he wanted to demonstrate, to the eyes of the whole world, the Catholic Church's unity. Three times in the 1860's the bishops of the entire world were invited to Rome: on the occasion of the canonization of the Japanese martyrs, for the eighteenth centenary of the martyrdom of Saints Peter and Paul, and, finally, for an ecumenical Council.

It was on January 18, 1862, the Feast of St. Peter's Chair, that Cardinal Caterini, Prefect of the Congregation of the Council, addressed a letter in the Pope's name to all the bishops "of the Catholic world," inviting them to come to Rome the following May for the ceremony to canonize twenty-six Japanese martyrs, killed *in odium fidei* on February 5, 1597, and the Trinitarian religious, Blessed Michel De Sanctis. This convocation made some governments uneasy. The French Ambassador to Rome, the Marquis de La Valette, expressed to Cardinal Antonelli his astonishment at not having been informed officially of a meeting of this kind. He feared it would provide an occasion for a solemn condemnation of French policy.

The Secretary of State reassured him by saying that this meeting of bishops with the Pope would be purely religious in character.[5] So the French
government allowed those French bishops who so wished to go to Rome,
but it required them to apply for exit passports. This meant that some of
them, who were tardy in making their arrangements, were prevented from
going. The Italian and Portuguese governments, however, prohibited their
bishops from going to Rome.

Notwithstanding these obstacles, the ceremonies were splendid. The
Civiltà Cattolica counted 43 cardinals, 5 patriarchs, 52 archbishops, and
186 bishops (including about 50 from France), a total of 286 members of
the episcopal hierarchy. This was a far higher number than at the promulgation of the dogma of the Immaculate Conception. One third of the
world's entire episcopate was present in Rome, as well as about 4,000
priests and 100,000 of the faithful from many countries. After the public
or semi-public consistories that were held at the end of May to prepare
for the solemn act of canonization, the event itself took place on June
8. When he had returned to Paris, Augustin Cochin, a liberal, summed
up the general impression in these words: "This demonstration of the
Church's power, unity, and extent was very impressive. One feels that the
funeral of such a vibrant, colossal body is not imminent. Events will take
their course; but God has shed such a ray of light upon the spiritual power
as to dazzle the most hostile observers."[6]

This canonization ceremony was not, however, simply a show of
strength. It was also an opportunity for all the bishops to meet with the
Pope. This took place the following day. In a long allocution the Pope solemnly recalled the condemnation of the "terrible ills, ever to be deplored,
by which the Catholic Church and civil society itself are lamentably tormented and oppressed, causing great harm to souls."[7]

The Pope denounced the errors of Rationalism, Pantheism, and what
would later be called Modernism. Pius IX did not use this term, but it corresponds to what he was stigmatizing. He denounced those who regarded
divine Revelation as "imperfect and therefore subject to a continual and
indefinite progress, corresponding to the progressive development of human reason. Furthermore they dare to suggest that the prophecies and
miracles set forth and reported in the sacred Books are poetic fables; that
the sacred mysteries of our faith are the result of philosophical investiga-
tions; that the divine books of the Old and New Testament contain nothing but myths, and that—horrible though this is to utter!—Our Lord
Jesus Christ himself is nothing but a mythical and fictional figure."

Those Pius IX had in mind here were the theologians and exegetes,
particularly in Germany, followers of David Friedrich Strauss, who were

---

[5] Falconi, *Antonelli*, pp.400-01.
[6] Letter to Msgr. Dupanloup, cited in Lagrange, *Vie de Mgr. Dupanloup*, II, 367-68.
[7] Allocution *Maxima Quidem*, Latin-French text in *Encycliques*, I, 503-20.

developing a rationalist exegesis. Strauss, in his *Leben Jesu, kritisch bear-beitet* (1835-36) (Life of Jesus, critically edited), had reduced the Gospels to the level of collective myths.[8] However, the Pope may also have been thinking of the provocation offered by Ernest Renan some months earlier. The Emperor had appointed Renan to the Chair of Hebrew at the Collège de France, and in his opening lecture course Renan had described Jesus as "an incomparable man, so great that I would not like to contradict those who, struck by the exceptional nature of his work, call him God." The following year he published his *Vie de Jésus,* which caused a scandal and reaped enormous success (there were twelve French editions in two years and eighteen different German translations). In it he denied in particular Christ's divinity and his miracles.[9] The work was condemned by many bishops in their pastoral letters, and Louis Veuillot answered it in his *Vie de Notre-Seigneur Jésus-Christ,* praised by Pius IX in a brief.

In his allocution to hundreds of bishops who had come to Rome, the Pope put the accent on what would be his chief battle in the years to come: the defense of Catholic doctrine. It goes without saying that everyone understood the importance of this allocution. When the Pope had finished speaking, Cardinal Mattei, Dean of the Sacred College, surrounded by several bishops, read an "Address of the Bishops" to the Pope. Msgr. Dupanloup, who, to his profound satisfaction, was considered among the bishops as one of the great champions of the pope's temporal power, had prepared a draft text insisting on this question; Cardinal Wiseman had written another draft, in which, while he also defended the temporal power, he also denounced revolutionary and liberal principles, in particular "those ridiculous freedoms of which modern nations are so proud."[10]

In the end a commission had conflated these two drafts and produced the "Address" read out by Cardinal Mattei.[11] In it, with a particular emphasis, the bishops manifested their attachment and fidelity to the "free Pontiff-King": "...You are, for us, the master of sacred doctrine, you are the center of unity, you are an indefectible light for the peoples, prepared by divine Wisdom; you are the Rock, the very foundation of the Church herself, against which the gates of hell will never prevail; when you speak, it is Peter we hear; when you decree, it is Jesus Christ we obey; in the

---

[8] René Zapata, "Strauss," *Dictionnaire des Philosophes,* under the direction of Denis Huisman (Paris: Presses Universitaires de France, 1984), II, 2448-49.

[9] Cf. Ernest Renan, *Histoire et parole,* in Oeuvres diverses, ed. L. Rétat, R. Laffont (Collection "Bouquins," 1984); also Y. Chiron, "La religion d'Ernest Renan," *Itinéraires,* January 1985, pp.105-15.

[10] Lagrange, *Vie de Mgr. Dupanloup,* II, 359-61, and further details in U. Maynard, *Monseigneur Dupanloup et M. Lagrange son historien* (Société générale de Librairie catholique, 1884), pp.130-31, and Aubert, pp.248-49.

[11] Latin-French text in *Encycliques,* II, 550-61.

midst of so many trials and tempests we admire you as, with serene mien and imperturbable heart, you accomplish your sacred ministry, invincible and steadfast."

The bishops also approved the doctrinal and temporal condemnations made by the Pope in his allocution: "We bishops condemn the errors you have condemned; We reject and detest the new and alien doctrines which are proliferating everywhere to the detriment of the Church of Jesus Christ; We condemn and reprove the sacrileges and plunderings, the violations of ecclesiastical immunity, and the other offences committed against the Church and the See of Peter."

An episcopate so loyal to the Pope and so much in accord with his temporal and doctrinal views was, in its vast majority, bound to accept the Syllabus and the dogma of papal infallibility which were to be Pius IX's two major doctrinal acts in the following years.

The Origins of the Syllabus

No act of the Church, at least in the nineteenth century, aroused such controversy, among both Catholics and non-Catholics, as the Syllabus (or "Syllabus of the Principal Errors of Our Time"), which was published on December 8, 1864, as an annex to the encyclical *Quanta Cura*.

The history of this Syllabus is long and complicated.[12] Cardinal Pecci (the future Leo XIII) was no doubt the first to suggest that the Pope should draw up this kind of catalogue of modern errors. This was in 1849, in the wake of the Roman revolution. The bishops of the Spoleto province were meeting at a provincial council and, having completed their work, at Cardinal Pecci's suggestion they wrote asking Pius IX to "tabulate all the errors against the Church, against authority and property, as they present themselves in our times, and to condemn them, specifying the relevant note of censure."

In 1851 a layman, Emiliano Avogadro della Motta, in a work published in Turin, *Saggio intorno al socialismo e alle dottrine e tendenze socialistiche* (Essay on socialism and the socialist doctrines and tendencies), also called for a global condemnation of the "huge and highly pernicious errors" of modern society. We have already seen how, in February 1852, when the dogma of the Immaculate Conception was being prepared, the editor of the *Civiltà Cattolica*, with the Pope's full agreement, suggested that a solemn condemnation of the errors of the times should be included in the Bull defining the dogma.[13]

---

[12] Cf. principally E. Amann, "Syllabus," *Dictionnaire de Théologie Catholique*, XIV, col.2877-2925; Aubert, pp.248-54; Martina, II, 287-347; and secondary sources which we shall refer to in the notes.

[13] P. Calvetti, "Congruenze sociale di una definizione dogmatica sull'Immacolata Concepimento della B. V. Maria," *Civiltà Cattolica*, February 1852.

The following May, on the Pope's order, Cardinal Fornari sent various people a questionnaire on these errors. "The Holy Father," he wrote, "has ordered that a study be made of the intellectual state of modern society, with regard to the errors generally held concerning dogma and its points of contact with the moral, political, and social sciences." The letter was accompanied by an initial "collection" (syllabus) of twenty-nine errors, of which his correspondents could take account in their reply. The questionnaire was sent to several bishops (including Msgr. Pie, Bishop of Poitiers, and Msgr. Geissel, Archbishop of Cologne), various theologians (including Dom Guéranger), and also to laymen—a sign that clericalism was not as absolute as its detractors were saying. Among the laymen consulted were Louis Veuillot, Editor of *L'Univers*; Count Avogadro della Motta, already referred to; and Donoso Cortès, one of the most important Spanish Catholic philosophers of the century, who had just published his main work, an "Essay on Catholicism, Liberalism, and Socialism," and was Spanish Ambassador in Paris.[14] Louis Veuillot's response is not known; that of Donoso Cortès became the subject of a book.[15]

Avogadro della Motta observed that "the Immaculate Conception was such a privilege that it seemed to call for a special Bull," and that it would therefore be better to separate the dogmatic definition from the systematic condemnation of errors. This opinion was shared—as we have already seen—by Dom Guéranger, who expressed it during his stay in Rome. Pius IX responded immediately. When the commission working on the dogmatic Bull had finished its work, the Pope instructed it to go on to prepare the future Syllabus.

New consultations took place. Fr. Smith, a Benedictine who was a consultor of several Roman Congregations, went to Solesmes on October 11, 1859, to ask Dom Guéranger for a report on the chief errors of the present time.[16] Fr. Smith then went to Louvain and made the same request to the rector of the Catholic University, Msgr. de Ram. At about the same time, in the Pope's name, Msgr. Fioramonti asked Msgr. Pie to prepare notes on two widespread errors: "The order of faith and of the supernatural sacrificed to the order of nature; and the practical and absolute separation of the religious order from the civil order, raised to the level of a dogma and hailed as progress."[17]

Each of the three persons consulted compiled a long memorandum. These works were read attentively and annotated by the Pope. We also know that Cardinal Geissel, Archbishop of Cologne, was again consulted

---

[14] Cf. Jules Chaix-Ruy, *Donoso Cortès: Théologien de l'Histoire et prophète* (Paris: Beauchesne 1956).

[15] *Lettre au cardinal Fornari,* re-edited in the series L'Age d'Homme in 1989.

[16] Delatte, *Dom Guéranger,* p.648.

[17] Maynard, *Monseigneur Dupanloup et M. Lagrange,* p.128.

at the beginning of 1860, but we do not know the nature of his reply. In January 1860, on the basis of these consultations, the commission drew up a collection of seventy-nine condemned theses under the title *Syllabus Errorum in Europa Vigentium.*

Some months later, on July 23, on his own initiative, Msgr. Gerbet, Bishop of Perpignan, published an *Instruction pastorale sur diverses erreurs du temps présent* (Pastoral instruction on various errors of the present time). In it he included a catalogue of eighty-five erroneous propositions that were to be condemned. Msgr. Gerbet, a former disciple of Lamennais, had submitted to the Roman decisions after the latter's condemnation. Msgr. Gerbet was the author of several apologetical works and had been for a long time a professor in Rome and Paris; he was one of the outstanding figures of the French episcopate. The Paris nuncio, Msgr. Sacconi, sent a copy of the pastoral instruction and its annexed catalogue to the Pope.

Pius IX was pleased with it, and decided that the catalogue of modern errors drawn up by Msgr. Gerbet should be used in preparing the Syllabus. Following a method of working previously used in the preparation of the dogma of the Immaculate Conception, another commission was created in May 1861, with the task of examining in more detail the eighty-five propositions indicated by Msgr. Gerbet. This new commission, presided over by Cardinal Caterini, Prefect of the Congregation of the Council, included three theologian-consultors: Msgr. Delicati; Fr. De Ferrari, a Dominican; and Fr. Perrone, the Jesuit whom one encounters at every major doctrinal juncture of Pius IX's pontificate. Eventually nine further consultors would be added to the group.

After a score or so of working sessions this commission compiled a list of sixty-one doctrinal propositions that were to be condemned; the particular censure incurred by each proposition was specified. When the bishops met in Rome for the canonization of the Japanese martyrs in June 1862, Pius IX had a copy of this list distributed to each of them, under the seal of secrecy. He required them to examine the condemned errors attentively and make their observations within two months; if there were further propositions that needed to be condemned, they should mention them. The majority of bishops approved the proposed text, and some indicated other propositions that should be condemned. However, about a third of the bishops consulted judged a condemnation of this kind inopportune, or expressed their disagreement concerning the censure to be applied to this or that error.

The vicar-general of Msgr. Dupanloup informs us that the latter showed himself far more critical: he expressed "his surprise that the Pope, having so many learned theologians at his disposal in Rome, instead of presenting the bishops with a Roman project, had submitted to them a catalogue borrowed practically word for word from the pastoral letter of a French bishop."[18] This reproach—no doubt inspired by his disappointment in not having been consulted in advance—was highly exaggerated, since the commission, which was entirely Roman, had spent a long time working at and refashioning Msgr. Gerbet's catalogue. Msgr. Dupanloup also feared "the storm which will not fail to be raised by such an act." Here he was correct, but Pius IX was not a man to fear "storms."

The secrecy demanded by Pius IX with regard to this Syllabus had not been respected by everyone. On July 19, no doubt informed by some bishop, the French Ambassador to Rome communicated the list of condemned propositions to his minister. Liberal Catholics began to be uneasy, while at the same time being sure of their victory: "The times are visibly working in our favor," wrote Léopold de Gaillard, a writer for the *Correspondant*; "Let us not be over-hasty, but let us not pull back either. Condemned or not, in twenty-five years' time the principles of [17]89 will constitute the spirit and the law of all civilized peoples. This future is assured, and it counsels us to be both prudent and firm."[19] Montalembert, at the same period, expressed the same disdain: "I understand that we are threatened with an avalanche of condemned propositions for the delectation of Messeigneurs Gousset, Pie, Gerbet, and others, who have so well grasped the reciprocal situation of the Church and the Empire. Rome could not do anything more calculated to embarrass her friends, bring joy to her enemies, and hasten her own misfortune."[20]

The main collaborators of the *Correspondant* met the following October 9 at Montalembert's property at La Roche-en-Brény. As well as their host, present were Augustin Cochin, the Count de Falloux, Théophile Foisset, and Msgr. Dupanloup. Later, their adversaries would speak of a liberal "plot."[21] Msgr. Dupanloup's vicar-general, who attended the meeting, rebutted this charge and published the "pious address" given by the Bishop of Orléans as he distributed communion to his friends.[22] The bishop had preached patience: God commands you "to be faithful and charitable; to be patient towards men, patient in the face of events, because both are in his hands. He attains His goal with strength and sweetness, but along paths which are not ours, and in a time-scale that is not that of

[18] Lagrange, *Vie de Mgr. Dupanloup*, II, 455.
[19] Letter of Léopold de Gaillard to the Marquise de Forbin d'Oppède, dated July 29, 1862, cited by Jean-Rémy Palanque, *Catholiques libéraux et gallicans en France face au concile du Vatican 1867-1870* (Aix-en-Provence: Publications des Annales de la Faculté des Lettres/Editions Ophrys, 1962), p.57.
[20] Letter from Charles de Montalembert to Msgr. de Mérode, September 13, 1862, in *Correspondance inédite 1852-1870* (Paris: Cerf, 1970), p.278; hereafter, *Correspondance*.
[21] Cf. Delatte, *Dom Guéranger*, pp.700-01, 863-67.
[22] Lagrange, *Vie de Mgr. Dupanloup*, II, 394-95.

our short life!" In other words, even if their liberal ideas would soon have to be condemned, God would vindicate them in the end.

Apart from this improvised homily, Abbé Lagrange tells us nothing of the other conversations which took place at this meeting—which Montalembert regarded as historic.[23]

Although there are no documents showing a link between the two events, one cannot ignore a coincidence of dates here: on October 9, 1862, the meeting with Dupanloup and Montalembert took place, and the same month a Turin weekly, the *Mediatore*, founded by the ex-Jesuit Passaglia, published in its columns the document that had been distributed to the bishops, energetically criticizing it in several articles. The polemic spread to many anti-clerical publications. It may be that this unwelcome divulging of the document's contents prompted the Pope to make a further modification of the Syllabus. A new version was drawn up.

Meanwhile the catalogue of condemned errors was enriched—if one can use the term—by further condemnations. In December 1862, in a Brief to the Archbishop of Munich and Freisingen, Pius IX condemned the theses of Fr. Jakob Frohschammer, professor of philosophy at the University of Munich.[24] The Pope cited two of the latter's recent books[25] and denounced two major errors found in them: "Firstly, the author attributes to human reason powers that in no way belong to it; secondly, he grants to this same human reason the liberty of thinking anything, and of always thinking audaciously, thereby entirely suppressing the Church's rights, functions, and authority." Frohschammer, the Pope continued, "not content with suggesting that the Church should never deal severely with philosophy, actually goes on to say that her duty is to tolerate its errors and leave it to correct itself...."

Philosophy went astray when it accorded absolute primacy to the human intellect and so made common cause with liberal Protestantism. In this same Brief, Pius IX expressed his disquiet as to the many Catholic philosophers and theologians in Germany who were calling for "a liberty to teach and write that is currently unknown in the Church." In fact, in recent years, several German works had been put on the Index: in 1857, a book by the same Frohschammer, *Über den Ursprung der menschlichen Seelen* (On the origin of human souls); in 1858 and 1859, works by Trebisch, Knoodt, and Batzer, all disciples of Günther, who had already been condemned in 1857; in 1859, a critique of Thomist theology by Oischinger;

---

23 After this meeting Montalembert had a commemorative plaque placed in his chapel; it bore his watchword, "A free Church in a free country," almost identical to that of Cavour, even if he claimed to give it an entirely different meaning.

24 The brief *Gravissimas Inter*, December 11, 1862, Latin-French text in *Encycliques*, I, 521-35, and Latin extracts and notes in Denzinger-Schönmetzer, pp.567-70.

25 *Introduction à la philosophie et fondement de la métaphysique*, 1858; *De l'Indépendance de la science*, 1861, and a journal, *Athenaeum*, which he edited from 1858.

in 1860, a book by Huber, a disciple of the historian Döllinger; in 1861, a work by Lassaulx, a Munich theologian. Since Frohschammer refused to submit to this new condemnation, the Archbishop of Munich withdrew his priestly faculties; soon Frohschammer left the Church.

In the wake of this condemnation of an entire current of thought in German philosophy and theology, the meeting (September 1863) of more than eighty "Catholic scholars" from Germany, Austria, and Switzerland, convoked by Döllinger, seemed to many to be provocatory. Certain bishops showed themselves hostile even to the idea of such a meeting, organized without their authorization, while others were more favorably inclined towards it once Rome, presented with a *fait accompli*, did not dare to prohibit it but demanded that a close watch be kept on the purport of the discussions.[26]

Döllinger, who gave a notable lecture on "Theology's past and its future," showed himself very daring in certain passages. He demanded complete "freedom of movement" for the theologian, denouncing the decadence of ecclesiastical sciences in the Latin countries and regarding Germany alone as having "theology's two eyes, that is, philosophy and history"—in virtue of which it could claim to be "the teacher of the nations." Not only did this address claim for the theologian a liberty that was unacceptable to the Pope, it was also profoundly contemptuous of the Catholic theologians and philosophers of the Latin countries, where the Thomist renaissance was beginning to bear fruit.[27] A part of the assembled company expressed its disagreement with Döllinger's position; after all, Germany also had its "Roman" school inspired by Thomism.[28]

The Pope, poorly informed of the exact thrust of Döllinger's ideas, and satisfied by the conclusion of the congress, which expressed complete fidelity to the Holy See, initially sent his congratulations, urging it to pursue "its authentically Catholic work." Later, following complaints from his nuncio in Munich and some German bishops, he wrote a much more reserved letter to the Archbishop of Munich.[29] He expressed his surprise that, at this congress of Catholic philosophers, theologians, and historians, no contribution had been forthcoming "from the initiative, authority, and mission of the ecclesiastical power." He reminded the Archbishop that it was not sufficient for the faithful to submit "to dogmas expressly defined by the Church": they should also "submit to doctrinal decisions emanating from pontifical congregations, and to points of doctrine which, by common and constant consent, are held in the Church as truths and as theological conclusions that are so certain that the contrary opinions,

[26] Aubert, pp.205-9; Martina, II, 316-319.
[27] Cf. Piolanti *Pio IX e la rinascita del tomismo*.
[28] Cf. Aubert, pp.209-10.
[29] Brief *Tuas Libenter*, dated December 21, 1863, in *Encycliques*, I, 569-85.

even if they cannot be qualified as heretical, nonetheless merit some other theological censure." This was a reply—albeit without naming names—to Döllinger and other German "Catholic scholars" who were demanding theology's "freedom of movement."

One month after this congress of Catholic scholars in Munich, the first "Congress of Belgian Catholics" was held in Malines. It too had given Pius IX cause for concern. Present were several cardinals, including Cardinal Ledochowski, nuncio in Brussels, and foreign bishops and delegations. The congress was to be an opportunity for the Belgian Catholic Church to affirm its unity in the face of governmental policy which was becoming ever more laicist and anti-clerical.[30] One of the invited speakers, however, was Montalembert, who wanted to use it to deliver his "political testament."[31]

The two addresses he gave, on August 20 and 21, constituted the prime event of the congress.[32] He praised "Catholic and liberal Belgium" for the welcome it gave him. He regretted the fact that too many Catholics in Europe had not "yet taken their part in the great revolution that has given birth to the new society, the new life of the peoples" and were preserving a mentality "of the *ancien regime, i.e.*, that regime which refuses to admit either equality, or political liberty, or freedom of conscience." He exalted the "immortal well-springs of freedom" and, advocating the separation of Church and State, he thought that "the merest appearance of too close an alliance between the Church and the throne was enough to compromise and weaken her." Finally, while rejecting "the ridiculous and culpable doctrine that all the religions are equally good,"[33] he praised freedom of worship and of conscience, "the most precious, the most sacred, the most legitimate, the most necessary freedom."

These addresses scandalized a number of those present, in particular Cardinal Wiseman and the Brussels nuncio. Soon Montalembert published them under the title *L'Eglise libre dans l'Etat libre* (A free Church in a free State), which was seen as provocatory. A Belgian friend of Veuillot's, Count du Val de Beaulieu, replied in a pamphlet entitled *L'Erreur libre dans l'Etat libre* (Freedom of error in a free State). Several bishops, includ-

---

[30] On May 20, 1850, in the allocution *Si Semper Antea*, Pius IX had protested against an education law which the Belgian government had just adopted. Latin-French text in *Encycliques*, I, 197-215.

[31] Letter from Montalembert to Foisset, August 1863, cited by Aubert, p.251.

[32] Extracts in Philippe Tollu, *Montalembert: Les libertés sous le Second Empire* (Albatros, 1987), pp.443-53.

[33] Perhaps he was thinking of an encyclical recently published by Pius IX entitled *Quanto Conficiamur*, dated August 10, 1863, in *Encycliques*, I, 537-56, in which the Pope once again indicated the precise meaning of the axiom "Outside the Church no salvation."

ing Msgr. Pie and Msgr. Gerbet, demanded an official condemnation of Montalembert's addresses.

Msgr. Dupanloup went to Rome to plead his friend's cause. He sent Cardinal Antonelli a long note, while Montalembert sent in a memorandum in which he declared his submission in advance to the decisions of the Holy See.[34] Pius IX had valued Montalembert's past battles for freedom of education in France and his recent writings in favor of the temporal sovereignty; in a letter, in former times, he had called him a "good soldier of Jesus Christ." Also, although his Malines addresses merited condemnation, the Pope did not wish it to be public. He sent a private letter to Montalembert *via* Cardinal Antonelli, rejecting his ideas, which were "in contradiction with the teachings of the Catholic Church and with the acts of various Sovereign Pontiffs." The Secretary of State also pointed out that "the head of the Church will not be able to keep silent on the merit of certain doctrines which are being propagated to the prejudice of the Catholic religion and society."[35] This was to signal the forthcoming Syllabus.

The liberals greatly feared this solemn condemnation, even if some of them, as we have seen, thought that the future would ultimately vindicate them. Adolphe Dechamps, one of the leaders of the Catholic party in Belgium and a friend of Montalembert, wrote a memorandum to Pius IX explaining that to condemn the very foundations of the modern constitutions would put the Church in danger of intensified hostility. The King of the Belgians, Leopold I, intervened with the same sentiments in a letter to the Pope.

For its part, the French government instructed its ambassador in Rome to make representations to Cardinal Antonelli.[36] In Rome, by contrast, others—notably Dom Pitra, recently made cardinal—were urging the Pope to act rapidly and solemnly.[37] In a memorandum sent to Pius IX some time during 1863 Cardinal Pitra presented the liberals as a "party" which "is assuming more and more the aspect of Port-Royal, sometimes timid, sometimes audacious, never straightforward. Like a sect, this party is versed in the art of subterfuge, of semi-retractations, of claims, of false reports, of rectifications in newspaper columns, of official and semi-official interventions, and of diplomatic maneuvers." He hoped for a clear

---

[34] Lagrange, *Vie de Mgr. Dupanloup*, II, 437-438. Msgr. Dupanloup's vicar-general does not mention this condemnation.

[35] Letter of March 5, 1864, cited by Tollu, *Montalembert*, p.451.

[36] Aubert, p.254.

[37] Dom Pitra, a monk of Solesmes and an author of very valuable historical works, had been called to Rome in 1858. He was created cardinal in 1863. Pius IX was hoping to make Dom Guéranger a cardinal also, but that would have deprived the Abbey of Solesmes of its Father Abbot. So Pius IX chose Dom Pitra, "the most learned of the Solesmes monks" (Robert).

and strong condemnation: "Infinitely respectable motives have led to hesitation and temporizing analogous to that employed by the Jansenist school. It is to be feared that the Church will have a new canker in her side unless an energetic remedy removes the danger."[38] The Cardinal wished that, rather than issuing a new encyclical or allocution, "the Holy See should speak in the magistral clarity of a dogmatic constitution."

By an irony of history it can be said that, indirectly, it is to the liberal Montalembert that we owe the Syllabus as published in 1864. In fact, the author of the final version of this famous document was a Barnabite religious, Fr. Luigi Bilio.[39] He had been teaching philosophy, theology, and canon law in several establishments of his order when, at the end of 1863, he was appointed consultor of the Congregation of the Holy Office. The first task entrusted to him was to examine the two addresses of Montalembert mentioned above. He communicated his observations in a long report of forty-two pages, concluding that the speaker had erred. This analysis resulted in the condemnation of March 5, 1864, to which we have already referred. It was not made public.

Fr. Bilio, whose clear, erudite analyses had been appreciated in the Montalembert affair, was charged with the task of finalizing the general condemnation which had been talked about for more than ten years. At the same time, encouragement to publish the long-awaited condemnation arrived from France: Msgr. Pie sent Pius IX the third synodal instruction he had just given to his clergy; it concerned the modern errors. Furthermore two bishops, Msgr. Doney, Bishop of Montauban, and Msgr. de la Bouillerie, Bishop of Carcassonne, sent the Pope a long joint letter urging the condemnation of liberalism.[40]

Several times Fr. Bilio thoroughly re-worked the existing catalogue. In six months, from June to November 1864, he produced three very different drafts. These came after the other, earlier, drafts compiled since 1860. His last draft broke radically with the criterion of selection used in the earlier drafts. Instead of drawing up a catalogue of condemned errors, or errors to be condemned, he had examined Pius IX's teaching since his first encyclical of 1846 and extracted a list of eighty-four propositions explicitly censured by the Pope. This resulted in a solemn recital of quotations, with references, concerning philosophical and theological questions and the relations between Church and State. This list was slightly modified.

---

[38] Memorandum cited by Albert Battandier, *Le cardinal Jean-Baptiste Pitra* (Paris: Sauvaitre, 1893), p.490.

[39] Martina, II, 321ff.

[40] This led to a fine eulogy of Msgr. de la Bouillerie by Pius IX some years later: Msgr. Ricard, *François de la Bouillerie* (Lille: Maison Saint-Joseph/Oeuvre de Saint-Charles, B-Grammont, n.d.), p.259.

Certain quotations were withdrawn on account of duplication, and others, taken from two recent acts of Pius IX, were added.

The first of these was a letter to the Archbishop of Freiburg-in-Breisgau, in the Grand Duchy of Baden. On June 29, 1864, the Baden government had adopted a law withdrawing public education from the Church's control. Very quickly, in this Brief dated July 14, Pius IX protested.[41] The second act was a letter to the Bishop of Mondovi dated September 29, praising him for having protested against a draft law of the Italian government suppressing the exemption from military service which clerics had enjoyed hitherto.[42]

In the end the Syllabus contained eighty-two condemned propositions, and the document, officially dated December 8 like the accompanying encyclical, had already been distributed to the cardinals, when Fr. Bilio, who had been instructed to have the document printed in its definitive form, on his own initiative, judged it opportune to withdraw two propositions which could be misunderstood. One concerned the constitutions, and the other concerned Italy.[43] Thus the definitive version of the Syllabus, after twelve years of work and eight different draft versions, contains eighty condemned propositions drawn from thirty-two encyclicals, allocutions, or letters of Pius IX.

Quanta Cura and the Syllabus

The Syllabus, formally without signature or date, was in fact sent to all the bishops of the world together with a new encyclical dated December 8, 1864, entitled Quanta Cura. It was not an annex, properly so called, although the two texts were combating similar errors.

In the encyclical,[44] Pius IX, having recalled the fact that his predecessors and he himself had "continually resisted the machinations of those evil men, who, 'foaming out their own confusion, like the raging waves of the sea,' and 'promising liberty, while they are themselves the slaves of corruption,' [endeavored…to subvert the foundations of Religion and civil Society]," explained that it was his duty to denounce "other erroneous opinions." This, he says, is *Naturalism,* which desires societies to be constituted and governed without regard to religion; it is the "liberty of conscience and of worship," which is nothing other than the "liberty of perdition," as St. Augustine says; it is the attempt to remove the education and instruction of the young from the Church's authority; it is the nega-

---

[41] Brief *Quum Non Sine,* in *Encycliques,* I, 587-97.
[42] Letter *Singularis Nobisque,* in *Encycliques,* I, 599-602.
[43] Martina, II, 344-46. Pius IX did not distance himself from this action of Fr. Bilio; in fact, he retained a great trust in him. He created him cardinal in 1866 and made him one of the presidents of the First Vatican Council.
[44] Latin-French text in *Encycliques,* I, 1-23.

tion of the Church's temporal rights and its subordination to the State. Ultimately, the Pope says, there are those who, "animated and excited by the spirit of Satan, have arrived at that excess of impiety as not to fear to deny Our Lord and Master Jesus Christ, and to attack His Divinity with scandalous persistence." Furthermore, "in view also of the terrible conspiracy of our adversaries against the Catholic Church and this Apostolic See," Pius IX exhorted the bishops to preach in defense of the true doctrine, to pray, and to encourage their faithful to pray. In order to prompt people to true piety and penitence he would grant a plenary indulgence in Jubilee form for the coming year, 1865. Finally, the encyclical being dated December 8, 1864, *i.e.*, ten years to the day after the definition of the dogma of the Immaculate Conception, the Pope invoked "the Immaculate and Most Holy Mother of God, the Virgin Mary, who has destroyed all heresies in the whole world...."

The "Syllabus of the Principal Errors of Our Time, which are censured in consistorial Allocutions, Encyclical and other Apostolic Letters of Our Most Holy Lord, Pope Pius IX" appeared in the form of eighty condemned proposition, in ten categories.[45] The first to be condemned were propositions of "pantheism," "naturalism," and "absolute rationalism," *i.e.*, those which say that "God and nature are the same thing," that "all things are God," that "there is no difference between spirit and matter, necessity and freedom, true and false, good and evil, justice and injustice" (prop.1); the view that rejects "all action of God upon man and the world" (prop. 2); the ideas that suggest that reason "is law to itself, and suffices, by its natural force, to secure the welfare of men and of nations" (prop.3); and that "the faith of Christ is in opposition to human reason" (prop.6).

A second group of condemned errors concerned "moderate rationalism." Here the Pope had in mind, in particular, the theories of Günther and Frohschammer and the views of Döllinger, though none of them were explicitly named. The Pope condemned those who say that "theological must be treated in the same manner as philosophical sciences" (prop.8); that "the decrees of the Apostolic See and of the Roman congregations impede the free progress of science" (prop.12); and that one can engage in philosophy "without taking any account of supernatural revelation" (prop.14).

"Indifferentism" and "latitudinarianism" were summed up in four condemned propositions. Thus, for instance: "Every man is free to embrace and profess that religion which, guided by the light of reason, he shall consider true" (prop.15), and "Man may, in the observance of any religion whatever, find the way of eternal salvation, and arrive at eternal salvation" (prop.16).

---

[45] Latin-French text in *Encycliques*, I, 24-50.

This was followed by reference to texts of Pius IX in which he had condemned "socialism, communism, secret societies, Biblical societies, and clerico-liberal societies."

No less than twenty propositions manifested "errors regarding the Church and her rights." It is a mistake to say that "it appertains to the civil power to define what are the rights of the Church, and the limits within which she may exercise those rights" (prop.19). It is false to claim that "the obligation by which Catholic teachers and authors are strictly bound is confined to those things only which are proposed to universal belief as dogmas of faith by the infallible judgment of the Church" (prop.22). It is an error to say that the Church "has not... any temporal power, direct or indirect" (prop.24), or that "National churches, withdrawn from the authority of the Roman pontiff and altogether separated, can be established" (prop.37).

A sixth section condemned "errors about civil society, considered both in itself and in its relation to the Church," such as these: "In the case of conflicting laws enacted by the two powers, the civil law prevails" (prop.42); "The civil authority may interfere in matters relating to religion, morality, and spiritual government" (prop.44); "Lay authority possesses of itself the right of presenting bishops" (prop.50); "The laws enacted for the protection of religious orders and regarding their rights and duties ought to be abolished" (prop.53).

Next came a list of nine erroneous propositions on "Natural and Christian ethics," e.g., "The science of philosophical things and morals and also civil laws may and ought to keep aloof from divine and ecclesiastical authority" (prop.57); that "Authority is nothing else but numbers and the sum total of material forces" (prop.60); that "It is lawful to refuse obedience to legitimate princes, and even to rebel against them" (prop.63).

Ten propositions summarized the "Errors concerning Christian marriage," notably those affirming that "The doctrine that Christ has raised marriage to the dignity of a sacrament cannot be at all tolerated" (prop.65); that "in many cases divorce properly so called may be decreed by the civil authority" (prop.67); or that "In force of a merely civil contract there may exist between Christians a real marriage" (prop.73).

"Errors regarding the civil power of the Sovereign Pontiff" were comprehended in two propositions, the second of which said that "The abolition of the temporal power of which the Apostolic See is possessed would contribute in the greatest degree to the liberty and prosperity of the Church" (prop.76).

Finally, section ten listed four "Errors having reference to modern Liberalism." The last of these is, no doubt, the most famous of the entire list: "The Roman Pontiff can, and ought to, reconcile himself, and come to terms with progress, liberalism, and modern civilization" (prop.80).

In 1974, during the beatification process of Pius IX, the Promoter-General of the Faith cited the Syllabus as one of the "difficulties" posed by the examination of the cause, referring to them as "difficulties...regarding the opportuneness of certain propositions which would eventually be criticized even by Catholic authors."[46] Indeed, there was strident criticism, even in certain Catholic circles.

Reactions

The encyclical, dated December 8, and the Syllabus, were sent to the bishops the following week and made public on December 21. Count de Sartiges, the French ambassador to Rome, had already sent a dispatch to his Minister of Foreign Affairs signalling the encyclical's content: "It is said to be more doctrinal than political, although indirectly it does touch on all the major questions. More particularly, it would strike at the doctrines of *Avenir* and of Falloux and Montalembert."[47]

It is true that the encyclical and the Syllabus struck a blow not only against the anti-clericals, agnostics, and atheists, but also against liberal Catholics. As Msgr. Pie—an authorized commentator—would say at a gathering of his clergy, "the act of December 8...has considerable range. True, it is directed against adversaries outside, but it is addressed even more, if that is possible, to those inside."[48]

The liberals were presented with a catastrophe. Even before he had learned the content of these two Roman acts, Alfred de Falloux expressed his dismay to Montalembert: "The Church has been brought to one of the most formidable trials she has ever had to undergo. I must admit how surprised I am, or rather, how profoundly wrong I have been. I had always refused to believe that Providence would allow this final catastrophe to occur, coming on top of so many others!"[49] Montalembert thought he would resign from the editorial team of the *Correspondant*, together with his most high-profile liberal friends (Falloux, Broglie, Cochin), in order to "make room for people less compromised and less defenseless."[50] In

---

[46] P. R. Perez, "Alcune difficoltà emerse nelle discussioni 'Super Virtutibus' del Servo di Dio Papa IX," in Carlo Snider, *Pio IX nella luce dei processi canonici* (Vatican City: Editrice la Postulazione, della causa di Pio IX/Libreria Editrice Vaticana, 1992), p.237. Snider replied to this difficulty in Chapters 7-9 of the work cited.

[47] Dispatch of December 15, 1864, to Edouard Drouyn de Lhuys, A.M.A.E., C.P., Rome 1028, f.276.

[48] Msgr. Pie, "Entretien avec le clergé," July 1865, in *Oeuvres de Msgr. l'Evêque de Poitiers*, V, 436.

[49] Letter of December 25, 1864, in Montalembert, *Correspondance*, p.313.

[50] Letter from Montalembert to Falloux, December 30, 1864, in Montalembert, *Correspondance*, pp.314-15.

the end the group did not protest publicly, as certain people were urging them to do; it was left to Msgr. Dupanloup to endeavor to propagate a minimalist interpretation.

In France, the government and anti-clerical press showed great hostility to the Pope's condemnations. *Le Siècle* stigmatized the "supreme insult offered to the modern world by a doomed papacy"; the *Revue des Deux-Mondes* protested: "Is it possible to issue such an anathema, the last gasp of political ambition, so alien to Christianity's origins, while invoking the Galilee Fisherman and Paul, the great man who converted the world while he worked with his hands?" (Jan. 1, 1865); the *Journal des Débats* was highly disturbed: "This pope who speaks so loftily to the whole world, who, in his Bulls, in Latin, treats kings as his lieutenants, evokes the nightmare of a papal power that would devour civil society" (Jan. 1, 1865). While all these newspapers were publishing extensive extracts from the Syllabus and commenting on it, on January 1, 1865, Napoleon III, through his Minister for Justice and Religions, Baroche, sent a circular letter to the bishops of France, prohibiting them from "making public these acts which contain propositions contrary to the principles underlying the Empire's constitution," and enjoining them to make it clear to their diocesan clergy that "they should abstain, in the present circumstances, from saying anything that could give cause for regrettable misinterpretation."[51]

The bishops' reactions varied. Some eighty bishops reacted one way or another. About thirty of them contented themselves with writing a letter of protest to the Minister. (There was one, however, the Bishop of Montpellier, who actually approved of the prohibition.) Others preferred the more classic forms of issuing a bishop's pastoral, addressing to the clergy or giving a pastoral instruction, which provided the opportunity of commenting on the encyclical and the catalogue of condemned errors. The first two French bishops to protest to the Minister, on January 2, were Msgr. Pie, Bishop of Poitiers, and Msgr. Doney, Bishop of Montauban, who had been among the most insistent in requesting the Pope to undertake this condemnation. Both of them commented on the pontifical documents in a pastoral letter or an address to their clergy.

Two bishops acted in contravention of the government's prohibition: Msgr. de Dreux-Brézé, Bishop of Moulins, and Cardinal Mathieu, Archbishop of Besançon. Both of them, celebrating the Feast of the Epiphany in their cathedrals on January 8, read out the entire text of the encyclical and the Syllabus. They were brought before the Council of State and

---

[51] Baroche's circular is published in *Encycliques*, II, 219. Also printed, pp.220-549, are the bishops' responses to this circular and the comments they made on the Syllabus. These responses, together with other documents, are also found in the collection *L'Encyclique et les Evêques de France* (Paris: E. Dentu, 1865).

condemned for a breach of the law.[52] However, the most famous episcopal
reaction came from Msgr. Dupanloup. Taking as his pretext an important
diplomatic accord that had been signed by France and Italy the previous
September 15—to which we shall return in the next chapter—he refuted
the attacks in the pro-government and anti-clerical journals and set forth
his own commentary on the encyclical and the Syllabus. He did this in a
bulky pamphlet, in which he explained that "the encyclical has not been
interpreted, it has been misrepresented. Furthermore, the government itself is strangely mistaken about it."[53]

In the case of Roman documents, he explained, it was necessary to observe "elementary rules of interpretation." The condemnation of a proposition "does not necessarily imply that its opposite is being affirmed," nor
should it be regarded as "universal and absolute." An unbiased reading
should pay attention to "all the terms and all the slightest nuances." Thus
Msgr. Dupanloup managed to say that the Pope had condemned only
"unlimited liberty," not "whatever is good in progress, whatever is truly
useful in modern civilization, whatever is truly liberal and Christian in
Liberalism." The Bishop of Orléans urged that "the Church is not the
enemy of 'political liberty'"; on the contrary, "I dare to say that, in this
regard, no spirit is more liberal than hers."

Announced on January 23 and available for sale on the 26th, Msgr.
Dupanloup's pamphlet was immediately a great success. In three weeks
it had sold 100,000 copies. Liberal Catholics saw it as a rehabilitation of
their struggle, and Catholics loyal to the Pope saw it as a skillful justification. Dupanloup's first biographer and practically all subsequent historians mention that the Pope wrote a Brief of congratulation to him, and
that 630 bishops from all continents wrote congratulating him on his
pamphlet.[54]

An attentive reading of Pius IX's Brief to the Bishop of Orléans, dated
February 4, which the latter had reproduced at the head of subsequent
editions of his pamphlet, shows that it did indeed contain praise for the
manner in which Msgr. Dupanloup had refuted "the calumnies and errors of the newspapers, which had so lamentably disfigured the meaning
of the teaching proposed by Us." One phrase, however, shows the Pope's
dissatisfaction: "We address the present testimony of our gratitude to you,
certain that…you will teach your people and make them understand the
true meaning of our Letters with even greater zeal and care than you have
shown in refuting the calumnious interpretations forced upon them."

[52] Paul Pelletier, *Pierre Simon de Dreux-Brézé* (Charroux: Editions des Cahiers
Bourbonnais, 1994), pp.303-4.
[53] Msgr. Dupanloup, *La Convention du 15 septembre et l'encyclique du 8 décembre* (Paris:
Charles Douniol, 1865).
[54] Lagrange, *Vie de Mgr. Dupanloup*, II, 471-73.

In other words, the celebrated pamphlet had not yet presented "the true meaning" of the encyclical and the Syllabus…

As for the letters from the 630 bishops, in the absence of a systematic analysis of them which has not yet been made, they were clearly far from representing a rallying to Msgr. Dupanloup's liberal standard. "Most of them, no doubt, were simply polite and grateful acknowledgments. Many of them, perhaps, expressed certain reserves. Others, indeed, contained more unequivocal praise, though such praise could only refer to the points praised by the Pope. Some, of course, mainly praised the commentary, designed for the use of liberal Catholics."[55]

Entirely contrary to Msgr. Dupanloup's interpretation was that of Louis Veuillot. Still without a newspaper, and hostile to the Bishop of Orléans's pamphlet, Veuillot published another in reply, identically printed and produced, entitled *L'Illusion libérale*.[56] He explained, in thirty-nine short chapters, that

> the liberal Catholic is neither Catholic nor liberal. What I mean by this—and I am not doubting his sincerity—is that he has lost both the true notion of liberty and the true notion of the Church. He may say that he is a liberal Catholic as much as he pleases, but he exhibits a much more well-known character, and all his features show us someone met with only too frequently in the history of the Church: his true name is SECTARIAN…. Catholic liberalism and the spirit of the world are of the same blood; they tend towards each other by a thousand slopes….Heresy, which does not deny all the truth at once, which does not affirm all the error at once, opens a watercourse for these futile springs; they converge on it from two opposite sides, and so the torrent swells. If heresy breaks its banks, there is only one solid ground, only one refuge: the ROCK…*Tu es Petrus…et non praevalebunt.*"

This work was neither a commentary on the encyclical and Syllabus, nor a refutation of Dupanloup's pamphlet as such; but it throws down the gauntlet to liberal Catholics and calls people to "rally around the Sovereign Pontiff, to follow his inspired directives unshakably, to affirm with him those truths which alone will save both our souls and the world." Pius IX really savored this work: "These are my ideas, utterly and absolutely."[57]

In France, other works were published to defend the encyclical, notably *L'Encyclique du 8 décembre 1864 et les principes de 1789, ou l'Eglise, l'Etat et la liberté* by Keller, the former Alsatian deputy, and *La doctrine*

---

[55] Maynard, *Monseigneur Dupanloup et M. Lagrange*, p.140.
[56] This work, which appeared in 1866, was republished in a new edition in 1989 with the addition of a bibliography: Éditions Dismas, Haut-le-Wastia, Belgium.
[57] Words cited by Aubert, p.25.

de l'encyclique du 8 décembre 1864, conforme à l'enseignement catholique by
Canon Peltier of Rheims.

Abroad, polemics were less animated. The anti-clerical press profited
from the encyclical to discredit the Church, and in Naples and Palermo
Freemasons were to be seen burning the two pontifical documents in a
public square, but generally the hostility of those opposed to it—from
whichever camp—was less in evidence. Initially the Austrian and Italian
governments tried to prohibit the publication of the pontifical documents,
but then they abandoned the attempt. A man like Döllinger felt himself
targeted by some of the propositions of the Syllabus, but the violent pamphlet he wrote at the time was not published until after his death.

In the German-speaking countries it was primarily supporters of the
Syllabus who made their voices heard. Cardinal Rauscher, Archbishop of
Vienna, in *Der Staat ohne Gott* (The State without God), praised the Pope
for having set his face against the separation of Church and State. The
Jesuits started a journal, *Stimmen aus Maria Laach,* to provide a commentary on the Syllabus, and another Jesuit, Fr. Clemens Schrader, a professor
in Rome and subsequently in Vienna, published a series of pamphlets
entitled *Der Papst und die modernen Ideen* (The Pope and modern ideas).

The Syllabus, together with the dogma of the Immaculate Conception and the First Vatican Council, was one of the three great milestones
of Pius IX's pontificate. In fact the Pope himself indicated the continuity
between the three events. The dogma was proclaimed on December 8,
1854, the Pope symbolically gave the Syllabus the date of December 8,
1864, and he opened the Council on December 8, 1869.

In the same way as the preparatory commission for the dogma was the
first preparatory commission for the Syllabus, anticipating the publication
of the encyclical *Quanta Cura* and its famous annex, it was on the occasion of a solemn session of the Congregation of Rites that Pius IX made
known his intention of summoning a General Council of the Church.

Propaganda Fide

It would be a mistake to interpret the Syllabus solely as the sign of a
papal authority anxious to create a unity, focused on itself, by firmly and
solemnly fixing the boundaries of Catholic doctrine.

Certainly, on all levels, doctrinal and liturgical, Pius IX did encourage this "movement towards Rome" which can be seen intensifying over a
long period from the first decades of the nineteenth century. At the same
time, however, he labored for the Church's expansion on all the continents; this is one of the characteristics of his pontificate.[58]

---

[58] Philippe Boutry has given a magnificent presentation, from the French perspective,
of this twofold movement: "Le mouvement vers Rome et le renouveau missionnaire"
in *Histoire de la France religieuse*, under the direction of Jacques Le Goff and René
Rémond (Seuil, 1991), III, 423-63.

Pius IX's missionary concern was expressed in a twofold direction: towards non-Catholic Christians (particularly Eastern Christians), who must be brought back to the See of Peter, and towards those peoples who had not yet been Christianized. The history of this twofold missionary thrust belongs to general Church history: it would go beyond the narrow confines of this biography. We shall content ourselves, therefore, with mentioning certain significant facts belonging largely to the years when the Syllabus was being actively prepared.

We have already referred to Pius IX's constant concern, manifested from the very first period of his pontificate, for the Oriental Churches, whether Catholic or not. The "union" of the Oriental Churches with Rome was close to his heart, and he worked for it throughout the whole span of his pontificate. This question was more particularly the responsibility of the Congregation of the Propagation of the Faith. From 1856, for almost twenty years, it was directed by a very active man, Cardinal Barnabo. His initiatives, together with those of the Pope, led to certain results, and some of these were lasting.

This concern for the return of the Orthodox Churches to the bosom of Catholicism was notably re-awakened when, in 1858, with the encouragement of the new Tsar of Russia, Alexander II, there was talk of abolishing serfdom—which affected more than twenty-two million Russians.[59] Pius IX foresaw that this event, by its very nature, would change the religious situation in Russia, and he sent Dom Pitra on a mission thither. He told him: "We must not lose sight of the fact that we are on the threshold of great events. I do not share the illusions of many people who view things, as they say, through rose-tinted spectacles. I am not very optimistic about Russia and its Emperor Alexander. Nonetheless the enfranchisement of the serfs is, in itself, a great event, even for religion. It will result in all sorts of movements in Russia, and it seems that God desires to play a part in this. In this case we must seek to see things as Providence does and make appropriate preparations."[60]

Dom Pitra's mission was entirely a scholarly one. He was to go and study and edit the canonical sources of the Orthodox. "After protracted studies," one of his biographers tells us, "he reached the conclusion that, up to the schism of Photius (or the steps taken that brought it about), the Oriental Church, and in particular the Church of Constantinople, had been closely united to the Roman Church."[61] However, it was not from Russia that the most striking conversions to Catholicism came in

---

[59] The abolition of serfdom did not take place until 1861.
[60] Cited by Dom Fernand Cabrol, *Histoire du cardinal Pitra* (Paris: Victor Retaux & Fils, 1893), p.223.
[61] *Ibid.*, p.225.

the 1860's. In January 1861, the Bulgarian Orthodox community in Constantinople made known its intention of "uniting with the Holy Roman Church."[62] Pius IX immediately let it be known, through a brief to Msgr. Brunoni, vicar-apostolic in Constantinople, that he would receive them with joy and that he would grant them what he had promised in the 1848 encyclical to the Orientals, that is, that they would be able to maintain their religious customs and their clergy. In April a Bulgarian delegation came to Rome, and the old *higumen* Sokolski, having made the Catholic profession of faith required of former Oriental schismatics, was consecrated archbishop by the Pope himself. The Turkish government recognized his authority and conversions to Catholicism soon multiplied (the figure would eventually rise to sixty thousand). Some months later, however, Msgr. Sokolski disappeared in Russia in grievous circumstances, no doubt the victim of the Orthodox authorities. Although Pius IX gave them a new archbishop in 1865, Msgr. Popoff, the number of Bulgarian Uniates dropped considerably.

In November 1861 another conversion greatly raised Pius IX's hopes. The Greek Archbishop Melethios converted to Catholicism. The Pope believed that it heralded a vast conversion movement in Greece. In January 1862, furthermore, in the apostolic letter *Romani Pontifices* he announced the creation of a Congregation for the Oriental Rite at the heart of the Congregation of the Propagation of the Faith.[63] The new Congregation was given the particular task of "examining the canons of the Oriental Church and Eastern books of all kinds, its versions of the Bible and discipline." It had the obligation of preserving the existing traditions in each Oriental Church united to Rome (each cardinal member of the Congregation was allotted a particular rite) and preparing to receive new Oriental communities.

Pius IX's anticipation of huge numbers of faithful returning to the Catholic Church was not fulfilled, however. It should be borne in mind that almost all the non-Catholic Oriental Churches were situated in two antagonistic empires: the Russian and Turkish Empires. Several Orthodox communities under the Turkish yoke saw the Russian Empire as their future liberator; they had no intention of forfeiting its protection and sympathy by allying themselves with Rome. There was also the negative example given to these Orthodox Churches by some of their neighboring Oriental Catholics. Under Pius IX's pontificate a number of ephemeral local schisms troubled the turbulent Oriental Catholic Churches, *e.g.*, in 1860 in the Patriarchate of Antioch (Holy Land Catholics of the Greek

---

[62] Letter of December 23, 1860 (according to the Julian Calendar), and subsequent documents in *Annales I*, 438ff.

[63] Text of the letter in *Annales I*, pp.467-70.

Rite); at the end of the 1860's several Armenian Catholic bishops were involved.

Missions to pagan peoples were not impeded by the same difficulties. Cardinal Barnabo "presided with competence, prudence, and energy over the marvellous missionary expansion which characterized the pontificate of Pius IX."[64]

Here we cannot go into the history of these missions on all the continents. All historians agree that the Pope had no hesitation in encouraging all the new initiatives and congregations. The missionary aspirations he had had as a young priest could now be realized by other founding figures. Without going into the details of the way he supported this or that enterprise, we mention only the help he gave in 1864—the year of the Syllabus—to Fr. Daniel Comboni, who had come to present an ambitious "plan for the regeneration of Africa." This was a large-scale missionary project aiming to combat slavery and foster an African clergy.[65] In 1867 Fr. Comboni, a missionary priest of Mazza's Institute [Verona], succeeded in founding the Institute of Missionaries for Black Africa (usually called "Combonians"), and in 1872 he founded the Institute of Pious Mothers. He is considered to have re-planted the Catholic Church in Sudan.

France's part in this missionary expansion in the second half of the nineteenth century was considerable. "At the death of Pius IX more than three-quarters of the priests and religious men and women engaged in missionary activity in the world were French."[66]

---

[64] Aubert, p.283.
[65] Fr. Pietro Chiocchetta, "Pio IX e le Missioni," *Atti del II. Convegno*, pp.51-68; Domenico Agesso, *Un prophète pour l'Afrique: Daniel Comboni* (Médiaspaul, 1994), pp.37-47.
[66] Boutry, "Le mouvement vers Rome," pp.445-46.

CHAPTER 13

THE ROMAN QUESTION

For a time, the Syllabus and the debates it prompted relegated the "Roman question"—*i.e.*, the fate of Rome and of the remainder of the Papal States in the Kingdom of Italy—to a place of secondary importance. Hitherto these States had enjoyed a stable existence, recognized by the majority of countries throughout the world.

Pius IX had never lost sight of this "Roman question." Even during the laborious preparation of the Syllabus, he had seized all the opportunities presented to him to remind people of the legitimacy of his temporal power and of his absolute refusal to accept being dispossessed of Rome and Latium. In May 1863 he had undertaken a journey to the provinces of the south of Latium, also called the Ciociaria. His twofold aim was to complete his great journey of 1957 by visiting towns which, at the time, had not received the Sovereign Pontiff, and to give support to a population that was suffering from what was then called "Neapolitan brigandage."

Situated at the frontier of the ancient Kingdom of Naples (which had now been integrated into the Kingdom of Italy), the Ciociaria had served as a refuge for troops who had remained loyal to the Bourbons of Naples. The guerrilla warfare of these soldiers, which was initially encouraged by Francis II (in exile in Rome), had become a veritable brigandry, to the detriment of the population of the south of the Papal States. Furthermore, the Italian government used the incursions of these "Neapolitan brigands" as a pretext for accusing the Pope of stirring up trouble and threatening the Italian State with military intervention.

Pius IX then sent in the papal troops, together with the French troops stationed in Rome, to curb this brigandage. He himself decided to visit the region's principle towns. In the space of ten days he visited Velletri, Valvisciolo, Frosinone, Veroli, Casamari, Alatri, Ceprano, Ferentino, and Anagni. Apart from the usual official ceremonies and the many liturgical functions he celebrated, the Pope received delegations from the towns visited, and also from the small country communities. This journey was a means of reassuring the anxious population and reaffirming his temporal rights over territories which Italy was coveting.

The September Convention and the Vegezzi Mission

Three months prior to the publication of the Syllabus a diplomatic event took place which reminded the world that the Roman question had remained unsolved. Napoleon III was still hoping that a congress of the great European powers, in which the Holy See would take part, could resolve the question in a peaceful manner. However, the principal powers had hardly any interest in this idea of a congress, which had been spoken of for a long time, and some of them (notably England) were categorically hostile to it.

Accordingly, Napoleon III decided to engage in direct and secret negotiations with the Kingdom of Italy. On September 15, 1864, the French and Italian governments concluded a "convention" to deal with the Roman question. The two governments had negotiated without even informing the principal interested party, Pius IX. What would henceforth be called the "September Convention" stipulated that Italy would engage "not to attack the Holy Father's present territory, and would obstruct, even by force, any attack coming from outside against the said territory"; it would forgo "all objections against the organization of a papal army, even if were composed of foreign Catholic volunteers," and declared itself ready to "bear the cost of a proportion of the debts of the former ecclesiastical states." France, for its part, would gradually withdraw her troops from the Papal States within the space of two years.

When the Pope learned of the contents of the accord, he was very concerned. If France were to withdraw her troops, currently stationed in Rome, the fate of the Papal States would be very precarious. What could the eight thousand soldiers of the papal army do against the tens of thousands of men Italy could enroll? At an audience with the French ambassador, Count Sartiges, Pius IX expressed his lack of faith in the Italian promises: "The French soldiers will not have crossed the frontier when the Papal State will be immediately assailed, first by irregulars, and then by regular forces."[1]

In private, nonetheless, Pius IX acknowledged that "there is some good in this Convention." In fact, instead of restoring to him the provinces of which his States had been despoiled, the Convention seemed to guarantee the intangibility of the existing frontiers. Even if the greatest prudence was always called for when dealing with Italian governments, which in the past had shown so much hostility to the Church, the Pope wanted to see this Convention as a gesture of goodwill on the part of Victor Emmanuel II.

Meanwhile, Pius IX was preoccupied with the dramatic situation in which most of the Italian dioceses found themselves. Ever since the various annexations, nine bishops or archbishops had been brought to trial and condemned, thirty others had been tried but acquitted, five others

---

[1]   Cited by Pietro Pirri, *Pio IX e Vittorio Emanuele II dal loro Carteggio privato*, 5 vols. (Rome: Pontificia Università Gregoriana, 1961), Vol.III, *La Questione Romana* (1864-1870), Pt.I, 23-24; hereafter, *Pio IX e Vittorio Emanuele.*

had been banished from their dioceses and held in Turin. Forty-one had chosen the path of exile. Added to this number there were tens of dioceses lacking a bishop, either because the Italian government was refusing to allow the consecrated bishops to take possession of their sees, or because the nominations, which initially depended on the civil authorities, had not been made.[2]

In all these dioceses lacking a bishop, religious life was necessarily upset, to say nothing of the dysfunctions provoked by the new laws which the Italian government had introduced. Pius IX tried to intervene in the most urgent cases, as witness a letter from this time to his brother Gaetano: he told him that he was putting three hundred écus per month into the Gualandi Institute in Bologna (a hospice for the deaf and dumb, founded by two priest-brothers in 1850), "because the State's local authorities are no longer paying for their citizens. I have not the heart to put so many poor creatures on to the streets...."[3]

In March 1865 two men highly regarded by Pius IX, Don Bosco and Msgr. Ghilardi, Bishop of Mondovi, one of Italy's most intransigent bishops, suggested that he re-establish contact with Victor Emmanuel with a view to putting an end, at least, to this disastrous situation in the Italian dioceses. The Pope followed these recommendations. On March 10, he wrote a letter to Victor Emmanuel indicating that he was "anxious to supply the vacancies in so many episcopal sees in Italy" and suggested that the King should send "a person of confidence" to Rome: "I would prefer a good and straightforward layman," the Pope specified, "rather than an ecclesiastic of weak character."[4]

The Pope's request was limited solely to the question of episcopal nominations. He made no reference to the other religious questions and the Roman question. In the Pope's judgment, this was the best way of arriving at an agreement. The spiritual needs of the faithful called for the swift appointment of bishops. The King replied to the Pope's letter, glad to re-establish relations which had been interrupted for five years, and announced that he was sending a negotiator, Francesco Saverio Vegezzi, a trained lawyer. He was, the King said, "my personal friend."

Vegezzi and another envoy, the lawyer Giovanni Maurizio, arrived in Rome in April. They were received by the Pope, but the real negotiations took place with the Secretary of State, beginning on April 21 and

---

[2] Complete list drawn up by Fr. Margotti in *Unità Cattolica* of April 4, 1865, translated in *Le Monde* of November 13, 1865, under the title "Martyrologe de l'épiscopat italien" and reproduced in *Annales I*, 602-606.
[3] Letter of Pius IX to Gaetano Mastai, November 14, 1862, published by Polverari, "Lettere di Pio IX ai familiari," in *Pio IX nel primo centenario*, pp.55-56.
[4] Letter of Pius IX and Victor Emmanuel's reply are published in Pirri, *Pio IX e Vittorio Emanuele II*, III, II, 51-53.

23 and May 3. Reading the long account provided by Cardinal Antonelli, one can see that the King's envoys showed themselves very conciliatory at that time; they gave him to understand that, with regard to a number of bishops who had been expelled or exiled (apart from two or three difficult cases), it would not be difficult to re-integrate them into their dioceses; nominations to the vacant sees could be made by the Pope himself after obtaining the agreement of the Italian authorities, and all of them would be dispensed from swearing an oath to the King.[5] In May, however, in the middle of negotiations, Vegezzi was summoned to Turin. Under pressure from the anti-clerical deputies, who were hostile to the course these discussions were taking—leading to permission for the return or the nomination of tens of bishops—the government gave the negotiators new instructions. Vegezzi returned to Rome in June and insisted that the bishops nominated or re-integrated would have to take an oath of allegiance to the King—a demand he had dropped a month before. The Holy See, which did not recognize the legitimacy of the Kingdom of Italy, could not accept this. Other difficulties surfaced, showing that the Italian government's position had suddenly hardened. This brought about the failure of a mission which Pius IX had wanted to succeed and which initially had been so full of promise.

Against Freemasonry

No historian, to our knowledge, has made the connection between this failure of Vegezzi's mission in June 1865 and the solemn condemnation of Freemasonry issued by Pius IX the following September. It does seem, however, that there is some link between these two events, even if not a direct one. In fact, the negotiations failed because the anti-clerical fringe of the Italian parliament was strong enough to impose its views on the government and on the weak King, Victor Emmanuel.

Anti-clericalism in Italy, as elsewhere in Europe, originated in Freemasonry, which had a large and powerful membership. Furthermore, the great artisans of Italian unity (Mazzini, Cavour, Garibaldi) were Freemasons;[6] and in the years to which we are referring, Italian Freemasonry, split into rival observances, was trying to achieve its unity. "A congress of all the Masons of Italy took place in Florence in 1864," wrote the French Freemason historian, Naudon, "representing seventy lodges and five observances (the four Supreme Councils—Naples, Sicily, Turin, and Livorno—and the Grand Orient of Turin). This congress succeeded, in part, in remedying the evil from which Italian Masonry was suffering,

---

[5]   Complete text of Cardinal Antonelli's report in Pirri, *Pio IX e Vittorio Emanuele,* III, II, 59-66.
[6]   Paul Naudon, *Histoire générale de la Franc-maçonnerie,* 2nd ed. (Paris: Office du Livre, 1987), pp.170-173, and Epiphanius, *Massoneria e sette segrete: la faccia occulta della storia* (n.p., n.d.), pp.131ff.

and establishing a certain unity. The Grand Orient was entrusted with the direction of this task. Turin became the seat of the new observance and, for a very brief period, Garibaldi was its Grand Master."[7]

This attempt at a Masonic union, followed by the failure of the Vegezzi mission, may have led Pius IX to consider that Freemasonry was more dangerous than ever; to say nothing of Freemasonry's power in other countries of Europe or America, notably in Prussia, where the royal princes directed the Grand Lodge of the Freemasons of Germany.

At a consistory on September 25, 1865, furthermore, the Pope gave an allocution entirely dedicated to denouncing Freemasonry.[8] It is true that, ever since his first encyclical in 1846, and then twice subsequently (in the consistorial allocutions of April 20, 1849 and December 9, 1854), he had denounced the doings of "secret societies." But this was in passing, in the midst of other concerns. Now the whole allocution was on the subject of "this perverse society of men, commonly called Masonic, which, initially existing in shadows and in obscurity, has finally come out into the light of day, to the ruin both of religion and of human society."

The Pope recalled the condemnations issued by his predecessors. He regretted that Catholic sovereigns had taken so little account of them. "Would to Heaven they had acted with less indulgence in such a grave matter!" There would not have been "so many seditious movements, nor so many incendiary wars setting all Europe on fire, nor would so many bitter evils have afflicted the Church—and be afflicting her still."

Today "the Masonic sect…has developed to such an extent that, in these difficult times, it shows itself with impunity everywhere, and is more brazen than ever." Certain minds are still deluded as to the nature of this secret society, believing that "this institution has no other aim but to help people and succor them in adversity." This is a grave error. "What claims are made by this association of men of all religions and all beliefs? What is the purpose of these clandestine meetings and this oath that is so strictly required of initiates, who commit themselves never to reveal anything about these matters? And what is the meaning of the terribly severe punishments incurred by initiates if they should fail to keep faith with their oath? Surely, any society which thus flees from the light of day must be impious and criminal; for, as the Apostle says, the man who does evil hates the light."

Pius IX solemnly recalled the prohibition against Catholics taking part in these "baneful assemblies," under pain of excommunication. In the months that followed this public condemnation of Freemasonry, several

---

[7] Naudon, *Franc-maçonnerie*, pp.171, 173.
[8] Allocution *Multiplices Inter Machinationes*, French translation in *Annales I*, pp.594-95.

Masonic publications in France and Italy, intent on revenge, propagated the story that Pius IX himself, in his youth, had been a Freemason.

Apparently it was the Lodge of Palermo that first put out the accusation: "There was a man called Mastai-Ferretti who received the Masonic baptism and swore fraternity and love for his brothers. This man was later created Pope-King under the name of Pius IX, and then we find him pronouncing a curse and excommunication against all those who are affiliated to Freemasonry! But the curse and the excommunication fall on his own head; furthermore, by this very act, he has become a perjurer. The pope has thus excommunicated himself." In France, the journal *Le Monde Maçonnique* immediately went into print with this information.[9] Subsequently this Masonic journal, and others, would take up the subject again and again.

In February 1868 *Le Monde Maçonnique* again referred to an Italian publication, *L'Umanitario,* the organ of the Palermo Supreme Council, in support of its accusation, promising to put "all the documents under the scrutiny of our readers."[10] Some months later the journal published a letter from the Masonic Lodge of Messina, affirming that the future Pius IX had been initiated at Philadelphia on his way back from his mission in Chile.[11] Of course these accusations provoked indignant rebukes from Catholic newspapers. The Masonic journal tried to obtain documents in support of its claims from the Lodge of Philadelphia. Soon it had to admit that no trace had been found of a Mastai-Ferretti being initiated at Philadelphia and that "the nearest name to it in the registers of the Grand Orient of Pennsylvania was that of a Martin Ferretty, who was accepted as a Mason in 1849 at Lodge No. 187 held at Cuba (Havana)."[12]

The question seemed to be closed. However, some months after the death of Pius IX another Masonic publication re-floated the accusation, adding certain stories of a kind in which the forger Leo Taxil excelled.[13] This time it was suggested that the initiation took place not in Philadelphia, but in France, at Thionville, when the future Pius IX was not yet a priest and was serving in Napoleon's armies. This was augmented by an account of some of his "amours."[14] This is the unlikely story we have already mentioned in connection with the future pope's years as a young man.

[9] Caubet, "Revue des journaux," *Le Monde Maçonnique*, December 1865, pp.466-67.
[10] *Ibid.*, February 1868, p.617.
[11] *Ibid.*, August 1868, pp.224-26.
[12] *Ibid.*, January 1869, pp.536-37.
[13] Leo Taxil, *Les amours secretes de Pie IX, par un ancient camérier secret du pape* (Librairie Anticléricale, 1881).
[14] *La Chaîne d'Union*, April 1878, pp.138-39.

Some decades later most of the Masonic publications actually distanced themselves from the myth of "Pius IX the Freemason."[15] For a long time, however, some of them continued to propagate these historically indefensible assertions. Thus, even in 1925, in the *Acacia,* the French Grand Orient's "monthly review of Masonic and social studies and action," a major article on Pius IX noted that "it was even said that it had been affiliated to a Carbonari lodge, which is improbable."[16] To say that Pius IX had been a "Carbonaro" was implicitly to say that he had been a Freemason, since the two organizations were very closely allied. The myth was reborn from its ashes.

The Birth of Catholic Action

The Pope's anti-Masonic allocution, quoted above, also contained a passage in which Pius IX pitted "the pious societies of the faithful which flourish in the Catholic Church" against Freemasonry, "a society which flees the light of day." He praised the former in these terms: "In them, there is nothing hidden, nothing secret. The rules governing them are open to everyone's eyes, and all can see the works of charity practiced according to the doctrine of the Gospel."

Thus he was discreetly paying homage to certain Catholic organizations that had recently come on the scene; they were the hub of what in Italy is called the "Catholic Movement," which would be exemplified by the various organizations of Catholic Action. If it was Pius XI who gave a great impetus to Catholic Action movements throughout the whole Church, it can be said that the one who initiated it was Pius IX.

The question of Catholics' participation in Italian political life became particularly acute once the Romagna, the Marches, and Umbria had been detached from the Pope and annexed. Should Catholics get themselves elected to the Italian Parliament in order to try to counterbalance the influence of the anti-clericals, or would it be better for them, until the "Roman question" had been solved, to abstain from all participation in political life? Pius IX urged the latter attitude. To participate in elections would be to recognize the legitimacy of the institutions of the "usurper" State. Don Giacomo Margotti, editor of the great Catholic paper *L'Armonia,* esteemed by Pius IX and in regular contact with him, crystallized this resistance in his headline of January 8, 1861: *"Né eletti né elettori"* ("neither elected nor electors"). Catholics must be neither election candidates nor should they participate in elections.[17]

---

[15] Cf. esp. Ch.-M.L., "Pie IX ne fut pas franc-maçon," *L'Acacia,* January-June 1904, pp.54-60.

[16] "Les quatre derniers papes et la France," *L'Acacia,* September 1925, pp.65-66.

[17] A formula with the same meaning, *Non expedit,* "it is not appropriate," or "it is not beneficial," was used for the first time in 1866 by the Sacred Penitentiary.

This abstention from political life did not mean that Catholicism was restricted to the private domain. Instead of having the opportunity to defend Catholic ideas in the Parliament, lay Catholics, in accord with the ecclesiastical hierarchy, set up associations for the purpose of defending the Church and the interests of Catholics in all the domains (social, economic, cultural, educational). This was all the more essential, as the religious orders who, for centuries, had devoted themselves habitually to caritative and educational tasks, found that their work was being prohibited or obstructed by the infamous "Law on the Convents," to which we have already referred. It was in these years—the 1860's—that the first organizations came into being.

In 1865 a journalist, Gianbattista Casoni—who, incidentally, had taken part in the Congress of Malines in 1863 and had been shocked by Montalembert's addresses—and a lawyer, Cesare Fangarezzi, created the Italian Catholic Association for the defense of the liberty of the Church in Italy. On April 4, 1866, Pius IX wrote a brief of approbation for the organization, urging it to defend "the liberty of the Church and resist, in the manner required by prudence and charity, the efforts of irreligious men." The Italian government, on the occasion of the war against Austria, which was soon to break out, prohibited the association and obliged its leaders to go into hiding.

In May 1867 another association was formed; it was to prove more durable. This was the Society of Catholic Youth. The two founders, Mario Fani, from Viterbo, and Giovanni Acquaderni, from Bologna, had been leaders in their cities' local Catholic associations. It was these "Catholic societies" which Pius IX had referred to, in his anti-Masonic allocution of 1865, as "wholesome, well-adapted to promote piety and come to the aid of the poor." In order to escape the attacks of the Italian government, the movement, which hoped to spread to all the towns of Italy, took a motto that expressed its purely religious motivation: "Prayer, action, and sacrifice." The Pope approved the new organization in the brief *Dum Filii Belial* of May 2, 1868. Once again he contrasted the Catholic movements with the "sons of Belial who are at great pains to spread their assemblies of darkness, particularly among the young," and he praised this "union of young people which brandishes the banner of religion, setting it up against the impetuous irreligion and restraining it...." The clearly anti-Masonic spirit of the early days of Catholic Action has been thoroughly forgotten by its current members.

The Tonello Mission

The end of the 1860's was one of the periods in Pius IX's pontificate in which reasons for satisfaction alternated with signs of uneasiness. As we have seen, the Convention of September 1864 had been both distressing and, in a certain way, promising. The failure of the Vegezzi mission had shown that Pius IX's distrust of the Italian authorities was still a justified one. The situation of the Papal States was more delicate than ever.

In October 1865, taking advantage of the grave illness of his pro-Minister for War, the loyal Msgr. de Mérode, Pius IX relieved him of his duties. The news gave rise to various interpretations and was reported in all the European newspapers. Some people accused the prelate of having had dreams of grandeur when, after the manner of Haussmann, he transformed the face of old Rome, using papal troops for the task. Others saw his "fall" as the Secretary of State's revenge. At the beatification process the Promoter of the Faith would cite this removal of Msgr. de Mérode as one of the "difficulties" obstructing the cause of Pius IX.[18]

In reality Msgr. de Mérode had not forfeited the Pope's esteem; in removing him Pius IX was exercising a political choice. Ever since entering the government, Msgr. de Mérode had frequently clashed with the Secretary of State. Their temperaments and their analyses of the situation were opposite.[19] The one remained at heart a soldier, the other a diplomat. People said of Mérode that he was "a firebrand rather than a man of justice," and his enemies called him *il matto* (the madman) on account of his ardent and intransigent temperament.

When the Convention of September was to be implemented and the French troops were to quit Rome, leaving it weakened *vis-à-vis* Italy, Cardinal Antonelli judged it preferable to adopt a "low profile" and not to exacerbate the existing situation by hastily reinforcing the papal troops. It would be better to employ diplomacy than expand the armed forces.

Pius IX accepted these view. He asked Msgr. de Mérode to resign, and he refused. The Pope then relieved him of his functions and appointed a layman, General Kanzler, to replace him at the Ministry of War. To show that he continued to have full confidence in him, Pius IX kept Msgr. de Mérode as a chamberlain and then made him his almoner, naming him titular Archbishop of Melitena *in partibus infidelium.*

One further time, events led Pius IX to follow the path of negotiations urged by his Secretary of State. In 1866 Prussia and Italy became allies in a war against Austria. Austria was defeated at Sadowa. The Kingdom of Italy was able to annex Venetia, and Prussia pursued its hegemony by assuming the leadership of a North German Confederation. Meanwhile, France continued to withdraw its troops from Rome, a process that was complete by December of that year.

---

[18] Pérez, "Alcune difficolta," in Snider, *Pio IX nella luce dei processi canonici,* p.237.

[19] Msgr. Besson, *Frédéric-François-Xavier de Mérode: Sa vie et ses oeuvres* (Paris: Desclée, De Brouwer, & Cie, 1898), pp.164-165; Aubert, pp.102-3, 284; Falconi, *Antonelli,* pp.413ff.

This new situation put Italy in a position of strength. On the initiative of Napoleon III the Italian authorities again sent negotiators to
Rome.[20] The two Italian envoys, Michelangelo Tonello, professor of Roman law (and former professor of canon law), assisted by the lawyer Cal-
legaris, arrived in Rome on December 10, 1866, which was the very eve
of the departure of the last French troops. In addition to two audiences
with the Pope, they had many discussions with Cardinal Antonelli, until
the following March. In these discussions Tonello skillfully avoided raising the question of the vacant episcopal sees at the level of principle, but
proceeded case by case. He was so successful that, in February and March
Pius IX was able, in consistory, to proceed to nominate thirty-seven bishops and archbishops: twenty in different Italian provinces, including the
sees of Turin and Milan, and seventeen in the dioceses of the Papal States.
These conversations also made it possible to regulate various questions
that, properly speaking, were not religious, such as the Italian State's tak-
ing-over part of the public debts contracted by the Holy See for the territories that had been annexed, or the improvement of railway traffic between the two States.

The Eighteenth Centenary of Saints Peter and Paul

These accords, limited as they were—Tonello's request that the annexations should be recognized as legitimate had been firmly rejected by
Antonelli—made it possible to remedy, in part, the great distress existing
in certain Italian dioceses.

Accordingly, the eighteenth centenary of the martyrdom of the Apostles Peter and Paul, which took place the following June, unfolded in a
spirit of relative optimism.

Pius IX had wanted this commemoration to be, once again, a great
demonstration of the Church's unity around the Chair of Peter. The preceding December he had invited all the bishops of the world to come to
Rome for this celebration, and announced that on that occasion he would
also proceed to canonize a number of martyrs, confessors, and virgins.
The canonized *beati* belonged to different historical periods, but common
to most of them was that they had been persecuted or had suffered trials
for their faith. In giving them as examples to the whole Church, Pius IX
had in mind the hardship suffered by faithful and clergy in Italy and many
other countries.

This second and last canonization ceremony of his pontificate would
honor Blessed Pedro de Arbués, the first Inquisitor of the Faith in the
Kingdom of Aragon, killed by lapsed Jews in 1485; twenty-nine priests

---

[20] Pirri, *Pio IX e Vittorio Emanuele II*, III, I, 144-65, and many documents published in
Pt. II; Falconi, *Il giovane Mastai*, pp.424-427.

and religious of Gorcum, Holland, strangled and dismembered by Calvinists in 1572; Blessed Josaphat, Archbishop of Polotsk, massacred by the Orthodox in 1623; Blessed Germaine de Pibrac, a humble shepherdess who died in 1601 at the age of twenty-two; Blessed Paul of the Cross, the eighteenth century founder of the Passionists (a religious congregation with which Pius IX had been closely associated since his youth, as we have seen); Blessed Leonard of Port-Maurice, a Reformed Franciscan who died in 1751, one of the great apostles of devotion to the Immaculate Conception; and, finally, Blessed Marie-Françoise of the Five Wounds, a Franciscan Tertiary who died in 1791.

When this new meeting of the bishops in Rome was announced, some of them were uneasy: wasn't the Pope going to use this solemn occasion to define a new dogma, the dogma of his infallibility?

This unease is evident in the pastoral letters written by a few bishops (Dupanloup, Ginoulhiac, Ketteler) prior to their departure for Rome. It is much more clearly expressed, however, in a letter of April 1867 from Msgr. Ginoulhiac to Msgr. Dupanloup, reporting a rumor that was going around at the time: "The plan, therefore, was to seek in advance, from the bishops assembled in Rome, signs of adherence and the expression of a desire which would authorize this definition, either immediately or subsequently."[21] The rumor was unfounded, but it cropped up again in Rome two months later.

The celebrations of June 1867 were attended by even greater crowds than those in 1854 and 1862. Bishops arrived from all continents. The recent accords with Victor Emmanuel's government made it possible for many Italian bishops, priests, and faithful to come to Rome. Only the Catholic bishops of Russia (most numerous in the Polish and Ukrainian territories) were prevented by their government from rallying to the Pope's standard. The Orthodox Church regarded the canonization of Blessed Josaphat as an insult.

The main issue, however, was that for several years the Russian government had been trying to attract Russian Catholics into the Orthodox Church (even in the years 1865-66, fifty thousand of the Catholic faithful changed to Orthodoxy) and to subordinate the Polish hierarchy and clergy to its complete control.[22]

In June, therefore, the Pope was surrounded by 46 cardinals, all the Oriental Patriarchs, almost 500 archbishops and bishops, 20,000 priests,

---

[21] Unpublished letter of April 25, 1867, Archives of St. Sulpice, Paris.

[22] In 1866 the Russian government had renounced the concordat signed twenty years earlier. Other decisions, and the arrest of bishops and priests, led Pius IX to protest, in the encyclical *Levate* of October 17, 1867, against the "calamities" affecting Russian and Polish Catholics (*Annales ecclésiastiques de 1867 à 1868*, ed. Joseph Chantrel [Paris: Gaume & Cie, 1896], pp. 673-678; hereafter, *Annales II*).

and about 150,000 of the faithful. As we have said, there had been a rumor for several months that the dogma of papal infallibility would be proclaimed at this solemn meeting.[23] There was no basis to the rumor, because no preparatory commission had met to write a draft decree. However, the rumor did manifest the hopes of many people and the fears of some.

One fact did give a certain substance to the rumor. On June 3, before most of the bishops and faithful had yet arrived in Rome, the *Civiltà Cattolica* suggested that its readers, and the faithful, should take a vow to defend papal infallibility. The vow contained the following definition of this doctrine: "That the Pope, when using his authority and as universal Teacher, defines EX CATHEDRA (as it is said) what is to be believed in matters of faith and morals, he is infallible; it follows that his dogmatic decrees are irreformable and binding in conscience, even before they have been followed by the Church's assent."[24]

To those who had doubts about this dogmatic definition, such a suggestion, under these circumstances, coming from a journal regarded as expressing the Pope's own thought, seemed to signal that some new dogma was about to be foisted in them. It was nothing of the kind.

The ceremonies began with the celebration of Corpus Christi, in which the Pope himself was seen to carry the Blessed Sacrament. The canonization ceremony took place on June 29.

On July 1, Pius IX, responding to the bishops who had come to present him with an address exalting the authority and magisterium of the Sovereign Pontiff,[25] officially announced that he would summon an ecumenical Council, although he did not fix the date. This was confirmation of the less solemn announcement made in December 1864. The religious celebrations ended on Sunday, July 7, with the beatification of 205 martyrs of Japan who died for their faith between 1517 and 1632.

At this time the Pope was also given very many gifts (mostly precious objects) and financial donations to replenish the papal coffers. Louis Veuillot, in *L'Univers,* which he had succeeded in re-launching two months ago, after a seven-year interruption of publication, reported to his readers on the magnificence of the ceremonies and the submission to the Pope of the entire episcopate—even if the word "infallibility" was not mentioned.

---

[23] Lagrange cites three letters from bishops who were uneasy about this dogma being decided upon "immediately and, as it were, in passing" (letter of Msgr. Ketteler, Bishop of Mainz) (*Vie de Mgr. Dupanloup*, III, 48-49).

[24] Complete translation of the vow in *Annales II*, 560-61.

[25] Cf. Lagrange on the important part again played by Msgr. Dupanloup in the drafting of this address (*Vie de Mgr. Dupanloup*, III, 57-60).

Mentana

Scarcely two months after the conclusion of the Roman ceremonies—symbolizing the Church's universality and unity centered on the pope—a "Peace Congress" took place in Geneva at the instigation of various European revolutionary movements. The guest of honor was Garibaldi. He produced a series of twelve propositions.[26]

The evident pacifism—"All nations are sisters"—was mixed together with the dream of world government—"Every nation will appoint a member of the Congress," and "The Congress must be permanent, central, and universal." In fact, this Peace Congress represented a threat of war. Indeed, one of the propositions was that "The slave has the right to make war against tyrants." Most significantly, Garibaldi showed great hostility to the Church by having the following propositions adopted: "We declare that the Papacy, the most noxious of sects, has fallen"; "The priesthood of ignorance and revelations must be replaced by the priesthood of enlightenment, truth, and justice." He concluded his address by saying that "There will be no improvement until priestcraft is defeated."

Expressions such as these, and the presence in Geneva of so many representatives of organizations hostile to governments, provoked protest on the part of certain newspapers. In the end, on September 12, the Swiss authorities prohibited the continuance of the Congress, after Garibaldi had left Geneva in a hurry.

For several months, however, Garibaldi had been recruiting volunteers in various towns near the Papal States. Initially the Italian government, directed by Urbano Rattazzi, did nothing about this. But when, at the end of September, Garibaldi's men made their first incursions into papal territory, their chief was arrested and detained on the island of Caprera, off the coast of Sardinia. A number of deputies immediately protested against the illegality of this arrest, and trouble surfaced in various Italian cities. In fact Rattazzi's attitude was more than ambiguous. It seemed likely that he would repeat the tactics employed by Cavour to get possession of the Marches and Umbria: he would let Garibaldi's men stir up unrest in the Papal States and in Rome, and then intervene under the pretext of re-establishing order.

Garibaldi's first incursions were repulsed by papal troops and were in no way supported by the populace. At the beginning of October the *Giornale di Roma* was able to publish a list of 115 Garibaldian prisoners. Unrest continued, however.

France, which was not fooled by the tactics of the Rattazzi government, decided on October 16 to send in troops to the Pope's aid. This intervention was justified by the Italian government's incapacity to respect

---

[26] Text in *Annales II*, 639.

the September Convention. Nonetheless the French troops did not leave Toulon until October 27. In the meantime, taking advantage of a change of government in Italy, Garibaldi had succeeded in escaping from Caprera. He assembled his volunteers in Florence, invaded the Papal States, and on October 26 gained possession of Monte Rotondo. Post and telegraph services were interrupted, and so-called "deserters" from the regular Italian army went over to the Garibaldians. In Rome, Garibaldi's men stirred up trouble and exploded a huge bomb in a barracks of the papal Zouaves, killing twenty-seven people.[27]

On October 29, the French expeditionary force commanded by General de Failly disembarked at Civita Vecchia, entering Rome on the 31st. Garibaldi's troops had made progress. They had taken possession of Viterbo and were threatening the north of Rome. What is more, the regular Italian troops seemed desirous of joining the Garibaldians, and they too entered the Papal States, occupying Acquapendente, Orte, and Frosinone.

It was decided that joint action should be taken by the French and the papal troops; this led to the victory of Mentana.[28] On November 3, 2,913 papal troops commanded by General de Courten and 2,000 French troops commanded by General de Polhès set out from Rome before daybreak. Before Mentana they encountered the first troops of Garibaldi. The latter were 9,000 strong according to General Kanzler's estimate, and 10,000 according to the French ambassador. (*L'Osservatore Romano*, with some exaggeration, put the number at 15,000.) Fighting took place from the end of the morning, initially involving papal troops and Garibaldians. The French were held in reserve, and did not intervene until the middle of the afternoon. In his report, General de Failly said that "wonders had been worked" by the new rifles (Chassepot rifles) with which the French army had been equipped. Garibaldi's men retreated to Mentana. French and papal troops laid siege to the town. On the morning of the 4th, when Garibaldi had already fled, the besieged forces surrendered. They left on the

---

[27] The culprits, Giuseppe Monti and Gaetano Tognetti, were arrested; in October 1868 they were condemned to death. Despite the pressure exerted on Pius IX by the Italian government and parliament to pardon the two condemned men or commute their punishment, they were executed on November 24. This double execution came up in 1974 as one of the "difficulties" put forward by the Promoter of the Faith in the beatification process of Pius IX. Cf. Perez, "Alcune difficolta," in Snider, *Pio IX nella luce dei processi canonici*, p.234.

[28] The Archives of the [French; translator's note] Ministry of Foreign Affairs contains a detailed account (wrongly catalogued under 1869) of this battle, drawn up by the French ambassador to Rome, as well as a map and other pieces related to Mentana (A.M.A.E., C.P. Rome 1044, ff.201ff.) General Kanzler's report to Pius IX and that of General de Failly to his minister of war were published in *Annales II*, 114-121. Finally, Paolo Dalla Torre produced a study entitled *L'anno di Mentana* (1st ed. 1938; Milan: Aldo Martello Editore, 1968).

field of battle about 1,000 dead and wounded; the papal troops counted 30 dead and 100 or so wounded, and the French reported 2 dead, 1 man disappeared, and 86 wounded. Viterbo and Monte Rotondo, abandoned by Garibaldi's troops, were soon reoccupied. The Italian troops, who had not taken part in the battle officially, vacated the Papal States. When the French and Papal Zouaves returned to Rome on November 6, they received a victor's welcome. Subscriptions were organized for the wounded and funeral services were held for the dead; the Pope had a new military medal struck (*Fidei et Virtuti*) to honor the bravest of the combatants.

In all the Catholic countries, Mentana seemed to have avenged Castelfidardo. Large meetings of up to 100,000 people were held to express gratitude to the heroes of Mentana and to adopt resolutions in favor of the pope's temporal power. These meetings were presided over by Cardinal Cullen in Dublin, Archbishop Manning in London, and Bishop Ketteler in Mainz. Many volunteers hastened to Rome to enroll in the papal armies (notably 300 Canadians).

While he shared in the general rejoicing, Pius IX could not help being uneasy. One month after the victory of Mentana, in a letter to his brother Gaetano, he wrote: "Here we have to be continually on watch, fearing new attacks."[29] In recent months the Italian government's hypocrisy and evasions had been as terrible as Garibaldi's actions. It was only due to French intervention that Rome had been saved, but how long would this support last?

Ut Unum Sint

Pius IX was well aware that a military victory, however striking it might be, could not put an end to the war being waged against him by certain elements. This was not only a war to deprive him of his last temporal possessions, but also a different war, on a broader front and at a much deeper level, going far beyond the frontiers of Italy: it was a war waged against the Church by her enemies.

Pius IX never separated these two wars. When certain historians today speak of the Papal States as "an anachronism" and say that the Roman question "accentuated the rigidity of the pope and many Catholics *vis-à-vis* liberalism and contributed to making the Church seem fundamentally hostile to modern ideas,"[30] they fail to recognize the fact that Pius IX, by intransigently defending his temporal sovereignty, was not conducting primarily a political struggle, but a religious one. In his mind everything was linked: his temporal and political sovereignty made possible the free exercise of his spiritual mission; in his view, those hostile to his temporal

---

[29] Letter of December 9, 1867, published by Polverari, "Lettere di Pio IX ai familiari," in *Pio IX nel primo centenario*, pp.60-67; hereafter, "Lettere."

sovereignty were in league with the Church's adversaries. His struggle was therefore indissolubly twofold.

This is how we should understand the great assemblies of bishops in 1854, and in particular those of 1862 and 1867. From the end of the 1860's onwards—and this phenomenon would be more marked after Rome was taken—we also see an increasing number of collective audiences given to important groups of the faithful; they provided an opportunity for the Pope to make a short allocution. To a greater extent than the solemn consistory discourses or the Encyclicals and Briefs, with their subjects precisely chosen (befitting the doctrinal context), these short, partly improvised addresses to pilgrims give us a better idea of Pius IX's immediate concerns and a more spontaneous expression of his thought.

Thus, at the Vatican on April 11, 1868, receiving in audience a thousand people—mostly laypeople—he spoke to them, urging them to be "united around the Holy See."[31] The aim of this unity is simultaneously the defense of the pope's temporal sovereignty, the defense of the faith against the Church's enemies, and the return of Protestants and Orthodox to the Holy See. By being united around the pope, the Church will be strong: "Be united and then you will be strong, strong against hell and against those evil men who attack you and what you are bound to defend and bound to love, namely, justice, truth, the Church, the Holy See."

The following June, in a more restricted circle, in the presence of the cardinals who had come for the anniversary of his election, Pius IX returned to the subject of this "unity." He spoke the following improvised words:

> The struggle between good and evil is as old as the world, and this struggle has followed the Church in her development down the centuries. We see this intense struggle before our very eyes, here in Italy, where profanations, spoliations, and insults succeed one another without interruption. It is most intense against Rome, which evil men have targeted. Here Satan is bending all his strength to destroy the center of Catholic unity, in order to set up the center of abomination. Yet, this ceaseless, pitiless war has produced a salutary reaction in our favor. People of high aspirations have come over to our side; all good men are coming forward in our defense. Every day we are visited by priests and bishops from the remotest lands. They come here seeking light and strength at the tomb

---

30 Aubert, p.80. The author also considers that "in blocking the energies of Catholics on the solution of a problem that was primarily political, the [Roman question] distracted them for many years from properly religious problems." All the great, specifically religious decisions and orientations of Pius IX's pontificate give the lie to such an assertion: the reform or creation of many religious congregations; the formidable expansion of the missions; the vibrant growth of pilgrimages and Catholic charitable works; not to mention the dogma of the Immaculate Conception.
31 Text of this allocution in *Annales II*, 776-77.

of the Apostles. This light and this strength are indeed here, in the Holy City.[32]

The Ecumenical Council being prepared would be a solemn opportunity to manifest this unity, a unity rendered visible in the presence of all the bishops of the world, and a unity in the faith expressed in the reaffirmation or definition of important points of Catholic teaching.

In April 1869, some months before the opening of the Council, Pius IX celebrated the fiftieth anniversary of his priestly ordination. Earlier, in September 1868, the powerful Association of German Catholics, largely organized by laymen, meeting at its annual Congress (the *Katholikentag*), had launched the project of celebrating the Sovereign Pontiff's priestly jubilee with fitting magnificence. The idea was taken up in Italy by the Catholic Association of Italian Youth. Ultimately people came to Rome from all the countries of Europe for this solemn day; significant sums were raised by subscription, expressions of homage were made, and sumptuous gifts were given. The German Catholics, in addition to a major financial gift, sent an address to the Pope signed by 1,217,000 signatures.

The ceremonies and festivities lasted for several days. There was a Solemn Mass in St. Peter's (where the Pope distributed Communion to 300 persons, giving a prominent place to nine children from the *Ospizio Tata Giovanni*); a banquet was given to 1,500 people (all the cardinals, many bishops and prelates, the King and Queen of Naples—in exile—and all the diplomats accredited to the Holy See, *etc.*); the Pope visited the *Ospizio Tata Giovanni* (where he had celebrated his first Mass) and said Mass there; and there was a visit to the Basilica of St. Agnes in memory of the miracle of April 12, 1855, without counting the popular festivities and various illuminations.

These ceremonies came to an end with an audience which the Pope granted on April 14 to the Catholic Association of Italian Youth, which had taken such a large part in the preparation for this jubilee. A thousand young people represented the groups that were found everywhere throughout Italy. The Pope addressed an allocution to them, including the celebrated lines: "I am with you, and you are with me. Together we must fight against error, we must confront our enemies and try to extirpate the poison from their hearts, and shield those who have not yet been affected by it."[33]

---

[32] Allocution of June 15, 1868, in *Annales II*, 798.
[33] Allocution cited in *Annales ecclésiastiques 1869-1873*, ed. Dom François Chamard, p.101; hereafter, *Annales III*.

CHAPTER 14

THE VATICAN COUNCIL

In the history of Pius IX's pontificate, the opening of the Vatican Council in December 1869 eclipsed the jubilee celebrations of April. As in the case of the Syllabus, the event was the result of lengthy and minute preparation. We shall describe this in detail. It also produced a multitude of writings. In the present work we have referred principally to two kinds of writings. On the one hand, the writings of some of those who took part in or witnessed the event: in particular an unpublished manuscript of 394 pages, which constitutes the very informative *Journal de mon voyage et de mon séjour à Rome* (Diary of my journey to Rome and of my stay there) by Henri Icard, Rector of the Seminary of St. Sulpice and Council theologian of Msgr. Bernardou, Archbishop of Sens;[1] and on the other hand the classic historians, Théodore Granderath,[2] Fernand Mourret;[3] Roger Aubert;[4] Giuseppe Alberigo.[5] Other manuscript or printed sources will be cited in the course of the chapter.

The Council's Origins

It seems that Cardinal Lambruschini was the first to suggest to Pius IX that he should consider calling an Ecumenical Council. This was in 1849, when Pius IX was still in exile in Gaeta. "I think," wrote the former Secretary of State, "that Your Holiness, in due time (which cannot be far off), will have to convoke a general Council to condemn recent errors, stir up the faith of the Christian people, and restore and re-affirm ecclesiastical discipline, which is so enfeebled in our day. The evils are wide-ranging, and therefore wide-ranging remedies are needed."[6]

In 1863 Cardinal Wiseman, on a visit to Rome, also suggested the summoning of a general Council. The Pope replied that he was thinking

---

[1]   Archives of Saint-Sulpice. Also consulted: Msgr. Manning, *Histoire du concile du Vatican* (Paris: Victor Palmé, 1872); Louis Veuillot, *Rome pendant le Concile* (Paris: Lethielleux, 1927) (a collection of his articles that had appeared in *L'Univers,* 1st ed. 1872).

[2]   Théodore Granderath, *Histoire du concile du Vatican,* 6 vols. (Brussels: Libr. Albert Dewit, 1907-1914) (German ed. 1903-1906).

[3]   Fernand Mourret, *Le Concile du Vatican* (Paris: Bloud et Gay, 1919).

[4]   Roger Aubert, *Vatican I* (Paris: Editions de l'Orante, 1964).

[5]   Giuseppe Alberigo, "Le Concile Vatican I (1869-1870)," *Les Conciles oecuméniques* (Paris: Cerf, 1994), 2 parts (Histoire des Décrets) in 3 vols.

[6]   Letter published in M. Manzani, *Il cardinale L. Lambruschini* (Rome, 1960), pp.525-26, cited by Aubert, *Vatican I,* p.39.

about it and praying for that intention, but he was afraid that his great age would not allow him to bring the project to fulfilment.[7]

On December 6 of the following year, as we have already noted, two days before the official publication of *Quanta Cura* and the Syllabus, Pius IX conducted a confidential discussion with the fifteen cardinals of the Congregation of Rites, meeting at a general session. He asked their advice as to whether it would be opportune to summon a Council, requiring them to keep absolute silence about this initial consultation. Their replies reached him in the weeks that followed: thirteen of the cardinals consulted favored the holding of a Council, one was opposed to it, and another left the Pope to judge for himself. Fr. Mariano Spada, Procurator-General of the Dominicans, was asked to produce a summary of the fifteen responses of the cardinals. It was printed.[8]

In March 1865 a commission of cardinals was set up, with the task of examining the problems associated with this future Council. This was the "Directing Preparatory Commission for the Affairs of the Future General Council." It was composed of five cardinals under the presidency of Cardinal Patrizi, who was Pius IX's vicar-general and Prefect of the Congregation of Rites, a man very close to the Pope.[9]

This Directing Preparatory Commission met for the first time on March 9. The *Quadro dei sentimenti* drawn up by Fr. Spada was distributed to the participants and they were asked four questions regarding (1) the need for convoking a Council, (2) the obstacles against it, (3) the arrangements to be made prior to its convoking, and (4) the subjects to be discussed if it were to take place. They were all agreed that it would be opportune to summon such a Council. They thought it would be useful to create an Extraordinary Congregation to prepare for the future Council, and that, after the official announcement had been made, bishops from different countries should be consulted as to what questions of doctrine and discipline, in their view, should be dealt with by the Council.

When, on March 13, Msgr. Giannelli presented his report on this first meeting, Pius IX was pleased that his project had met with their assent. However, he judged it preferable not to wait for the Bull of Convocation to be published, but to consult with the bishops immediately. He hoped that this consultation, which had to remain secret, would get under way without delay.

On April 20, 1865, the Prefect of the Congregation of the Council wrote a confidential letter to thirty-six European bishops—eleven Italians, including Cardinal Pecci, Archbishop of Perugia, the future Leo XIII; nine Frenchmen, including Msgr. Pie and Msgr. Dupanloup; seven Spaniards; five Austrians; two Bavarians; one Belgian; and one Englishman. Their replies were published in the *Rapporto sulle riposte date da varii Vescove alla lettera del 20 Aprile 1865 diretta ai medesimi dall'eminentissimo Cardinale Prefetto della S. Congregazione del Concilio intorno alla idea di un futuro Concilio ecumenico.*[10]

At least one bishop, Msgr. Dupanloup, was hesitant as to the opportuneness of calling a Council.[11] This initial hesitation contrasted with the eagerness he would show at the future Council.

In general the bishops who were questioned thought that the danger came, not from a specific new heresy, but from the widespread calling into question of the very principle of revelation and of the Church's various doctrines. They thought it was necessary to reaffirm the fundamental truths of Christianity and point out the many errors that were current throughout society. Cardinal Pecci listed the following, which needed to be specifically reprobated: naturalism, rationalism, freethinking, indifferentism, and the superstitions of magnetism and spiritualism. Seven bishops called for the dogmatic definition of infallibility. Some also hoped that the Syllabus would be solemnly reaffirmed. In a number of responses there was an insistence on the need to define the relationship between Church and State, and to condemn the subjection of the spiritual power to the temporal power, which existed in several countries.

Various questions of ecclesiastical discipline were also frequently mentioned, as was the reform of moral conduct on the part of the faithful. As Msgr. Pie said, "the future assembly should draw up decrees against the excesses of luxury and pleasure, against this thirst for wealth which, in an effort to obtain the quickest possible gratification, has recourse to speculation; against the abandonment of family life, the profanation of marriage, the disregard of Sunday and holy days, and the neglect of the Church's services. Other prelates will say the same."[12]

The bishops consulted also devoted considerable attention to problems of ecclesiastical discipline. The points most often referred to are these: "improvement of clerical formation; a stricter observance of their rule on the part of religious, and the relationship of many new congregations with the diocesan authorities; the need to keep a watch on the press; the dimi-

---

[10] Summary in Granderath, *Histoire du concile du Vatican,* I, 54-65; further information in Aubert, *Vatican I.*

[11] "In his reply he limited himself to setting forth the reasons for and against, without drawing any conclusion," Lagrange, *Mgr. Dupanloup,* III, 53.

[12] Granderath, *Histoire du concile du Vatican,* I, 59.

nution of censures and other ecclesiastical penalties; the unification of the catechism; the question of schools; and, above all, the problems regarding marriage, i.e., the limitation of the number of impediments, rules on mixed marriages, the practice of civil marriage."[13]

At the beginning of 1866 a complementary inquiry was made of nine Oriental bishops: the Patriarch of Jerusalem; the Maronite, Melkite and Syrian Patriarchs; two Armenian prelates; two Romanian bishops from Transylvania; and the Vicar Apostolic of Constantinople. Some of their suggestions coincided with those made by the European bishops. Most expressed the wish that the future Council would address the question of the return of the Oriental schismatics to the bosom of the Catholic Church. Certain European bishops had already formulated the same request, notably Cardinal Pecci.

For a moment, the Pope had it in mind to cause the opening of the Council to coincide with the ceremonies commemorating the eighteenth centenary of the martyrdom of Saints Peter and Paul. But in 1866 several European countries, and the Papal States themselves, found themselves in a worrying or conflictual situation (the Austro-Prussian war, in which Italy was involved, and the withdrawal of French troops from Rome). The Pope judged it more prudent not to convoke the Council for the following year. As we have said, however, the solemnities of June 1867 provided an opportunity for the official announcement of the Council to all the bishops present, without any date being fixed. The announcement was made on July 1 in Pius IX's response to the bishops' address.

One month before, on June 6, Cardinal Caterini, Prefect of the Congregation of the Council, had sent a questionnaire to all the bishops present in Rome asking how certain precepts of the Church were observed in their dioceses (*Quaestiones quae ab Apostolica Sede Episcopis proponuntur*).

Seventeen precise questions were asked. They concerned the prohibition on allowing heretics or schismatics to be godparents in baptisms; various canonical prescriptions on marriage; the formation of clerics; the new congregations; the sanctions to be applied to clergy and to cemeteries.[14] This questionnaire was submitted to the bishops without any reference to the future Council; it was left to the Pope to make the next mention of it. Only 224 bishops replied to it; no systematic analysis of their responses has been made.

Preparatory Work

The following September various preparatory commissions were created and began to meet. There were five of them, each presided over by

---

[13] Aubert, *Vatican I*, p.42.
[14] Complete text of the circular in *Annales II*, 174-76.

a cardinal: the Doctrinal Commission; the Commission for the Missions and the Oriental Churches; the Commission for Ecclesiastical Discipline; the Commission for Religious; and the Politico-ecclesiastical Commission. A further commission would be set up, the Commission of Rites and Ceremonies, more particularly concerned with the arranging of the Council's sessions. The Directing Preparatory Commission of cardinals was composed of the cardinal presidents of the six Commissions, plus two other cardinals.

The names of these different Commissions were a good indication of what were to be the main preoccupations of the future Council. Each Commission was composed of several consultors (members of Congregations, professors or rectors of seminaries, university professors). In total there were ninety-six consultors. While a large majority of these consultors were Italians (fifty-nine) the number of foreign consultors was not negligible (thirty-seven). On several occasions Pius IX had expressed the wish that these foreign consultors should not come solely from Catholic countries. As a result, they exhibited a certain universality: thirteen Germans, six Frenchmen, five Spaniards, four Austrians, three Englishmen, one Russian (residing in Paris), one Dutchman, one Swiss, one American, one Guatemalan (living in Spain), and one Syrian.

This great geographical diversity went hand in hand with a real diversity of origin. There was no dominance of Jesuits in the Council's preparation, as their enemies claimed. Of the ninety-six consultors, only eight were Jesuits. The secular clergy were represented as well as the religious clergy (in the person of the most important orders), although it must be admitted that the Jesuit influence was considerable in the Doctrinal Commission—itself the most important Commission—because of the part played in it by the Jesuit consultors Perrone, Franzelin, and Schrader. They took an active part in the preparation of the major drafts of the doctrinal decrees.

It was certainly the case that those theologians Rome considered suspect were excluded. Döllinger, for instance, in a letter to Msgr. Dupanloup, tells him that the Archbishop of Prague, Cardinal Schwarzenberg, and the Archbishop of Breslau, Msgr. Förster, had asked the Pope to name him as one of the consultors.[15] Döllinger had no hope of this two-pronged request's being successful. He did not feature among the consultors; in fact, from his base in Germany, he was one of the Council's most resolute opponents.

On June 29, 1868, Pius IX published the Bull *Aeterni Patris* convoking the Council for December 8, 1869, the Feast of the Immaculate Con-

---

[15] Unpublished letter of December 28, 1868, Archives of Saint-Sulpice.

ception.[16] The Church was undergoing a "terrible tempest" and society
was suffering from "immense evils":

> The Catholic Church and her salutary doctrine, her venerable power,
> and the supreme authority of this Apostolic See, are attacked and trod-
> den underfoot by the embittered enemies of God and men. All sacred
> things are cast out and scorned, and the Church's goods are despoiled and
> squandered. The pontiffs, most venerable men, consecrated to the divine
> mystery, people eminent for their Catholic convictions, are tormented in
> every way. Religious communities are annihilated; godless books of all
> kinds and pestilential journals are spread everywhere; the most pernicious
> sects are everywhere multiplying, and in all kinds of forms. Practically
> everywhere the clergy have been forbidden to engage in teaching the un-
> fortunate youth and, what is worse, these young people are in many places
> entrusted to teachers who propagate error and iniquity.
>
> As a result of all this, to Our profound sorrow and the sorrow of all
> men of good will on account of the loss to souls—for which no amount
> of tears would suffice—we are faced with impiety, the corruption of mor-
> als, unbridled licence, the contagion of all kinds of perverse opinions, of
> all vices and crimes, and the violation of divine and human laws. These
> things have been propagated to such a point that our most holy religion
> and human society itself are wretchedly troubled and confused.

Faced with "such a concourse of calamities," the Ecumenical Council

> will have to undertake a most painstaking examination and determine
> what should best be done, in such difficult and hostile times, for the great-
> er glory of God, for the integrity of faith, for the beauty of the divine cult,
> for men's eternal salvation, for the discipline of the secular and regular
> clergy and their wholesome and solid instruction, for the observance of
> ecclesiastical laws, for the reformation of morals, for Christian education
> of youth, for peace among men, and for universal concord.
>
> We must also exert every effort, with the help of God, to remove all
> evil from the Church and from civil society. We must bring back to the
> right path of truth, justice, and salvation those unfortunate men who
> have wandered astray; we must reprobate vices and reject errors....For
> the influence of the Catholic Church and her doctrine not only avails for
> men's eternal salvation, but also—and no one can ever refute this—it con-
> tributes to the temporal well-being of peoples, to their genuine prosperity,
> to the maintaining of order and tranquility, and even to the progress and
> solidity of the human sciences....

This solemn convocation had been preceded by discussion regarding
the participants: Who should be invited, and who could participate in the
Council's debates? Compared with earlier councils, the number of participants was increased. Those invited were not only residential bishops (who
numbered slightly more than 700) but also all those who were bishops

---

[16] Text of the bull in *Annales II*, 178-181.

in virtue of their consecration, even if they were not heads of dioceses. So those invited included nuncios, vicars apostolic, prelates of the Curia, auxiliary or missionary bishops, *i.e.*, about 250 prelates. Also invited were abbots general, the generals of orders and presidents of monastic congregations (but not abbot superiors of single monasteries nor the superiors of religious congregations).

One fact shows the Pope's severity and, at the same time, the limits of his power. On March 8, 1869, receiving the secretary of the Directing Preparatory Commission, he had observed that certain titular bishops were less than exemplary in their conduct, and he hoped that the convocation would be executed in such a way that these bishops, who were unworthy of attending the Council's sessions, should be excluded. The Directing Preparatory Commission did not grant the Holy Father's wish, expressing the view, in its session of March 14, that only an excommunicated bishop could be excluded from the Council. Pius IX gave in.[17]

Some criticized the decision to invite vicars apostolic (who do not have responsibility for a diocese) to the Council. They were afraid that such men, directly depending on the Holy See, often isolated in vast missionary territories, would constitute a blunt instrument in the Pope's hands. But Louis Veuillot justly observed that it would be wrong to keep these men out of the Council—men who had not only received episcopal consecration but were holding the front lines of Christendom.

In comparison with the Council of Trent, there was a further innovation: the sixty-one bishops of the Oriental Rite were also invited. Their presence was fully justified by the development of Oriental Christianity, and the improvement of the means of transport made it a possibility. It is significant, finally, that the temporal sovereigns who, in the Middle Ages and during the Counter-Reformation, had been participants in councils, either in person or by representatives, were not formally invited. The Directing Preparatory Commission, which had to decide this question, had been divided. Pius IX himself came to help in the deliberations and, during the course of an extraordinary session, it was decided that the princes would not be expressly invited, but those who wished to collaborate in some way would be offered the chance to do so. Hence the expression in the Bull of Convocation: "The sovereigns and heads of all peoples, in particular the Catholic princes, will not only refrain from preventing our venerable brothers, the bishops, and other persons mentioned below from attending the Council, but on the contrary will be pleased to help and assist them with their cooperation...."

---

[17] Granderath, *Histoire du concile du Vatican*, I, 114-15.

No sovereign participated, therefore, in the sessions of the Ecumenical Council. Louis Veuillot interpreted this fact as an official sign that Christendom had come to an end:

> The bull summoning the Ecumenical Council does not call sovereigns to sit in this legislative assembly. The omission is striking, indeed, remarkable! Implicitly it affirms that there are no longer any Catholic crowns, *i.e.*, that the order on which society has been based for more than ten centuries has now ceased to exist....A new era has begun. Church and State are *de facto* separated, and both sides acknowledge this....It is done, and it is not a good thing. It was the State, not the Church, which wanted it. Soul and body are no longer united.[18]

Pius IX would explain this, in less direct language, to a French diplomat who regretted this exclusion: "The relationships between the powers and the Holy See have changed so much since the last council that it seemed to him difficult to convoke certain governments, who were increasingly uninterested in religious questions."[19]

Slightly more than two months after the official bull convoking the Council, the Pope wrote two apostolic letters to the Christians separated from Rome. Their tone was very different. The first, dated September 8, 1868, was addressed to "all the bishops of the Oriental Rite who are not in communion with the Apostolic See," that is, the Orthodox, Copts, Nestorians, Jacobites, *etc.*[20] Pius IX recognized them as "Churches," but those who were "alienated and separated from the communion of the Holy Roman Church, which is spread throughout the entire universe." Consequently, he invited these bishops to come to the Council "so that the laws of former affection may be renewed, so that the peace of our fathers, this heavenly and salutary gift of Jesus Christ, which time has weakened, may take on a new vigor, and that so, after a long night of affliction and after the dark shadows of a prolonged division, the serene light of the desired union may shine forth to the eyes of all."

The second letter was very different in spirit. Dated September 13, it was addressed to "all Protestants and other non-Catholics," *i.e.*, members of different Protestant denominations (Anglicans, Lutherans, Calvinists, *etc.*) and other schismatic communities (Jansenists, *etc.*).[21] This time Pius IX did not address himself to "Churches" but—in his own expression—to "religious societies," that is, to all the members of these societies, and not to bishops (Anglican, Episcopalian, *etc.*), whom the Holy See refused to regard as such. In addition the Protestants and "non-Catholics" were not

---

[18] Article of July 11, 1868, reprinted in *Rome pendant le Concile*, p.34.
[19] Dispatch of the *chargé d'affaires*, de Croy, to the French Minister of Foreign Affairs, September 1,1869, A.M.A.E., C.P., Rome 1044, f.80.
[20] Apostolic letter *Arcano Divinae Providentiae*, published in *Annales II*, 181-83.
[21] Apostolic letter *Jam Vos Omnes Noveritis*, published in *Annales II*, 183-85.

invited to the Council, but invited simply to "offer the most fervent prayer to the God of mercies, that he would break down the wall of division, dissipate the shadows of error, and bring them to Holy Mother Church...."

These invitations to the separated Christians received little response. The Patriarch of Constantinople, while he agreed to receive the Pope's envoys, refused to accept the letter of invitation they brought with them. The Orthodox patriarchs and metropolitans depending on Constantinople acted with the same disdain. In Russia Pius IX's Apostolic Letter was published by several newspapers; in general people were glad that the Pope had not used the word "schismatic," but the Orthodox hierarchy refused to give a favorable reply. The divisions in Protestantism were such that a common response was impossible. Furthermore Pius IX had not invited them to come to the Council but to convert to Catholicism. There were some positive echoes, but they did not go as far as conversion.[22] The Dutch Jansenists, to judge from their leadership, seemed favorably disposed, but this attitude did not last.

In England, finally, reaction was generally more lively. The *Morning Post* said that "the whole letter is an insult to the good sense and religious sentiments of all Christians who do not recognize Pius IX as the direct successor to St. Peter," and the *Times* took an ironical line.[23] However, when a Presbyterian pastor, Dr. Cumming, wrote to the Pope asking if Protestants would be able to express themselves freely at the Council and put forward their points, Pius IX did not let this first initiative go without a response. In two letters to Msgr. Manning, Archbishop of Westminster, he confirmed his desire to see the Protestants return to the bosom of the Catholic Church, adding that he was disposed, not to admit them to the Council sessions, but to designate competent theologians who were ready to debate with them in Rome itself.[24] The Pope had thus manifested his good will.

During this period the Preparatory Commissions were engaged in intensive work, in particular the Doctrinal Commission. The many reports they received were the raw material they used to elaborate draft decrees. Memoranda on very varied subjects were submitted to the Doctrinal Commission: three on papal primacy, one on the temporal power, one on infallibility, others on pantheism and naturalism (including an analysis by Cardinal Pecci); on liberty of conscience; on secret societies; on the Trinity, Christology, Communism; *etc.* At the end of fifty-seven meetings the Doctrinal Commission had succeeded in editing four draft decrees: on the

---

[22] Joseph Chantrel cites the writings of the German Protestants W. Menzel, R. Baumstark (*Annales II*, 214-15).

[23] Quotations in *Annales II*, 218.

[24] Letters of the Pope cited in *Annales III*, 189-90.

Church, on the Pope, against modern errors originating in rationalism, and on Christian marriage.[25]

It should be noted that the first schemas had been written with the following preamble: *"Pius Episcopus, servus servorum Dei, sacro approbante concilio"* (Pius, Bishop, servant of the servants of God, with the approval of the holy Council). This formula, which had already been used in preceding councils (notably at the fifth Council of the Lateran), seemed to stamp the matters to be discussed with the seal of pontifical authority. Pius IX did not like it, and required the formula to be modified.[26] The Directing Commission, after several discussions, did not withdraw the initial formula but added the complementary: *"Schema constitutionis... quod Patribus examinandum proponitur"* (Scheme of the constitution... which is proposed for examination by the Fathers).

The other Commissions also prepared very many draft decrees. The Commission for Ecclesiastical Discipline produced twenty-two draft decrees; that of Religious, eighteen; the Commission for Missions and Eastern Rite Churches prepared a draft decree on the missionary apostolate, another on rites, and a third on the extraordinary minister of confirmation. The Politico-Ecclesiastical Commission drew up eighteen draft decrees (notably one "On the relief to be offered to the wretched state of the poor and the workers").

All the draft decrees were examined by the Directing Commission, which had the power to suggest or impose modifications. It was also given the task of drawing up the procedure to be applied during the Council sessions. One of those consulted was the great German historian Hefele, professor at Tübingen, who in 1855 had begun to publish a monumental *History of the Councils,* which is still an authority today.

As well as the questions of protocol and ceremonial, the question of the presidency had to be decided. By right the Pope was president of the Council; at "general congregations" he would be represented by a council of six presidents, and at "solemn sessions" he would intervene personally. It was the Sovereign Pontiff's right alone to raise matters for discussion at the Council; the Council Fathers could only express their wishes, which would be submitted to the Pope for his agreement. The discussions would take place between Council Fathers, and there would be no parallel meetings of *theologi minores* as there had been at the Council of Trent. The procedural regulations were published in the constitution *Multiplices In-*

---

[25] Finally the decree on the pope was inserted into the schema on the Church "so that the doctrine of the Mystical Body should not appear to be distorted by dealing on the one hand with what belongs to the body and on the other hand with what belongs to the head."

[26] Granderath, *Histoire du concile du Vatican,* I, 492ff.

ter, dated November 27, 1869, and were brought to the cognizance of the Fathers during the pre-synodal session of December 2.[27]

Anxieties and Maneuvers

The announcement of the Council had worried a good number of liberal Catholics, who feared that their ideas would be condemned once again. Some of them were hostile to papal infallibility, and sensed that it would be one of the important questions raised. Once the holding of a Council had been publicly announced, in 1867, their anxieties had surfaced.

Montalembert, echoing the fears of the Bishop of Dijon on his return from Rome, wrote: "He thinks that the Roman prelates, bishops, and cardinals, are more inclined to extend the scope of the Syllabus than to restrict it. Archbishop Manning is banking on the imminent Council to give us the *coup de grace.*"[28] At the same time Montalembert, in an address to the Congress of Belgian Catholics again meeting in Malines, publicly praised the Pope's initiative: "With goodwill and respect I salute this providential inspiration of Pius IX, who has thus set a crown upon the grandeurs of his pontificate. At the very moment when treachery and abandonment are aggravating all the perils that surround him, he responds to threats of death with threats of life; in the eye of the storm, he floods us with strength, confidence, and light."[29]

Montalembert's fears, kept private for the moment, were shared by another liberal, the English Lord John Acton. In Rome during the Council, this disciple of Döllinger would be one of the liberals' champions. The day after the Council had been announced, he wrote in an article: "For the advocates of Roman ideas, concern to preserve authority is more important than the propagation of the faith."[30]

As for Msgr. Dupanloup, now that he had recovered from his former antagonism to the Council, he began to display all-out activity. In August and September 1867 he went to Malines to talk to Msgr. Deschamps (who would soon declare himself to be one of the warmest defenders of infallibility); then he went to Mainz to meet Msgr. Ketteler and to Cologne to visit Msgr. Geissel, two other important personalities at the future Council. In 1868 he published a first pastoral letter on the subject, intended to be reassuring to liberals, and founded a newspaper, the *Français,* making the liberal Augustin Cochin its editor. This paper would finally give him a daily platform; it would enable him to reply, sometimes anonymously,

[27] Text of the constitution in *Annales III*, 233-43.
[28] Letter of July 17, 1867, cited by Aubert, *Vatican I*, p.71.
[29] Letter from Montalembert to Falloux, September 5, 1867, which would be read out at the Congress, in Montalembert, *Correspondance*, p.356.
[30] *The Chronicle*, July 13, 1867, cited by Aubert, *Vatican I*, p.72.

both to the government's newspapers and to the Ultramontane press, notably *L'Univers,* so widely read by the French clergy.

It was during 1869, the year that saw the opening of the Council (in December), that the controversies came out into the open. The first were prompted by the publication, in the *Civiltà Cattolica* of February 6, of a "Letter from France" which made a great stir.[31] This consisted of long extracts from two memoranda written by French priests who had been sent to Rome by the apostolic nuncio in Paris. Significantly, the published extracts carried the statement that Catholics "properly so-called" desired "the future Ecumenical Council to proclaim the teachings of the Syllabus...by means of affirmative formulas and with the requisite developments," and that they would "gladly welcome the proclamation by the future Council of the dogmatic infallibility of the Sovereign Pontiff." On this latter point, "We are aware, of course, that the Sovereign Pontiff, by a sentiment of august reserve, might not wish to take the initiative in a matter which seems to concern him personally. It is our hope, however, that the unanimous explosion of the Holy Spirit, by the mouth of the Fathers of the future Ecumenical Council, will define the teaching by acclamation." Finally it was stated "that a great number of Catholics have expressed the wish to see the future Ecumenical Council complete the cycle of solemn expressions of homage given by the Church to the Immaculate Virgin, by a proclamation of the dogma of her glorious Assumption."

Some saw in this article a Jesuit move in favor of a definition of infallibility by acclamation, without prior discussion by the Council. It was in fact a blunder: the journal, very closely associated with the Pope, seemed to be attributing to him the observations and wishes that had been anonymously expressed. "In any case," notes R. Aubert, "people such as the Jesuit General or the Master of the Sacred Palace explicitly regretted that the unfortunate correspondence had been published."[32] Nonetheless, the polemics multiplied in many countries.

In France Msgr. Dupanloup had two articles published on the subject in the *Français,* denying any authority or representative status to the published correspondence and regarding the definition of the dogma of infallibility as inopportune.[33]

In Germany, Döllinger published five anonymous articles in the *Allgemeine Zeitung* between March 10 and 15.[34] In the face of the claims expressed in the *Civiltà Cattolica,* Döllinger said, there was need for "an act

---

[31] Complete [French; translator's note] translation of the article in Aubert, *Vatican I,* pp.261-269.

[32] Aubert, *Vatican I,* p.78.

[33] Lagrange mentions the articles but does not say that he was the author (under the name "F. Beslay") (*Mgr. Dupanloup,* III, 125).

of legitimate defense, an appeal to thinking Christians, a protest—based on history—against a threatening future, against the plans of a powerful coalition...." The reprobated article is only the manifestation of a tendency that is solidly established in the Church: "About eighty years ago a movement of reaction began to make itself felt in the Catholic Church; by now it has become a strong current...." Döllinger situated himself within the liberal current: "We share in a community of ideas with all those who are convinced that the Catholic Church must not adopt a hostile attitude towards the principles of liberty and political, intellectual, and religious autonomy." He felt that "a great and profound reform of the Church was necessary and inevitable." Finally he denounced the "ecclesiastical revolution" that was in preparation, denouncing the doctrine of infallibility and that of the papal primacy as theologically unfounded.[35]

Döllinger was persuaded that a plot was being prepared to impose these doctrines on the Church. He explains this in a private letter to Msgr. Dupanloup, basing his conviction on report from a German priest who had returned from Rome:

> According to what he has seen and heard, the Jesuit faction led by Cardinal Reisach and favored by the Pope believes itself sure of victory. The roles have already been cast: an English prelate (whom you will have no difficulty in guessing) has promised to take the initiative, and once the Council has opened he is publicly and energetically to beseech the Pope to deign to declare his own infallibility. Then the bishops will follow by general acclamation; the Pope will yield to this enthusiasm—a manifestation of the Holy Spirit—and the Catholic world will be enriched by a new dogma infinitely more important than the Immaculate Conception. It will be followed by the articles of the Syllabus, etc.[36]

In Germany, in the following months, more publications relayed Döllinger's criticisms, showing more or less moderation.[37] One of them, originating in Coblenz, hoped that people would reject any dogmatic definition that would separate the Catholic Church even more from the Protestant communities, and proposed four priorities for the future Council, namely, to bring the laity more into the life of the Church, to raise the clergy's intellectual level, to break with the medieval theocracy, and to suppress the Index. Of course, it was not the case that all German-speaking Catholics shared the views of this manifesto, but a certain number of German bishops were not too far from them.

---

[34] They would be developed and reprinted as a book entitled *Der Papst und das Konzil.* The work was published at the end of August 1869 in Leipzig under the pseudonym "Janus" and translated into several languages.

[35] Cited by Granderath, *Histoire du concile du Vatican,* I, 219ff.

[36] Unpublished letter of April 2, 1869, Archives of Saint-Sulpice. The English prelate to whom Döllinger refers is probably Msgr. Manning.

[37] Texts cited by Granderath, *Histoire du concile du Vatican,* I, 219-43.

In September 1869, at their annual meeting in Fulda, a majority of them gave it as their opinion that the definition of infallibility would be inopportune. Fourteen of Germany's nineteen bishops wrote a joint letter to the Pope expressing their apprehension at the prospect of a dogmatic act of this kind. Pius IX was annoyed with this letter because it showed hostility towards an issue that was not officially listed in the Council's schedule.

In fact, while some feared that it would be raised at the Council (such as the Bishops of Bohemia and of Hungary, who also wrote joint letters to the Pope), others hoped that it would be. These men also let their voices be heard. Most prominent among them was Msgr. Deschamps, Archbishop of Malines, who was to become one of the leaders of the "infallibilists." In June 1869 he published a pamphlet entitled *L'Infaillibilité et le Concile général.* The Pope was so very pleased with it that he himself paid for its translation and printing costs in Italy.[38]

The most important work of the adversaries of papal infallibility (prior to another pamphlet of Msgr. Dupanloup, to which we shall return) was that published in September in two large volumes by Msgr. Maret, *Du Concile général et de la paix religieuse.*

Msgr. Maret had been linked to the liberals ever since 1848 when, with Lacordaire and Ozanam, he had founded a newspaper, *L'Ère Nouvelle,* which represented a very minor and ephemeral Christian-Democrat current of thought. He was one of the most influential theologians of the time in France. A defender of the Gallican theories which had had their hour of glory in the seventeenth century, and which were characterized by wild assertions of independence *vis-à-vis* Rome, Msgr. Maret was also on the best terms with Napoleon III, who prided himself on his neo-Gallicanism. He summarized his doctrine in four points: (1) independence of the secular power *vis-à-vis* all political jurisdiction attributed to the Church; (2) the legitimacy of the principles of 1789 and of the constitution of modern society; (3) spiritual sovereignty to reside in the episcopal corps united to the Sovereign Pontiff; (4) the Papal monarchy to exhibit a temperate character.[39]

Maret had been Dean of the Faculty of Theology in Paris since 1853. Despite the insistence of Napoleon III, Pius IX refused, in 1861, to appoint him Bishop of Vannes. At the most, he had agreed to appoint him Bishop of Sura *in partibus, i.e.,* conferring upon him the episcopal dignity without entrusting the care of an existing diocese to him. Msgr. Maret's influence had continued to increase among a certain clerical fringe, but

---

[38] De Croy, the embassy attaché, who was received in audience on August 16, reports the fact in a dispatch to his minister of September 16, 1869, A.M.A.E., C.P., Rome 1044, f.85.

[39] Cited by Palanque, *Catholiques libéraux,* p.29.

also with the Emperor, to whom he had suggested a number of episcopal nominations, including Msgr. Darboy, another Gallican, for the position of Archbishop of Paris.

In 1862, Msgr. Maret had thought that the calling of a Council would be the ultimate remedy, "the only legitimate, honorable means of getting out of the present difficulties, of re-establishing justice in the Church, of avoiding a schism in Italy, of reforming the Church, and of bringing about conciliation and peace.... It is the only way to put an end to the scheming of the absolutist, theocratic party."[40] Furthermore, the two volumes he published—thanks to financial assistance from Napoleon III—less than three months before the opening of the eagerly awaited Council, were only a more elaborate expression of ideas that had been around for a long time. This time, he hoped, if all the bishops of Christendom were meeting in Rome, these ideas had some chance of being heard. In his book he explained that the bishops held their jurisdiction from God and not from the Pope, that the infallibility enjoyed by the Pope was not "personal" and "separated," and that it could only be exercised with the bishops' consent. Finally he stated that the Pope was not above the Council, even if he had the privilege of convoking it and presiding over it. He also suggested that, in order to reconcile the papacy and the episcopate, and permit the latter to play its full part in governing the Church, a General Council should be held every ten years.

Msgr. Maret had sent his book to all the French bishops. Some of them, who owed their nomination to him and shared his neo-Gallican ideas, congratulated him by private letter. Other and contradictory voices, however, made themselves heard publicly. First of all, on September 28, Msgr. Pie, in a homily to his clergy on the twentieth anniversary of his elevation to the episcopate, refuted the work without naming it. *L'Univers* published the homily. Other bishops publicly approved of the response of their brother of Poitiers. *Etudes,* the famous journal of the French Jesuits, published a series of articles by Fr. Matignon refuting Msgr. Maret's ideas.

Msgr. Maret was dismayed when he was told that his work had been passed on to two consultors of the Congregation of the Index. He immediately invoked his powerful protectors.[41] On October 19, to Napoleon III, he wrote a "Note on the situation in which the Bishop of Sura has been placed." He said that he was fearful that his book was threatened with imminent condemnation, demanded to be heard by the Pope himself before being judged, and urged the Emperor to instruct his Foreign Minister to intervene in his favor by "telegraphic means." Napoleon III agreed to

---

[40] Cited by Palanque, *Catholiques libéraux*, p.31.
[41] Documents relating to this affair are held in the Archives of the [French; translator's note] Ministry of Foreign Affairs, A.M.A.E., C.P., Rome 1044, ff.153-180.

intercede in favor of Msgr. Maret. On October 20 the minister addressed an enciphered telegram to the French ambassador in Rome, asking him to intervene with Cardinal Antonelli. On October 22 De Croy replied by telegraphic dispatch to the effect that, after he had consulted Antonelli, who had himself raised the matter with Pius IX, "as of today, no one has volunteered a verdict on the Bishop of Sura's book." Only two months later, in the event, the work seems to have been submitted to examination by two theologians. By this time, however, the Council had opened and the refutation of Msgr. Maret's theories would be performed during the debates, as a result of the many interventions of the "infallibilists."

Other voices were raised in the wake of Msgr. Maret's. On October 10 the liberals' major journal, the *Correspondant,* had published a very long manifesto (Montalembert called it an "article-manifesto") soberly entitled "The Council" and signed "for the editorial committee: P. Douhaire." In actual fact it was a joint effort by the journal's principal collaborators, apart from Montalembert. While "restraining its style with the most scrupulous prudence,"[42] the journal expressed its hope that the Council would reject the definition of infallibility as inopportune, and that the Pope would not endeavor to impose it, "because Pius IX will be no less concerned than Pius IV with fraternal concord." The journal pronounced itself, like Msgr. Maret, in favor of a periodical meeting of the Ecumenical Council. The article prompted public censure by several bishops, notably those of Poitiers and Cambrai, and the irony of Louis Veuillot, who wrote a vengeful article on the "French Janus."[43]

Msgr. Dupanloup had acted with discretion for several months, even if his adversaries accused him of having inspired the *Correspondant* article. But on November 11, before leaving for Rome, he published a 60-page booklet entitled *Observations sur la controverse soulevée relativement à la définition de l'infaillibilité au prochain Concile* (Observations on the controversy surrounding the definition of infallibility at the next Council): "I am not discussing infallibility, but whether its definition would be opportune." He thought that a dogmatic definition of infallibility would risk alienating the Orthodox and Protestants even further from the Catholic Church, and "stirring up the former mistrust" on the part of governments. The doctrine itself was not easy to define, and by proclaiming papal infallibility there was danger of weakening the role of the episcopate in the Church.

This publication, which Msgr. Dupanloup had sent to all the Council Fathers, made a great stir. The international press printed extensive ex-

---

[42] Letter from Falloux to Montalembert, November 20, 1869, published in Montalembert, *Correspondance,* p.416. On the article cf. Palanque, pp. *Catholiques libéraux,* pp.97-100.

[43] Article of October 31, 1869, reprinted in *Rome pendant le Concile,* pp.58-64.

tracts from it. It also awakened certain controversies. Louis Veuillot gave it as his view that "the campaign against the infallibility of the Vicar of Jesus Christ is getting under way" and that Msgr. Dupanloup's little book "contributes a regular and official episcopal intellect to those taking up arms."[44]

Was it an exaggeration on Louis Veuillot's part to associate Msgr. Dupanloup with the *Correspondant* article, Msgr. Maret's work, and the writings of Döllinger? An analysis of the positions of each of these men shows that, on certain matters, they were in disagreement. On the other hand, they did share hostility towards infallibility, and Msgr. Dupanloup, in virtue of his high profile, was *de facto* their head. Döllinger recognized him as such. After the Bishop of Orleans had already left for Rome, Döllinger urged him in flattering terms: "Keep on being the Knight without fear and without reproach, the episcopal Bayard in this Council. All eyes are turned towards you; you are looked upon as the center of all sincere friends of truth present at this assembly.... Be the Church's *Fabius Cunctator*."[45] Not all, however, appreciated the action of the Bishop of Orleans. A burlesque was soon going the rounds in Rome to the effect that "Msgr. Dupanloup treats the bishops as if he were the pope, the pope as if he were only a bishop, and the Council as if he himself were the Holy Spirit."[46]

First Meetings

The bishops began arriving in Rome from November onwards. The Holy See looked after the living expenses of the poorest bishops—a number of Italian bishops deprived of their income by the government, Oriental bishops or bishops from missionary territories, *etc.* Ultimately four out of every ten bishops were paid for by the Holy See. To this were added the running expenses of the Council itself: a room 75 feet by 155, made of wooden partitions, was erected in the right transept of St. Peter's Basilica, against two pillars of the baldacchino; texts and bulletins had to be printed, *etc.* The Council cost 5,000 francs per day, which soon prompted Pius IX to remark, "I do not know whether the pope will emerge from this Council fallible or infallible, but assuredly he will be bankrupt."[47] Several European newspapers, notably *L'Univers,* opened subscriptions to help the Pope meet the Council expenses. One hundred and eighty-four issues of Veuillot's paper, until May 1870, carried long lists of subscriptions. Often the donor accompanied his gift with a declaration in favor of infallibility or some other mark of veneration for Pius IX.

---

[44] Article of November 17, 1869, reprinted in *Rome pendant le Concile*, p.72. Msgr. Dupanloup responded with a very energetic and bitter *Avertissement à M. Veuillot.*
[45] Unpublished letter of November 29, 1869, Archives of Saint-Sulpice.
[46] Aubert, *Vatican I*, p.92.
[47] *Ibid.*, p.94.

At the opening of the Council the Church had 55 cardinals, 6 Oriental patriarchs, 964 bishops, 6 abbots *nullius,* 24 abbots general, and 29 generals of orders or congregations. All were members by right of the Council, but 292 of them did not come to Rome, either for reasons of health or because they were only auxiliary bishops, who had to stay in their diocese, or because they were prevented by their government (this was the case with several Portuguese bishops and the seventeen bishops of the Russian Empire). This meant that the number of Council Fathers varied, depending on appointments made or deaths occurring during the Council, and because some of the participants had to return home.

In the first months there were about 700 Council Fathers, and in the final month, July 1870, about 600. It was the largest and most universal Council in the Church's history. The last Council, held at Trent in the sixteenth century, had only a third of this number of participants, all Europeans. This time a third of the bishops came from other continents. The Latins were still dominant, however, the biggest number being Italians (285, or 35%) and Frenchmen (131, or 17%). The influence of the latter was therefore considerable, all the more so since they included men well known in other lands (such as Msgr. Dupanloup) or highly thought of by the Pope (such as Msgr. Pie).

The French government was fully aware of the important role to be played by its bishops. It also hoped, through them, to have some influence over the Council. When the Council opened, the French Minister of Justice and Religion, Duveyrier, wrote to his colleague, the Minister of Foreign Affairs, La Tour d'Auvergne, anxious that he would give clear instructions to the French ambassador to Rome, Banneville. Duveyrier insisted "that M. de Banneville should be urged to use all his influence to prevent a decision which would have extremely disagreeable consequences."[48] The "decision" in question was that of defining papal infallibility. The French government was hostile to this, and the minister gave three reasons: the power of bishops would be diminished; "the increase in the number of beliefs imposed on Catholics would tend to alienate the faithful from the Church's bosom and push them towards freethinking and materialism"; and, finally, a dogma of this kind would harm the concordat. The Minister of Foreign Affairs immediately wrote to the ambassador in Rome, citing the same arguments.[49] The Council's outcome showed that the French government was not in a position to impose its views.

A first meeting with the Pope took place on December 2 in the Sistine Chapel. About five hundred bishops and other Council Fathers were already present. This was not the Council's official opening, which had

---

[48]   Letter from Duveyrier to La Tour d'Auvergne, December 11, 1869, A.M.A.E., C.P., Rome 1044, ff.312-313.
[49]   Letter of December 12, 1869, A.M.A.E., C.P., Rome 1044, ff.314-315.

been fixed for six days later, but a pre-Synodal meeting. In it the Pope gave an important address that shows his clarity of mind. He referred to the obstacles that would not fail to surface:

> We shall infallibly have to undergo disputes and conflicts. The enemy, who only asks to sow cockle along with the good grain, will not rest; but we must remember the strength and perseverance of the Apostles, who received this praise from the Master: "You have remained faithful to me in my tribulations" (Luke 12:28), and we must recall the Savior's words when he said: "He who is not with me is against me" (Matt. 12:30). Let us remember our duty and exert ourselves to follow Christ with an unbreakable faith and firm sentiments, remaining closely attached to him.[50]

The text of this instruction was distributed.

The Pope had designated five members of the Organizing Preparatory Commission to preside in his place at the future general sessions. They were Cardinals Reisach, De Luca, Bizzarri, Bilio, and Annibal Capalti; the first died shortly afterwards and was replaced on December 30 by Cardinal De Angelis. A secretary was appointed in the person of Msgr. Fessler, Bishop of Sankt-Pölten (Austria); he would play a prominent part in the running of the Council. This choice of a Germanic bishop for such a key post might upset the bishops of the other countries, remarked Cardinal Caterini, Prefect of the Congregation of the Council. He would have preferred an Italian to be nominated for this post since the Italian bishops were in a majority at the Council. Pius IX insisted on his choice, but agreed that an Italian should be named sub-secretary: Msgr. Ludovico Jacobini. It was also decided that there would be four Deputations of twenty-four Fathers.

This first meeting displeased some people. Icard reports a conversation he had with Msgr. Darboy. The Archbishop of Paris was already showing his ill-humor: "To accept this regulation would be to concede defeat; it would have been better to let us stay at home."[51]

The same author, who was in daily contact with many bishops, gives prominence to the fears expressed by some of them, that at the first general session, December 8, they would be asked to vote on decrees they had not examined. Their fears were groundless.

On December 8, after a day's fasting and abstinence, the solemn opening took place. Thousands of pilgrims from all over Europe were present at the ceremony at St. Peter's. A few privileged people were accommodated on special stages erected around the assembly room: the Empress of Austria, the ex-King of Naples, some other members of royal families, and the diplomats accredited to the Holy See. After Solemn Mass of the

---

[50] Cited by Granderath, *Histoire du concile du Vatican,* II, I, 10-11.
[51] Henri Icard, "Journal de mon voyage et de mon séjour à Rome," Archives of Saint-Sulpice Seminary, Paris, December 4, 1869, f.23.

Immaculate Conception, sung by the Dean of the Sacred College in the
hall of the Council, the Pope intoned the opening prayers.

Next, two entirely formal decrees were adopted by acclamation, not
by written vote: a decree proclaiming the Council open, and another fixing the next general session for January 6. Then Pius IX gave an address
in which he pointed out the dangers of liberalism, reminded those present
that the Council had been convoked to apply remedies to the Church's
ills, reaffirmed the necessity of the temporal power, and finally urged the
Council Fathers to be united to the Holy See.

He exhorted them in these terms:

> Courage then, Venerable Brethren, be strong in the Lord; and in the
> name of the august Trinity, sanctified in the truth, clothed with the armor
> of light, teach together with Us the way, the truth, and the life, to which
> the human race cannot refuse to aspire, despite all its agitations and all
> sorts of wretchedness. Work with Us, so that kingdoms may find peace
> once again; barbarians, a law; monasteries, repose; the Churches, order;
> clerics, discipline; and so that God may find a people according to His
> desire.[52]

It should be noted that, while Pius IX called for unity, he did not in-
tend to restrict the freedom of speech during the sessions. In 1974, during
the process of beatification, the Promoter of the Faith would refer to "the
liberty of the Fathers at the First Vatican Council" as one of the "difficulties" posed by the cause of beatification.[53] The reproach was unjustified.
Even before the opening session, Pius IX had been at pains personally
to reassure the bishops who might have been anxious. As Icard notes on
December 5, "the bishops admitted to audience yesterday were all quite
happy: the Pope had given evidence of his kind disposition and had told
them that he wanted them to be free."[54] As the Council debates unfolded,
all opinions were expressed, and at considerable length.

Several tendencies emerged as the debates got under way. As was natural, meetings of language groups were held regularly outside the plenary
sessions. Italy was an exception here: it was divided into two main groups:
"The central Italian group, where the Tuscans set the tone, and which was
distinguished for its moderation on several occasions; and the northern
group under the presidency of the Patriarch of Venice, but where a certain
number of Piedmontese and Lombard bishops were characterized by their
liberal tendency and their independence *vis-à-vis* the dominant views in
Rome."[55] The Germanic group, consisting of the German, Austro-Hungarian, and Swiss bishops, was initially numerous: seventy-eight Fathers;

[52] Cited by Granderath, *Histoire du concile du Vatican,* II, I, p.32.
[53] Perez, "Alcune difficolta," in Snider, *Pio IX nella luce dei processi canonici,* p.237.
[54] Icard, "Journal," December 5, 1869, f.26.
[55] Aubert, *Vatican I,* p.103.

but some of them stopped attending meetings of the group when the latter showed itself to have a majority hostile to the definition of papal infallibility. The Hispanic group (Spain and Latin America) decided, at its first meeting, to propose the definition of papal infallibility if it were not officially put on the program.

The French group, bathed in the prestige of some of its bishops, of the world-wide extension of its missionary congregations, and of Napoleon III's action in favor of the pope's temporal power, was nonetheless very much divided between liberals and neo-Gallicans, on the one side, and Ultramontanes on the other. Only one joint meeting took place, after which there were meetings of the different tendencies: the Ultramontanes gathered around the Archbishop of Bourges at the French Seminary; the adversaries of the definition of infallibility were led by Cardinal Mathieu at the Palazzo Salviati; the moderates met with Cardinal de Bonnechose in the church of San Luigi dei Franceschi.

Above all, it was the question of infallibility which rapidly caused people to speak of a "majority" and a "minority" at the heart of the Council. (From December 22 onwards these two terms appear in Icard's diary.) Even before work began, everyone knew that the number of bishops favorable to a definition of papal infallibility by the Council was much larger than the number of bishops who, for various reasons, were opposed to it. Nonetheless the cleavage between these two great tendencies did not arise solely over the question of infallibility. More often, it had its origins in other differences of view on the more general idea of the Church and of the relations between Church and State.

The majority consisted of bishops from traditionally Catholic countries (Italy, Spain, Galicia, Tyrol, Ireland, Latin America), but also of bishops from countries where they were struggling against Protestantism or liberalism (all the bishops of Belgium; Holland; most of the Swiss; a certain number of French, English, North American, and German bishops), and a great number of Oriental and missionary bishops.

At the start of the Council, according to Roger Aubert's calculations, the minority consisted of about 140 members. Some of them were hostile to the doctrine itself, and considered it theologically unfounded; this was the case with Msgr. Maret. Others, without being fundamentally hostile to it, judged that its definition would be inopportune; they feared that it would poison the relations between Church and State even more. This was the view of Msgr. Ketteler, Archbishop of Mainz, or of Msgr. Simor, Primate of Hungary. The greater number of this minority were German and Austrian bishops. Its heart was Cardinal Rauscher, Archbishop of Vienna ("the minority's spiritual director," in the words of Johann Friedrich Schulte, professor of canon law at Prague University).[56] The second im-

---

[56] Cited by Aubert, *Vatican I*, p.114.

portant group of the minority was made up of French bishops under the influence of Cardinal Mathieu, Msgr. Darboy, Msgr. Maret, and Msgr. Dupanloup.[57] These minority French bishops knew that the vast majority of their priests did not understand their position; furthermore, once the dogma had been proclaimed, they all rallied to it, with more or less good grace.

Significantly, one of the minority's kingpins was a layman, Lord Acton, already mentioned. A liberal and an opponent of infallibility for historical reasons, he came to Rome in order to see his ideas triumph. "Helped by many international connections and his knowledge of languages, he was eager to bring together the main leaders of the opposition, several of whom hardly knew each other when they arrived in Rome. Where necessary he acted as their interpreter, showing them possibilities of joint action that had at first seemed daunting to many of them, making them realize that governmental support might be had not only from Paris, Vienna, and Munich, but even from London."[58]

Outside, the majority's most vehement opponent was Döllinger. Under the pseudonym of *Quirinus* he published in the *Allgemeine Zeitung* from December 17, 1869, to July 19, 1870, a series of "Letters from Rome" which caused a considerable commotion.[59] Material for Döllinger's chronicles came from the many letters he received from his friends in Rome, notably Lord Acton, and also from dispatches of the Bavarian and Prussian ambassadors, whose governments furnished him with copies.

Finally we should note that, from the very first days of December, Msgr. Haynald, a Hungarian bishop hostile to infallibility, suggested to Msgr. Dupanloup that an "international committee" should be set up to defend their ideas.[60] The Bishop of Orléans was seduced by this project and promoted it eagerly, but not without much hard work. The meetings in language groups and the first tasks of the Council had already begun when this "international committee" started to operate. Icard mentions it for the first time on December 29. He describes it as dominated by the Archbishops of Vienna and Prague, and notes that several French bishops (Darboy, Dupanloup, Ginoulhiac) figured in it, as well as Germans, Italians, and Americans.[61]

Regulations stipulated that several commissions should be constituted to examine in greater depth the major topics under discussion. Only one of them, composed of twenty-six members, the so-called Commission of

57 Icard, a moderate Ultramontane, often describes the Bishop of Orléans as being "over-excited."
58 Aubert, *Vatican I*, p.121.
59 The seventy-nine letters published in the *Allgemeine Zeitung* were published as a collection: *Quirinus: Römische Briefe vom Konzil* (Munich: 1870).
60 Lagrange, *Mgr. Dupanloup*, III, 156.
61 Icard, "Journal," December 29, 1869, f.76.

Postulates, with the task of receiving and examining the Fathers' proposals before transmitting them to the Pope, was appointed directly by the Pope himself. The others, each composed of twenty-four members, were elected: the Deputation of the Faith (or Dogmatic Commission) on December 14, the Deputation of Discipline the same day, the Deputation of Religious on December 20, the Deputation for the Oriental churches and the missions on January 14.

The election of the Deputation of the Faith gave rise to the first serious disagreement between majority and minority. Prior to the vote, the most determined elements of each of these two tendencies had drawn up a list of candidates. The list of the partisans of infallibility, revised by certain champions of the cause (Deschamps, Manning, etc.) and by Cardinals De Angelis and Patrizzi, easily obtained a very large majority of the votes cast. Most of the Fathers, who were not acquainted with one another, judged it wiser to vote for a list made up solely of defenders of the papal cause and which seemed to have the approval of high authority. The minority felt pushed to one side and, when the election of the remaining Deputations was carried out, only a very reduced number of its representatives were elected.

It is worth pointing out again, without lapsing into hagiography, that Pius IX had a concern for justice: he would have liked Msgr. Dupanloup, who appeared to be one of the leaders of the minority, to be a member of one of the important commissions. But Msgr. Manning was hostile to this idea, and nothing came of it.[62]

First Discussions

The first schema distributed to the Fathers on December 10 was a draft dogmatic constitution, *De Doctrina Catholica contra Multiplices Errores ex Rationalismo Derivatos* (On Catholic doctrine, against the many errors derived from rationalism). This was a long text in eighteen chapters, largely written by Fr. Franzelin, professor at the Gregorian University. First of all it condemned several theories: materialism, pantheism, absolute rationalism, and its opposite, traditionalism.[63]

Next it set forth the great problems of fundamental theology: Scripture and Tradition; the sources of revelation; the necessity of a supernatural revelation; the distinction between the knowledge of faith and science; the immutable character of dogma; *etc.* Finally several important points of

---

[62] Granderath, *Histoire du concile du Vatican,* II, I, 92.
[63] In the nineteenth century, "traditionalism" referred to a doctrine which denied that the reason was able to know anything about God except through Revelation and the tradition of the Church. This doctrine had already been condemned by a decree of the Congregation of the Index, in June 1855, against the theses of Augustin Bonnetty: Denzinger-Schönmetzer, pp.562-63.

dogmatic theology were redefined: the Trinity, Creation, Incarnation and Redemption, the nature of man, the supernatural order, sin and grace. The discussion of this schema began on December 28.

The first speaker was Cardinal Rauscher. He spoke for more than an hour on a point of order. The errors referred to, he explained, had already been condemned several times. Furthermore, the doctrinal text proposed was too professorial. During the day several other speakers criticized the schema: "quite apart from its excessive length and its debatable structure, its tone was too polemical and its language too technical, largely beyond the grasp of the faithful."[64] Other criticisms were formulated in the following days, so much so that, on January 7, the Deputation of the Faith, at its first meeting, decided to withdraw the draft and entirely refashion it.

Now that the first draft constitution had been rejected, the Fathers went on to examine several schemas presented by the Commission for Ecclesiastical Discipline. A first schema dealt with the duties of bishops, their obligation to reside in their diocese, pastoral visitations and visits *ad limina,* provincial or diocesan synods, and vicars general. A second schema was concerned with the problems posed by the vacancy of an episcopal see. The discussion of these first two schemas presented an opportunity for the opponents of Roman centralization to raise their voices. Msgr. Dupanloup, speaking for the first time, complained that the decrees of provincial councils were sometimes modified unilaterally by Roman congregations. Msgr. Strossmayer, Bishop of Diakovo (Bosnia), one of the minority's best orators, urged that ecumenical councils be held periodically.[65]

A third disciplinary schema raised questions of detail concerning the tonsure, the soutane, retreat houses for aged priests, *etc.* Roger Aubert observes that, while some discussions got lost in questions that were too local, others approached the problem with a praiseworthy breadth of perspective, which would be confirmed by future events. Msgr. Gastaldi, for instance, Bishop of Saluzzo, called for the editing of a single code of canon law that would be easy to use; it should harmonize the different current prescriptions, which were scattered throughout different collections of rules and were sometimes antiquated. A fourth project considered the production of a universal catechism in Latin to replace the multitude of diocesan catechisms. These four drafts were discussed in turn in Janu-

---

[64] Roger Aubert, Michel Gueret, and Paul Tombeur, *Concilium Vaticanum I. Concordance, Index, Listes de fréquence, Tables comparatives* (Louvain: Publications du Cetedoc, 1977), p.vii.

[65] In doing so he was once more raising the old conciliarist claim that Msgr. Maret had resurrected some months earlier, and which certain participants in the Second Vatican Council would put forward again a century later.

ary and then in the first three weeks of February; finally they too were withdrawn for emendation, the Deputation of Discipline being charged with responsibility for modifying the original texts. Only two of the four schemas would be re-presented to the Council before the latter was interrupted, namely, that on the catechism, at the end of April, and that on the government of dioceses in a period of vacancy.

The Constitution *Dei Filius*

In the meantime, other subjects were occupying the minds of the Fathers. On January 21, 1870, a new draft dogmatic constitution was distributed to them, entitled *De Ecclesia Christi,* and at the end of February they were given six other schemas: two came again from the Deputation of Discipline and concerned the Mass and ordination titles, and four came from the Deputation of Religious.

The aim of the new dogmatic constitution, in fifteen chapters, was to set forth the nature, properties, and power of the Church, and then to go on to condemn errors regarding ecclesiology. In it, the Church was defined as the mystical Body of Christ and presented as "a spiritual society, of an absolutely supernatural order," but also "a visible society" equipped with a visible magisterium, cult, and priesthood. It was explained in detail how the axiom "Outside the Church no salvation" should be understood. While the pope's primacy in the Church was the theme of a long chapter, the question of papal infallibility—a matter of controversy at that time—was not mentioned, because it had not yet been officially inscribed in the order of the day of the Council debates. The justification of the pope's temporal sovereignty was re-iterated and the schema ended with three long chapters on Church-State relations. If the legitimacy of "many and diverse forms of civil society" was acknowledged, the separation of Church and State was rejected as an error. Not only should the State draw inspiration from Christian morality, it should also respect the rights of parents over their children (notably in the field of education) and the rights of the Church over the faithful.

The definition of the Church as the "mystical Body of Christ," though drawn from writings of the Church Fathers, baffled some bishops, who asked that it be replaced by some more usual definition. Others regretted that the Church's foundation by Christ had not sufficiently been emphasized, and that the function proper to the episcopate had been eclipsed by the importance given to the papacy. Even bishops regarded as Ultramontane agreed on this latter point; thus Msgr. Pie said, "The schema is reprehensible on account of its silence regarding the bishops. This silence will prove troublesome."[66] This schema, too, was withdrawn and profoundly

---

[66] Icard, "Journal," f.188.

re-shaped. The Council's suspension some months later meant that the new text was never distributed to the Fathers.

The first doctrinal schema on Revelation, sent back to the commission on January 10, had been totally refashioned "to give it a less professorial appearance and to avoid any condemnation of an opinion that is open to free discussion."[67] Three men took a prominent part in this: Msgr. Deschamps, Msgr. Pie, and Msgr. Martin, assisted by eminent theologians, notably Fr. Kleutgen, a German Jesuit and Thomist.

This schema on Revelation was reduced to nine chapters and then finally divided into two distinct constitutions. The first, *Dei Filius,* was concerned with "the Catholic Faith" and was distributed to the Fathers on March 14. They began to debate it in the forum of the general congregation four days later. The discussion lasted for a month, allowing various nuances and precisions to be introduced, even if a certain number of bishops complained that the 281 amendments proposed were examined far too quickly. Finally, on April 24, in a solemn session presided over by the Pope, the 667 Fathers present unanimously approved the constitution. The minority, who had hesitated a few times right up to the eve of the vote, joined in.

Some opponents who could not be convinced, like Msgr. Strossmayer, preferred not to come and take part in the vote. This was the first constitution to be approved by the Council. Once the result had been obtained, Pius IX rose and said: "The decisions and canons contained in the constitution that has been read have received the approval of all the Fathers, without exception; and for Our part, with the approval of the Holy Council, We define these decisions and canons as they have been read, and confirm them in virtue of Our apostolic authority."

This constitution has been judged severely by some bishops who voted for it half-heartedly, and denigrated by certain historians who criticized it for its formalism. A specialist in contemporary Catholicism like Roger Aubert, who is rarely given to praise, recognizes that *Dei Filius* "constitutes a remarkable achievement, presenting a dense and luminous exposition of the Catholic doctrine on God, Revelation, and the Faith, in opposition to modern pantheism, materialism, and rationalism."[68]

A well-structured prologue recalled the principal errors that had proliferated in modern times, against which the Church had to struggle: Holy Scripture regarded as "fables and fictions" (this had in mind, without naming them, the exegetes and historians who wanted to "demythologize" Christianity: Strauss in Germany and Renan in France, *etc.*); the rationalism or naturalism which leads to "the abyss of pantheism, materialism,

[67] Aubert, *Vatican I*, p.182.
[68] *Ibid.*, p.191.

and atheism" and also those Catholic theologians who, "erroneously con-
fusing nature and grace, human knowledge and divine faith, are involved
in giving dogmas a different meaning from that which is held and taught
by Holy Church, their Mother, putting in peril the integrity and purity
of the faith."

Faced with these various errors, four short chapters reaffirmed the
Catholic doctrine: "God, creator of all things," "Revelation," "Faith," and
"Faith and Reason." Eighteen canons were annexed to the constitution
itself in order to anathematize those who professed heresies in direct contradiction with the truths of faith presented in the four chapters.

The Dogma of Infallibility

While the disciplinary schemas and the Constitution *Dei Filius* were
being debated, the question of infallibility had already been discussed
outside the Council sessions and was the object of different kinds of maneuvering. As we have seen, the Preparatory Dogmatic Commission had
decided not to submit to the Fathers a draft schema on papal infallibility
lest it appear that the question had been suggested by the person most
concerned in it, *i.e.* the Pope. It was up to the bishops themselves to call
for it, if they judged such a definition to be theologically well-founded
and opportune. On December 18, Msgr. Pluym, a Dutch Passionist, pa-
triarchal vicar of Constantinople, had presented a petition to the Commission of Postulates asking that the question of infallibility be included
in the debates.

A few days later Cardinal Rauscher circulated a handwritten *exposé* of
his objections. From then on there was an incessant clash of infallibilists
and anti-infallibilists (or "fallibilists," as Veuillot ironically termed them)
using petitions, memoranda, and debates.

At the end of January an influential work was published: *De la Monar-
chie pontificale à propos du livre de Mgr. de Sura,* (On the Papal Monarchy,
with reference to the book by Msgr. de Sura) by Dom Guéranger.[69] The
Abbot of Solesmes, an *ex officio* member of the Council since he was the
head of a congregation, preferred not to attend the Council for reasons of
health. Nonetheless he wished to reply to Msgr. Maret's book and defend
the possibility of a doctrinal definition of the Sovereign Pontiff's personal
infallibility. In passing he also refuted the assertions of the *Correspondant,*
of Döllinger, and of Msgr. Dupanloup. Dom Guéranger's book came just
at the right time. When Pius IX was told what it contained he was delighted and desired it to be distributed "in large numbers." In this he was
anticipated by the Bishop of Le Mans, who had already ordered three
hundred copies. After reading the book, Pius IX wrote a letter to Dom

---

[69]   Cf. Delatte, *Dom Guéranger,* pp.804-807.

Guéranger which was more than a eulogy: it was an energetic critique of
the anti-infallibilists:

> The adversaries of infallibility are men who, while being proud to be
> called Catholics, show themselves to be completely imbued with corrupt
> principles and keep trotting out quibbles, calumnies, and sophisms in
> order to undermine the authority of the supreme leader whom Christ has
> given to the Church—for they do not believe in his prerogatives. They
> do not believe, as other Catholics do, that the Council is governed by
> the Holy Spirit; heedless as they are, full of folly, unreason, impudence,
> hatred, violence, they seek to enthuse people like themselves by organiz-
> ing activities by which they get hold of votes in popular assemblies. They
> undertake to refashion the Church's divine constitution and adapt it to
> the modern forms of civil governments.[70]

Pius IX's severe criticism was justified in the case of opponents of infallibility such as Msgr. Maret, who was preaching a neo-Gallicanism and
a liberalism that were contrary to the Church's constitution. It was exaggerated, no doubt, where it failed to distinguish them from those who,
like Msgr. Ketteler, were hostile to the definition because they thought it
inopportune. In fact, when Pius IX stigmatized the anti-infallibilists for
"organizing activities by which they get hold of votes in popular assemblies," he could have addressed the same reproach to the partisans of infallibility: both parties operated by compacts, maneuvering, and petitions. It
appears that the first text to circulate was the work of the anti-infallibilists.
On January 15, Icard reported that several bishops had met to prepare a
letter asking the Pope to withdraw the question of infallibility. Thirty-
three French bishops signed this letter.[71]

The response was of the same caliber: on January 28, a postulate was
presented in favor of the dogmatic definition of papal infallibility. At the
instigation of Anthony Peter IX Hassoun, the Armenian Patriarch, and
Msgr. Ledochowski, Archbishop of Gnesen and Posen, four copies of this
postulate were circulated and 380 signatures were collected. If one adds
a request of the bishops of the old Kingdom of Naples, which attracted
69 signatures, a similar request of the 17 bishops of the Franciscan Order,
and various other individual or collective postulates, one arrives at the
significant figure of 480 Council Fathers who were expressly asking for a
dogmatic definition of infallibility.[72]

The postulate of the 380 proposed the following formula of definition: "The authority of the Roman Pontiff is exempt from all error when,
in a matter of faith or morals, it determines and prescribes what all the
faithful must believe and hold, or reject and condemn." This formula,

---

[70] Cited by Maynard, *Mgr. Dupanloup et M. Lagrange*, p.264. Cardinal Pitra wrote to
Dom Guéranger that this energetic brief was in fact a much milder version of a text
which had already known two far more virulent drafts (Delatte, p.815).
[71] Icard, "Journal," January 15, 1870, f.127.

which was judged to be too absolute—since it made no mention of the necessity of communion in the faith of the Church, nor was there any precise specification of the exact conditions for such infallibility—meant that certain bishops preferred to sign the alternative drafts we have referred to.

These petitions caused disquiet in the ranks of the anti-infallibilists. A delegation of forty of them managed to obtain an audience with Pius IX and asked him not to proceed with the petitions that had been submitted to the Commission of Postulates. Having listened to them, the Pope replied: "My Brothers, entrust yourselves to the Council; give your votes from your hearts and in conscience, expose your ideas to your colleagues in the general congregation, and leave the rest to God and the Holy Spirit, who will never, absolutely never, abandon the Church of the Son of God, but will surely enlighten the assembly."[73]

The anti-infallibilists continued to agitate. No doubt the aforementioned "International Committee" did not want to appear, by circulating a single text, to be an opposition bloc; it was at the level of national groupings that the opponents of the definition produced their documents. By doing this, they were able to present different arguments in turn and so gather a larger number of signatures. Five distinct documents were drawn up against having the question debated, some insisting on doctrinal difficulties, others maintaining that the time was not opportune. The anti-infallibilist petitions gathered 136 signatures. This was a minority of the Fathers, of course, but it was not insignificant (about 20% of the Council) and included some very celebrated figures, often representing important dioceses. During this time, together with Cardinal de Rouen, Icard worked on a conciliatory text which had, however, hardly any success.

On February 9, despite the considerable number of opposing voices, the Commission of Postulates transmitted, to the Pope, the petitions in favor of the definition together with its own favorable advice. Pius IX hesitated for almost three weeks before taking his decision. Some people thought that he would not dare to proceed in the face of such an important number of opponents. They mistook the situation.

A story reported by Granderath and others gives a good illustration of the Pope's state of mind at this time. Cardinal Schwarzenberg, at an audience with the Pope, tried to show him that the definition was inopportune and full of danger. Pius IX interrupted him: "I, Giovanni Maria Mastai, believe in the Sovereign Pontiff's infallibility. As pope, I do not look to the Council for anything. The Holy Spirit will enlighten the Fathers."[74]

---

[72] Granderath, IV, *Histoire du concile du Vatican,*168-69.
[73] *Ibid.*, II, I, 374.
[74] *Ibid.* p.372. The author says that "we cannot certify the exactitude of this account," but regards the statement as indicative of the Pope's mind.

On March 1, furthermore, the Pope informed Msgr. Fessler, secretary to the Council, of his desire to have infallibility debated in session. On March 6 a first draft of the definition was distributed to the Council Fathers. At this moment there took place an episode which, while it had no effect on the course of the Council, clearly illustrates the exasperation felt in certain liberal circles. Montalembert, who had fallen out with his friends at the *Correspondant,* whom he regarded as too timid, and was now putting his hope in Msgr. Dupanloup, published an extremely poisonous letter in the *Gazette de France* of March 7 and in the *Journal des Débats* of March 9. In it he was replying to the charge of having abandoned his anti-Gallican views of 1847:

> How could we have suspected in 1847 that the liberal pontificate of Pius IX, acclaimed by all the liberals of both worlds, would turn into the pontificate represented and personified by *L'Univers* and the *Civiltà?...* Who could have foreseen the enthusiasm of the majority of Ultramontane doctors for a renaissance of Caesarism?...Who could have predicted the permanent triumph of these lay theologians of absolutism, who began by throwing away all our liberties, all our principles, all our former ideas, under Napoleon III, and are now sacrificing justice and truth, reason and history, as a holocaust to the idol they have erected at the Vatican.[75]

These were Montalembert's last public words. On March 13 he died. A number of historians mention the fact that Pius IX, irritated by this damaging article, forbade the holding of a funeral service planned by Msgr. de Mérode, Montalembert's brother-in-law, for the sanctuary of Ara Caeli in Rome.[76]

None of them, however, reports the end of the story, which shows that, in the event, Pius IX did not forget the demands of charity. In fact Icard relates that, on March 18, the Pope was present at a funeral service he directed to be celebrated for Montalembert at the Church of Santa Maria Transportina. One of the Pope's domestic prelates explained the Pope's attitude to Icard:

> The Holy Father did not sanction the proposed service for M. de Montalembert at the Ara Caeli, because there had been a lack of propriety in announcing it without informing him or the Cardinal Vicar, which should have been done under the circumstances....But in order to show that he was not forgetful of the services which this man had given the Church, and that he was still charitably disposed towards him, he desired a solemn Mass to be sung at Santa Maria Transportina, at which he himself would be present. He was present, albeit on a gallery; and since no notification had been made, practically no one else was there; those who were there did not even know for whom this requiem was being sung.[77]

---

[75] Cited by Palanque, *Catholiques libéraux,* pp.125-26.
[76] Tollu, *Montalembert,* p.523; Palanque, *Catholiques libéraux,* p.126; Aubert, *Le Pontificat de Pie IX,* p.345.
[77] Icard, "Journal," ff.277-278.

All the same, the Montalembert affair had no influence on the infallibility debate in progress.

The draft distributed on March 6 was not a new constitution but a complementary chapter to be inserted into the schema on the Church, after the chapter on the papal primacy. The text, modified by the Preparatory Commission, had been edited by Cardinal Bilio and submitted to Pius IX's approval. Cardinal Bilio's work was based on two earlier proposals made by Dechamps and Manning. Initially the Council Fathers had ten days in which to present their observations. There were a number of meetings, often in national groups, to draw up joint responses. For instance, the German-speaking bishops met with Cardinal Rauscher practically every day.

On March 11, the International Committee wrote a letter to the Council presidents asking for a further postponement and for the setting-up of a special commission composed of delegates of the Deputation of the Faith and representatives of the minority. The first request was granted and the date for producing amendments was put back to March 25; but the second request was turned down: a commission of this kind would have been in contradiction with the rule requiring the Council debates to be public.

Chapter 9 on the papal primacy received 88 amendments, and the text on papal infallibility, which was linked with it theologically, was subject to 139 amendments. This shows the vigorous nature of the controversy. Infallibilists thought that the definition of the pope's infallibility could easily be justified by texts of Holy Scripture and by arguments drawn from the great scholastic theologians, from St. Thomas Aquinas to St. Robert Bellarmine. Others cited the needs of the present situation.

In this context it is significant to recall the arguments put forward some months earlier by Msgr. Mermillod, Bishop of Geneva, to Msgr. Dupanloup after the latter had published his anti-infallibilist pamphlet:

> An infallible center is the precondition for the unity of the faith. Furthermore, at the present time of sentimentalism in the faith, precise and well-formulated doctrines constitute a barrier, both to the enthusiasm which errs by excess and to the rashness that entertains doubts. There is another danger in the current life of the Church; the central doctrinal power is a rampart against the bureaucratic mentality that is infiltrating the episcopate. In times of democracy and statolatry, which diminish men, the Church needs liberty and dignity; the infallible center is the refuge and support of the episcopate.[78]

As for the anti-infallibilists, they presented a great variety of arguments. Some of them judged a definition of this kind inopportune: the pope's doctrinal authority was not under threat; councils, they said, only

---

[78] Unpublished letter of December 26, 1869, Archives of Saint-Sulpice.

defined truths of faith when they were gravely imperiled. Others, hostile
to the very principle behind the definition, put forward historical and
theological arguments: certain of them expressed the fear of seeing the
episcopate's authority weakened or the fear of schism; others, again, notably a number of American bishops, feared that a dogma of this kind
would reinforce the hostility of Protestants or—the view of Msgr. Strossmayer—would widen the gulf with the Orthodox.

An anonymous pamphlet, *Quaestio*, circulated by Msgr. Ketteler, re-
stated the Gallican theses: the Church is a moderate monarchy in which
the pope only has the major share in the power given to the Church; the
bishops also have their share. The pope can only exercise an infallible
magisterium if he does so in collaboration with, and with the approval
of, the bishops. The circulation of this pamphlet gave rise to an incident.
The pamphlets had arrived by post, in a chest. When the Master of the
Sacred Palace was informed, he seized it. Msgr. Ketteler then had to try
to get hold of it.

Pius IX was told about the affair. Once again, his reaction shows that
he was not the authoritarian "idol" denounced by Montalembert and others. The Pope related to Msgr. Senestrey, Bishop of Regensburg, a defender of infallibility, how he let Msgr. Ketteler decide, according to his
own soul and conscience, how to act: "The pamphlet had been written
against me; so I asked the Bishop of Mainz if he thought that, in my
own house, I should hand over, to my enemies, weapons that were to be
used against me. At all events, I had the chest of pamphlets returned to
him, asking only that he would kneel before his crucifix and meditate on
the decision he should take regarding them."[79] Msgr. Ketteler, who subsequently declared that he did not share the views expressed in the pamphlet, had it distributed, despite the Pope's warning, "so that the question
could be studied." This pamphlet circulated by Msgr. Ketteler was only
one of some two hundred pamphlets on the subject of the Council which
have been identified in Germany; seventy-one of them deal explicitly with
the question of infallibility.

In France, too, the "war of pamphlets" was raging. The anti-infallibilists (Frs. Gratry, Gaduel, Lagrange, *etc.*) were answered by the infallibilists
(A. de Margerie, Dom Guéranger, who had written a new book entitled
Défense de l'Eglise romaine contre les accusations du P. Gratry [Defense of the
Roman Church against Fr. Gratry's accusations]). In the anti-infallibilist
camp it was the writings of Döllinger which most assiduously wielded
invective. According to Döllinger, infallibility was something desired by
a pope who was temperamentally inclined to autocracy. By its very injus-

---

[79] Granderath, *Histoire du concile du Vatican*, III, I, 39, n.1.

tice, one of the portraits of Pius IX he drew at this period illustrates his thesis:

> Pius, *totus teres atque rotundus,* is firm, unshakable, simultaneously polite and as hard as marble; his intellect is very mediocre; he lacks ideas; he is ignorant; he understands nothing of humanity's state of mind and its present needs; he does not even suspect the existence of different nationalities; but, with the faith of a nun and the most profound veneration for his own person—the repository of the Holy Spirit—his whole being breathes absolutism. He is filled by one single thought: Me, and outside me—no one.[80]

The day after the text on infallibility had been distributed, a rumor went around that it would be voted on by acclamation at the next general congregation. Even if this idea was floated by a very zealous prelate of the infallibilist party, Pius IX was not at all in favor of such a suggestion. He wished the Council to follow the normal debating procedures in this matter also. At the end of March he declared to Cardinal de Bonnechose that, far from wanting to impose a formula, he wished "the terms in which the power of the Roman Pontiff may be defined to be freely studied."[81]

If the order of work were to be respected, the text on infallibility would not be discussed in general session for several months. At this period the Constitution on Revelation and Faith, which we have already mentioned, was still being discussed, and the eleven chapters of the Constitution on the Church would have to be debated before dealing with the additional text on infallibility. Furthermore, many infallibilists began to hope that this text on infallibility would be put to a debate as soon as the Constitution *Dei Filius* had been voted on, and some even suggested making it a distinct constitution, separate from that on the Church. Their arguments were not unfounded. The question of infallibility, which was much disputed, was creating constant agitation. If it were dealt with immediately and given a definitive answer, the Council would acquire the necessary calm for it to be able to examine the other subjects scheduled. On the other hand, if the pre-arranged order of work were followed, the text on infallibility would doubtless not be examined before the spring of the next year; by then some bishops who had come from far countries would have returned to their dioceses, whereas the infallibility issue merited as broad a debate as possible.

From the first fortnight of March, almost two hundred Council Fathers showed themselves to be in favor of bringing forward the examination of infallibility. The minority were hostile to bringing it forward: they saw this as a ploy to interrupt discussion on the subject. The Council presidents were split on the issue. The decision had to be made by the Pope.

---

[80] *Römische Briefe,* p.626, cited by Granderath, *Histoire du concile du Vatican,* II, II, 254.
[81] Cited by Aubert, *Vatican I,* p.201.

He was approached both by those in favor and those against bringing the debate forward. Some were still hoping that, ultimately, infallibility would not be dealt with at the Council. Icard reports that the Secretary of State took action along these lines at the end of March: "Seriously concerned at the consequences a definition might have in the present circumstances, [Cardinal Antonelli] has met with a number of cardinals he frequently consults on political affairs. They agreed to go to the Holy Father and earnestly beg him to withdraw this notorious question from the Council. The Pope did not entertain their suggestions. He told them: I have the Blessed Virgin with me, and I shall go ahead."[82]

Pius IX ordered Council officials to study the best way of facilitating the examination of the many texts under discussion. On April 27 (three days after the vote and promulgation of the Constitution *Dei Filius*), he announced, by the mouth of Cardinal Bilio, that the texts on the papal primacy and infallibility would be the object of a separate constitution, the *Constitutio Prima de Ecclesia Christi* (First Constitution on the Church of Christ), and that they would soon be put to a debate. Seventy-one members of the minority signed a petition drawn up by Msgr. Ketteler, protesting against the decision, but they did not ask the Pope to reconsider.

At the time that the new decree on the Sovereign Pontiff was being planned, the Council Fathers were examining the re-worked text of the Decree on the Catechism, from April 29 to May 14. On May 4 there was a vote on the whole of the schema: 491 *placet,* 56 *non placet,* 44 *placet juxta modum.* Among those who were opposed or hesitant, some were hostile on principle to the idea of a single catechism for the entire Church; others would have preferred it to be optional, and others again were demanding that it should not be edited solely by Roman theologians under the Pope's authority, but that bishops delegated by the Council should be associated in drawing it up. The solemn session which was to promulgate this Decree on the Catechism never took place, as a result of the Council's being interrupted. On May 9 the draft Constitution on the Sovereign Pontiff was distributed to the Council Fathers.[83]

The discussion was opened on May 13 with a general report that had been entrusted to Msgr. Pie. This report was clear and nuanced, with the intention of reassuring anti-infallibilists in good faith or those who were hesitant. The schema in its entirety was debated during fourteen sessions, from May 14 to June 3. One innovation was well received because it enabled the debate to proceed with greater dispatch: each session was

---

[82] Icard, "Journal," March 27, 1870, f.298.
[83] Full text published in Granderath, *Histoire du concile du Vatican,* III, I, 406-16, Appendix II, with the first draft prior to its revision by the Deputation of the Faith.

opened by an address given by a representative of the Deputation of the Faith, who replied in detail to the objections proposed by the speakers of the day before. The debates were lively, and sometimes tense. Msgr. Foulon, Bishop of Nancy, wrote to a correspondent on May 23: "I have the impression that several speakers are talking with clenched fists or with their finger on the trigger of a revolver."[84]

The minority fielded its most incisive or most profound orators, in a sequence that had been long in preparation. It was the task of Msgr. Hefele, Bishop of Rottenburg, a brilliant historian of councils, to set forth the historical difficulties of the proposed definition; Msgr. Strossmayer and Msgr. Maret were to present the theological arguments.

On June 3, after three weeks, and when sixty-five Fathers had had the opportunity of speaking from the dais (twenty-six of these were from the minority), the Council presidents decided to close the general discussion, even though a further forty members had notified their intention of speaking. The presidents rightly feared that the repetition of arguments already heard would become tedious and would delay the necessary discussion of the text chapter by chapter.

This discussion would allow an examination of the terms in which the doctrine of infallibility should be put forward. Those opposed to the definition were hoping that the discussion would shed light on the theological difficulties to which it would lead.

It would be simplistic to portray anti-infallibilists and infallibilists as two factions entirely opposed in everything. At times there were attempts in both "camps" to reach a conciliatory formulation. We have already referred to the attempt made by Icard and Cardinal de Rouen in January-February. At the same period, Louis Isoard, an auditor of the Rota (and future Bishop of Annecy) was at the center of a "third party" which was trying to produce a draft that would reconcile adversaries and partisans of infallibility.[85]

Roger Aubert has shed light on other meetings that began in the third week of May. Present were determined partisans of the definition (notably Msgr. Dechamps and Msgr. Senestrey, Bishop of Regensburg) and opponents (notably Msgr. Simor, Msgr. Dupanloup, and some other French bishops). "At one moment the Archbishop of Malines believed that agreement was in sight, while Dupanloup, for his part, was not without hope."[86] However, fundamental questions were still dividing the parties, despite a certain rapprochement between the points of view.

When Chapter 6, which dealt specifically with infallibility, came under discussion on June 15, the great diversity of positions was clearly

---

[84] Cited by Aubert, *Vatican I*, p.213.
[85] Icard, "Journal," January 29, 1870, ff.152-53.
[86] Aubert, *Vatican I*, p.219.

evident, even within each camp. To what degree do the bishops share in the Church's infallible magisterium? Under what conditions can the pope exercise an infallible magisterium? In exercising his supreme jurisdiction, does the pope have the principal part or does he have complete fullness of power? Must he confer with the episcopate before defining a truth of faith? These and other points found neither the majority nor the minority speaking with one voice, and so they were the object of several amendments.

One of the most memorable speeches was that of Cardinal Filippo Guidi, Archbishop of Bologna. The members of the minority were delighted that one of the most illustrious Italian cardinals joined with them in opposing the definition. In reality Cardinal Guidi's position was not hostile to the definition of infallibility; he regarded the latter as certain, but expressed an entirely personal opinion on the conditions under which it could be exercised. Guidi was not of the view of certain Gallicans, that the pope should have to obtain the assent of the bishops before making an infallible definition, as if he shared his authority with them. But, according to Granderath's summary, Guidi affirmed that "the pope must ask the bishops what is the common understanding of the Church, and the tradition of the particular Churches, on the truth in question; he must ascertain whether this truth has been believed everywhere and always, more or less explicitly or implicitly. In a word, the pope, before delivering his supreme and definitive judgment, must hear the Church's judgment, must know what is the belief of the daughter-churches, and whether this belief is in accord with the Mother-Church, the Roman Church."[87]

This opinion was entirely personal, and it was contradicted by history. While the definition of a new dogma is, of course, preceded by a study of the question, nothing obliges the pope to consult the bishops. He may be content to submit the question to theologians, or he can study the matter himself. Cardinal Guidi's assertion created quite an uproar in the aisles. Some advocates of the definition interrupted him, calling him a *birbante* (scoundrel) or a *brigantino* (brigand). Those opposed to the definition, on the other hand, encouraged him. Some authors claim that in the wake of this speech the cardinal was summoned by Pius IX and reprimanded. When Guidi cited "tradition" in defense of his position, Pius IX is said to have been quick to interrupt him, retorting, "I am Tradition."[88] While there is good evidence for the audience at this date, Pius IX's retort must be treated with caution.

On July 4, discussion on Chapter 4 was suspended. A new definition of infallibility was drawn up, taking account of certain objections of the

---

[87] Granderath, *Histoire du concile du Vatican,* III, II, 19-20.
[88] Words reported by the Old Catholic historian Friedrich, cited by Granderath, *Histoire du concile du Vatican*, III, II, 23.

minority; this was the sixth draft in four months. This is proof, if proof were needed, that Pius IX did not impose a rigid formula. In it the union of pope and Church was better affirmed, and the expression *ex cathedra*, in particular, laid down with greater precision the conditions under which the pope can exercise his infallibility.

A first vote was taken on the amendments, and then, on July 13, a provisional vote was taken on the whole text. About fifty Fathers preferred not to come to St. Peter's, so that they would not have to give their vote. A huge majority (601) approved the text; 88 voted against it and 62 voted *placet juxta modum* (and about 20 of the latter were infallibilists who were not happy with the concessions given to the minority). Among the 88 there were heads of some of the most important dioceses in Christendom at that time (Paris, Lyons, Cologne, Munich, Milan). On the very day of the vote, Veuillot expressed the feelings of many infallibilists when, in a letter, he wrote:

> The 88 *non placets* caused some astonishment, and even consternation here and there, but no discouragement. Rather, they produced the opposite effect. Heretical infatuation has been seen for what it is, we have seen how futile concessions are, and any modifications as a result of the votes *juxta modum* will be in the direction of firmness.[89]

Each camp sent delegations to Pius IX to ask for modifications to the text. The anti-infallibilists went to the Pope in the evening of July 15, asking for an addition to the text making it clear that the Church's consent had a role in the exercise of papal infallibility. The delegation was led by Msgr. Darboy and included Msgr. Simor, Msgr. Ginoulhiac, Msgr. Ketteler, Msgr. Scherr, Msgr. Rivet: these were high-profile representatives of the minority, and by taking this action they showed that they were prepared to submit if they were given some satisfaction. Pius IX did not want to give them a definitive answer himself. He advised the deputation to present its wishes in writing. This was done the following morning, at the earliest possible hour, by Msgr. Darboy.

Certain members of the majority, on the contrary, were at pains to insure that it was made clear that the Church's consent was not necessary for an infallible decision on the part of the pope. Pius IX passed on this request to Cardinal Bilio, expressing his approval, with such effect that the dogmatic definition was modified once more. The text on which the Fathers were to give a definitive pronouncement was formulated as follows:

> We teach and define that it is a dogma divinely revealed: that the Roman Pontiff, when he speaks *ex cathedra*, that is, when in discharge of the office of Pastor and Doctor of all Christians, by virtue of his supreme apostolic authority he defines a doctrine regarding faith or morals to be

[89] Cited by Aubert, *Vatican I*, p.229.

held by the Universal Church, by the divine assistance promised him in Blessed Peter, is possessed of that infallibility with which the Divine Redeemer willed that His Church should be endowed for defining doctrine regarding faith or morals: and that therefore such definitions of the Roman Pontiff are irreformable of themselves, and not from the consent of the Church.

When there was no longer any doubt that the text would be voted for by the Council by a very large majority, Msgr. Dupanloup tried a last effort. He wrote a letter to the Pope suggesting that he should act as follows: the Pope would receive with gratitude the Fathers' vote on the prerogatives of the Roman See and papal infallibility, but he would immediately declare that, given the circumstances and the disquiet of minds, it was preferable, for the present, not to confirm the vote and not to promulgate the dogma. Dupanloup went on: "Such a course of action, full of wisdom, so simple and unexpected, would forestall inevitable and absolutely certain evils at the eleventh hour; it would astonish the world and elicit universal gratitude and admiration, and redouble the love which men bear to Your Holiness. Governments and peoples would be obliged to be grateful for having been delivered from a new source of disagreements at a moment when the whole of Europe may be on the eve of an upheaval. His Holiness's fatherly authority would be greatly enhanced thereby."[90]

The Pope could not accept this proposition. Sixty bishops preferred to leave Rome rather than persist in their opposition at the definitive ballot. Certain diplomatic representatives of countries hostile to infallibility—the ambassadors of France and Austria, the plenipotentiary ministers of Prussia and Bavaria—showed their disapproval of the projected vote by absenting themselves from the solemn session.

On the day itself, July 18, only 2 of the 535 Fathers present still voted against.[91] This massive endorsement of the constitution *Pastor Aeternus,* despite the notable absences, elicited thunderous acclamation and applause which extended to the outside of the basilica, where a vast crowd of faithful and priests were gathered. At the same time an unusual storm imparted a strange atmosphere to the day. Prior to the *Te Deum* which concluded the ceremony, Pius IX pronounced a brief allocution in which, most of all, he wanted to reassure those who were uneasy. "This supreme authority of the Roman Pontiff, venerable Brothers, does not crush you: rather it supports you."

Once this new constitution had been adopted, the Fathers were authorized to take their leave until November 11, so that they would not

---

[90] Cited by Granderath, *Histoire du concile du Vatican,* III, II, 134.
[91] Msgr. Luigi Riccio, Bishop of Cajazzo, and Msgr. Edward Fitzgerald, Bishop of Little Rock. The latter is supposed to have said *"Nunc placet*–now I agree," which was understood to mean *"Non placet*–I do not agree" (Aubert, *Vatican I,* p.232).

have to endure the great heat of Rome, and would be able to spend some time in their dioceses. The Council was not suspended, however: during the summer a draft constitution on the missions was distributed and the text of the schema on the vacancy of episcopal sees was refashioned; but the work was carried on at a slower pace and in the presence of an assembly that was becoming increasingly reduced.

On September 1, there were only 104 Council Fathers present. This general congregation, the eighty-ninth, was the last. France had declared war on Prussia on July 19, and this would have consequences in Italy. On September 20, Victor Emmanuel II ordered Italian troops to occupy the remaining Papal States and Rome. The Pope found himself a "prisoner of the Vatican" and the Council was interrupted.

CHAPTER 15

THE "PRISONER OF THE VATICAN"

On July 22, 1870, three days after France had declared war on Prussia, Pius IX wrote to William I, King of Prussia, and Napoleon III.[1] In his letter he asked them to cease hostilities and offered himself as a mediator. Both refused. In August, Napoleon III decided to withdraw the garrison he had kept in Rome since the 1867 intervention. On September 2, the French army capitulated at Sedan, and the Emperor, Marshal MacMahon, 39 generals, and 105,000 men were taken prisoner. This was the end of the Second Empire and the advent, on September 4, of the Third Republic.

Victor Emmanuel took advantage of this situation to annex the remains of the little Papal State. On September 6 he denounced the September Convention and explained to the other Powers that the occupation of Rome was necessary. Then all the governments declared their non-intervention and Austria, through its Chancellor, Beust, even voiced its encouragement of the Italian government.[2]

The End of the Papal States

Beginning on September 8, Italian troops moved into the Papal States from various points.[3]

Victor Emmanuel II had already appointed a commissar-general of the Roman States to represent his authority there: Count Ponza di San Martino. On September 10, the latter requested an audience with the Pope so that he could give him a letter from Victor Emmanuel. The King was demanding that Pius IX should renounce his own rights. The Pope could not accept this. His reply to the Count was animated, and echoed throughout the corridors. According to the Sovereign Pontiff's private sec-

---

[1] Letters, and replies from the sovereigns, are published in Pirri, *Pio IX et Vittorio Emanuele*, III, II, 231-33.

[2] Salvatorelli, *Histoire de l'Italie*, p.518.

[3] For a detailed presentation of the events of September cf. Paolo Dalla Torre, "La difesa di Rome nel 1870," in *Pio IX nel primo centenario*, pp.485-662. Dalla Torre fully reproduces the 124 documents left by Major Fortunato Rivalta, General Kanzler's Joint Chief of Staff, and the "family memoirs" of Rudolf Kanzler, the son of Pius IX's Army Minister. We shall cite other sources in the notes.

retary, Ponza di San Martino staggered from the audience and had to be supported and assisted out of the building.

The Count, in his official report of the audience, naturally gives a version more to his advantage, but he does give a precise account of the reasons for Pius IX's refusal: he wrote that he found "the pope calm and dignified, but absolutely and inflexibly resolved not to enter into any arrangement. [He] protested with considerable energy that the current situation, being perfectly normal and peaceful, in no way justified the decision taken by the King." When the Count protested that the Pope would not dare to maintain his resistance until blood began to flow, "the Holy Father protested that, in truth, he had a horror of blood, but that he did not have the right to give the troops orders that would dishonor them. It was necessary for Europe to know that the Holy See would only give way in the face of unjust aggression."[4]

In fact, two solutions seemed to present themselves to Pius IX. Either he would give the order for armed resistance to an unjust invasion, or he would allow the occupation to take place and content himself with issuing a protest. Actually he chose an intermediate solution. The chief of staff of the papal armies, having ascertained the state of the available troops, reported that the Sovereign Pontiff could count on only 8,860 officers and men.

He could not hope for help from abroad. Even if thousands of volunteers were recruited from Catholic countries, it would be weeks before they could be in Rome and in readiness for combat. Nor could he hope for help from the great Catholic Powers: for years now, Austria and Spain had been run by governments that had shown themselves hostile to the Church; France, now a republic, was preoccupied with devoting itself to a war with Prussia—a war it refused to regard as lost.

Abandoned by all governments, Pius IX decided that, without making his soldiers fight until they were exhausted, he should nonetheless not let them surrender without showing some resistance. In this way their honor would be intact and the whole world would see that the Holy See was the victim of unjust violence.

Pius IX knew that the hours of the temporal power were numbered. On September 10, after giving the audience to Count Ponza di San Martino to which we have referred, he went to Rome, to show that he was not intimidated by the threat hanging over his States, and to reassure the populace. There he carried out two inaugurations that had been planned several months ago: that of the aqueduct of Acqua Marcia (which had just been restored) and that of the Termini fountain. These were his last two acts as a temporal sovereign.

---

[4] Cited in Dalla Torre, "La difesa di Rome nel 1870," p.525.

General Cadorna, at the head of a strong Italian army, had received the order to march on Rome. On September 12, Lt. Col. de Charette was obliged to quit Viterbo with his Zouaves and turn back to Civita Vecchia, a fortified naval base where, in the past, outside help had disembarked. Soon, however, he was given the order to proceed to Rome, where the army minister, General Kanzler, was hoping to concentrate his troops. On September 16 the Italian troops took Civita Vecchia, defended until the final hour by the Spaniard, Jose Serra y Navarro, in the papal service since 1862. On the 18th, several corps of Italian soldiers converged on Rome.

In a letter dated September 14 to General Kanzler, Pius IX, after deploring what had happened to the Papal States ("a great sacrilege and the most enormous injustice"), indicated what kind of resistance should be shown to the invader: "As to the duration of the defense, it is my duty to order that it should consist solely in a protest against violence and nothing more, *i.e.*, negotiations for surrender should be opened at the first cannon shots. At the moment when all Europe is mourning very high numbers of victims in a war between two great nations, it will never be said that the Vicar of Jesus Christ, even when unjustly attacked, has consented to any blood being spilt." However, General Kanzler and Brigadier-Generals Zappi and De Courten had protested that they could not order their troops to surrender without a fight. So, on September 19, Pius IX agreed to modify certain terms in his letter: where it had read "at the first cannon shots," he substituted "after the opening of a breach" (in the ramparts); and instead of refusing to countenance "any blood being spilt," he substituted the expression "much spilling of blood."[5]

What Pius IX finally authorized was thus a "symbolic" resistance. What could his 8,800 men do, together with some hundreds of Roman volunteers, against the 70,000 men sent by Victor Emmanuel II against the Papal States?

On September 19, for the last time in his life, Pius IX went around the streets of Rome. His final visit was to the Scala Santa and the monastery of the Passionists who look after this sanctuary, which the Pope had venerated ever since his youth. Pius IX also gave his benediction to the troops defending the nearby San Giovanni Gate. On his way back to the Vatican he was accompanied by small groups of people who called to him: *"Forte, Santo Padre! Si difenda! Coraggio! Corragio!"* (Be strong, Holy Father! Defend yourself! Courage! Courage!)

[5] On September 21, after the fall of Rome, the *Civiltà Cattolica* published the second version of the letter. When the first version became known, certain historians believed that it had been written on the 19th, and that the journal had subsequently altered the text. Hence the polemics accusing Kanzler of having disobeyed the orders of Pius IX. These polemics were futile, as is shown by the documents published by Dalla Torre, "La difesa di Rome nel 1870," pp.600, 621-23, which explain the whole affair.

On September 20, at 4:30 in the morning, Italian troops rushed in a body against the city gates. At 5:15 the cannonade began, lasting for two-and-a-half hours. When the Pope was told, towards eight o'clock, that the wall of the Porte Pia had been breached, he gave the order to stop fighting. Surrender was quickly negotiated between the military chiefs of the two camps. Rome was declared occupied "except that part bounded on the south by the bastions of the Holy Spirit, including the Vatican hill and the Castel Sant'Angelo and consisting of the Leonine City." The Italians also demanded that the foreign soldiers in the Pope's service should leave the city. At ten o'clock a white flag was hoisted in different parts of the city and on the cupola of St. Peter's Basilica. This was the end of the most ancient state in Europe, reckoned according to the uninterrupted succession of its sovereigns.

This date, September 20 ("*XX settembre*"), has remained in Italian history as a glorious day, as the consummation of an historical process that allowed Italy to be completely unified, with Rome as its capital city.

As for the Church, this day marked the end of her temporal power. On the centenary of this event the Jesuit Fr. Angelo Martini, in two "authorized" publications, gave what may be regarded as the official verdict of today's Church on this historic event.[6] In them he explains that the annexation of Rome had become "ineluctable" and that it was "an intervention of Providence in the course of the history of the Church and the world," "a sword-thrust, cutting the knot" which bound the Church to temporal interests and to problems from which she had become incapable of extracting herself.

Pius IX, faced with this event, had an entirely different reaction. The day after Rome was seized, he wrote a short note to his nephew Luigi: "It's all finished! Without liberty, the Church cannot be governed. Pray for me. I give you my blessing."[7]

Vatican Captive

On September 21, in St. Peter's Square, the papal troops were mustered for the last time. In the final skirmish they had counted 16 dead and 58 wounded—for ever, in Catholic history, symbolizing devotion to the Holy See. When the troops had already been given the order to march, Pius IX suddenly appeared at a window, unexpectedly, and blessed them once more. Then, very moved, he covered his weeping face in his hands and withdrew. The Zouaves and other papal soldiers waved their berets, shouted acclamations, and fired a few rifle shots. Generals De Courten

---

[6] Angelo Martini, "XX settembre 1870," *Civiltà Cattolica*, September 1870, reproduced in *L'Osservatore Romano*, September 20, 1970.

[7] Letter of September 21, 1870, published by Polverari, "Lettere," in *Pio IX nel primo centenario*, p.64.

and Zappi led the columns as they left Rome. At the Gate of St. Pancras they passed before the victorious General Cadorna, who had them disarmed. The papal soldiers were taken by train to various towns in Italy, where they were kept for some days, or for some months in certain cases, before being freed.

Pius IX thus found himself without an army, his territory reduced to that of the Vatican. The picture of the "prisoner Pope" became a symbol for those fighting for his cause.

Ever since the Lateran Accords, signed in 1929 between Pius XI and Mussolini, Catholics have been accustomed to regard the Vatican State as a small piece of territory that is sufficient to enable the Pope to exercise his spiritual mission. In 1870, however, the Papal States still consisted of 4,600 square miles (equivalent to two French "departments") and 600,000 inhabitants.

At the time, therefore, depriving the Pope of them and leaving him with the Vatican as his sole possession, seemed, to most Catholics, not only an unjust spoliation but also a grave infraction of his liberty. Pius IX, too, regarded himself as henceforth deprived of liberty. He said this on September 21 in the short letter to his nephew we have already quoted, and he said it publicly in his first official act after the fall of Rome. On September 29, in a letter to cardinals, he deplores the fact that "We find Ourselves now without that liberty which is absolutely indispensable for governing the Church of God and maintaining her rights."[8]

Soon, in a long encyclical addressed to all the bishops, dated November 1, he would use the word "captivity" to describe his situation.[9] Literally speaking, the term was an exaggeration. Pius IX was free to leave the Vatican, to go to foreign countries, for instance. Morally, however, it was impossible for him to leave the Vatican. In fact, as Pius IX writes in his encyclical,

> since that day We have seen unfolding before Our eyes actions that cannot be recalled without exciting the just indignation of all men of goodwill; infamous writings full of lies, turpitude, and impiety, for sale cheaply and disseminated everywhere; many newspapers dedicated to propagating the corruption of minds and the corruption of morals, scorn and calumny against religion, and to inflaming opinion against Us and against this Apostolic See; disgusting images and other works of the same kind with the aim of publicly ridiculing sacred things and persons; honors and monuments decreed for those who, guilty of the most grave crimes, have been judged and punished in conformity with the law; the Church's ministers, against whom all manner of hatred is fomented, subject to insults, some of them being even struck and injured; several religious houses despoiled; Our Quirinal Palace violated, and one who lived there, a cardinal of the

---

8   Brief of September 29, 1870, published by Auguste Roussel, *Actes et paroles*, p.5.
9   *Ibid.*, pp.9-20.

Holy Roman Church, violently ejected; other ecclesiastics of Our household obliged to leave this residence after all sorts of vexations; laws and decrees enacted that violate and trample upon the liberty, the immunity, the property, and the rights of the Church of God. So great are these evils that, unless God in his mercy prevent it, We shall have the pain of seeing them increase, while We find Ourselves incapable of applying any remedy, given the state of captivity that We are in. We no longer have the full exercise of liberty except by agreeing to address lies to the world: thus the attempt is made to make people believe that We are allowed to exercise Our apostolic ministry, while the officious government preens itself on having given what it calls necessary guarantees.

In Rome, Rome was no longer itself. Pius IX no longer had the liberty to act to protect his clergy and faithful from physical attack or moral aggression; nor could he leave the Vatican without exposing himself to "such a vast conspiracy against the Church of God and against this Holy See." Thus the Pope considered himself a "captive." The events of the first weeks of the occupation of Rome had clearly shown, furthermore, that the Italian government wished to impose itself on Rome once and for all, eliminating all vestiges of the ancient temporal power, by brute force if necessary.

At the end of September, violating the terms of surrender, Italian troops had occupied the Leonine City and the fortified square near the Vatican, the Castel Sant'Angelo, where they got their hands on the papal treasury (4 million écus). Then they took over the Apostolic Quirinal Palace, where the last three conclaves had taken place, and ejected those living there—a cardinal and several prelates and clerics; the Palace had been destined to become the residence of the King once Rome had been declared the capital of Italy. Now the Pope only had the palaces of the Lateran and the Vatican.

In order to give a certain legitimacy to the invasion of the Papal States and Rome, a plebiscite had been organized for October 2. In Rome, according to the official figures, 40,785 persons approved of Rome being attached to the Kingdom of Italy and only a mere 46 were opposed to it. Several contemporary historians cite these figures as showing an "unanimous approval."[10] In fact, quite apart from the "very strong abstention" referred to by Fr. Martina, attention must be drawn to the irregularities surrounding this vote. The voting booths had no screen and the public vote had to take place under the vigilant eye of partisans of the annexation, who applauded those who voted "yes" and hurled invective at those who voted "no."[11] There was an absence of electoral lists; there was the massive presence of about 10,000 "patriots" from all regions of Italy, "equipped

---

[10] Martina, III, 250. Cf. also Aubert, *Le Pontificat de Pie IX*, p.360, and Salvatorelli, *Histoire de l'Italie*, p.518.

with tickets issued by prefects and sub-prefects...; they were conveyed to Rome free of charge"; and there was multiple voting, in three or four different voting stations.[12] Thus the "unanimous approval" given by the vote of October 2, 1870, is nothing but an historical myth. This is also proved by a kind of contra-plebiscite which was organized some months later by the Society of Catholic Interests. In every parish of Rome, registers were signed by men of voting age who disapproved of the annexation of Rome; 27,161 signatures were collected and presented to the Pope.[13]

It is clear, therefore, that the numbers opposing the new regime were much bigger than the official results of the October 2 vote would suggest. Nonetheless, on October 9, a royal decree stipulated as follows:

Art. 1. Rome and the Roman provinces are an integral part of the Kingdom of Italy;

Art. 2. The Sovereign Pontiff retains the dignity, inviolability, and personal prerogatives of a sovereign;

Art. 3. An *ad hoc* law will establish the conditions necessary to guarantee—including territorial franchises—the Sovereign Pontiff's independence and the free exercise of the spiritual authority of the Holy See.

Before the projected law could be adopted, another law had been presented to the Italian Parliament in December 1870 concerning the transfer of the capital of the Kingdom of Italy to Rome. It spoke of the expropriation, from "corporations and moral persons, of those buildings, situated in Rome, which will be adjudged to be of public utility for the location of administrations and ministries." On March 4, 1871, a decree authorized the Ministry of Public Works to occupy eight convents belonging to different religious orders. Tens of others were expropriated in the following months. Furthermore, when the law "guaranteeing...the Sovereign Pontiff's independence and the free exercise of the spiritual authority of the Holy See" was elaborated, Catholics feared the worst.

This law regarding so-called "guarantees" was approved by the Chamber on May 9, 1871, and promulgated on May 13.[14] It recognized the person of the Sovereign Pontiff as "inviolable and sacred" and therefore accorded him complete immunity: he could not be cited to appear before tribunals, either as accused or as witness. Those "public offenses and injuries" of which he could be the victim were regarded as public violations of law to be heard at the Court of Assizes, but "discussion on religious

[11] *Civiltà Cattolica*, VIII, No.1 (1870), pp.214-16; cited in Polverari, III, 20.
[12] Chamard, *Annales III*, 426.
[13] Chamard gives a detailed presentation of this counter-plebiscite of July 24, 1871 (*Ibid.*, pp.426-27).
[14] Text of the law in Chamard, *Annales III*, 502-504, and a detailed juridical analysis in D. Le Tourneau, "La Loi des garanties (13 mai 1871): portée et contenu," *Revue des Sciences Religieuses*, April-July 1988, pp.137-58.

matters is entirely free." The law guaranteed that the pope could continue to reside in the palaces of the Lateran and the Vatican and in the residence of Castel Gandolfo—although it did not recognize them as his property—and also guaranteed that the Italian State would give the Holy See an annual grant of 33,225,000 lire (equivalent to the "Roman budget" made public in 1847-48, *i.e.*, a quarter of a century earlier...). The pope was guaranteed free communication with the outside world and diplomatic immunity for his representatives.

On the part of the Italian State this "law of guarantees," which contains inconsistencies acknowledged by jurists, was a series of concessions poorly covering up a total questioning of the temporal sovereignty. Ten years after the promulgation of these guarantees Emile Ollivier, who was a determined opponent of the temporal power of the popes, acknowledged that: "They can be compared to a railway on which no catastrophe has yet occurred, for the simple reason that no train has yet traveled along it." Citing this verdict, Dominique Le Tourneau comments: "The 'guarantees' are only valid so long as they are not invoked; if the pope were to risk going out into the streets of Rome, the guarantees would go up in smoke."[15]

Pius IX had protested against the decree of annexation of October 9, 1870, and in the encyclical of the following November 1 he had renewed the excommunications against those who had despoiled his States; he also rejected this "law of guarantees" of May 13, 1871. On May 15, in the encyclical *Ubi Nos,* he uttered his *non possumus:*

> We will not admit, We shall never accept any immunity or guarantee whatsoever, which, under the pretext of protecting Our sacred power and Our liberty, may be offered Us in exchange and in place of that temporal sovereignty with which divine Providence has willed the Apostolic Holy See to be equipped and fortified, and which is assured to Us by legitimate and unquestionable titles and by the possession of more than eleven centuries.[16]

In the Wake of the Council

After the vote on the Constitution *Pastor Aeternus,* on July 18, 1870, the next solemn session of the Council had been fixed for November 11. During the second fortnight of August some general congregations had taken place, some of them with a very limited participation. The occupation of Rome on September 20 had interrupted the work. After the royal decree of October 9 proclaiming the annexation to Italy of Rome and its province, Pius IX regarded the Council's liberty as no longer assured. On

---

[15] Le Tourneau, "La Loi des garanties," p.156.
[16] Text in *Actes et paroles*, pp.42-51.

October 20 he officially declared the Council prorogued *sine die*. Some bishops suggested continuing the work at Malines, where it had been customary to organize large assemblies in the wake of Catholic congresses, but the idea was not taken up.

The Council, though truncated, profoundly influenced the Church in subsequent decades. The Constitution *Dei Filius*, Roger Aubert observes, "had a profound influence on theological teaching, particularly on the burning issue of the relationship between reason and faith. After 1870 the treatises *De Religione Revelata* and *De Fide* could not be the same as before."[17] It should be added that Pius IX had prepared the way, in previous years, for this important constitution by condemning the erroneous and opposite theories on the subject (the condemnations of Frohschammer and of traditionalism, *etc.*).

As for the Constitution *Pastor Aeternus*, it had dealt with the question of papal infallibility in precise terms. The doctrine, which was accepted by the majority prior to the Council, was strictly circumscribed as a result of being dogmatically defined. The succeeding history of the Church has shown that the dogmatic definition of 1870 has facilitated clearer distinctions as to the nature, scope, and authority of the different acts of the Magisterium. In the event, all the opponents of this doctrine submitted, except Döllinger.

In May 1870, even before the dogma had been defined, Msgr. Fessler, secretary of the Council, had gone to Munich to see Döllinger.[18] Döllinger believed it to be a personal visit. Msgr. Fessler, in the course of several discussions, urged him to either cease his attacks on the dogma in preparation, or submit. Then in June Professor Laemmer, from Breslau, went to see him, this time carrying a message from Pius IX: "The Pope had ordered him to stop off in Munich and tell me that he continued to bear good will towards me and that he prayed for me every day."[19] Here again is a sign of the charity which animated Pius IX regarding his adversaries, even if this charity towards persons did not mean tolerance of their erroneous ideas. Döllinger, however, remained obstinate.

Returning to his diocese after the adoption of the new dogma, the Archbishop of Munich invited the professors of the Faculty of Theology to "work for Holy Church."

Döllinger replied, "Yes, for the old Church!"

"There is only one Church," said the Archbishop, "not a new Church and an old Church."

"But they have made a new one!" retorted Döllinger.[20]

---

[17] Aubert, *Le Pontificat de Pie IX*, p.361.
[18] Döllinger indicates this in an unpublished, undated letter, probably written to Msgr. Maret or Msgr. Dupanloup, kept in the Archives of Saint-Sulpice.
[19] The same document.

Döllinger rallied around him some professors of theology or canon law, and finally he was excommunicated on April 23, 1871. In the months that followed, a schismatic community was set up, the "Old Catholic" movement. At its height, around 1875, it had some 52,000 adherents in Germany and Austria, and 73,000 in Switzerland. However, the movement declined rapidly and evolved into a radical reformism that corresponded to Döllinger's wish, expressed in 1869, for a "great and profound reform of the Church."

The "Old Catholic" movement ran out of steam because it did not get the support of any of the bishops who had opposed infallibility during the Council. They all, sooner or later, made known their acceptance of the new dogma. On August 1, 1870, Msgr. Melchers, Archbishop of Cologne, published the dogmatic constitution in his diocesan magazine, and at the end of the month all the German bishops except five, at their meeting in Fulda, signed a pastoral letter inviting the faithful to embrace the new dogma. However, the five reluctant bishops refused to support Döllinger and finally, one by one, they submitted over the following months.

In France, letters of submission from the heads of dioceses came in rather more slowly. Cardinal Mathieu and Msgr. Ginoulhiac did so in the month of August 1870, but it was not until February 18, 1871, that Msgr. Dupanloup made his submission known to Pius IX: "I only wrote and spoke against the opportuneness of the definition. As for the doctrine itself, I have always professed it, not only in my heart, but in my published writings."[21] Msgr. Darboy, impeded by the siege of Paris, could not make his submission known to the Pope until March. Only much later, after receiving a letter from Pius IX dated November 28, 1870, threatening to put his book on the Index, did Msgr. Maret submit, in August 1871; nor did he withdraw his book from bookshops until several months had passed.[22]

The bishops of the Austro-Hungarian Empire also had a number of determined opponents among their number. Some of them rallied to infallibility after Msgr. Fessler, in a pamphlet published in 1871 entitled *The True and the False Infallibility of the Popes,* had explained the technical and restrictive sense in which the word "define" should be understood in the dogmatic formulation. The pamphlet received Pius IX's formal approbation. The last opponents of the definition did not submit until October 1871 (Msgr. Haynald) and December 1872 (Msgr. Strossmayer).

The interruption of the Council left incomplete a great quantity of reflections and reforms, from which much had been expected. Fifty-one

[20] Anecdote reported by the historian Friedrich, a disciple of Döllinger, and cited by Aubert, *Le Pontificat de Pie IX*, p.365.
[21] Cited by Granderath, *Histoire du concile du Vatican*, III, II, 255.
[22] *Annales III*, 523.

schemas, twenty-eight of them disciplinary in nature, were ready; it had not been possible either to discuss them or vote on them. Nonetheless, this preparatory work, and the suggestions of the Council Fathers to the Commission of Postulates, would not be all consigned to oblivion.

Pius IX was concerned to give satisfaction to those who had called for the extension of the cult of St. Joseph. Many religious institutes created during his pontificate were dedicated to St. Joseph (five female congregations in France alone). During the Council three successive petitions had been circulating, asking that St. Joseph should be proclaimed "Patron of the universal Church." These petitions had collected a total of 314 signatures.[23] On December 8, 1870, the Congregation of Rites declared St. Joseph Patron of the universal Church and raised his feast to a Double of the First Class.[24] On July 7, 1871, Pius IX, in the Apostolic Letter *Inclytum Patriarchum,* confirmed this decree. Also, during the Council many bishops had requested that the Church should be consecrated to the Sacred Heart. Pius IX also granted this request, on June 16, 1875. The very same day, in Paris, the foundation stone of the Basilica of Sacré Coeur was laid; this was in response to a "national vow to the Sacred Heart of Jesus to obtain the deliverance of the Sovereign Pontiff and the salvation of France."[25]

Other preparatory projects of the Council were brought to completion in succeeding pontificates. One schema of the Dogmatic Commission had Christian marriage as its object: Leo XIII consecrated an important encyclical, *Arcanum,* to it in 1880. At the Council there had also been a call for the regrouping and unification of the multiplicity of canon laws; in the following years first Pius IX, and then Leo XIII, were at pains to regulate "first of all the most urgent matters that seemed to concern discipline more closely," and after this a complete re-ordering of legislation was envisaged.[26] It was under the pontificate of St. Pius X that a Code of Canon Law was elaborated; it was promulgated by his successor in 1917.

"The Great Pius IX"

In 1871 the pontifical jubilee of Pius IX was celebrated. He was the first pope in the Church's history since St. Peter to have reigned for twenty-five years in Rome, thus giving the lie to the traditional adage recalled in the ceremony of papal coronation: *Tu non videbis annos Petri* (You will not see the years of Peter). The exceptional longevity of the pontificate,

---

[23] *Annales III,* 444.
[24] That day the Catholics of Rome celebrated the Feast of the Immaculate Conception with particular splendor: it was the first great religious solemnity since the occupation of Rome. A band of revolutionaries attacked the faithful coming out of St. Peter's Basilica and wounded five people.
[25] Cf. Alfred Van der Brule, *Le Sacré-Coeur de Montmartre* (Paris: Téqui, 1995).

together with the dramatic situation to which the Pope had been reduced, inspired Catholics to celebrate the anniversary of the election with great enthusiasm. It was also an opportunity to renew the great ceremonies of unanimity seen in the 1860's.

The twenty-fifth anniversary of the pontifical election fell on June 16. On June 4, in an encyclical letter, after repeating his protest against the annexation of Rome, the Pope thanked all the faithful for their devotion and fidelity to the Holy See.[27] He went on:

> After so many vicissitudes, by the protection of the most clement God, We already see approaching the anniversary of Our promotion, when, as the successor of Blessed Peter in his See, We find Ourselves, remote from him in merit though We be, to have spent the same number of years in apostolic service. This is assuredly a new, singular, and very great grace, coming from the divine munificence; in such a long series of Our most holy predecessors, for nineteen centuries, this grace has been accorded, by the disposition of God, only to Us.

So that this anniversary could be celebrated fruitfully, Pius IX granted "a plenary indulgence of all their sins" to the faithful who would make their confession and communion on the occasion of his pontifical jubilee.

During the whole month of June successive delegations came to the Vatican, representing different Catholic associations, or from foreign countries. The Pope gave short addresses, more or less improvised, to each group. The address to the French delegation on June 16 caused a great stir in France and led to polemics. The group consisting of about twenty-four persons was led by Msgr. Forcade, Bishop of Nevers; it included two cardinals and several prelates. While France had supported the Holy See on several occasions, it had precipitated the fall of the temporal power by suddenly withdrawing its troops at the commencement of the war with Prussia. Subsequently it had experienced great upheavals, culminating in the installation of a revolutionary power, the Commune, in Paris from June to May 1871. In addition to causing considerable destruction by fire, the insurgents had shot fifty-two hostages, including Msgr. Darboy.[28]

No doubt Pius IX was thinking of all these events when he received the French delegation; perhaps he also recalled Montalembert's last public statements and the strong French opposition—neo-Gallican and liberal— at the Council. Thus, in his short allocution, there was an alternation of praise and reproach:

---

[26] Preface to the *Code de droit canonique* (Paris: Centurion-Cerf-Tardy, 1984), p.xix.

[27] Text of the encyclical in *Actes et paroles*, pp.52-58.

[28] This caused Pius IX to say, on hearing of the death of the Archbishop of Paris, who had been one of the anti-infallibilists: "He has washed his faults in his own blood and has put on the robe of martyrdom" (*Annales III*, 518).

I love France; she is always impressed upon my heart. I pray every day for her, chiefly at this great, holy sacrifice of the Mass; she is always present to my thoughts. I have always loved her and always shall! I know how she has always given such evidence of the most tender devotion, and how great is her charity and compassion for the misery of the poor, for the misery of the Church, and how many charitable institutions she has founded; in particular I know what a great ardor is shown in France for good works, among men also, but especially among women.

Then, continuing his clearly improvised address, Pius IX expressed what was on his mind:

But I must tell France the truth....My dear children, I must find words to tell you what is in my heart. What afflicts your country and prevents it from meriting God's blessings is this mixture of principles. I must say this, and not hide it: what I fear is not these wretches of the Paris Commune, veritable demons from hell walking about on the earth. No, it is not that. What I fear is this unhappy politics, this Catholic liberalism which is the real scourge....Of course we must practice charity, we must do what we can to bring back those who are astray: but to do that there is no need to share their opinions.[29]

Pius IX had often condemned liberalism in all its forms, but here, for the first time, he specifically named "Catholic liberalism."[30]

The Catholic press in France got involved with controversies on this issue, and Msgr. Dupanloup's *Annales du diocese d'Orléans* reproduced the allocution, but omitting the passage on "Catholic liberalism." This aroused lively polemics with *L'Univers* and Msgr. Pie's *Semaine Liturgique de Poitiers.*

Readers will have noted the allusion to the Commune in this allocution. Pius IX returned to it a little later in a letter to Thiers. The latter, as chief of the Republic's executive power, had written a letter of congratulation to Pius IX, in the name of the government, on the occasion of the twenty-fifth anniversary of his pontificate. In it he saluted "his great faith," "the brilliance of his apostolic virtues," and his "memorable pontificate."[31]

Pius IX replied by a friendly, handwritten letter in Italian, in which he urged: "I beg you to do all that is in your power to exalt the honor of our most holy religion, and especially to give an eminently Catholic character

---

[29] Allocution of June 16, 1871, in *Actes et paroles*, pp.65-67.
[30] When, on February 17, 1870, during the Council, Pius IX was inaugurating the Roman exhibition of religious antiquities and art, he had already upset the liberal Catholics by declaring: "According to some people, religion must change with the times, and also needs its '89. I say that this is a blasphemy...." It was felt that he was referring to something Falloux had said. Through the mediation of Msgr. Freppel the Pope let Falloux know that this was not the case, but that he was sticking to his condemnation. Cf. Montalembert, *Correspondance*, p.427, n.140.

to education. This will be a powerful means of opposing the Commune, the *Internationale*, and all these institutions which are destructive of society."[32] Noteworthy is the significance attached to Catholic education as a remedy for the evils of modern society. This will be a recurrent theme in talks and discussions during the last years of Pius IX's pontificate.

The ceremonies on the twenty-fifth anniversary of his election were marked, in certain provincial towns, by several incidents provoked by the anti-clericals; but in Rome and in all the Catholic countries the dominant note was one of respectful veneration. The festivities were brought to an end when Pius IX learned that a committee had been formed, under the leadership of the Marquis Cavaletti, a Roman senator, to offer him a golden throne and give him the appellation "the Great," along the lines of certain popes in history who had received this title posthumously (St. Leo I, St. Gregory I, St. Nicholas I).

In a letter to the Marquis Cavaletti Pius IX refused these two expressions of homage. He requested that the sums already collected for the construction of a pontifical throne of gold should be used instead to pay for seminarians to be exempted from military service (a recent imposition upon them). As to the title "the Great," Pius IX, in the spirit of sincere humility often found in him, rejected it in these terms:

> One word of the divine Redeemer comes to mind. While he was going through the country of Judaea clothed in human nature, someone, admiring his divine virtues, called him "Good master." But Jesus immediately replied: "Why do you call me good? God alone is good." Now, if Jesus Christ, speaking of himself as man, has declared that God alone is good, how can his unworthy Vicar do other than say that God alone is great? Great by the favors He has shown to this same Vicar; great by the support he gives to his Church; great by the infinite patience with which He treats his enemies; great by the reward He is preparing for those who abandon the ways of sin to cultivate the exercise of penitence; great by the severity of His justice in chastising unbelievers and all the stubborn enemies of His Church.[33]

The Pope's state of mind in these last years of his life was not at all triumphalist. Nor was he flattered by the signs of adulation shown him here and there. In the latter years of his pontificate we see him making lucid and critical assessments of some of his temporal actions. From the beginning of the 1870's, however, he shows himself in his personal letters to be both humble and trusting. Thus in 1872, replying to his brother, who

---

[31] The rough draft of this letter—corrected by Jules Favre—and the copy of the text actually sent are to be found in the Department of Manuscripts of the Bibliothèque Nationale, N.A.Fr. 20623, ff.223-225.

[32] Unpublished letter of July 2, 1871, B.N. ms. N.A.Fr. 20622, ff.261-262. The handwriting is already a little shaky.

[33] Letter of August 8, 1871, in *Annales III*, 550-551.

was hoping to see the imminent triumph of the papacy over its enemies, he wrote: "God will grant it when and how He judges it opportune." He placed himself under "the protection of God, who animates the nations and every day brings more hearts back towards this center of truth. May His will be always done!"[34]

Against the *Kulturkampf*

Pius IX's last great battle was directed against the policy of laicization undertaken by Germany in the 1870's, a policy its advocates called the *Kulturkampf* (the "struggle for civilization").

From the 1850's and 1860's onwards, as we have seen, certain German states had tried to increase the State's control over the Church. The Catholic Church had protested against this. On January 18, 1871, the day after his country's victory over France, in the Gallery of Mirrors in the Versailles Palace, William I, King of Prussia, was proclaimed Emperor of a Germany which would now consist of twenty-five states. Quite naturally, the last Chancellor of the Kingdom of Prussia, the Protestant Bismarck, became the first Chancellor of this Empire, which was dominated by Prussia. Under the influence of the National Liberals, in favor not only of greater state control but also of the laicization of society, the German government, in the months and years that followed, introduced more and more laws that were unacceptable to Catholics. The latter closed ranks around their bishops and around a party, the *Zentrum,* principally inspired by the deputy, Windthorst. Pius IX supported this resistance on the part of German Catholics.[35]

The first measures were taken against Catholics in the summer of 1871. On June 29, Bismarck prohibited the bishops from removing "Old Catholic" professors. On July 8, the Catholic section of the Ministry of Religions was suppressed; this was an administrative division which, in the old Prussian government, had acted as a "buffer" between the State and the Catholic Church. Then, on December 16, Bismarck succeeded in getting the Reichstag to vote on what is known as the *Kanzelparagraph* (the pulpit paragraph), a law aimed at punishing preachers with either a fine or prison if they criticized an act of government.

---

[34] Letter of June 2, 1872, to Gaetano Mastai, published by Polverari, "Lettere," in *Pio IX nel primo centenario,* pp.69-70.

[35] Cf. principally G. Bazin, *Windthorst, ses alliés et ses adversaries* (Paris: Bloud & Cie, n.d.; 1st ed. 1896); Aubert, *Le Pontificat de Pie IX,* pp.384-96; Msgr. B. Gherardini, "Pio IX, episcopato e *Kulturkampf,*" *Pio IX,* 1, 1977, pp.22-59, and Paul Colonge, "Ludwig Windthorst, âme de la résistance catholique dans l'Allemagne bismarckienne," *Les Résistances spirituelles* (Actes de la X. Rencontre d'histoire religieuse de Fontevraud) (Angers: Presses de l'Université d'Angers, 1987), pp.135-53.

At the beginning of 1872 a new Minister of Religions was appointed: Adalbert Falk, "a rigid theoretician, stubborn in his conception of the State's all-powerful rights in church matters, and who, from his childhood in a pastor's family, had imbibed a profound antipathy towards Catholicism."[36] The following March, Falk had a law adopted by the Prussian Assembly which removed priests or pastors from their position as inspectors of primary schools, giving it to State officials. The following June, a circular excluded all religious orders from teaching in public schools—a measure which affected almost nine hundred educational establishments. Finally, on July 4, the Reichstag adopted a law stipulating: "Art. 1. The members of the Society of Jesus or of orders affiliated to it (Redemptorists, Vincentians, Holy Ghost Fathers, Sacred Heart Congregation) may be excluded from the territory of the Empire by a simple police measure, even if they possess German citizenship; Art. 2. The Society of Jesus and the congregations connected with it are banished from the Empire."[37]

The "struggle for civilization" of which Bismarck and his ministers were so proud was in fact directed against Catholics, who were considered "barbarians" and *Vaterlandlos* ("without fatherland") according to language frequently used by the government press.

Several times during 1872 Pius IX denounced these anti-Catholic laws, introduced by a "country seduced by the mirage of the anti-Catholic spirit and a spirit of ambition" (April 13, 1872). Then, on December 23, in his consistorial end-of-year allocution, commenting on different countries, he protested against "the cruel persecutions" from which the Church in Germany was suffering; "Attempts are being made to destroy it root and branch, not only by hidden maneuvering, but by overt force." He encouraged the Catholic hierarchy, the German clergy, and faithful to continue in their resistance. The Pope concluded: "May it please God that the public authorities, taught by long experience, may finally learn that, among their subjects, none are more anxious than Catholics to render to Caesar what is Caesar's, precisely because they apply themselves religiously to render to God what is God's."[38]

The German government was greatly displeased by this allocution. The German *chargé d'affaires* at the Holy See was recalled to Berlin. The Interior Minister confiscated those Catholic newspapers which had published the Pope's discourse, and some days later, on January 9, 1873, Falk set before the Reichstag four draft laws reinforcing the anti-Catholic persecution. These laws, adopted the following May, have gone into history under the name "the May laws." They have been compared to the Civil Constitution of the Clergy that the French Revolution imposed on the

---

[36] Aubert, *Le Pontificat de Pie IX*, p.386.
[37] Cited by Bazin, *Windthorst*, pp.74-75.
[38] Text of the allocution in *Actes et paroles*, pp.291-301.

Church. Inspired by Protestant lawyers and Freemasonry, which at that time was very influential in Germany, they affected Lutheran communities as well as the Catholic Church. But while the former had always been under State control and therefore did not see their activity profoundly modified, it was quite different for the Catholic Church. Neither the Holy See nor the German bishops had been consulted in advance, so the "May laws" caused havoc in the organization of the Catholic Church in Germany.

The first law concerned the formation and appointment of the clergy, and stipulated that only German subjects could exercise an ecclesiastical function—thereby excluding all foreign priests and religious from German territory; minor and major seminaries were "placed under State inspection"; seminarians would have to do three preliminary years of study at university; the "academic examination," indispensable for anyone wishing to exercise an ecclesiastical function, would be administered by a commission appointed by the Minister of Religions; and all ecclesiastical nominations would have to be made with the agreement of the provincial civil authorities.

The other laws reduced the bishops' power of jurisdiction, notably by forbidding them on their own initiative to proceed with sanctions against their clergy or to pronounce public excommunications. Instead a "court of justice for ecclesiastical affairs" was set up, dependent on the State, where clerics could appeal against their superiors' decisions.

Encouraged by the Pope, the German bishops refused to observe these laws, which were applied with greater or less rigor, depending on the States of the Empire: it was primarily in Prussia, Hesse, and Baden that the civil authorities proved most intransigent. Many trials took place, fines were imposed, and priests and bishops were imprisoned. The first of these was Msgr. Ledochowski, Archbishop of Posen and Gnesen (today's Poznan). He had protested against the prohibition of teaching the catechism in Polish in the primary schools and Polish territories then annexed to Germany. He was arrested, condemned to two years detention, and deposed from his see. He would be compelled to go into exile in Rome, where Pius IX made him a cardinal.

Many other bishops would be arrested and imprisoned. One of them, Msgr. Eberhardt, Bishop of Trier, died in prison. Other measures were taken to increase the persecution. Many parishes found themselves without a priest and most of the episcopal sees became vacant. In Prussia all the religious orders except the Hospitalers were expelled, and a law on "the administration of vacant Catholic dioceses" proposed that, where parishes were without a priest (and one in four were so), the priest would be elected by the population, Catholic or not. Both clergy and faithful were more or less united in refusing to obey these laws. In Prussia, out of 4,000 priests, there were only a score of so-called *"Staatspfarrer"* (State parish priests).

In all the other States of the German Empire, Catholics persevered in their resistance. Many priests had to carry out their ministry clandestinely, and exiled bishops continued to direct their dioceses secretly from Belgium, Holland, Austria, or Rome. The *Zentrum* inspired this resistance at the public level. Until his death in 1891 Windthorst was the redoubtable Reichstag orator who fought against Bismarck, his ministers, and his laws. His party gained a greater hearing: at the second Reichstag elections he doubled his number of votes and went from 58 to 90 seats. Some Protestant conservatives, hostile to the laicist policy being conducted by the government, gave their votes to the Catholic party. Windthorst managed to encourage the Catholic press to develop and defend Catholic interests, filling the gap left by the now gagged voices of the priests and bishops. The number of Catholic newspapers doubled during the *Kulturkampf.*

After the various interventions we have mentioned, Pius IX dedicated one whole encyclical, on February 5, 1875, to denouncing the "May laws" and the persecutions.[39] He raised his voice in accusation against these laws and against the evil acts they caused and would go on causing. Solemnly he declared: "These laws are null and void because they are entirely contrary to the Church's divine constitution. For the Lord has subordinated the bishops of his Church, in what concerns his sacred service, not to the earth's mighty ones, but to Peter, to whom he has entrusted his lambs and sheep (Jn. 21:16-17)." He also exhorted priests and faithful not to submit to these laws, and declared that those clerics who accepted a ministry at the hand of the German government were "subject to major excommunication *de facto* and *de jure.*" The order to be followed by everyone was: "We must obey God rather than men," because no wrong is done to the civil government "by refusing to give to Caesar what is God's." Not until almost ten years after the death of Pius IX was an accord brought about between Rome and Berlin.[40]

A number of Swiss cantons were inspired by the German *Kulturkampf* to impose new religious legislation with the purpose of reducing the Church's influence. The difference here was that Switzerland introduced these discriminatory measures against Catholics in a new constitution, in 1874, which had consequences lasting for almost a century.[41] In doing this, they found support among some priests and many faithful who had rejected the dogma of infallibility. Msgr. Lachat, Bishop of the diocese

---

[39] Full text of these laws in *Annales III*, 737-42.
[40] Full text in *Annales ecclésiastiques 1873-1879*, Dom François Chamard (Paris: Gaume & Cie, 1896), pp. 256-58; hereafter, *Annales IV*.

of Basel, was dismissed by the cantonal authorities for having suspended from their functions two priests who had rejected the Council decrees. In many parishes of the five cantons within the diocese, parish priests faithful to their bishop were dismissed and replaced by Old Catholic priests. In fairness it must be observed that the Lucerne canton authorities gave asylum to Msgr. Lachat and permitted him to exercise his office on their territory. In the cantons within the diocese of Basel (Solothurn, Aargau, Bern, Thurgau, and Basel-rural), great numbers of Catholics remained faithful to their exiled bishop and refused to accept the priests foisted upon them. A clandestine religious life was organized, which lasted for several years.

The canton of Geneva had to go through an equally serious persecution. The President of the Council of State, Carteret, was a Freemason, very hostile to the Catholic Church. He went as far as to say, "It would be best for us if the Catholic Church were to go off with its sticks and bundles."[42] A law of February 3, 1872, obliged religious congregations to request state authorization in order to continue to exist, which made it possible to "deconfessionalize" the schools: the Christian Brothers were expelled and the Sisters of Charity were prohibited from teaching. Next, religious congregations were forbidden to accept new members. On August 30 of the same year the Geneva Council of State prohibited Msgr. Mermillod, Bishop of Geneva, from exercising any episcopal function.[43]

In September, further decrees deprived him of his functions as vicar-general and parish priest of the Church of Our Lady, and forbade the clergy of the canton to have any hierarchical relations with him. This unjustified attack elicited a response that preserved the interests and rights of the Genevan Catholics: in a Brief dated January 16, 1873, Pius IX appointed Msgr. Mermillod vicar-apostolic, as if Geneva were a mission territory. When he refused to renounce his ecclesiastical functions, Msgr. Mermillod was arrested the following February 11 and expelled from the country. A decree of the Council of State prevented him from returning to Swiss territory. So Msgr. Mermillod established himself on the frontier, at Ferney (as Voltaire had once done), and from there, for ten years, he administered his diocese.

---

[41] Two Marian apparitions on German soil should be mentioned in the context of the *Kulturkampf*: that of Marpingen, in 1876-77, not so far recognized by the Church, and that of Dietrichwalde (today Gietrzwalde in Poland), in 1877, recognized as authentic. Cf. Y. Chiron, *Enquête sur les apparitions de la Vierge* (Paris: Perrin-Mame, 1995), pp.232-35.
[42] Cf. principally Mourret, *Histoire générale de l'Eglise*, VIII, 603-8, despite its errors of detail and its omissions; Aubert, *Le Pontificat de Pie IX*, pp.395-96; G. Félix, *S.E. le cardinal Mermillod* (Tours: Alfred Cattier, 1893); and Conzemius, *Segesser*.
[43] Cited by Mourret, *Histoire générale de l'Eglise*, VIII, 603.

On May 30, 1873, the Grand Council of Geneva adopted a "law reorganizing the Catholic Church" at the very moment when Germany was adopting its famous "May laws." The coincidence of dates only serves to underline the striking similarity of intention: to put the Church under State control. Henceforth the State would have the right to "suppress parishes or create new ones"; parish priests would be elected by a parish assembly; the ecclesiastical hierarchy would have to obtain advance authorization, from the civil authorities, for all pastoral measures and instructions.

In practice, the "reorganization law" had a much more ambitious purpose. It aimed to replace the Catholic Church with a "National Catholic Church" independent of Rome and subject to the State. An appeal was made to Old Catholic priests or those who had broken with the Church, such as the Carmelite Hyacinth Loyson, who was elected as parish priest of Geneva the following October. On November 21 Pius IX published the encyclical *Etsi Multa Luctuosa* denouncing this Swiss *Kulturkampf* and the "wretched sectarians" of the "National Catholic Church." In reprisal, the federal authorities expelled the apostolic nuncio from Bern, breaking diplomatic relations with the Holy See. Some months later, opposition to Catholicism was made official by a new federal constitution, adopted by an overwhelming majority of the Swiss on April 19, 1874. The prohibition of the Society of Jesus was confirmed, associations "affiliated" to it were also prohibited, and it was announced that "this prohibition may be extended by federal decree to other religious orders whose activities present a danger to the State or threaten inter-denominational peace"; the foundation of new convents was declared illicit, as was the creation of new bishoprics; civil marriage was made obligatory and ecclesiastical jurisdiction was abolished.

Pius IX had no choice but to protest again, in an encyclical dated March 23, 1875, addressed to "the bishops, clergy, and faithful of Switzerland who are in grace and communion with the Holy See."[44] This unusual turn of phrase was necessary in view of the support the "Old Catholics" had received from the civil authorities getting themselves into parishes and supplanting the Catholic clergy. Pius IX solemnly put people on guard against "these wretched sectarians." He told the bishops:

> Employ all the means at your disposal to keep the unity of faith among the faithful entrusted to your care. Remind them unceasingly that they must keep away from these dangerous enemies of Christ's flock and their poisonous pastures. They must flee from their religious ceremonies, their

---

[44] In 1864 Msgr. Mermillod was appointed auxiliary bishop of Msgr. Marilley, Bishop of Lausanne, with particular responsibility for the canton of Geneva. When consecrating him bishop, Pius IX told him, "Go, ascend the seat of St. Francis de Sales; go to this Geneva which is not afraid to call itself the Protestant Rome, and convert it."

teaching, their pestilential pulpits, which they have the audacity to set up to betray sacred doctrines; they must avoid their writings and avoid contact with them. They must have no dealings, no relationship with the usurper-priests and apostates who dare to exercise the functions of the ecclesiastical ministry, absolutely lacking all jurisdiction and all legitimate mission. They must abominate them as aliens and thieves who come only in order to steal, assassinate, and destroy.

The Pope also denounced the final terms of the Helvetic Constitution "which are opposed to the canonical requirements on marriage, and entirely abolish ecclesiastical authority and jurisdiction."

The Pope's severity was justified. Above all, he was concerned to defend the unity of faith and the Church in Switzerland. The attempts to form a "National Catholic Church" were doomed to failure, but the anti-Catholic attitude of the Swiss State persisted officially for decades. Relations between Switzerland and the Holy See were not resumed until 1920, and it was not until 1973 that Articles 51 and 52 of the Constitution, referring to Jesuits and convents, were abrogated.[45]

Without going into the religious history of all the countries, which was not our intention in the present book, we must nonetheless mention the difficult situation of the Catholic Church in Austria in these years after the Council. These difficulties were felt by Pius IX with particular bitterness. As a result of a change of government, Catholic Austria, which had signed such a favorable concordat in 1855, had begun to adopt a hostile attitude to the Church since the end of the 1860's. After the promulgation of the dogma of papal infallibility, the Austrian Minister of Religions, Stremayr, in a long report to Emperor Franz Josef on July 25, 1870, set forth the reasons why Austria should renounce the 1855 concordat. "The infallible pope," he explained, "is not the pope with whom Austria concluded the concordat." Five days later the Emperor Franz Josef replied, saying that the concordat was "shaky," and he instructed his Minister of Religions to "prepare draft laws that will be necessary with a view to regulating the relations between the Catholic Church and my Empire, in conformity with fundamental laws and having regard to the conditions indicated by history."[46]

The offensive being prepared against the Church must not be linked with the anti-Catholic *Kulturkampf* in Germany and Switzerland. Rather, it must be seen as a resurgence of Josephism. Austria was still overwhelmingly Catholic, unlike Germany and Switzerland, and the Emperor was not planning to go so far as the separation of Church and State.[47] It was more that he and his government wanted a great control over the Austrian Church, which, since the vote on infallibility and the submission to the

[45] Texts in *Annales IV*, 266-67.
[46] Philippe Chenaux, "La Suisse," in *Histoire du Christianisme*, XII, "Guerres mondiales et totalitarismes (1914-1958)" (Paris: Desclée/Fayard, 1990), pp.554ff.

pope of very many anti-infallibilist bishops, they feared would become a vassal of Rome.

On July 27, 1873, the universities, all of which were founded by the Church, were placed under state control, and bishops were excluded from any role in their administration. The following year a series of "religious laws" was presented to the Austrian parliament with the aim of submitting ecclesiastical appointments, all episcopal pastoral measures and the practice of divine service, to governmental control. On March 7, 1874, while these laws were still being debated, Pius IX wrote a personal letter to the Emperor and, the same day, published an encyclical. In his letter to Franz Josef he urged him not to open "the path to a disastrous future for the Church and for the well-being of his peoples," and he raised the specter of excommunication. In the encyclical addressed to the Austrian bishops, *Vix dum a Nobis,* the Pope defended the value of the concordat of 1855 and invited the episcopate to study the most effective means of defending the Church's liberty.

It is important to note that, in the event, Pius IX took account of the services rendered hitherto by Catholic Austria, and that he left it to the Austrian bishops, whose determination he had been able to observe at the preceding Council, to attend to and deal with the threat to the Church. Even prior to the encyclical, Cardinal Rauscher, Archbishop of Vienna, had refused to get involved in a trial of strength with the government and had promoted the opening of discussions with the Minister of Religions. His auxiliary bishop, Msgr. Kutschker, succeeded in getting certain measures of the draft laws withdrawn. The Emperor himself, no doubt viewing the possibility of excommunication with some apprehension, yielded to certain episcopal demands.

When, at the beginning of 1876, a law presented in 1874 on the suppression of convents came up for discussion, Cardinal Schwarzenberg, Archbishop of Prague and leader of the Austrian episcopate since the recent death of Rauscher, protested energetically. The law was voted in, but Franz Josef refused to sign it. Perhaps he recalled Pius IX's warning, given at an allocution on March 11, 1875: having denounced "these Catholic governments that exceed Protestant governments in the shameful career of religious oppression," he had added: "God will tell the Protestant persecutor: You have sinned, and sinned gravely. But to the Catholic persecutor he will say: You have sinned even more gravely: *majus peccatum habes.*"[48]

One of the pontificate's last victories should be mentioned, namely, the re-establishment of the episcopal hierarchy in Scotland. As was formerly the case in England, Scotland no longer had bishops to rule the

---

[47]   Letter of July 30, 1870, cited by Mourret, *Histoire générale de l'Eglise,* VIII, 609-10; cf. also Aubert, *Le Pontificat de Pie IX,* pp.392-94, and Martina, III, 427-34.

approximately 380,000 Catholics found there. Scotland was treated as a mission territory, with three vicars-apostolic in charge of these faithful and their 257 priests. In the 1860's Scottish priests and faithful had begged the Pope to appoint bishops. In view of the reticence of the vicars-apostolic themselves and of Cardinal Manning, Pius IX had not acceded to their request. However, when a delegation of Scottish clergy went to Rome in 1877 and renewed their petition, Pius IX initiated negotiations.[49] On January 28, 1878, a decree of the Congregation of Propaganda Fide re-established the two ancient archdioceses of Glasgow and Edinburgh and the four dioceses of Aberdeen, Dunkeld, Galloway, and Argyll. Pius IX died the following month, and it was his successor, Leo XIII, who announced the news and proceeded to appoint bishops to these titles, in a Bull of 1878.

The Last Years of the Pontificate

Almost forty years ago, drawing up a balance-sheet of Pius IX's pontificate, Roger Aubert wrote:

> Pius IX, very poorly advised by those around him, did not succeed in adapting the Church to the profound political evolution that was transforming, root and branch, the organization of civil society in the course of the nineteenth century. Nor did he take sufficient account of the urgent necessity of adapting to another evolution, *i.e.*, the progressive transformation of the ancient agricultural economy in an industrialized world, and the urban proletariat's awareness of its own wretchedness (and of its own strength) as its numerical importance grew from year to year. Fortunately, Catholics and bishops did begin to face the problem, in Germany and then in Austria, France, and England. But it is regrettable that the Holy See, too preoccupied with the struggle against doctrinal and political liberalism, and against the last vestiges of Gallicanism and Josephism, gave no detailed direction in the matter of either principles or pastoral organization.[50]

In 1974 the Postulator of the Faith raised this same topic as one of the "difficulties" presented by Pius IX's cause of beatification: "The 'social question'...seems to have been foreign to Pius IX's concerns and pastoral priorities."[51] These severe verdicts amount to reproaching Pius IX with not having written the great social encyclical *Rerum Novarum* that his successor would publish in 1891.

This is to fail to see that there is no break between Leo XIII and Pius IX in any matter, and that "social Catholicism," of which Leo, by his

---

[48] On August 25, 1870, he wrote to his mother: "I fervently desire to reach a new accord with Rome, but with the present pope it is impossible," cited by Martina, III, 430.

[49] Cited by Mourret, *Histoire générale de l'Eglise*, VIII, 613.

[50] *Ibid.*, p.618, and Aubert, *Le Pontificat de Pie IX*, p.397.

encyclical, was the standard-bearer, was not antipathetic to the "intransigent Catholicism" of Pius IX. Quite the contrary. The day after *Rerum Novarum* was published, Georges Goyau, an historian and perspicacious observer of the Catholicism of his time, noted: "The newspapers are saying that Leo XIII is coming closer to the modern world, whereas Pius IX had isolated himself from it. Such language is full of improprieties....It seems to imply that the Syllabus condemns democracy and the encyclical *Rerum Novarum* canonizes liberalism."[52] Many Italian and French studies in recent decades have confirmed that Pius IX's intransigent Catholicism provided the rich soil for the growth of social Catholicism, and that, far from being opposed to one another, they were united in the same rejection of liberalism in all its forms.

We have already pointed out that at the end of the 1860's Pius IX encouraged what can be regarded as the first stirrings of "Catholic Action," even if this expression was not used at the time. One of these movements proved durable and experienced rapid expansion: Acquaderni's Society of Catholic Youth. In the last years of Pius IX's pontificate the Italian *movimento cattolico* continued to develop, encouraged by the Pope.

In December 1870, the Society of Catholic Youth was complemented by the "Society of Catholic Interests," directed by one of the founders of the *Civiltà Cattolica,* Fr. Curci, and a layman, Prince Chigi. In 1872 the "Society for the Promotion of Good Works" was created, directed by Girolamo Cavaletti. Then, on the initiative of Catholic Youth, the first "Italian Catholic Congress" was held in Venice, from June 12 to 16, 1874, following the idea of the Congresses that had been organized by Belgian and German Catholics for some years. On this occasion Acquaderni set forth the field of operation of "the lay Catholic in this terrible quarter of an hour that society is going through," namely, religious works, caritative works, works of instruction and education, the press, and the arts.[53]

In 1875 the "Work of the Congresses" appeared—the most comprehensive Catholic movement of these decades. Two of the participants in the Venice Congress, Vito D'Ondes Reggio and Giuseppe Sacchetti, decided to found an organization, independent of Catholic Youth, that would create a federation of local initiatives in several areas. Its establishment was officially announced at the second Italian Catholic Congress, held in Florence in August 1875 under the presidency of Duke Salviati. Some little-known words of Pius IX show the encouragement he gave unceasingly to the *movimento cattolico*: receiving in audience a number of

[51] Aubert, *ibid.*, pp.499-500.
[52] Perez, "Alcune difficolta," in Snider, *Pio IX nella luce dei processi canonici*, p.237.
[53] Cited by Jean-Marie Mayeur, *Catholicisme social et démocratie chrétienne* (Paris: Cerf, 1986), pp.27-28.

Sacred Heart nuns during the Florence Congress, he recalled some advice he had given to the Congress president:

> I told him to take, as his model, Ireland, which keeps demanding and demanding. Demand that the Church be at liberty in education, where the government has the monopoly; demand that the Church be free in the choice of her ministers and in the vocation of her clerics....Demand that a brake be put on the license of the press, the source and origin of so many mortal sins....Whenever I have the opportunity to speak, I keep repeating that unity is necessary if demands are to be successful: if people keep campaigning, they will obtain what they are asking for. As you see, in the end I am becoming a bit of a republican myself![54]

Pius IX's advice was followed a little later when the Society of Catholic Youth set up a "League of Daniel O'Connell" (named after the great Catholic Irish patriot) to campaign for freedom of education. In particular it organized a petition with 30,000 signatures and sent it to the Italian Parliament. The Italian Catholic Congresses took place every year. The third was organized in Bologna in 1876, but was brutally dispersed by the civil authorities after incidents created by the city's republicans. The fourth, which was the last during Pius IX's lifetime, was held at Bergamo in October 1877. On this occasion the Pope wrote a letter of encouragement to the Congress president, urging him "to promote the Catholic Congresses, which need to be more frequent nowadays, given the increasingly deplorable conditions of religious and civil society."[55] One participant at this Bergamo Congress was the young Giorgio Montini, secretary of the Padua University group of Catholic Youth. Giorgio Montini would become one of the principal representatives of the *movimento cattolico* in Brescia, and the father of the future Paul VI.[56]

As for the "Work of the Congresses," it was an expression of "intransigent" Catholicism, hostile to the so-called "transigent" Catholics who favored a "conciliation" between the Pope and the Italian State, but its anti-liberalism led it to act in many different ways in social matters. In its early days, *i.e.*, towards the end of Pius IX's pontificate, the "Work of the Congresses" coordinated a multiplicity of initiatives in different regions of Italy (particularly Lombardy and Venetia): it created, or was involved in creating, not only caritative activities, but also people's banks, mutual societies, peasant leagues, and newspapers.[57] All this activity was at a local level. Bishops and laypeople often worked together, and if Pius IX did not have the time to produce the great encyclical setting forth the teaching on this Catholic social action in all its fullness, he certainly encouraged the

---

[54] Cited by N. Bertazzoni, "Pio IX e l'Azione Cattolica Italiana," *Atti del II. Convegno*, p.376.
[55] *Summarium* §584.
[56] Letter of September 24, 1877, in *Annales IV*, 659-60.

work. There can be no doubt that the "social question" was indeed one of his "concerns" and "pastoral priorities."

The special position in which Pius IX found himself from 1870 on-wards, as a "prisoner of the Vatican," partly explains a certain slowing-down of activities and initiatives that can be observed in the last years of his pontificate. We must also take into account the advanced age he had reached—a longevity that was rare at this period of history.

Pius IX alluded to his health for the first time, it seems, in the famous allocution to French pilgrims of June 16, 1871, on the twenty-fifth an-niversary of his pontifical election. What he said was this: "I do not wish to prolong this discourse: neither my strength nor my age will allow it."[58] He was seventy-nine. For several years those close to him had noticed the effects of old age on him. In particular he suffered from a tumor in his leg: "The pains were such that, when they afflicted him, his features were distorted," reported Cardinal Nocella.[59] At first he used a stick when walking, then crutches, and finally a wheelchair. He was not one of those old men who are given to complaining constantly of their deteriorating health. It was not until after his death that ulcers were found on his arms, which he had neglected to have dressed.[60]

As Pius IX grew old he was well aware that a period of the Church's history was coming to an end. He saw some of his closest collaborators vanish one after another: in 1874 Cardinal Barnabo and Msgr. de Mérode, in November 1876 Cardinal Antonelli. As a replacement for the latter at the Secretariat of State he chose Cardinal Simeoni, who was already old, specifically in order to give his successor a free hand. The Pope is sup-posed to have said, "I have chosen Simeoni, but it will not be for long. By picking a cardinal who is destined neither for the papacy nor for political functions, I am giving complete liberty to the future conclave and to my successor."[61] In fact, Simeoni, who until then had been pro-nuncio in Madrid, simply continued the policies of Antonelli.

Pius IX accepted his physical decline with a serenity that is attested by many witnesses. Speaking familiarly to those near to him, he often re-ferred to himself as "this poor man." In 1875 he had made a will, desiring particularly to be buried in the Basilica of San Lorenzo outside the Walls,

---

57 A. Fappani, "Montini, Giorgio," in *Dizionario storico del movimento cattolico in Italia (1860-1980)*, 3 pts. in 6 vols. (Turin: Marietti, 1982), pp.399-400.

58 Cf. the very informative entries in the *Dizionario storico del movimento cattolico in Italia (1860-1980)*. It would go beyond the limits of this biography to discuss the initiatives undertaken in foreign countries, but a history of the Church in the years 1860-70 would have to deal with the activities of La Tour du Pin and his "Oeuvre des Cercles" in France, of the "Fédération des sociétés ouvrières catholiques" in Belgium, of Msgr. Ketteler in Germany, of Baron von Vogelsang in Austria, *etc.*

59 *Actes et paroles*, p.66.

60 *Summarium* §38.

a shrine dear to his heart: he had closely followed the work of restoration, which had begun in 1850. Later codicils provided for certain legacies to institutions he cherished: he left his principal library to the Roman Seminary and his personal library, consisting mainly of ascetical books, to the Passionists of the Scala Santa; precious objects were given to the collegial church of Santa Maria in Via Lata, where he had been a canon, to the cathedrals of Senigallia, Santiago de Chile, and Imola. Items of religious art were left to several princes and Catholic sovereigns who had shown unshakable attachment to the Pope (notably the Count de Chambord, the King of Naples, Isabella of Spain, and Alphonsus of Bourbon). Finally a sum of 100,000 lire was to be distributed to the poor.

At the same time various bulls had been issued to set the rules to be followed for the election of his successor: after those of August 1871 and September 1874, the last, in October 1877, was promulgated by Pius IX the very month he added a last codicil to his will.

The illness that was to carry him off—bronchial catarrh—seized him the following month, November 1877. Periods of remission alternated with crises that confined him to bed and forbade all activity, even the celebration of Mass. Then newspapers began making suppositions about his death and the chancelleries began wondering who would succeed him.

On January 4, 1878, the French Minister of Foreign Affairs, Waddington, sent a long dispatch to Baron Baude, French Ambassador to the Holy See, giving him instructions in the event of a conclave.[62] In it he specifically asserted that France, though having become a republic, had no intention of waiving its traditional right of veto. He also raised a question that had already been discussed discreetly: Would the conclave take place in Rome or, given the fear of Italian interference, elsewhere? Various other locations were considered, such as the Principality of Monaco, or one or other of the Swiss cantons.

Contrary to all expectation it was not Pius IX whose death was imminent, but that of Victor Emmanuel II. The latter was much younger than the Pope: only fifty-eight. His death was sudden. The King was compelled to take to his bed on January 5, the victim of a high fever produced by pleuro-pneumonia. On January 6, as soon as Pius IX became aware of the serious illness of the man he had excommunicated for usurping his States, he sent his confessor and sacristan, Msgr. Marinelli, to the Quirinal "to have news of the King and put himself at his disposal."[63] The Pope was hoping that, on his deathbed, the King would repent of his faults and would be reconciled with God and the Church. However, on that day Msgr. Marinelli could not gain access to the King. The next day, January

---

[61] *Summarium* §151.
[62] Words reported by the Belgian minister in Rome, cited by Falconi, *Antonelli*, pp.530-31, and in a similar version by Aubert, *Le Pontificat de Pie IX*, p.498.

7, Pius IX ordered Msgr. Marinelli to return to the Quirinal, telling him: "If I were well, I would go myself to absolve him. My desire is, absolutely, for this soul to be saved and I pray every day for this intention."[65] Once again, however, the King's entourage would not let the Pope's envoy enter. It was the court chaplain, Fr. Anzino, who, on January 9, was able to receive the confession of the King of Italy, his death being imminent, and gave him absolution and communion after he had renounced his faults.

These last moments of the life of Victor Emmanuel gave rise to polemics. The government newspapers endeavored to take the good out of the King's final repentance, reporting him as saying: "In all that I have done, I have always been conscious of carrying out my duty as a citizen and a prince and doing nothing against the religion of my fathers." Pius IX immediately ordered his Secretary of State to rectify this deceitful presentation of the facts by a long circular to the diplomats present in Rome and to all the nuncios and representatives of the Holy See in Europe. Cardinal Simeoni explained how the King's verbally expressed repentance was a real act of retractation of his errors and a sincere repentance for his acts of spoliation of the Holy See.[66]

The Italian government and Umberto, the inheritor of the Kingdom, refused to recognize this retractation. On the very day his father died, Umberto, having been proclaimed King, made a declaration in which he promised to follow the "great examples" given by the deceased King: "devotion to my country, love of progress, and faith in our free institutions." Pius IX ordered his Secretary of State to protest by an official note sent to the diplomats accredited to the Holy See.[67] Once again the Pope denounced the "iniquitous spoliation" and asserted that he would "maintain intact...–the Church's right over her ancient Roman possessions, which have been destined by Divine Providence to guarantee the independence of the Roman Pontiffs, the full liberty of their apostolic ministry, and the peace and tranquillity of Catholics all over the world."

Pius IX remained inflexible in asserting the Church's temporal power. However, it was on a more strictly religious note that his life came to an end. On February 2, the Feast of the Purification, he delivered his last public allocutions. As on the same date every year, he received a delegation of the Roman clergy, religious orders, and ecclesiastical colleges, who came to give him the traditional candle for Candlemas. He spoke a few words to them, urging them carefully to teach children the catechism.[67]

---

[63] A.M.A.E., C.P., Rome 1063, ff.8-15.
[64] Dispatch of Baron Baude to Waddington, dated January 9, 1876, A.M.A.E., C.P., Rome 1063, ff.22-26.
[65] *Summarium* §39.
[66] Circular of January 28, 1878, in *Annales IV*, 698-699.

That day was also the seventy-fifth anniversary of his First Communion. It will be recalled how vivid was his memory of the religious emotion of that event. He had agreed that this anniversary would be marked by special ceremonies, not for self-glorification but out of devotion to this sacrament. All the parishes of Rome organized First Communion Masses that day and, in the Vatican, Pius IX received a group of first communicants from different parishes. He gave them a little talk. It is significant that Pius IX's public life came to its conclusion with him giving Eucharistic instruction to children. This links him to one of his successors, St. Pius X, who would be the great apostle of the Eucharist at the beginning of the next century.

It is well known that, in the nineteenth century, First Communion was made late, at the age of twelve to fourteen, and that it was not until the pontificate of St. Pius X, by the decree *Quam Singulari Christus Amore* (August 8, 1910), that this age was lowered "to seven years, more or less," provided the child could also satisfy the precept of confession and "knows how to distinguish the eucharistic bread from ordinary physical bread."[69]

This same decree, however, reminds us that it was Pius IX who first began to question the custom of leaving First Communion to a relatively late age. On March 15, 1851, the Congregation of the Council corrected a chapter of the Rouen provincial council which forbade children being admitted to Communion before the age of twelve, and on March 12, 1866, Secretary of State Antonelli wrote to the bishops of France reprobating the custom "of deferring First Communion until a late and fixed age."

Similarly, it was under the pontificate of St. Pius X that a decree, *Sacra Tridentina Synodus* (December 20, 1905) was issued, encouraging the faithful to receive Communion daily, provided that the required dispositions were present, namely, "the state of grace and a right intention."[70] The decree referred back to the teaching of the Council of Trent on this subject.[71] Nonetheless, says the decree, in succeeding centuries, "piety having declined and, later, the poison of Jansenism having spread everywhere, a debate began as to the dispositions necessary to approach Holy Communion frequently and daily: great and difficult requirements were made of those who wished to do so."

This was still the situation under the pontificate of Pius IX, but minds began to change, notably under the influence of a growing Eucharistic devotion and of certain authors. One of the latter was Msgr. de Ségur,

---

[67] Text of the note in *Annales IV*, 698-99.
[68] Text of the allocution in *Annales IV*, 698-99.
[69] Decree published in *Documents pontificaux de Sa Sainteté saint Pie X* (Publications du "Courrier de Rome," 1993), II, 651-56.
[70] Decree published in *ibid.*, I, 673-76.
[71] The Eucharist, in the words of this Council, is "the antidote that delivers us from daily faults and preserves us from mortal sins."

who was very close to Pius IX. When Msgr. de Ségur published his *La Très Sainte Communion* in 1860, to spread the practice of frequent communion, Pius IX wrote him a letter of approbation.[72] So, in the field of Eucharistic practice, Pius IX was a precursor of St. Pius X.

Death

These public audiences of February 2 were the last. In the following days he still received some cardinals, but on the 6th, being particularly exhausted, he was obliged to receive them from his bed. On the morning of the 7th, after a disturbed night, he was shivering and his breathing got faster.[73] Immediately the Cardinal Vicar of Rome had the Blessed Sacrament exposed in all the churches of Rome, while the bells summoned the faithful to prayer.

The Pope knew well that the hour of his death had arrived. He asked for the last sacraments to be given to him. It was nine o'clock in the morning. The situation deteriorated in the afternoon and, at 5:35, when the bells of Rome were ringing the Angelus, Pius IX breathed his last. The cardinal *camerlengo* was Cardinal Pecci (the future Leo XIII, elected a few days later). He carried out the prescribed ceremonial, and then the death was announced to the Romans by the great bell of the Capitol. The deceased's body was embalmed the next day and lay in state in the Vatican Palace and subsequently in the chapel of the Blessed Sacrament in St. Peter's Basilica. For three days the faithful could come and render him their last respects.

Provisionally, Pius IX was buried in the crypt of St. Peter's while the tomb was being built in St. Lawrence Outside the Walls. His body was not transferred there until July 13, 1881, an event that gave rise to riotous and scandalous incidents.[74]

In order that the daily life of Rome should not be disturbed and no pretext should be given for provocations, it had been agreed that Pius IX's body should be transferred during the night. More than 100,000 faithful crowded together along the route, reciting the Rosary and litanies or throwing flowers from their windows. However, hostile groups infiltrated among the faithful as the cortege left St. Peter's Square.

When the funeral convoy was crossing the bridge of Sant'Angelo there was much unseemly pushing and shoving as hostile insults were

---

[72] Letter of September 29, 1860, B.N. ms. N.A.Fr. 22833, ff.24-25.

[73] The most detailed testimony regarding the death and funeral of Pius IX is that made by one of his private secretaries, Msgr. Francesco Salesio Dalla Volpe in the canonization process, *Summarium* §§312-36; cf. also *Annales IV*, 699-704.

[74] Cf. the testimony of Dalla Volpe in *Summarium* I, §§329, 330. For other testimonies cf. §173.

redoubled: "Long live Italy! Long live Garibaldi! Into the river with the carrion! Into the Tiber with the swine!"

Similar incidents were repeated all along the route, with some individuals going as far as to attack the cortege with sticks. The police proved particularly timid and ineffectual.

Leo XIII protested. A petition circulated in Rome, collecting more than 100,000 signatures, and finally King Umberto presented official apologies to the Vatican. Even after his death, therefore, Pius IX was a "sign of contradiction," and remains so today, in large measure.

However, even an opponent such as the liberal Charles de Mazade had to agree, on the day after the Pope's death: "Today he enters history accompanied by the world's respect and religious feeling. He leaves us, having provided the spectacle of this astonishing longevity on the Chair of St. Peter, which enabled him to see and know everything: he saw the most profound revolutions, national crises, changes of fortune, hopes and false hopes, exaltation and bitterness. He quits the scene, having played the part of a European and universal personage, in the most agitated, the most tortured period of the century."[75]

---

[75] "Chronique de la Quinzaine," *Revue des Deux-Mondes,* March 1, 1878, pp.953-64. The liberal Mazade tempered his praise by saying that "No doubt, from a human viewpoint, this was not a policy of the first class."

CONCLUSION

TOWARDS THE
CANONIZATION

The judgment to be given by historians on Pius IX and his pontificate is founded on criteria and assessments in which the objectivity of facts must come first. Were the Pope's actions favorable to the Church, to her vigor and independence? Was he able to resolve the many problems posed in the realm of faith, society, *etc.*?

The Church, however, when she proclaims one of her members first blessed, then a saint, is making a judgment of a different nature. This verdict rests on criteria and assessments that are of a spiritual and doctrinal order. How did the person under consideration practice the theological virtues of faith, hope, and charity, and the cardinal virtues of prudence, justice, fortitude, and temperance? Such a verdict is reached after a long examination of acts and words that takes place during the beatification or canonization process.

Pius IX had not yet been buried when, on February 8, 1878, the members of the Vienna Third Order of Franciscans sent a telegram to the Holy See requesting the introduction of his cause of beatification and canonization. (Pius IX, as we have seen, was a member of the Franciscan Third Order.) Then, on February 11, the faithful of Palermo sent a similar request to their bishop. The first request on the part of the hierarchy, made to Leo XIII, came from eight bishops from the Venice area, together with their Patriarch, Cardinal Agostini. In a long letter dated May 24, 1878, *i.e.*, less than four months after the Pope's death, they gave it as their view that "the unique length of the pontificate in history" was a sign of divine Providence and that "Pius IX practised the theological and moral virtues to such a high degree that he merits being proposed as a model and venerated as a saint."[1]

They called for the opening of a canonical process. That same year, similar requests were formulated by Neapolitan and Canadian bishops. Others would be made in subsequent years, but Leo XIII did not accede to them, no doubt for political reasons.

His successor did not have the same hesitations. In 1904, one year after his election to the pontificate, and on the fiftieth anniversary of the dogmatic definition of the Immaculate Conception, St. Pius X began the

---

[1] Extracts from this letter in *Annales IV*, 732-35.

canonical process, ordering an enquiry into Pius IX's reputation for sanctity, his virtues and the miracles attributed to him.

In 1907 a first Postulator of the cause was appointed, Msgr. Cani, and
the informative processes began. The ordinary process in Rome interrogated 83 persons between 1907 and 1922; the process in Senigallia interrogated 16 persons between 1908 and 1915; the process in Spoleto interrogated 24 persons in 1916; the process in Imola interrogated 29 persons
from 1908 to 1916; and the process in Naples interrogated 91 persons
from 1907 to 1913.[2] A total of 243 direct witnesses, clerics or laypeople,
were interrogated at length on the various stages of Pius IX's life and on
his practice of the different virtues. The detailed responses were collected
together in twelve large volumes.

In 1952 the Advocate of the cause, Msgr. Giuseppe Stella, extracted
the most important responses from these twelve manuscript volumes, producing the *Summarium,* in 1,159 pages of large format. This constituted
the first part of the *Positio,* which we have frequently cited in this book.
On December 7, 1954, the decree was promulgated, officially introducing
the cause.

In 1955 and 1956 the apostolic process took place, examining the
virtues and miracles. A further nineteen testimonies were added. Subsequently the Postulation of the cause, directed at that time by Msgr. Canestri, was in a position to publish a collection of reports on the 133 miracles
attributed to the intercession of Pius IX.

After the informative processes, the opening of the cause, and the apostolic processes, the fourth canonical stage began on October 25, 1956,
with "the exhumation, identification, and reposition of the body of the
Servant of God, Pius IX." In the presence of the Cardinal-Vicar Micara,
Cardinal Cicognani, Prefect of the Congregation of Rites, Cardinal Valeri,
Prefect of the Congregation of Religious, Msgr. Canestri, Postulator of
the cause, and other prelates, the tomb was opened. The triple coffin (of
chestnut, lead, and cypress) in which Pius IX had been buried was recovered, not without some difficulty. The coffins were opened in the crypt
and, to the great joy of those present, the body was found to be intact.
Journalists present also confirmed this fact. The body was re-buried on
November 23.

The Congregation of Rites next had to examine the virtues and miracles attributed to Pius IX. This was done by three congregations (ante-
preparatory, preparatory, and general ordinary).

The first took place on October 2, 1962, the second on May 28,
1963. The third was late in meeting. Paul VI had become pope and the
Second Vatican Council was being held–a Council which, on many

---

[2] "Index Testium et Summarii," in *Summarium,* pp.1-50.

points, seemed contrary to the teaching of Pius IX. For example, with regard to the Declaration on Religious Liberty, one of the Council's principal theologians, Fr. Congar, admitted: "It must be acknowledged that what this text says is materially different from the 1864 Syllabus, and is even practically opposed to what is asserted in Propositions 15, 77, and 79 of that document."[3]

In 1971, after the death of Msgr. Canestri, a new Postulator of the cause was appointed: Msgr. Piolanti, rector of the Lateran University. He did much to reactivate a cause that had been allowed to slumber. In 1972 appeared the first issue of the trimestrial journal *Pio IX,* devoted to historical studies on the various aspects of the life and pontificate of Giovanni Maria Mastai. In 1975 Msgr. Piolanti created a collection of *Studi Piani,* published by the Editions of the Vatican Library, which, so far, have produced nine historical studies of great interest.

Meanwhile, on April 15, 1974, following a petition signed by four cardinals (Parente, Guerri, Mozzoni, and Palazzini) requesting Paul VI to take up the cause of Pius IX again, the Promoter general of the Faith, Fr. Perez, communicated to the Postulation of the cause thirteen "difficulties" that had surfaced at the two congregations (ante-preparatory and preparatory) convened in 1962 and 1963.[4]

The Postulation of the cause appointed a new advocate, Carlo Snider, to answer these "difficulties." Swiss by nationality, Snider was a lawyer at the Congregation of the Cause of Saints, and had previously been involved with other celebrated causes, notably those of Frédéric Ozanam, Cardinal Ferrari, Emperor Charles of Austria, and Msgr. Darboy. On October 7, 1984, he presented his response to the thirteen "difficulties," entitled *"La nota della santità nella vita e nel pontificato di Pio IX."* Then Msgr. Piolanti, Postulator of the cause, succeeded in getting the third congregation (the "ordinary general" congregation) to meet, at last, on December 11 following. At the conclusion of its session it concluded that in his life Pius IX had exercised in "heroic manner" (according to the canonical formula) the theological virtues of faith, hope, and charity and the cardinal virtues of prudence, justice, fortitude, and temperance.

Finally, on July 6, 1985, Pope John Paul II promulgated the decree on the heroic exercise of the virtues.[5] From that time Pius IX was accorded the title of "Venerable."

The process of beatification continued. The acknowledgment of a miracle attributed to the intercession of the Venerable was, in fact, necessary for him to be proclaimed "Blessed." This acknowledgment was given in January 1986. On January 15, 1986, the Consulta dei Medici attached

---

3   Yves Congar, *La Crise de l'Eglise et Mgr. Lefebvre* (Paris: Cerf, 1976), p.54.
4   Texts in Snider, *Pio IX,* pp.234-38.
5   Latin text in *Pio IX,* 1-2 (1986), pp.3-10.

to the Congregation for the Cause of Saints certified, unanimously, that by the intercession of Pius IX a French nun, Sr. Marie Thérèse de Saint-Paul, of the Carmel of Nantes, had been miraculously cured. After a scrupulous medical examination of the documents and testimonies in their possession, the doctors of the Consulta established that this nun, born at the end of the last century, was suffering from a fracture of the right kneecap, which had never been set, and that this fracture had become a "pseudo-arthrosis with diastasis of the fragments," causing her great suffering. Because of her devotion to Pius IX—her father, two of her uncles, and two of her cousins had been papal Zouaves—she had begun a novena on February 11, 1910, to ask for a cure through the intercession of Pius IX. The pain suddenly disappeared. Sr. Marie Thérèse was able to engage in normal activities once again, going up and down stairs, kneeling, walking without effort, all the things which, previously, she could not do. The cure had been sudden, complete, without relapse, and obtained without medical help—conditions required if a cure is to be regarded as miraculous.

Official recognition of this miracle attributed to the intercession of Pius IX permitted his beatification. In 1987, John Paul II judged it advisable to institute a special committee of seven members with the task of studying and pronouncing whether it would be "opportune" to beatify his predecessor. Fr. Giacomo Martina, whose historical studies on Pius IX we have often cited—not without pointing out the debatable nature of some of his verdicts—was one of the seven-member commission. After four working sessions the commission put the matter to a vote: five of the members thought that the beatification was "opportune," one pronounced himself favorable *juxta modum,* and one declared himself opposed to it.[6] The latter was Fr. Martina.

Fr. Martina has explained his opposition to the beatification of a pope to whom, as an historian, he had dedicated so many years of his life, by arguing that public opinion, above all in Italy, would not understand why the Church would elevate to her altars a man who was so opposed to the process of national unification. Furthermore, he believed that the Church cannot beatify and then canonize someone who, in the Syllabus, condemned the principles on which, nowadays, all modern societies are founded. Finally, he judged that the beatification of Pius IX would reinforce the currents of traditionalist opposition in the Church. Rather than beatifying Pius IX, Fr. Martina thought it would be better to "venerate him in silence, without any noisy show."[7]

This personal opinion, however, did not bind the Church since, on September 3, 2000, Pope John Paul II judged it opportune to proceed to the joint beatifications of Pius IX and John XXIII, the popes who con-

---

6   Tommaso Ricci, "Beato in pectore," *30 Giorni,* June 1991, p.65.
7   Interview given to the Italian magazine *Jesus,* April 4, 1991, p.69.

vened the most recent councils, Vatican I and Vatican II. In his sermon during the Mass of beatification the Pope, besides emphasizing the great devotion of John XXIII for Pius IX, pointed out that the newly beatified Pius IX:

> ...Amid the turbulent events of his time, was an example of unconditional fidelity to the immutable deposit of revealed truths. Faithful to the duties of his ministry in every circumstance, he always knew how to give absolute primacy to God and to spiritual values.

> His lengthy pontificate was not at all easy and he had much to suffer in fulfilling his mission of service to the Gospel. He was much loved, but also hated and slandered. However, it was precisely in these conflicts that the light of his virtues shone most brightly: these prolonged sufferings tempered his trust in divine Providence, whose sovereign lordship over human events he never doubted. This was the source of Pius IX's deep serenity, even amid the misunderstandings and attacks of so many hostile people. He liked to say to those close to him: "In human affairs we must be content to do the best we can and then abandon ourselves to Providence, which will heal our human faults and shortcomings."

> Sustained by this deep conviction, he called the First Vatican Ecumenical Council, which clarified with magisterial authority certain questions disputed at the time, and confirmed the harmony of faith and reason. During his moments of trial Pius IX found support in Mary, to whom he was very devoted. In proclaiming the dogma of the Immaculate Conception, he reminded everyone that in the storms of human life the light of Christ shines brightly in the Blessed Virgin and is more powerful than sin and death.

BIBLIOGRAPHY

Archives

Archives of the Ministry of Foreign Affairs, Paris:
  Political Correspondence, Rome: 986, 987, 994, 1028, 1044, 1045, 1063.

Archives of the Saint-Sulpice Seminary, Paris:
  Henri Icard, *Journal de mon voyage et de mon séjour à Rome*, 394 manuscript pages.
  Letters of Msgr. Dechamps, Ignaz Dollinger, Msgr. Ginoulhiac, Msgr. Manning, Msgr. Maret, Msgr. Mermillod, Msgr. de Mérode to Msgr. Dupanloup.

National Library, Paris:
  N.A.Fr. 11911, 20622, 20623, 22833, 22953.

Acts of Pius IX

No complete French translation of the Pontifical Acts of Pius IX exists. A critical Latin edition of his encyclicals with an Italian translation is to be published by Dehoniane Publishers of Bologna in the series *Enchiridion delle encicliche*. Listed below are the different collections referenced in this work.

Actes et paroles de Pie IX captif au Vatican. Ed. Auguste Roussel. Paris: Victor Palmé, 1874.
Les Actes pontificaux cités dans l'encyclique et le Syllabus du 8 décembre 1864 suivis de divers autres documents, ed. Joseph Chantrel. Paris: Librairie Vve. Poussielgue & Fils, 1865.
Annales ecclésiastiques de 1846 à 1866. Ed. Joseph Chantrel. Gaume & Co., 1887.
Annales ecclésiastiques de 1867 à 1868. Ed. Joseph Chantrel. Gaume & Co., 1896.
Annales ecclésiastiques de 1869 à 1873. Ed. Rev. François Chamard. Gaume & Co., 1893.
Annales ecclésiastiques de 1873 à 1879. Ed. Rev. François Chamard. Gaume & Co., 1896.
Denzinger, H. and A. Schönmetzer, eds. *Enchiridion symbolorum definitionum et declarationum de rebus fidei et morum.* 36th ed. (Barcelona-Fribourg-Rome: Herder, 1976).

Encycliques et Documents en français et latin. Ed. Rev. Raulx. 2 volumes. Bar-le-
Duc: L. Guérin, 1865.
L'Encyclique et les Évêques de France. Complete collected letters. Paris: E. Dentu,
1865.

Works or Articles About Pius IX and His Pontificate

As yet no complete bibliography of works devoted to Pius IX exists,
as there are for other popes. Nonetheless, in the second edition of Roger
Aubert's *Pontificat de Pie IX,* besides the general bibliography that appeared in the first edition (1952), there is an important "Bibliographical
Supplement." Moreover, in the first volume of *Pio IX* (1974), the Rev. Giacomo Martina included an introductory chapter, "Interpretazioni di Pio
IX: Storia di una storiografia," which gives a very ample, critical, though
incomplete, historiography. Finally, the review *Pio IX* (Rome) and especially the *Revue d'Histoire Ecclésiastique* (Louvain-la-Neuve) regularly publish reviews of articles or books devoted to Pius IX and his pontificate.

Below we list only the works or articles consulted for this biography.
For the acts of colloquia, we only cite the generic title without giving the
specific reference of each of the communications that the reader found
cited in chapter notes. Similarly, we do not repeat here the specific titles of
the numerous articles found in the review *Pio IX* (the first issue of which
was published in 1972) which have been cited in the chapter notes.

Atti del II Convegno di ricerca storica sulla figura e sull'opera di Papa Pio IX, Octo-
ber 9-11, 1977. Senigallia: Centro Studi Pio IX.
Pio IX nel primo centenario della sua morte. Ed. la Postulazione della causa di Pio
IX/Libreria Editrice Vaticane, 1978.
Positio super Introductione Causae, Vol. 1: *Tabella testium et Summarium.* Sacred
Congregation of Rites, 1954.
Grâces obtenues par l'intercession de Pie IX depuis l'époque de sa mort. Bologna:
Archdiocesan publ., 1884.
Aubert, Roger. *Le Pontificat de Pie IX.* 2nd edition. Paris: Bloud & Gay, 1963.
————. *Vatican I. Histoire des conciles oecuméniques,* Vol. 12. Editions de
l'Orante, 1964.
Aubert, Michel Gueret, Paul Tombeur, and Roger. *Concilium Vatican I: Concor-
dance, Index, Listes de fréquence, Tables comparatives.* Louvain: CETEDOC
Publications, 1977.
Ausenda, Claudio Vila Pila and Giovanni. *Pio IX y las escuelas pias.* Rome: Editio-
nes Calasanctianae, 1979.
Bogliolo, Luigi. *Pio IX profilo spirituale.* Libreria Editrice Vaticane, 1989.
Brunetti, Manlio. *Pio IX: Giudizio storico-teologico.* Senigallia: Edizione dell'Opera
Pia Mastai Ferrretti, 1992.

Calm, Lillian. *El Chile de Pio IX: 1824.* Santiago du Chili: Editorial Andres Bello, 1987.

Cempanari, Maria Angela Luzi and Mario. *La Biblioteca privata di Pio IX alla Scala Santa in Roma.* Fratelli Palombi Editori, 1995.

Canestri, Msgr. Alberto. *L'Anima di Pio IX.* 4 volumes. Marino: Tipografia santa Lucia, 1965-1967.

Cani, Msgr. *Procès romain pour la cause de béatification et de canonisation du serviteur de Dieu le pape Pie IX.* Paris: Maison de la Bonne Press, 1910.

Cittadini, Giovanni. *Giovanni Maria Mastai-Ferretti: Lettere III.* Pieve-Torina: Mierma, 1993.

——————. *Giovanni Maria Mastai-Ferretti: Lettere IV.* Acquasanta-Frascati, 1994.

Corteville, Fernand. *Pie IX, le Père Semenenko et les défenseurs du message de Notre-Dame de La Salette.* Diffusion Téqui, 1987.

Dupanloup, Msgr. *Lettre M. le Vte. de La Guéronnière.* Paris: Charles Douniol, 1861.

——————. *La Convention du 15 septembre et l'encyclique du 8 décembre.* Paris: Charles Douniol, 1865.

Falconi, Carlo. *Il giovane Mastai.* Milan: Rusconi, 1981.

Fernessole, Pierre. *Pie IX.* 2 volumes. Lethielleux, 1960, 1963.

Ferri, Mario Gregorio. *L'Opera pia Mastai Ferretti: Bilancio di un secolo.* Senigallia: Edizione dell'Opera Pia Mastai Ferretti, 1992.

Granderath, Théodore. *Histoire du Concile du Vatican.* 3 tomes in 5 volumes, and 1 vol. *Appendices et documents.* Brussels: Libr. Albert Dewit, 1907-14.

Huguet, R.P., *L'Esprit de Pie IX.* Lyons-Paris: Felix Girard, 1866.

Ideville, The Count of. *Pie IX: Sa vie, sa mort, souvenirs personnels.* Paris-Brussels: Victor Palmé/J. Albanel, 1878.

Le Tourneau, Dominique, "La Loi des Garanties (13 mai 1871): Portée et contenu," *Revue des Sciences Religieuses,* April-July, 1988, pp. 137-158.

Manning, Msgr. *Histoire du Concile du Vatican.* Paris: Victor Palmé, 1872.

Maret, Msgr. *De la Papauté.* Paris: Gaume Frères & J. Duprey, 1860.

Martin, Msgr. Jacques. "Pie IX et le néo-gallicanisme: Le cas de Mgr. Darboy," *L'Osservatore Romano,* June 17, 1986, pp.5-8.

Martina, Rev. Giacomo. *Pio IX: 1846-1850.* Rome: Università Gregoriana Editrice, 1974.

——————. *Pio IX: 1851-1866.* Rome: Università Gregoriana Editrice, 1986.

——————. *Pio IX: 1867-1878.* Rome: Editrice Università Gregoriana, 1990.

Mencucci, Msgr. Angelo. *Pio IX et Senigallia.* Senigallia: Adriatica, 1987.

——————. *La genealogia della famiglia Masta-Ferretti.* Senigallia: Rotary Club, 1992.

Montalembert, Count of. *Pie IX et la France.* Paris: Jacques Lecoffre & Co., 1859.

Mourret, Fernand. *Le Concile du Vatican*. Bloud & Gay, 1919.

Parocchi, Cardinal Lucido M. *Pio IX caro a Dio e agli uomini*. Libreria Editrice Vaticana, 1986.

Piolanti, Msgr. Antonio. *Pio IX e la rinascita del tomismo*. Libreria Editrice Vaticana, 1984.

Pirri, Pietro. *Pio IX e Vittorio Emanuele II dal loro carteggio privato*. 5 volumes. Pontifical Gregorian University, 1948-61.

Polverari, Msgr. Alberto. *Vita di Pio IX*. 3 volumes. Editrice la Postulazione della Causa di Pio IX/ Libreria Editrice Vaticana, 1986-88.

Retamal-Fuentes, Fernando. *Escritos Menores de la mision Muzi*. Santiago: Pontificia Universidad Catolica de Chile, 1987.

Ricci, Tommaso. "Beato in pectore," *30 Giorni*, June 1991, pp.64-67.

Robert, Dom Leo. *Dom Guéranger chez Pie IX 1851-1852*. Association des Amis de Solesmes, 1960.

Saint-Albin, Alex. de. *Histoire de Pie IX*. 3 volumes. Paris-Brussels: Victor Palmé/ Joseph Albanel, 1878-1879.

Saint-Hermel, E. de. *Pie IX*. Paris: L. Hachette, 1854.

Ségur, Marquis de. *Les Martyrs de Castelfidardo*. Paris: Tolra, 1891.

Serafin, Alberto. *Pio Nono*. Tipografia Poliglotta Vaticana, 1958.

Snider, Carlo. *Pio IX nella luce dei processi canonici*. Editrice la Postulazione della Causa di Pio IX/Libreria Editrice Vaticana, 1992.

Veuillot, Louis. *Le Pape et la diplomatie*. Paris: Gaume Frères & J. Duprey, 1861.

———————. *Le Guêpier italien*. Paris: Victor Palmé, 1865.

———————. *A propos de la guerre*. Paris: Victor Palmé, 1866.

———————. *Rome pendant le Concile*. Volume 12 of *Complete Works*. P. Lethielleux, 1927.

———————. *Pie IX*. Volume 10 of *Complete Works*. P. Lethielleux, 1929.

———————. *L'Illusion libérale*. B-Haut-le-Wastia: Dismas, 1989.

Vibrac, Rev. Dominic. "Le Vénérable Pie IX, Pape de l'Immaculée, Bon Pasteur et grand spirituel," *La Pensée Catholique*, Nov.-Dec. 1992, pp.46-53.

———————. "Pie IX: Le pape 'Bon Pasteur'," *La Nef*, July-August 1995, pp.30-31.

Other Works Consulted

Agasso, Domenico. *Un prophète pour l'Afrique: Daniel Comoboni*. Mediaspaul, 1994.

Alberigo, *Les Conciles oecuméniques*. 3 volumes in 2 tomes. Cerf, 1994.

Anonymous. *Histoire civile, politique et religieuse de Pie VI*. Avignon, n.d.

Antonetti, Guy. *Louis-Philippe*. Fayard, 1994.

Barbier, Rev. Emmanuel. *Histoire du catholicisme libéral et du catholicisme social en France*. Vol. 1. 1923.

Battandier, Albert. *Le cardinal Jean-Baptiste Pitra*. Paris: Sauvaître, 1893.

Bazin, G. *Windhorst, ses alliés et ses adversaires*. Paris: Bloud & Cie, n.d.

Bernet, Anne. *Bernadette Soubirous.* Perrin, 1994.

Besson, Msgr. *Frédéric-François-Xavier de Mérode.* Société de Saint-Augustin, 1898.

Billet, Dom Bernard. "Culte et dévotion à la Vierge Marie dans l'ordre monastique aux VIIIe-IXe siècles," *Esprit et Vie,* May 11, 1972, pp. 299-303.

Bonvin, Bernard. *Lacordaire-Jandel.* Cerf, 1990.

Bosco, Don. *Souvenirs autobiographiques.* Médiaspaul, 1995.

Boulenger, Rev. A. *Histoire générale de l'Eglise.* Vol. 9: *XIXe et XXe siècles.* Lyons-Paris: Librairie Catholique Emmanuel Vitte, 1947.

Boutry, Philippe. "Le mouvement vers Rome et le renouveau missionnaire." *Histoire de la France Religieuse,* vol. 3. Seuil, 1991.

Brasseur. *Libermann 1802-1852.* Cerf, 1988.

Brule, Alfred van der. *Le Sacré-Coeur de Montmartre: Hubert Rohault de Fleury.* Téqui, 1995.

Cabrol, Dom Fernand. *Histoire du cardinal Pitra.* Paris: Victor Retaux & Fils, 1893.

Carcel Orti, Vincente. "Le cardinal Mercier et les études ecclésiastiques en Espagne," *Revue d'Histoire Ecclésiastique,* Jan.-June 1995, pp.104-112.

Catta, Etienne. "L'ordre social chrétien et le cardinal Pie," *La Pensé Catholique,* No. 10, 1949, pp.48-83.

Celier, Gregory. *Essai bibliographique sur l'antilibéralisme catholique.* Riddes, Switzerland: Procure Séminaire St-Pie X, 1986.

Cerbelaud-Salagnac, Georges. *Les Zouaves pontificaux.* France-Empire, 1956.

Chaix-Ruy, Jules. *Donoso Cortès: Théologien de l'histoire et prophète.* Beauchesne, 1956.

Chiron, Yves. *Enquête sur les apparitions de la Vierge.* Perrin-Mame, 1995.

Colonge, Paul. "Ludwig Windthorst, âme de la résistance catholique dans l'Allemagne bismarckienne," *Les Résistances spirituelles.* Acts of the 10th Conference on Religious History of Fontevraud. University of Angers Press, 1987.

Conzemius, Victor. *Philipp Anton von Segesser.* Beauchesne, 1991.

Crete, Jean. "Vie du cardinal Pie," *Itinéraires,* No. 247, 1980, pp.85-104, & No. 248, 1980, pp.118-35.

Dansette, Adrien, *Histoire religieuse de la France contemporaine.* Flammarion, 1948.

Delatte, Dom. *Dom Guéranger, abbé de Solesmes.* Revised and expanded ed. Solesmes, 1984.

Epiphanius. *Massoneria e sette segrete: la faccia occulta della storia.* Albano Laziale, Italy: Cooperativa Adveniat, n.d.

Falconi, Carlo. *Il cardinale Antonelli.* Milan: Arnoldo Mondadori, 1983.

Felix, G. *S.E. le cardinal Mermillod: Vie intime et souvenirs.* Tours: Alfred Cattier, 1893.

Frenaud, Dom Georges. "Dom Guéranger e le projet de bulle *Quemadmodum Ecclesia* pour la définition de l'Immaculé Conception," *Virgo Immaculata*. Rome: Academia Mariana Internationalis, 1956, II, 337-86.

Girard, Louis. *Napoléon III*. Fayard, 1986.

Gizzi, Stefano. *Il Cardinale Tommaso Pasquale Gizzi*. Amministrazione Provinciale de Frosinone, 1993.

Goyau, Georges. *Autour du catholicisme social*. Libr. Acad. Perrin, 1909.

Johnson, Dom Cuthbert. *Dom Guéranger et le renouveau liturgique*. Téqui, 1988.

Jouette, André. *Toute l'histoire par les dates et les documents*. Perrin, 1989.

Kosyk, Wolodymyr. *L'Ukraine et les Ukrainiens*. Paris: Publications de l'Est Européen, 1993.

Lacordaire and Montalembert. *Correspondance 1830-1861*. Cerf, 1989.

Lagrange, Rev. Fr. *Vie de Mgr Dupanloup*. 3 volumes. Paris: Libr. Poussielgue Frères, 1884.

Lottman, Herbert R. *La Dynastie Rothschild*. Seuil, 1995.

Mayeur, Jean-Marie. *Catholicisme social et démocratie chrétienne*. Cerf, 1986.

Maynard, Rev. U. *Monseigneur Dupanloup et M. Lagrange son historien*. Paris: Société Générale de Librairie Catholique, 1884.

Merklen, Léon. "Civilta Cattolica," *Catholicisme*. Letouzey & Ané, 1950. II, col.1153-54.

Montalembert, Charles de. *Correspondance inédite 1852-1870*. Cerf, 1970.

Mourret, Fernand. *Histoire générale de l'Eglise*. Vol. 8: *L'Eglise contemporaine*. Bloud & Gay, 1922.

Naudon, Paul. *Histoire générale de la franc-maçonnerie*. Office du Livre, 1987.

Newman, Cardinal John Henry. *Choix de lettres*. Téqui, 1990.

Palanque, Jean-Rémy. *Catholiques libéraux et gallicans en France face au concile du Vatican 1867-1870*. Publications des annales de la Faculté des Lettres. Aix-en-Provence: Editions Ophrys, 1962.

Pelletier, Paul. *Pierre Simon de Dreux-Brézé, Évêque de Moulins: 1850-1893*. Charroux: Editions des Cahiers Bourbonnais, 1994.

Pius X, Saint. *Documents pontificaux de Sa Sainteté Pie X*. 2 volumes. Publications du *Courrier de Rome*, 1993.

Pie, Msgr. Louis-Edouard. *Oeuvres de Mgr l'Evêque de Poitiers*. 10 volumes. Paris-Poitiers: H. Oudin, 1883-1894.

Plessis, Alain. *De la fête impériale au mur des fédérés: 1852-1871*. Editions du Seuil, 1973.

Renault, François. *Le cardinal Lavigerie*. Fayard, 1992.

Ricard, Msgr. *François de la Bouillerie*. Lille: Maison St-Joseph/Oeuvre de Saint-Charles, B-Grammont, n.d.

Soria, Diego. *Histoire générale de l'Italie de 1815 à 1850*. 3 volumes. Nîmes: n.p., 1861.

Salvatorelli, Luigi. *Histoire de l'Italie*. Editions Horvath, 1973.

Soltner, Dom Louis. *Les débuts d'une renaissance monastique: Solesmes, 1831-1833*. Solesmes: Association "Les Amis de Solesmes," 1974.

——————. "Pie IX et Solesmes," *Lettre aux amis de Solesmes*, No. 4, 1978, pp.6-30.

Stern, Jean. *La Salette: Documents authentiques*. Volume 3. Cerf, 1991.

Tollu, Philippe. *Montalembert: Les libertés sous le Second Empire*. Albatros, 1987.

Valognes, Jean-Pierre. *Vie et mort des Chrétiens d'Orient: Des origines à nos jours*. Fayard, 1994.

Virebeau, Georges. *Les Papes et la franc-maçonnerie*. Documents et Témoignages, 1977.

Woodward, Kenneth L., *Comment l'Église fait les saints*. Grasset, 1992.

Articles from Dictionaries and Encyclopedias

Dictionnaire de la Papauté (Fayard): "Pie X" (G. Martina), "Veto" (J.-B. d'Onorio).

Dictionnaire Pratique des Connaissances Religieuses (Letouzey et Ané): "Dupanloup" (J. Bricout), "Papes contemporains" (J. Bricout), "Pouvoir temporel du Pape" (Y. de La Brière), "Syllabus" (J. Rivière).

Dictionnaire de Théologie Catholique (Letouzey et Ané): "Conclave" (T. Ortolan), "Pie IX" (G. Mollat), "Syllabus" (L. Brigué).

Enciclopedia Cattolica (Cité du Vatican): "Bernetti Tommaso" (A. M. Ghisalberti), "Gizzi Pasquale Tommaso" (M. De Camillis), "Lambruschini Luigi" (F. Fonzi), "Macchi Vincenzo" (M. De Camillis), "Pio IX" (P. Pirri).

Enciclopedia Europea (Rome: Ed. Garzanti): "Pio IX."

New Catholic Encyclopedia (New York: McGraw-Hill): "Pius IX, Pope" (R. Aubert).

INDEX